HURT FEELINGS

Hurt feelings are universal and are present in human beings as well as in animals. These feelings are usually avoided by human beings and overlooked by the scientific and professional mental health communities. Yet, if unresolved and not shared with loved ones and professionals, they tend to fester in our bodies and affect our functioning. If not expressed and shared with caring others, anger, sadness, and fear often serve as the foundation of mental illness. Developmentally, each of these feelings, respectively, gives rise to antisocial acts, depression, and severe mental illness. This book suggests that instead of traditional one-on-one, face-to-face, conversation-based interventions, distance writing will allow mental health professionals to assign interactive practice exercises specifically focused on hurt feelings.

Luciano L'Abate, Ph.D., is Professor Emeritus of Psychology at Georgia State University in Atlanta, where he developed the first doctoral Family Psychology Program in the world. He is a Diplomate and former Examiner of the American Board of Professional Psychology as well as a Fellow and Approved Supervisor of the American Association for Marriage and Family Therapy. Author or coauthor of more than 300 papers, chapters, and book reviews in professional and scientific journals, he is also author, coauthor, editor, or coeditor of 46 books, with 6 other books at various stages of production. His work has been translated in Argentina, China, Denmark, Finland, French Canada, Germany, Italy, Japan, South Korea, and Poland. In 2003, he received a Silver Medal from the President of the University of Bari and the Renoir Prize from the University of Lecce in Italy for Outstanding Achievement. In 2009, Dr. L'Abate was the recipient of the Award for Distinguished Professional Contributions in Applied Psychology from the American Psychological Association.

Hurt Feelings

THEORY, RESEARCH, AND APPLICATIONS IN INTIMATE RELATIONSHIPS

Luciano L'Abate

Georgia State University

CAMBRIDGE
UNIVERSITY PRESS

CAMBRIDGE UNIVERSITY PRESS
Cambridge, New York, Melbourne, Madrid, Cape Town,
Singapore, São Paulo, Delhi, Tokyo, Mexico City

Cambridge University Press
32 Avenue of the Americas, New York, NY 10013-2473, USA

www.cambridge.org
Information on this title: www.cambridge.org/9780521141413

© Luciano L'Abate 2011

First published 2011

Printed in the United States of America

A catalog record for this publication is available from the British Library.

Library of Congress Cataloging in Publication data
L'Abate, Luciano, 1928–
Hurt feelings: theory, research, and applications in intimate
relationships/Luciano L'Abate.
p.   cm.
Includes bibliographical references and index.
ISBN 978-0-521-19364-1 (hbk.)
1. Intimacy (Psychology)   2. Pain.   3. Interpersonal relations.
I. Title.
BF515.L32   2010
158.2–dc22   2011012052

ISBN 978-0-521-19364-1 Hardback
ISBN 978-0-521-14141-3 Paperback

This book is dedicated to Mario Cusinato who, from the very outset in 1988, when he invited me to be Visiting Professor in the Department of General Psychology at the University of Padova, has tirelessly and critically evaluated empirically some models of the Relational Competence Theory. He devised and developed novel ways and means to validate those models together with a host of enthusiastic collaborators and students, among many: Walter Colesso, Eleonora Maino, and Claudia Scilletta. Without his and their continuous and contagious belief in the provisional validity of the Relational Competence Theory, this theory might have never reached any relevant position in the conceptualization and research of hurt feelings in intimate relationships.

I cannot ever forget how, many years ago, Mario and I spent a whole day in Washington, DC, during an annual meeting of the American Psychological Association, arguing about whether to use the term "hurt feelings" or "wounds." He capitulated on wounds, and I prevailed on hurts because I had already used that term in two earlier publications. In this way, he made sure that my feelings would not be hurt and that I would instead find excitement and pride in the entire enterprise of connecting theory with evidence and evidence with practice, a process that is still occurring during the waning years of my life.

Grazie mille, Mario, senza di te non ce l'avrei mai fatta!

Contents

Preface

The purpose of this book is to gather and integrate under one cover what is presently known to this writer about hurt feelings scientifically and professionally. What is the relationship of these feelings to relational competence, socialization, mental health, and applied disciplines, such as self-help, health promotion, prevention, psychotherapy, and rehabilitation? These feelings are *approached*, admitted, disclosed, expressed, and shared in *intimate communal* (close, committed, interdependent, and prolonged) relationships but are *avoided* (denied, neglected, repressed, or suppressed) either in agentic, instrumental exchanges or in dysfunctional relationships. These feelings must be considered within a ratio of joys and hurts received throughout a lifetime. One cannot consider hurt feelings separately from joys.

I have argued that hurt feelings are avoided by many people, including also functional ones, and by the scientific and professional communities that use a variety of circumlocutions, analogies, or inconsistent avoidance of these feelings. This avoidance has been found in the scientific and professional literatures, as expanded in this volume and in previous publications (L'Abate, 1997, 1999a, 2009b), using terms that avoid dealing directly with hurt feelings, namely distress, negative emotions, social pain, and emotional disturbances. As far back as thirty years ago (L'Abate, 1977), I argued that hurt feelings are at the bottom of our existence, underlying anger, sadness, fears, and disgust. With two students, showed that functional couples preferred disclosure and sharing of these feelings over rational problem solving (Frey et al., 1979).

Since those early publications, a whole literature has slowly been accumulating to make hurt feelings an important topic of research relevant to intimate relationships, mental health, and personality socialization (Feeney, 2004, 2005; Leary & Leder, 2009; Leary, Springer, Negel, Ansell, & Evans, 1998; Vangelisti, 2009b). More recently, my collaborators and I

(De Giacomo, L'Abate, Pennebaker, & Rumbaugh, 2010) have argued that these feelings may constitute the so-called unconscious, especially in psychopathology, at various levels of awareness.

Instead of paper-and-pencil, self-report questionnaires, which are a major source of information about intimacy and hurt feelings (Cusinato & L'Abate, 1994; Mashek & Aron, 2004; Prager, 1995; Schaefer & Olson, 1981; Stevens & L'Abate, 1989), I have also argued that intimacy must be defined behaviorally rather than just by such questionnaires (L'Abate, 1986, 1994, 1997, 1999a, 2005, 2009b). Consequently, I am admittedly involved in demonstrating the validity of my original definition and formulation above and beyond what my collaborators and I have done empirically thus far (Cusinato & L'Abate, 2012; L'Abate et al., 2010).

By constructing specific and verifiable models for hurt feelings at the subjectively receptive input side, I have been able to put together most of the literature on hurtful feelings, as distinguished from emotions at the expressive output side, into systematic verifiable models. By defining hurt feelings operationally, I have also developed two sets of written interactive practice exercises or workbooks about the causes and nature of these feelings. One series of interactive exercises has been administered on an experimental basis to undergraduates, inmates, and addicts by my collaborator, Prof. Eleonora Maino, and her graduate students at the University of Padua. Results from her research will be published elsewhere (Cusinato & L'Abate, 2012). These two sets of exercises are now part of a larger encyclopedia of interactive practice exercises developed over the last twenty-five years (L'Abate, 2011b). I would have liked to cover joyful feelings as well, but including them in this volume would have subtracted from concentrating solely on hurt feelings. Nonetheless, joyful feelings will be covered in a more joyful publication (L'Abate, 2011c).

By developing an operational definition of hurt feelings and two interactive practice exercises (L'Abate, 2011b) to study them in a laboratory and in a clinic, this verifiable model will allow us to evaluate much more specifically than heretofore possible other existing models – that is, whether the model and its definition are valid. If the combination of two models[1 & 15] of the Relational Competence Theory (RCT) is valid, then it would be responsible in part for the validity of the RCT from which it derives.

There are no other secondary sources about this topic that I know of except for Anita L. Vangelisti's (2009b) distinct contribution. That edited volume, however, does not contain applied contributions about the role of hurt feelings in self-help, health promotion, prevention, psychotherapy, and rehabilitation. Work by David Bakan and other worthwhile pioneers and researchers, for instance, does not cover clinical and nonclinical application of these feelings.

If we accept the thesis that hurt feelings are at the foundation of our experience and existence, it stands to reason that they need to be dealt with by health promoters, preventers, and psychotherapists, even though until recently these feelings have been avoided by the scientific and professional communities, as discussed throughout various chapters of this volume. Consequently, this work would contribute to the field of feelings and emotion not only by integrating past knowledge, but also by furnishing a specific method of evaluating hurt feelings in the laboratory as well as in clinical applications by various mental health disciplines.

In addition to Dr. Vangelisti's excellent contribution (2009b) and her chapter (Vangelisti & Beck, 2007) where, to my knowledge, there are no clinical applications, this book should provide a thorough background to the theory and practice of hurt feelings in both the scientific and professional literatures.

PLAN OF THE BOOK

When intimacy is defined behaviorally and observationally as the sharing of joys and hurts as well of the fears of being hurt, then *intimacy* is really what this book is about. As argued in Chapter 1, intimacy lies at the bottom of relationships requiring being able to be aware of, accept, express, and share hurt feelings with those we love and who love us. Joys, victories, and triumphs are easily shared. However, hurt feelings are much more difficult to share than joys and triumphs. When intimates are not available communally or otherwise, professional helpers come to the fore. This chapter also introduces an operational definition of hurt feelings as well as two additional visual models: an hourglass model of the nature of emotionality and the experience of feelings in general, and an upside funnel model of how hurtful and joyful feelings are at the bottom of most constructive and destructive feelings and their expression into emotions.

Part One involves possible antecedents of hurt feelings, including Chapter 2 on how hurt feelings are avoided in functional and dysfunctional relationships as well as in the scientific and professional communities. In this chapter, I introduce a tripartite model that serves as the basis for the rest of the volume. Chapter 3 includes all the possible antecedent "causes" or origins of hurt feelings, including abuse in its many forms, abandonment, criticism, neglect, and rejection, among others. Chapter 4 reviews the developmental aspects of hurt feelings from infancy to old age throughout various stages of the life cycle. Chapter 5 considers how the family or substitute or alternative intimate relationships contribute to whether or not hurt feelings are expressed and shared.

Part Two reviews the scientific bases of hurt feelings in their historical, conceptual and biological foundations, including their pioneers in Chapter 6, who "discovered" hurt feelings and acknowledged their existence and importance through conceptually relevant and empirical research. Chapter 7 includes a review of the biological foundation of hurt feelings. The incredible growth of neuroscience in the first decade of the twenty-first century made it impossible for me to even try to cover this topic. Through the good auspices of my colleague John Cacioppo, I was fortunate to enlist the contribution of three distinguished neuroscientists, Antoine Bechara, Dana Smith, and Lin Xiao, to write that chapter. Chapter 8 reviews the many gender and individual differences that exist in the experience, processing, expressing, and sharing of hurt feelings. As shown in Chapter 9, these individual and gender differences are the outcome of culture, as mediated, of course, by the family and intimate relationships. The avoidance (denial, repression, suppression) of hurt feelings, as shown in Chapter 10, has significant implications for physical and mental heath, including forgiveness.

Consequently, in Part Three, Chapter 11 reviews how sharing hurt feelings in self-help, health promotion, and prevention are necessary to decrease, if at all possible, the deleterious effects of the causes of unexpressed hurt feelings. Chapter 12 starts with a review of how hurt feelings have been avoided in the professional literature and what can be done to help people who need to become aware of, disclose, and share hurt feelings with loved ones or professionals.

In Part Four, Chapter 13, I try to look over all the possible advances that could occur at various levels of functioning, intimate/nonintimate, intra- and interpersonal, that will acknowledge the universal nature of hurt feelings. After that acknowledgment, I try to connect multifarious definitions and models of the antecedent, causes, and correlates of hurt feelings within the confines and requirements of sixteen models in the hierarchical (RCT). This attempts to give a theoretical cover to hurt feelings within a conceptual and empirical framework. Therefore, this volume constitutes the expansion of the RCT model,[15] where *intimacy has been defined behaviorally and observationally as the sharing of joys, hurt feelings, and fears of being hurt.* As shown in the final chapter of this volume, all sixteen models of the RCT help us understand hurt feelings in their multifarious manifestations and interpretations.

READERSHIP

The primary audience for this book might consist of advanced graduates in courses and seminars on feelings and emotions. Secondary audiences, where this book could be added as supplementary reading, would consist of courses on personality psychology, abnormal personality, psychopathology, and theories of personality. Tertiary audiences could be found in applied courses on health psychology, prevention, and psychotherapy. Fourthly, given that this volume covers the literature of both scientific and professional sources, it would be of interest to major researchers and professionals in most mental health disciplines: clinical psychology, psychiatry, social work, counseling, school and pastoral counseling, and psychiatric nursing, among others.

Luciano L'Abate
Atlanta, Georgia
July 31, 2011

Acknowledgments

The people to whom I owe the most for help writing this book are anonymous. I am grateful for the critically helpful feedback I received from two readers for Cambridge University Press and three referees from *Emotion Review* under the direction of its editor, Lisa Feldman Barrett.

Among those who are not anonymous but who helped me most directly have been Jeanie Lee of Cambridge University Press, who kept me honest and made sure I obtained the permissions necessary for all the epigraphs I have used throughout the chapters of this book. I owe Tiawanda Williams my gratitude for helping me organize the references and producing the Author Index, and Karen Viars for helping me to produce the Subject Index. I am also grateful to Sarah Steiner and Dana Smith for finding references that would have taken me days to locate – and that they managed to find in mere hours.

INTRODUCTION

The Nature of Hurt Feelings: What Is Intimacy?

It is increasingly apparent that a complete understanding of any emotional process is going to require attention paid to multiple levels of analysis, from the cultural to the behavioral, psychological, experimental, physiological, and molecular.

Coan & Allen (2007, p. 8)

Joys	*Hurts*
Feeling like breathing in a rainbow of diverse hues that warm a happy heart	Feelings that get to the tippity-top Like a hallowed hole on heavy hearts
And living life simply without falsity	A dive into the deep sea sponge mop
So every sentiment flows freely outward	All gooey because feelings have no smarts
For eternity, forgetting woes	I feel radiating pangs that spread out
And being heard by someone who listens	Leaving emptiness in the inner core
Not minding that earth's terrain ages about	Suff'ring means so much that I'd
Now that the moon is the timeless sage	While weeping, wishing I'd suffer no more
When sunlight bursts forth from a florid chest	This seems to be the result of long life
One with nature, and doing its very best	In which I can never be satisfied
Loveable lullaby flows into the universe strife	Spasms of a racing heart breathing

Rhythm's head gently rests on one of   Always presuming breath's dis
    many books
Caressing music with warm tender   If vision were bright as love
    looks.
Thus, joy awaits.   Maybe hurt feelings would
                                 understand me

Dr. Laura Sweeney

This chapter presents and supports a behavioral definition of intimacy in contrast to definitions of intimacy obtained through self-report, paper-and-pencil questionnaires. In no way is this contrast meant to diminish the value of questionnaires. It merely means that there are many ways to define intimacy that lead to different findings, implications, and conclusions. When intimacy is defined as the sharing of joys, hurts, and fears of being hurt, this definition implies also that hurt feelings exist at the foundation of our existence (Cusinato & L'Abate, 2012; L'Abate, 1977, 1986, 1994, 1997, 1999a, 2003, 2005, 2009b; L'Abate, Cusinato, Maino, Colesso, & Scilletta, 2010; L'Abate & Sloan, 1984).

What are hurt feelings, and what is intimacy? In one way or another, and at various intensities and depths, we are all hurt and wounded human beings. We are *needy* of others in the process of wanting to be close and to decrease the load of hurt feelings – that is, in the process of searching for intimacy. We are susceptible and *vulnerable* to being hurt by those we love, as much as we are also *fallible* in hurting those very same ones we love, and who love us (Jones, Kugler, & Adams, 1995; L'Abate, 1999a, 2005).

THE MEANING OF HURT FEELINGS

This chapter, therefore, introduces, elaborates, and expands on three models of hurt feelings defined operationally by a list of related hurtful feelings (Table 1.1), as well as visually by a multilayered-hourglass (Figure 1.1) and funnel-like models (Figure 1.2). The definition of intimacy in close relationships as *the sharing of joys, hurts, and fears of being hurt* seems the only behavioral one available versus many paper-and-pencil, self-report measures of intimacy and close relationships (Collins & Feeney, 2004; Fehr, 2004; Heyman, Feldbau-Kohn, Ehrensaft, Langhinrichsen-Rohling, & O'Leary, 2001; Laurenceau, Rivera, Schaffer, & Pietromonaco, 2004; Mashek & Aron, 2004; Praeger, 1995), including self-attributed intimacy motivation (Craig, Koestner, & Zuroff, 1994). Originally, a paper-and-pencil self-report questionnaire was developed to deal specifically with hurt feelings (Stevens

& L'Abate, 1989), whereas another intimacy questionnaire dealt mostly with hurt feelings (Descountner & Thelen, 1991).

Hurt feelings are a catch-all term covering the subjective experience of traumas, losses, betrayals, rejections, psychological injuries, threats, and dismissals we receive during the course of our lives. The prototype of hurt feelings is crying when sincere, nonmanipulative, and shared with loved ones to produce intimacy (Hastrup, Baker, Kraemer, & Bornstein, 1986; Hendriks, Nelson, Cornelius, & Vingerhoets, 2008; Kraemer & Hastrup, 1983a, 1983b; Lutz, 1999; Nelson, 2008). Crying about hurt feelings without sharing them with loved ones means keeping those feelings inside and allowing them to fester, with negative consequences for the individual and for one's intimate relationships.

Crying in helpless battered children and wives and in assaulted victims of predators is matched by the helplessness of battering parents and male predators themselves, who do not know how to deal with crying and tears (Bugental, 2010). A survey of undergraduates concerning frequency, intensity, antecedents, and consequences of crying supports the interpretation that in some individuals, some families, and perhaps some cultures, crying is viewed as a noxious stimulus, to be avoided, suppressed, and repressed. For instance, additional physical assault during rapes may be more likely to occur when the victim is crying; also witness how many children are abused and even killed to make them stop crying (Bell & L'Abate, undated). Stereotypically, many men perceive crying as a sign of weakness. It is acceptable for women to cry, but not for "real" men.

Before defining hurt feelings in particular, feelings or affects in general are defined as self-contained phenomenological experiences that include subjective sensory modalities that may (or may not) be independent of evaluative thoughts or images, what has been called the embodiment of feelings and affects (Ping, Dhillon, & Beilock, 2009). The evaluative part of this definition includes giving a name to a feeling to distinguish one feeling from another, and transforming feelings into emotions (Helm, 2009). Feelings of anger may be different from feelings of fear, just as much as both feelings may be different from sadness (Wierzbicka, 2009a, 2009b). An important differentiation lies in distinguishing feelings as internal intrapsychic experiences from emotions, that is, how feelings are expressed externally: verbally, nonverbally, or even in writing. Feelings, when aroused, can include pleasant and unpleasant sensations and can vary in their intensity.

Consequently, hurt feelings in particular are defined here as *unpleasant, painful, and harmfully subjective affects experienced from objectively aversive or negatively perceived life events.* Sensory modalities may include increase in blood pressure, heart palpitation, sweating, muscle rigidity, "butterflies in the stomach," and nonspecific psychosomatic visceral and cerebral sensations that sometimes may be detectable to individuals and sometimes may not be. Some sensations may occur below the level of awareness or below the level of understanding language and knowing how to speak, as in infancy (Glenberg, Webster, Mouilso, Havas, & Lindeman, 2009; Katz, 2009; Wierzbicka, 2009a, 2009b). We are more vulnerable to being hurt by those we love and who love us than by strangers (Fitness & Warburton, 2009). The latter, accidentally or intentionally, can inflict physical wounds with emotional concomitants that inevitably leave hurt feelings festering in us. Those feelings, however, can be alleviated and may even dissipate by sharing them with most intimates, family, and friends (Bersheid & Ammazzalorso, 2003; Hardcastle, 1999). When that process is deemed impossible, sharing them with mental health professionals, either verbally, nonverbally, or in writing, may be the next best alternative.

Instead of relying on indirect, paper-and-pencil, self-report questionnaires that constitute the mainstay and mainstream of intimacy research, including fear of intimacy (Firestone & Catlett, 1999; Firestone & Firestone, 2004 Sherman & Thelen, 1996; Vangelisti & Beck, 2007), a direct observational approach of actual behaviors can be relatively more fruitful theoretically and more relevant preventively and clinically. The operational definition of hurtful terms based on their frequencies of citation in PsycINFO is included in Table 1.1. This table shows how distress and trauma are cited more often than all other equivalent or similar terms, whereas hurts is the least-cited term. So much has been written about feelings included in Table 1.1 that to expand on them individually would make it impossible to write about anything else.

However, the choice of using the lowest common denominator of hurts was consciously made to relate it to its most frequent usage in the population at large and to encompass the widest range of possibly hurtful terms as contained in Table 1.1 as well as additional, possibly relevant terms not contained in that list, such as despair (Shabad 2001) or agony, among other feelings contained in most chapters of this volume.

An examination of similar terms in the King James Bible produced the following results: anguish – 25 matches; bereavement or bereaved – no matches (except for some in other editions); desperation or desperate – 7 matches; devastation or devastated – no matches; distress – 67 matches; grief – 46 matches; hurt – 103 matches; sorrow – 129 matches; suffering – 37 matches; suffer – 227 matches; trauma – no matches; upset – no matches. Sorrow, suffering, suffer, and hurts were mentioned more often than any other painful terms, with hurts as the closest contextual equivalent for sorrow and suffering.

When the term hurt includes suffering, at least three major sources come to the fore:

1. Bakan's (1968) seminal and extremely influential work, in which his main contribution was to argue for the dichotomy between community and agency rather than for suffering itself, which belongs within the communal rather than agentic realm – a dichotomy that will appear again and again in this volume.
2. Gilbert's (1992) contribution tries "… to explain the basis of human suffering as arising from maladaptive deviations in the expression of our individual humanness" (p. 4). Unfortunately, this definition was related only to internal deviations rather than just representing our overall socialized humanness. Strangely enough, Gilbert not only failed to define what he meant by suffering, but the term – even though present in the title – was not even included in the subject index.
3. Mayerfeld's more recent review (1999) defined suffering as a "disagreeable overall feeling" (p. 14), arguing for happiness and suffering as "absolute, not relative, terms" (p. 34). Mayerfeld's work also differentiated suffering as being "distinct from the frustration of desire" (p. 43) and "from the subjective opinion of suffering" (p. 50), indicating how suffering cannot be conceived as a rational experience but rather as a subjective one.

Once hurt feelings are defined behaviorally, one must define them accurately and comprehensibly. Here, however, a major distinction must be made between the *experience* of feeling hurts at the internal, subjectively receptive input side versus the external *expression* of hurts at the visible and objective output side that constitutes emotions (L'Abate, 1997, 2005). Feelings of whatever kind may remain dormant inside an organism unless they are elicited by self or by external others and events (Barrett, Mesquita, Ochsner, & Gross, 2007; Coan & Allen, 2007; Goldie, 2009; Rumbaugh & Washburn, 2003). Emotions, on the other hand, are visible externally when expressed, shown, and shared. When hurt feelings are not experienced and expressed, they cannot be shared and tend to remain inside, influencing the organism and festering in toxic and deleterious ways, containing the *unconscious* (De Giacomo, L'Abate, Pennebaker, & Rumbaugh, 2010). In some cases, the expression of hurt feelings is unacceptable and denied in their importance, as in self-silencing, especially in women (Jack, 1987, 1991, 2001; Jack & Dill, 1992).

Caprara and Cervone (2000, pp. 284–310) were exemplary among the few in emphasizing this distinction. Eventually, the emotion research community has acknowledged the importance of this distinction by devoting a whole issue of its premier journal to it (Reisenzein & Doring, 2009), as well as mentioning it in an important chapter (Barrett et al., 2007). This distinction will appear repeatedly throughout the course of this volume, the hope being that this frequency might counterbalance in some ways the still persistent failure to differentiate between feelings and emotions. The former is incorrectly equated with the latter, uniting them together as one entity. Feelings and emotions constitute two completely different processes. Without this differentiation, circularity remains as the only alternative, such as in "Emotion elicits the social sharing of emotion" (Rime, 2009a). Would it not be more specific and clearer to admit that "[c]ertain feelings elicit their social sharing as emotions"? Not all feelings emerge and transform themselves into emotions. Some feelings are kept inside and are not expressed and, therefore, not shared, without any resolution as to their toxic, internal existence (Clore & Huntsinger, 2009; Jack, 1987, 1991, 2001; Jack & Dill, 1992).

The overall term used to include whatever feelings are experienced internally by the self is *emotionality*, the condition of experiencing feelings of any kind. Whether and how those feelings are expressed and perhaps shared with others as emotions remains an important aspect of emotion theory and theorizing (Gross, 2007; Lewis, Haviland-Jones, Barrett, 2008). There may be a limit to the number of hurt feelings we can experience, but there is a myriad ways in which those feelings can be expressed outwardly to become emotions. Because the general literature on how emotions are expressed is so incredibly large, to the point of being unmanageable theoretically and empirically, this volume will attempt to concentrate specifically on the internal, subjective experience of hurt feelings in particular rather than just their overall outward expression as emotions.

Emotionality includes the experience of joys as well as of hurt feelings and of fears of being hurt. Hence, three feelings must be considered here: *joys*, *hurts*, and *fears* of being hurt. However, we need a model of how feelings in general are experienced before focusing particularly on those three feelings. Consequently, an hourglass model was constructed (1) to understand the process of experiencing feelings, that is, of *emotionality*.

This hourglass model demonstrates how two principles of equifinality and equipotentiality surround the whole Figure 1.1 in both upward

TABLE 1.1. *PsycINFO search for related terms to denote painful feelings*

Feeling	Frequency
Anguish	595
Bereavement	4,241
Desperation	193
Devastation	201
Distress	25,719
Grief	9,617
Hurts	50
Sorrow	588
Suffering	19,132
Trauma	26,450
Upset	1,238

```
-------------------------------------------------------------------
           Complex relational and nonrelational feelings
           ----------------------------------------------------
                   Altruistic and self-oriented feelings
                   --------------------------------
                           Basic feelings
                           ----------------
                           Gate keepers
                             ---------

                        Experiencing feelings

                            --------
                          Cerebral levels
                          -----------------
                          Visceral levels
                       -------------------------
                       Physiological levels
                    -------------------------------
                           Cellular levels
              -----------------------------------------------
                           Molecular levels
              ------------------------------------------------------
```

FIGURE 1.1. An hourglass model of emotionality as the basis of our existence and experience.

and downward directions (L'Abate, 2005). In the lower half of the model, from the molecular level upward, biological foundations are necessary to understand how feelings in general culminate and are experienced leading toward their equifinality in their experience (Panksepp, 1998a, 1998b). From this equifinal experience, there is an upward expansion and developmental equipotentiality of more refined and more complex feelings, as shown in the upper half of the model. In the lower part of the hourglass model (Figure 1.1), biological levels underlie the experience of hurt feeling.

The upward process of equifinality and equipotentiality does not end at the intermediate level of experiencing feelings. There is a downward, reverse process occurring according to the principle of synthetic integration that includes both upward and downward processes – interactionism and reductionism, respectively (Capitelli, Guerra, L'Abate, & Rumbaugh, 2009). Levels in the upper half of Figure 1.1 feedback downward to the equifinal experience of feelings, that is, to emotionality. How we experience feelings at their various levels of the upper half of the figure influences directly the experience of feelings underlying biological levels. From that experience at higher levels, there is a downward, equipotent process effecting biological levels, as discussed in Chapter 7 of this volume.

Therefore, the experience of feelings functions to direct circularly both upward and downward processes of equifinally and equipotentially. Both upward and downward processes indicate how emotionality – the experience of feelings in general – is crucial to our survival, let alone our enjoyment. We are all emotional human beings. However, individual differences in how we experience and express feelings into emotions makes the whole enterprise worth all that has been performed on this topic, in the last half-century and earlier, since Darwin's days and even before him.

A MULTILAYERED FUNNEL MODEL OF JOYS, HURTS, AND THEIR DERIVATIVES

The upper part of Figure 1.1 is expanded in Figure 1.2. Consequently, if we were willing to accept, approach, and include emotionality, composed by both joyful and hurt feelings, as the essence of our existence, even provisionally, then a model (Figure 1.2) different from those offered by previous theorists would be proposed. This model is in keeping with Tomkins's (1962, 1963) original amplification view. In Figure 1.2, hurtful and joyful feelings can be visualized via an upright vertical funnel starting at the base with hurts and joys and enlarging and expanding upward to the top, with supraordinate levels stemming from bottom-most hurts and joys. The visual model presented in Figure 1.2 needs further verbal elaboration because it includes different levels of feelings that do in fact belong together experientially and empirically.

Hurtful and joyful feelings exist at the narrow bottom of the funnel-like figure where activation/deactivation, pleasantness/unpleasantness,

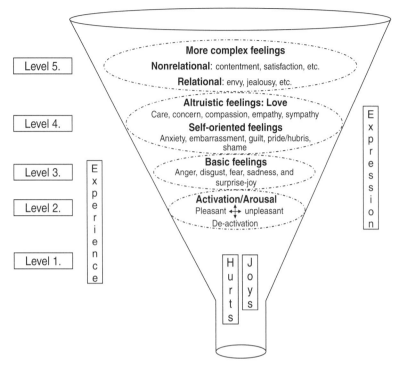

FIGURE 1.2. A funnel model of hurt feelings and their derivatives.

as well as intensity or powerfulness/ powerlessness serve as gatekeepers, either allowing or not allowing hurt feelings to enter awareness and influence basic feelings of anger, sadness, disgust, fear, joy, and surprise. From this primary level emerge more complex levels of feelings. This model is being evaluated with two series of written practice exercises deriving from the list of hurt feelings and from their antecedent sources (Eleonora Maino, personal communication, July 15, 2008, research in progress). Implications and limitations of this model are discussed for its further expansion to underlying biological factors, gender, individual, and cultural differences, as shown in Figure 1.1 and elaborated in other chapters of this volume.

Visually, therefore, hurts and joys are included in the narrow base of the funnel-like model (Figure 1.2) drawn under three dimensions of activation, pleasure, and intensity. The third dimension of intensity is missing from this figure because it was difficult to draw it there. This visual difficulty should not in any way diminish the importance of this third dimension.

These three dimensions function as gatekeepers for hurt feelings furnishing the bases for supraordinate levels of more nuanced feelings along an upward amplification and enlargement of the funnel, as originally envisaged by Tomkins (1962, 1963). The first level above the three gate-keeping dimensions is comprised of anger, disgust, fear, surprise-joy, and sadness. From these five basic feelings spring upwardly more complex feelings, such as altruistic feelings of love (care, concern, compassion, and consideration) and self-oriented feelings (anxiety, embarrassment, guilt, shame, pride/ hubris). At a higher level, there would be even more nuanced nonrelational (contentment, satisfaction) and relational (envy, jealousy) feelings.

Six criteria differentiate feelings along the supraordinate levels of this model: (1) *depth* or vertical up-down direction from the bottom to the top of the figure; (2) *width* or horizontal narrow-wide direction, starting with experiencing input but not including how feelings are expressed at the output side as expressed emotions; (3) *complexity*, including subtlety and indirection, starting with basic feelings at the bottom and including more complex, nuanced feelings on the ascent; (4) *direction*, from "internality," that is, intrapsychic, to "externality," that is, directed toward self first, and then relationally toward other persons, objects, or activities (Rime', 2009a, 2009b); (5) *openness*, as in how many feelings can be included at each level or at additional supraordinate levels, including those presented by Widen and Russell (2008) among others; and (6) *developmental* stages of maturation starting from early dependency in childhood through to denial of dependency in adolescence, to interdependence in adulthood, and finally to a return to dependency in old age (Saarni, 1999, 2008). This last criterion, however, would hypothetically bypass chronological development and instead consider levels of progressive personality differentiation, ranging from the simple basic feelings at the lowest level of differentiation and ascending to more, differentiated and nuanced, feelings at higher levels of development (Harris, 1989; Izard, 1979).

AMPLIFICATION OF THE FUNNEL-LIKE MODEL: FROM BASIC-LEVEL FEELINGS UPWARD

The literature on basic feelings – from joyful and hurtful feelings at the bottom of the funnel (Figure 1.2), to more complex pleasant and unpleasant feelings (Lindquist & Feldman Barrett, 2008) – is so vast that nothing new can be added that has not already been written, except to outline their being included in most texts already cited.

Basic-level feelings include:

Anger: Leading to acting out, aggression, hostility, externalizations, and murder
(Lemerise & Dodge, 2008).
Disgust: Leading to avoidance (Rozin, Haidt, & McCauley, 2008).
Fear: Leading to psychopathology (Ohman, 2008).
Sadness: Leading to internalizations, depression, and suicide (Bonanno, Goorin, & Coifman, 2008).
Surprise and Joy: Leading to pleasure, enjoyment, and functionality (Fredrickson & Cohn, 2008; L'Abate, 2011a).

Note, however, that surprise and joy have to overcome the negative influences of the other four pathogenic feelings: anger, disgust, fear, and sadness. Consequently, one must have a strong and wide repertoire of surprise and joys to overcome the negative influence of the other four feelings; who knows, perhaps a ratio of five joys to offset one hurt? (Gottman et al., 1997).

Even though love has been the object and subject of endless publications, the feelings included in this section are not usually found in the psychological literature on feelings and emotions, even though they are more likely to be found in relationship science (Stets & Turner, 2008). However, they are included in Davitz's pioneering work (1969) and in various chapters of Lewis et al. (2008).

Care: Caring as a feeling for someone, including self, implies its application in actual behavior: caregiving. Nonetheless, we may care for someone but be unable to transmit that feeling into action, as in the case of distance, sickness, or handicap (Clark & Parris Stephens, 1996; Oatley & Jenkins, 1996). Caregiving, of course, as an expression of caring, can be associated also with marital satisfaction (Feeney, 1996; Feeney & Hohaus, 2001). The major distinction is whether caregiving is voluntary or involuntary (Carnelley, Pietromonaco, & Jaffe, 1996; Gillath, Shaver, Mikulincer, Nitzberg, Erez, & van Ijzendoorn, 2005). Here, care is considered a feeling, but when expressed outwardly, it becomes a behavior.

Concern: It is difficult to differentiate care from concern except to view the latter as being tinged by some degree of anxiety and thus appearing slightly somewhat different from care (Oatley & Jenkins, 1996).

Compassion: This feeling, like the preceding ones, does appear often in the literature on feelings and emotions (Fehr & Sprecher, 2009; Gilbert, 2005; Lewis et al., 2008; Oatley & Jenkins, 1996, pp. 48, 49, 54, 91, 260, 309), and is present in relationship science (Sprecher & Fehr, 2005). This feeling arises when we see deficits or missing needs in another human being, including oneself. However, this feeling should be distinguished from empathy.

Consideration: This feeling involves including self as well someone or something else as being important in one's life, to the point of thinking about and planning for the welfare of that person or of that activity. This feeling is not included in more emotion treatises, but it is included in one Selfhood Model[11] of the RCT, as are the three previous ones (L'Abate et al., 2010).

Empathy: Implies putting oneself in another person's shoes, so to speak, as included in Eisenberg's seminal work (1986) and elaborated by Ickes (1997, 2007; Hakansson & Montgomery, 2003; Hoffman, 2008; Ickes, Dugash, Simpson, & Wilson, 2003; Ickes, Gesn, & Graham, 2000; Kilpatrick, Bissonnnette, & Rusbult, 2002).

Sympathy: This feeling suggests a positive understanding of another's position or personality, as included in Eisenberg's work (1986).

Self-Oriented Feelings

Except for anxiety (Rapee, 1996) and shyness (Carducci, 1999), feelings included in this level have been covered partially by Nathanson (1992) and completely by Tangney and Fischer (1995) and by Lewis (2008). Shyness, as a behavior rather than a feeling, can stem from fear, anxiety, shame, or guilt, just as worry and rumination can.

Anxiety: Most texts on feelings and emotions include this affect as separate from fear (Ohman, 2000, 2008). However, one could argue that anxiety perhaps is not as intense a feeling as fear, and belongs in the same class as sadness.

Embarrassment: This affect is most often cited in professional sources (Lewis, 2008; Parrott & Harre, 1996).

Grief and Bereavement: These two affects are cited in Bonanno, Goorin, and Coifman (2008), Field, Hart, and Horowitz (1999), Power and Dalgleish (1997), and Stearns (1993), among many others.

Guilt/Remorse: Guilt is cited in Eisenberg (2000), Lewis (2008), and Taylor (1996) among many others, whereas remorse is cited by Davitz (1969) as an offshoot of guilt.

Pride/Hubris: There are few references about pride (Davitz, 1969; Lewis, 2008; Power & Dalgleish, 1997).

Shame: Gilbert and Andrews (1998), Lewis (2008).

More Complex Feelings

These feelings are more difficult to locate in the scientific and professional literature, and this distinction might be impossible to sustain conceptually. The main distinction that can be made is whether complex feelings are relational or nonrelational (Butler & Gross, 2009). This distinction may be relative. For instance, one could experience satisfaction from the defeat of an adversary, death of an enemy, or disappearance of a rival, as in schadenfreude.

Nonrelational Feelings
One could argue that there are no nonrelational feelings, because all feelings derive from and are related to relationships (Lewis et al., 2008; Rimé, 2009a, 2009b).

Contentment: This feeling is essentially personal rather than relational, even though it could derive from one's communal relationships or from other instrumental sources. Nonetheless, it is not included in most sources relevant to feelings and emotions (Davitz, 1969).

Satisfaction: Relational satisfaction is achieved when there is reciprocity of positive feelings and behaviors. Nonrelational satisfaction is present when positive feelings are generated from personal task achievements, performances, and productions attained on one's own with minimal or no external influence. If this is the case, contentment and satisfaction are more refined experiences of pride and hubris. Satisfaction could be personally and generally internal – a culturally determined feeling about life – but it could also be specifically related to forgiveness in relationships (Kachadourian, Fincham, & Davila, 2004), loneliness (Goodwin, Cook, & Yung, 2001; Newall et al., 2009), sexual satisfaction (Lawrance & Byers, 1995), or attachment (Knobloch, Solomon, & Cruz, 2001).

Relational Feelings
Surely many more feelings can be included in this category (Eisenberg, 1986). Yet two different categories of relational feeling seem basic to positive and negative relationships. For instance, on the positive side one could consider the following:

Benevolence: Feeling kindly and positively toward somebody's actions or words.

Gratitude: Feeling overwhelmed by what someone has said or done positively toward us (Emmons, & McCullough, 2003; Tooby & Cosmides, 2008;

pp. 131–132) as shown in acknowledgment, feelings of obligation, grateful-ness, and thankfulness (Lambert, Graham, & Fincham, 2009).

On the negative side one could consider:

Animosity: This feeling represents bitter resentment toward someone's actions or words (Oatley, 2009a; Smith & Mackie, 2008, p. 429).

Envy: Comparing the performance or production of another to oneself is considered briefly in Stearns (2008, p. 28) and Lewis (2008, p. 318f).

Jealousy: The relationship science literature is replete with studies about this topic, to the point that only a few recent references can be given here (Bersheid & Ammazzalorso, 2003; Buunk & Dijkstra, 2001; Davitz, 1969; Oatley & Jenkins, 1996; Sagarin & Guadagno, 2004).

We should be able to trace most of these complex feelings to their basic sources. For instance, envy to anger and hostility, depression to sadness, and severe psychopathology to fears, as discussed in greater detail in the next chapter of this volume.

Limitations of the Funnel Model

Among the limitations of this model, the most glaring one relates to progressive levels of emotional differentiation and cognitive maturation in personality and in emotional intelligence (Bearison & Zimiles, 1986; Clark & Fiske, 1982; Salovey, Woolery, & Mayer, 2003; Shapiro & Weber, 1982). It seems difficult to obtain evidence to support such a develop-mental progression. Feelings within each level should correlate more significantly, negatively or positively, with each other than with feelings in lower or higher levels depending on their direction and grouping. For instance, guilt and shame would correlate negatively with pride and hubris but positively with sadness. Contentment would correlate nega-tively with embarrassment but positively with satisfaction, among other possibilities. Now that a list of hurt feelings exists (Table 1.1), it should be relatively easy to see how younger or older participants can recognize and describe them to arrive at a developmental understanding of these feelings.

Consequently, further expansions of this model should concentrate on whether such a progression exists and, if so, whether it is conceptually ten-able and empirically valid. If hurt feelings are accepted as a fundamental affect, then their underlying physiological and cerebral processes need fur-ther specification from expressed emotions, including gender, individual, and cultural differences.

Fears

There is not sufficient space to include what has been written about fears in the past and in the present (Ohman, 1993, 2000, 2008). Briefly and perhaps simplistically, fear is the expectation that something dreadful, threatening, and hurtful will happen to self or intimates. However, how can we differentiate between fears and hurts? Fear represents either the proximal or distal possibility that something hurtful might or will occur in the future, whereas hurt feelings means that that possibility has indeed occurred. Temporally, fears represent the present and future. Hurts represent the present and past. What we were afraid might happen has indeed happened. The prototype for fear is avoidance of intimates or of activities, objects, and tasks that may tax and threaten the individual, as found prototypically in avoidant personality disorders as well as in severe psychopathology (L'Abate, 2005; L'Abate et al., 2010).

Joyful Feelings and the Important Ratio of Joys to Hurts

Joys represent one extreme of a hedonic dimension of pleasure-pain, or if one likes, two separate, possibly orthogonal dimensions, one pertaining to various degrees of pleasant, pleasurable, and joyful experiences, and a second dimension pertaining to various degrees of unpleasant and painful experiences. Joyful and pleasurable feelings are just important as hurts because the latter are only relevant in their comparison with how many joyful experiences one has experienced, exchanged, given, and received throughout a lifetime. One prominent colleague and friend, for instance, who is living alone after two divorces, could not remember or recount two pleasures in his life. Hence, within the process of emotionality, the ratio of hurts to joys is the basic dimension to consider.

If hurt feelings are not counterbalanced by joys, then their prevalence will tip the balance toward dysfunctionality (Franks & Hefferman, 1998; Fredrickson & Losada, 2005). If joys outnumber hurts, it will be much easier to forget the latter and remain functional. Therefore, it does matter how many joys we experience in comparison to how many hurts. Joys cannot be separated from hurts. Both feelings are intrinsically linked together and affect individual and relationship functioning. The more frequent, intense, and long-lasting joys and pleasures will tend to offset the detrimental effects of hurt feelings (L'Abate, 2011c).

The prototype for joys is laughter and humor with intimates and in the approach to activities and tasks, including work and play (Bennett,

Zeller, Rosenberg, & McCann, 2003; Chapman & Foot, 1976; L'Abate, 2009c, 2011c; Sahakian & Frishman, 2007; Stearns, 1972). The frequency of pleasures received from infancy to old age work in the long run to counteract and offset the influence of inevitable losses and hurts. The more natural sources of enjoyment and pleasure are the best antidotes for hurts, for example, literary and visual art and hobbies like food, music, exercise, and sex and sensuality (L'Abate, 2007, 2009c, 2011c). The strength of "positive affectivity" offsets the effects of "negative affectivity" (Gordon & Baucom, 2009).

The importance of this ratio of accentuating and focusing on positive rather than negative aspects of life has been highlighted by recent research by Cohn, Fredrickson, Brown, Mikels, and Conway (2009). After questioning eighty-six undergraduate men and women about their levels of resilience and life satisfaction, these investigators asked the participants to track their feelings every day for a month and each evening. Participants were to indicate in computer form which positive feelings (such as amusement, gratitude, joy, and pride) and negative feelings (such as anger, fear, guilt, and sadness) they had experienced in the previous twenty-four hours. At the end of the month, participants were reevaluated with the same instruments administered at the beginning of the study. The results from the pre- and post-study evaluations, were pretty straightforward: Participants who reported each day the highest number of positive feelings in comparison to those who reported the lowest number of positive feelings demonstrated significantly higher levels of resiliency and greater life satisfaction, whereas levels of negative feelings seemed to have a negligible impact on resilience and no effect on life satisfaction.

The term used by Cohn et al. (2009) was "emotion," a term that was changed here into "feeling" because of the distinction made earlier about two different processes underlying each term. Comparative analysis of various theoretical models may be necessary, but ultimately the verifiability, applicability, and fruitfulness of a model to produce research and applications will prevail over strictly conceptual comparisons without applications. Cohn's et al. (2009) results tend to support the original studies of Emmons and McCullough (2003) on the positive effects of gratitude on emotional well-being.

This argument will allow us to consider further the avoidance of hurt feelings in human beings and to evaluate the scientific and professional literature on this topic. Therefore, the multilayered, funnel-like model of hurts and joys that includes most feelings relevant at the receptive, subjective side of experience is presented in Figure 1.2. These feelings may be part and parcel of what Russell and Barrett (1999) called "core affects." These are defined as being consciously accessible but in their more hurtful valence constitute our unconscious (Stegge & Terwogt, 2007) or perhaps vary along a dimension of awareness ranging from unconscious to semiconscious, preconscious, and fully conscious. Even if fully conscious, they may be expressed or remain unexpressed (Bargh, 2005, 2007; Bargh & Williams, 2007; De Giacomo et al., 2010; Hassin, Uleman, & Bargh, 2005; Wiens & Ohman, 2007). Hurts are stored and buried in memory unless there are more frequent and numerous joyful experiences to offset them.

Some of these concerns are answered within a horizontal information-processing Model[1] of RCT (Cusinato & L'Abate, 2012 L'Abate, 1986, 2005; L'Abate et al., 2010) that includes five components: (1) *Emotionality*: how feelings are experienced inwardly (Lambie, 2009); (2) *Rationality*: how feelings are appraised and processed cognitively (Clore & Ortony, 2008); (3) *Activity*: how feelings are expressed outwardly, verbally, nonverbally, and in writing, as emotions; (4) *Awareness*: how feelings have been expressed directly or indirectly, positively or negatively, verbally or nonverbally, and how their expression can or ought to be corrected (Stegge & Terwogt, 2007); and (5) *Context*: whatever spatially and temporally proximal or even distal factors are subjectively present at the time of experiencing feelings and expressing them (Mesquita, Barrett, & Smith, 2010).

This model has been evaluated and validated extensively through a paper-and-pencil self-report test, the Relational Answers Questionnaire (Cusinato & L'Abate, 2012; L'Abate, 2005; L'Abate et al., 2010; Maino, research in progress).

DEFINITIONS OF INTIMACY: A HISTORICAL BACKGROUND

This is not the first, nor will it be the last, attempt to define intimacy. Register and Henley (1992) commented about the importance of intimacy with respect to many aspects of relationship theory and a variety of academic disciplines. These authors found a great deal of research about the topic "but little consensus on even such basic issues as a definition of intimacy" (p. 467). On the basis of interviewing "ordinary people" about the meaning of intimacy, Register and Henley found seven major components of intimate experiences: (1) nonverbal communication, (2) presence, (3) time, (4) boundary, (5) body, (6) destiny/surprise, and (7) transformation. Consequently, these findings add to the many multidimensional definitions of intimacy without specificity and without links to immediate practical applications, all of which have contributed to a Tower of Babel about intimacy.

Moss and Schwebel (1993) attempted to reach a conclusive multidimensional definition of intimacy developed after a literature review and analysis of published definitions of intimacy. These investigators found (p. 32) that themes of mutuality and cognitive awareness and expressiveness were included in more than half of sixty-one unique definitions of intimacy found in the literature. The other half of general and multidimensional definitions also included themes of affective awareness/expressiveness and communication/self-disclosure. Furthermore, multidimensional definitions, which focused on committed romantic relationships, also emphasized themes of physical awareness/expressiveness and commitment/cohesion. Both factors distinguish intimacy in romantic relationships from intimacy in other types of relationships, such as friendships or therapist-client relations. Based on their search and analysis of the literature, Moss and Schwebel arrived at the following definitions: "Intimacy in enduring romantic relationships is determined by the level of commitment and positive affective, cognitive, and physical closeness one experiences with a partner in a reciprocal (although not necessarily symmetrical) relationship" (p. 33). According to its authors, this definition specifies five components of intimacy: (1) commitment, (2) emotion, (3) cognition, (4) physical contact, and (5) mutuality. Clearly, this conclusion represents an improvement over past definitions, but according to this writer's opinion, as represented by the definition already presented from the outset of this chapter, Moss and Schwebel's definition is not specific enough. As is the definition developed by Prager (1995) presented later, it is too rational and too general to lead to any specific intervention.

When intimacy is defined as "the potential to establish close relationships involving high levels of communication, closeness, and commitment," Weinberger, Hofstein, and Whitbourne (2008, p. 551) found that gender correlated with intimacy in sixteen couples evaluated thirty-four years after college graduation in predicting marital status at midlife. Women, but not men, with low intimacy in college were at higher risk of divorce in this sample.

The reason there has been so much written about intimacy without any consensus or a great deal of controversy lies in the possibility that no unifying behavioral and operational definition has been considered in the extant literature, except the one proffered originally more than thirty years ago (Frey, Holley, & L'Abate, 1979; L'Abate, 1977, 1986, 1999a). Instead of a behavioral definition, many paper-and-pencil self-report questionnaires, as already noted, have been created to foster whatever research is present at the base of each creation. Prager (1995), for instance, reviewed (pp. 31–43) paper-and-pencil measures of intimacy and related constructs classified according to whether they evaluated intimate behaviors (7), intimate experiences (3), relational closeness (10), affective-cognitive measures (6), behavioral measures (4), measures of individual differences in intimate relationships (9), and selected measures of related constructs (6). She defined intimacy (p. 67) "as a positively cathected psychological relation between two people in which partners share that which is private and personal with one another." Prager herself acknowledges that "[l]ike any superordinate concept, this one is broad and abstract, making it difficult to operationalize" (p. 67). If that is the case, what is the use of any definition if it cannot lead to verification and validation? This very question can be raised about the earlier definition by Moss and Schwebel (1993).

Not contained in Prager's original list was Stevens and L'Abate's (1989) Sharing of Hurts Questionnaire, which was further expanded and validated by Cusinato and L'Abate (1994). Stevens and L'Abate found six factors: vulnerability, hurt proper, conflict resolution, private values, social desirability, and imperfection. On the basis of their spiral model, Cusinato and L'Abate (1994) proposed a more complex model (p. 109) composed of (1) the ability to love and negotiate; (2) three modalities related to Being Present, Doing or Performing, and Having or Producing (money and goods); (3) the prerequisites of commitment, equality, and reciprocity; (4) enhancement factors in the ability to love (communicating values, respect for feelings, accepting limitations, affirming potentialities, sharing hurts, and forgiving errors; and (5) enhancement factors related to the ability to negotiate (authority versus responsibility, orchestrational versus instrumental decisions, and their contents: having and doing).

The multiplicity of definitions and measures by Prager (1995) illustrates a chaotic Tower of Babel that was expanded further by additional measures contained in Mashek and Aron's (2004) compendium as well as by other questionnaires published since that time (Laurenceau, Barrett, & Rovine, 2005). There is no agreement or consensus about what intimacy is or might be. Consequently, given this confusing state of affairs, it is important to review the pros and cons of a behaviorally concrete operational definition proffered here versus numerous paper-and-pencil self-report definitions of intimacy or related constructs contained in previous publications cited herein.

Unidimensional versus Multidimensional Definitions of Intimacy

The behavioral and operational definition given here is based on three sets of experienced feelings: joys, hurts, and fears, comprising one single affective, rather than cognitive, dimension of intimacy. This process implies and involves mutuality or reciprocity (Dunn, 1994). The actual sharing of hurt feelings is a process that occurs in most functional relationships, in social support, and in psychotherapy, when elicited (L'Abate, 1999b). It is inadequate, incomplete, or nonexistent in dysfunctionality.

Most other definitions, such as those listed earlier and in Moss and Schwebel (1993), Prager (1995), and Mashek and Aron (2004), consist of a wide range of intimacy terms or statements somehow related to the conceptual model developed by researchers. From these lists of items or statements, through statistical analysis, those items or statements that pertain mostly to intimacy, closeness, or related constructs emerge. Once the final format of the questionnaire is administered to a wide range of participants, it is possible, through factor analyses, to pare down those items to a variety of factors that comprise intimacy. Consequently, different factors derive from the original definition of the multidimensional model of intimacy, as illustrated previously, for instance, by Stevens and L'Abate (1989) and by Cusinato and L'Abate (1994), among many others.

Static versus Processual Definitions of Hurt Feelings

Most paper-and-pencil self-report measures of intimacy are static in the sense that they assess intimacy indirectly, with whatever emotional biases, intellectual limitations, or cultural opinions such that may exist in participants, including the effects of social presentation, impression management, and limited awareness of the process. Once this task is completed, then the whole instrument, or factors of it, are correlated with other paper-and-pencil self-report tests, and are all subjected to the same biases found in that kind of reporting. Additionally, no clinical interventions are possible, limiting these instruments in their possible applicability to evaluate self-help, health-promotion, or psychotherapy, but there are no direct interventions. These instruments can be applied to measure pre- and post-scores before and after any possible intervention. However, even seemingly inert and static self-report paper-and-pencil tests can be easily transformed into dynamic and interactive ways to intervene at various tiers of self-help, health-promotion, prevention, and especially in face-to-face (F2F), talk-based (TB) psychotherapy (see Chapters 11 and 12).

THE GATE KEEPERS OF FEELINGS

Above the experience of hurtful and joyful feelings (Figure 1.2) there are three dimensions that serve as gate keepers, allowing or disallowing (avoiding, denying, repressing, or suppressing) these feelings to surge and be expressed at supraordinate levels and forcing these feelings into deadlock to fester inside the organism. This gate-keeping function cannot be separated from self-regulation (Baumeister & Vohs, 2004) or emotion regulation (Gross, 2007).

Putative defenses based on avoidance, such as denial, repression, or suppression, have been used to indicate the functions of whatever gate-keeping mechanisms or processes are operating here. A more objective choice is to include dimensions of (1) approach-avoidance to signify contact or no contact with, or awareness or unawareness of, feelings in general and of hurt feelings in particular, in addition to (2) being able to express (discharge) or not express (delay) them explicitly or implicitly, directly or indirectly (Chapter 13 of this volume; Cusinato & L'Abate, 2012; Edelstein, & Shaver, 2004; L'Abate, 2005; L'Abate et al., 2010; Wiens & Ohman, 2007).

Osgood, May, and Miron (1975) proposed three cross-cultural clusters of feelings: evaluation, potency, and activity. Evaluation contained a hedonic component. Potency referred to intensity of feelings. Activity referred to activation of feelings. These three factors have been replicated with different methodology and names by Thayer (1989, 1996), and they constitute fundamental dimensions necessary to understanding their functions as gate keepers for underlying painful affects, moods, and hurt feelings, namely: (1) activation-deactivation, (2) a hedonic continuum of pleasure versus displeasure, and (3) tenseness-tiredness or powerful-powerless. Although there is no doubt about the first and second dimensions being present in many classifications of emotions reviewed later, one wonders whether the dimension of tenseness-tiredness could be subdivided into a third dimension of intensity or power.

Additionally, Shaver, Mikulincer, Lavy, and Cassidy (2009) conceptualized emotions as "organized sets of thoughts, feelings, and action tendencies supported and colored by physiological changes in the brain and body-changes that are generated by the appraisal of external or internal events in relation to a person's goals and concerns" (p. 93). In addition to this definition, these researchers added support to the function of gate keepers necessary to ward off hurt feelings: "Both generation and expression of emotions are affected by *regulatory efforts* (italics mine), which can alter, obstruct, or suppress appraisals, concerns, action tendencies, and subjective feelings"

(p. 93). Shaver, Schwartz, Kirson, and O'Connor (1987), as summarized by Shaver et al. (2009, p. 94), expanded on how

> regulatory efforts can alter the entire emotion process. If there is no reason to postpone, dampen, redirect, or deny the emerging emotion, the action tendencies are automatically expressed in congruent thoughts, feelings, and behaviors. However, when there are other goals in play (social norms, self-protective defenses) that make the experience and expression of a particular emotion undesirable, *regulatory efforts* are called into service to alter, obstruct, or suppress the emotion and bring about a more desirable mental state *or at least the outward appearance of a more desirable mental state.* (italics mine)

Hence, I am not alone in postulating the necessity of including gate-keeping functions specifically for hurt feelings. No gate keeping is necessary for joys and pleasures. The latter are absorbed directly in the organism without any regulatory effort when they are experienced, expressed, and shared with intimates and professional helpers.

The Hedonic Continuum: Joyfulness-Hurtfulness

Whether this continuum is controversial, as defined by two independent or related polarities, is really not as important as the relative functions of these polarities (Prinz, 2010; Russell & Carroll, 1999a, 1999b). We approach pleasant and joyful events and experiences. We avoid unpleasant, harmful, and painful experiences and especially hurt feelings (Gross, 2007). Aspects of the latter cannot be avoided anymore than death and taxes. Even though such an equation may seem simplistic at first blush, it still remains the most direct way to address such a dimension (Eaton & Funder, 2001).

Approach means dealing with, getting in touch with, and bringing into awareness feelings; it means cognitively appraising pros and cons of a painful or unpleasant experience and how that experience can, could, or should not be expressed (Clore & Ortony, 2008; Greenberg, 2008). This process occurs automatically and continues to exist and affect behavior below the level of awareness (De Giacomo et al., 2010; Fitzsimons & Bargh, 2004). Avoidance means keeping painful experiences or events buried inside the organism, yet outside of awareness, in spite of the patently negative effects this may have on our chemical, cerebral, and physiological functioning (Coan & Allen, 2007; Diefenbach, Miller, Porter, Peters, et al., 2008; Watson, 2000). Such avoidance may produce unexplained idiopathic physical or psychosomatic symptoms in Axis II Cluster C internalizing personality disorders, or sudden and seemingly unexplained impulsive explosions or acting out in Axis II Cluster B externalizing personality disorders (Kring, 2008). In Axis I, this avoidance is so powerful that any external attempt to recover or resurrect such feelings might produce a psychotic reaction (L'Abate, 2009b).

The Activation-Deactivation Continuum

Thayer (1989, 1996), more than anyone else, is responsible for contributing conceptually and empirically to this dimension of arousal/nonarousal. Clearly, he deserves the credit for introducing the importance of affect and moods into the relevant literature. However, if and when feelings and moods are equated with emotions, then the function of arousal may not be considered as critical as it should be. Moods, however, should be differentiated from feelings in a generality-specificity dimension. Moods are generally negative overall states without any specific source or identifiable stimulus. Feelings, on the other hand, unless below the level of awareness, are specific to the point that they can usually be named and can be distinguished from one another, depending, of course, on one's vocabulary and cultural background (Wierzbiska, 2009a 2009b). This distinction is made by Thayer by considering a relationship between moods and thoughts. In addition to the function of arousal/nonarousal, Thayer also introduced a dimension of tense-tired that refers to the intensity or strength of feelings reviewed in the following section.

The Intensity Continuum: Powerless and Powerful

Even though this continuum is not included in Figure 1.2 for lack of space, it is important enough to include here (Frijda, Ortony, Sonnemans, & Clore, 1992). Dimensions of activation and pleasantness are not sufficient in and of themselves to account for their gate-keeping functions. How strong or weak a traumatic or nontraumatic but hurtful experience is might determine whether it will be forgotten or stored in long-term memory and allowed to surface if and when necessary to be appraised and reappraised (Kensinger & Schacter, 2008). Such judgment becomes part of a ratio of positive and negative memories that we store within ourselves, which affect relationships with intimate and nonintimates (Gottman et al., 1997). This is the reason for including pleasant feelings at the same level with hurts – they are already included in joys (Figure 1.2). No gate-keeping function is necessary with joys, because pleasant, pleasurable, and positive feelings do not need any constraint or effort to be remembered. However, when the intensity and frequency of hurts overwhelm positive feelings, hurts offset and eradicate any pleasure and joy (Knobloch & Solomon, 2002).

Here is where awareness and memory play an important function (Kensinger & Schacter, 2008). The more we avoid hurtful experiences, the greater the ratio of negative to positive memories and the greater their effects on emotional and relational functioning (Gross, 2007). Pleasant memories do not need the effort of avoidance, denial, repression, or suppression that hurtful memories require; these avoidances produce the so-called unconscious or not-so-conscious motivation for certain behaviors (Bargh, 2008; De Giacomo et al., 2010; Hassin et al., 2005; Eisenberg, Smith, Sadovsky & Spinrad., 2004; Eisenberg, Hofer, & Vaughn, 2007; Wiens & Ohman, 2007). Intensity of hurt feelings, therefore, depends on the ratio of joyful to hurtful feelings. The more the joys, the less the intensity of hurtful feelings. The latter is more intense if not mitigated by the former.

PREVIOUS CLASSIFICATIONS OF BASIC FEELINGS AND EMOTIONS

An exhaustive review of the literature would find many other classifications (Barrett, 2006; Thamm, 2006). Hence, the one presented next is not the last, but it will need a nuanced rationale for its inclusion here. Hurts are those included in Table 1.1 and Figure 1.2. They are fundamental to whatever supraordinate feelings stem from the base of the funnel. Any discussion of basic feelings must include previous classifications, but there are perhaps as many classifications as there are textbooks on feelings and emotions (Ekman & Davidson, 1994; Thamm, 2006).

Multilevel models were briefly considered by Power and Dalgleish (1997) and by Berenbaum, Raghanvan, Le, Vernon, and Gomez (2003). Lazarus and Lazarus (1994) classified emotions (not feelings) into the following categories: (1) nasty emotions, including anger, envy, and jealousy; (2) essential emotions including anxiety, fright, guilt, and shame; (3) emotions provoked by unfavorable life conditions, including relief, hope, sadness, and depression; (4) emotions provoked by favorable life conditions, including happiness, pride, and love; and (5) empathic emotions, including gratitude, compassion, and those aroused by aesthetic experiences.

Another classification of feelings and emotion was suggested by Sanford (2007) as borne of Buck's (1999) developmental interaction theory. Buck distinguished hard, selfish emotions such as anger, domination, and power from soft, prosocial emotions such as sadness and hurt (pp. 65–66), which relate to the experience or expression of vulnerability. Such a distinction also posits different hemispheric dominances – right hemisphere for selfish emotions and left hemisphere for prosocial emotions. These dominances may lead to the distinction between externalizing and internalizing tendencies in criminality and psychopathology respectively (L'Abate, 2005).

A distinction that Sanford attributes to his own previous work and to Bradbury and Fincham (1989) pertains to the proximal versus distal effects of emotions: Proximal effects are "immediate, changeable, event-dependent aspects of a particular situation, whereas distal effects have to do with stable characteristic of the person" (p. 67). Proximal implies within-person variance, whereas distal implies between-person variance. In an important study relevant to a classification of feelings rather than emotions, Sanford and Rowatt (2004) followed up on this classification by distinguishing among three types of negative emotion (hard, soft, and fear-based) that are integral to functioning in close interpersonal relationships. Hard emotions include anger, soft emotions include feeling sad or hurt, and fear-based emotions include feeling anxious or threatened.

Married participants in Studies 1 and 3 and college roommates in Study 2 rated the extent to which they would feel different emotions in response to a variety of negative partner behaviors. Confirmatory Factor Analysis supported the distinction between three types of emotion. Although hard and soft negative emotions are highly positively correlated, they had opposite effects when used to predict relationship functioning. After controlling for shared variance between the emotions, soft emotion was associated with positive relationship functioning (high satisfaction, low conflict, and low avoidance). Hard emotion was associated with negative relationship functioning (low satisfaction, high conflict, and high avoidance). In contrast, fear-based emotion was strongly, positively, and uniquely associated with relationship anxiety.

Thamm (2006) presented a multileveled model of emotions after an exhaustive review of various approaches to emotion classification. He proposed four formal criteria fundamental to formal dimensions and levels of emotion differentiation according to these six levels:

Level I. Positive and Negative "Kingdoms" of Emotions.
Level II. Normal and Abnormal "Phyla" of Emotions.
Level III. Static and Dynamic "Classes" of Emotions.
Level IV. Expectations and Sanctioning "Orders" of Emotions.
Level V. The Comparative "Families" of Emotions.
Level VI. The "Genera" of Subtle Emotions.

Thamm's outline reproduced here does not do justice to the classification of emotion; to discover whether it is empirically feasible to be evaluated in detail conceptually and empirically will require wider attention by emotion theorists and researchers.

Another classification based on relationship closeness and disruptions potential was proffered by Bersheid and Ammazzalorso (2003, p. 323). They separated intense "hot" emotions, such a fear, jealousy, anger, frustration, passion, joy, and excitement, from less intense, weak "feeling states," such as sadness, loneliness, happiness, need, and contentment. Such a classification puts together emotions and feelings that seem separate from each other. For instance, at least conceptually, joy and excitement should be correlated with happiness and perhaps contentment, whereas fear, jealousy, and anger might correlate with sadness and loneliness. Furthermore, criteria to discriminate between intense emotions and weak feelings do not seem sufficiently validated to warrant what seems a rather questionable dichotomy; such a distinction requires a more sophisticated conceptual and empirical revision.

A recent hierarchical trilevel classification comes close to the one presented in Figure 1.2 (Widen & Russell, 2008, p. 349). It consists of a supraordinate level comprising a dimension of pleasure, hedonic neutrality, and displeasure. At a lower basic level, pleasure is related to happiness; neutrality is related to surprise; and displeasure is related to fear, anger, disgust, and sadness. At a subordinate level, happiness can be divided into excitement and contentment; surprise can be divided into startle and shock; fear can be divided into terror and anxiety; anger into fury and indignation; disgust into contempt and repulsion; and sadness into remorse and sorrow. Widen and Russell included a circumplex model of emotion comprising two orthogonal axes of high arousal/sleepiness and pleasure/displeasure (p. 349). Distress is located in the displeasure/high-arousal quadrant. Excitement is located into the high-arousal/pleasure quadrant. Depression is located in the displeasure/sleepiness quadrant. Finally, serenity is located in the sleepiness/pleasure quadrant.

Both models are interesting and relevant to the historical aspects of emotion classifications. However, the same error is mentioned repeatedly, that is, the equating of feelings at the receptive side with emotions at the expressive side and not distinguishing between the two separate processes – internal and external. Furthermore, the hierarchical model is not exhaustive and self-sufficient in and of itself, because an additional circumplex model is needed to account for feelings and emotions not considered in that hierarchical model.

Comparisons between both models and the one presented earlier in this chapter are inevitable in terms of their respective pros and cons. Inevitably, a question relevant to all three models will query which model can encompass the others. However, an open model, such as the one described in Figure 1.2, may integrate the models presented previously.

CONFLICTS AND CONTROVERSIES ABOUT HURT FEELINGS

Controversies arise over the most frequently used terms, such as *distress, negative emotions, social pain*, and even *emotional disturbances*, because of their inconsistent use in the extant literature and because they represent circumlocutions that avoid dealing directly with specific hurt feelings in favor of using pell-mell undefined and generic terms; they fail to distinguish between feelings on the receptive, subjectively receiving input side and emotions on the expressive output side, as well as hurt feelings, which remain inside unless they are elicited experimentally, experientially, or clinically (Coan & Allen, 2007; L'Abate, 1997, 1999a, 2005, 2009b). If terms such as distress, negative emotions, social pain, or emotional disturbances are left unspecified and are inconsistently used, how can we hope to relate them to physiological, cerebral, gender, individual, and cultural differences? How can we measure these feelings if we do not have an operational definition that is specific and clear? If hurt feelings constitute the essence of our existence, we will not be able to study them using terms inconsistently and controversially defined.

At least three major hierarchical classifications of emotions, each with its pros and cons, have been proposed, one by Berenbaum et al, (2003), a second by Widen and Russell (2008), and a third presented here and elsewhere (L'Abate, 2009b). The first two already have been compared and contrasted. It will be important to compare and contrast all three empirically once they have been compared and contrasted conceptually. Ultimately, a conceptual comparison of these three representative models would require more space than has been allotted.

However, without such a conceptual analysis, the ultimate criteria of any theoretical model is its empirical verifiability and its clinical applicability to various populations varying in levels of functionality/dysfunctionality. From these criteria it is a short distance from progress to fruitfulness in how productive a model is in eliciting research on underlying cerebral and physiological factors as well as individual, gender, and cultural correlates. For instance, the list defining hurt feelings has already been used as a practice exercise with Italian undergraduates and has been used with addicts and inmates (Maino, research in progress). Another list of practice exercises in English dealing with the antecedent causes of hurt feelings is still experimental. How will proponents of other feeling classifications verify the validity of these models? If a model is valid in the laboratory, how applicable will it be to semiclinical and clinical populations?

HURTFUL FEELINGS AND THE "UNCONSCIOUS"

Why concentrate on hurtful rather than on nonhurtful feelings? This concentration is based on the hypothesis that it takes more effort to avoid and suppress hurtful feelings than nonhurtful ones (Bargh & Williams, 2007; Baumeister, Zell, & Tice, 2007; Campbell-Sils & Barlow, 2007; Eisenberg et al., 2004, 2007; Fitzsimmons & Bargh, 2004; Loewenstein, 2007). Pleasant and pleasurable experiences may not need avoidance, repression, suppression, or cognitive reappraisal. They may be stored in long-term episodic memory and may be accessed at will whenever there is an occasion to be reminded of them (Fredrickson & Cohn, 2008; Kensinger & Schachter, 2008; Lucas & Diener, 2007). Positive feelings, therefore, may be forgotten, but no effort is needed to avoid, deny, repress, or suppress them. Any adequate classification of feelings needs to include pleasurable feelings in order to differentiate natural, functional forgetting from dysfunctional avoidance, denial, repression, and suppression of hurtful feelings (Fredrickson & Cohn, 2008; Isen, 2008).

Thus, hurtful feelings may constitute the so-called *unconscious* because they are avoided, whether through denial, repression, or suppression. As Greenberg (2008) concluded: "Awareness of emotion also involves overcoming the avoidance of emotional experience" (p. 91) or intimacy (Firestone & Catlett, 1999; Vangelisti & Beck, 2007). Hurtful feelings are stored within the organism, both cerebrally and physiologically, with deleterious health-damaging outcomes (Consedine, 2008; Diefenbach, Miller, Porter, Peters, Stefanek, & Leventhal, 2008; Kemeny & Shestyuk, 2008). Outside of our awareness, these feelings may affect our behavior to a much greater degree than pleasurable experiences (Laird & Strout, 2007; Wiens & Ohman, 2007). What is relevant here is the ratio of positive to hurtful feelings when one overwhelms the other in frequency and intensity (De Giacomo et al., 2010; Nielsen & Kaszniak, 2007; Wiens & Ohman, 2007).

THE NATURE OF INTIMATE RELATIONSHIPS

Emotionality, that is, how feelings are experienced first and how emotions are eventually expressed, is imbedded in intimate relationships. What are intimate relationships and how can they be characterized in relation to hurt feelings? Starting with a distinction between communal/expressive and agentic/exchange/instrumental characteristics (Bakan, 1968), intimate relationships tend to focus on their communal/expressive rather than on their agentic characteristic, in spite of the latter characteristics being just as important. This means that to be intimate, certain relationships should fulfill at least four requirements: closeness, commitment, interdependence, and duration. Nonintimate relationships are characterized by the lack of these four requirements.

Closeness

How can we differentiate between closeness – a quality denoting individuals living under the same roof and sharing financial and practical responsibilities – from intimate ones? Individuals could be linked by legal, financial, and practical responsibilities within the confines of a physical structure, yet they may be distant with respect to their emotional availability to each other in times of stress and distress (Clark, Fitness, & Brissette, 2003; Dresner & Grolnick, 1996; Parks & Floyd, 1996). Hence, we need to differentiate between physical and emotional closeness. The latter is developed through actual caring, not just words (Seltzer & Heller, 1997). Physical closeness is not synonymous with emotional closeness. Many individuals in jails and hospitals live in close quarters, but it is frequently questionable whether or not there is intimacy. This distinction will be expanded at the end of this section.

Commitment

Since the classical article by Stanley and Markman (1992), commitment has achieved a prominent place in the literature and research on relationships. As Fehr (2003) reviewed this requirement, she found it difficult to separate commitment from love, raising questions about the nature of love, a topic necessary to consider in close relationships (Branje, Frijns, Finkenauer, Engels, & Meens, 2007; Etcheverry & Le, 2005; Etcheverry, Le, & Charania, 2008; Kurdek, 2008; Le & Agnew, 2003; Marston, Hecht, Manke, McDaniel, & Reeder, 1998; Rusbult & Buunk, 1993; Rusbult, Kamashiro, Coolsen, & Kirchner, 2004). There are individuals who are afraid or unwilling to commit themselves wholeheartedly to a relationship, perhaps to avoid sharing hurt feelings with someone who may belittle or criticize them for those feelings (Acker & Davis, 1992; Birnie, McClure, Lydon, & Holmerg, 2009; Ogolsky, 2009; Weigel & Ballard-Reisch, 2002). Of course, having a satisfying romantic relationship is not always feasible, particularly if and when, with time, one discovers a partner's less-than-perfect characteristics. For instance, it is possible for less committed partners to be more vulnerable to negative partner characteristics than are highly committed partners.

In another instance, Arriaga, Slaughterbeck, Capezza, and Hmurovic (2007) had forty-one dating couples individually indicate their commitment level and then assign them to receive positive- or negative-false feedback about the partner's personality, and then indicate their post-manipulation satisfaction and uncertainty levels. Negative partner feedback affected the satisfaction level of less committed but not of highly committed individuals. Feeling uncertainty about the relationship mediated less committed partners' increase in vulnerability to negative partner information. The association between uncertainty and commitment was curvilinear and stronger under conditions of relationship threat. Self-esteem did not predict response to threat.

Interdependence

This characteristic means that there is a continuous mutual give-and-take exchange within and without the Golden Rule of reciprocity (Burger & Milardo, 1995: Holmes, 2002; Kelley & Thibaut, 1978; Murray & Holmes, 2009; Rusbult, Arriaga, & Agnew, 2003; Rusbult, Kamashiro, Coolsen, & Kirchner, 2004; Rusbult & Van Lange, 2003; Segrin, Badger, Meek, Lopez, Bonham, & Sieger, 205) without a partner proclaiming his or her autonomy and independence from loved ones, as some adolescents may do (Dresner & Grolnick, 1996). Once we live under the same roof in close and committed relationships, interdependence is inevitable. Everybody has to depend on everybody else for survival as well as for enjoyment. No one is exempt from participating reciprocally unless seriously sick or handicapped (Kurdek, 2007). This interdependence extends to parent-child bidirectionality (Lollis & Koczynski, 1997; Pettit & Lollis, 1997) as well as in families (O'Connor, Hetherington, & Clingempeel, 1997). Interdependence, however, should not be equated with reciprocity. One could be very dependent on someone else but deny such a dependency at the same time (Uehara, 1995).

Duration

Once the three previous characteristics are fulfilled, the chances of a relationship surviving for a long time may be high, but it is not always certain. There are always unpredictable, unexpected events that occur suddenly and that derail the duration of the relationship. Accidents, death, job loss, and other misfortunes will stress, and in many cases distress, a group of people living under the same roof and who fulfill the three previous characteristics.

These four characteristics/requirements, however, say nothing about the level of functionality in relationships of this kind. Many relationships may possess all four characteristics but also function erratically, inadequately, and ineffectively – if not destructively. Here is where intimacy, as defined in this work, must be considered as the positive glue that links individuals with other individuals, because only in most functional relationships is intimacy present (Levine, 1991). Of course, given the wide range of possible relationships, intimacy may be present all the time, most of the time, sometimes (at funerals and weddings), almost never, and never (L'Abate et al., 2010).

CONCLUSION

Hurtful and joyful feelings are fundamental to psychological and relational functioning. The scientific and professional avoidance of hurt feelings thus far mirrors what happens to most of us. We approach pleasure and avoid pain. This scientific and professional avoidance, however, cannot be ignored or overlooked any longer. Whether they are called traumas, sufferings, sorrows, or distress, and although they are attributed a negative valence, hurt feelings must be addressed scientifically and professionally, lest emotion scholars and professional helpers continue to remain irrelevant to the human condition. This admittedly strong statement represents my convictions, which will be backed up with evidence throughout this volume. Semantic analysis is not sufficient to discover consistencies, inconsistencies, and contradictions in emotion science. Critical analysis of basic constructs is necessary before entertaining empirical comparisons of existing hierarchical frameworks. It may take time and space to arrive at an integration of various theoretical models before embarking on and producing the research necessary to support them. As much as one would want to consider in greater detail joys and pleasures, one can only devote time, space, and energy to one topic at a time. Therefore, only hurt feelings will be considered in the rest of this volume, in spite of the admitted importance of joys and pleasures in their own rights. This same writer will cover joys and pleasures in a more adequate fashion that, by necessity, cannot be considered here (L'Abate, 2011c).

PART ONE

BACKGROUND

Most of what is known to this writer about hurt feelings, their avoidance, and their approach will be considered in this section.

2

Hurts: The Avoided Feelings

There is substantial experimental evidence to indicate that other mammals are affective creatures. Probably all vertebrates that exhibit strong instinctual emotional behaviors experience affects.

Panksepp (2008, p. 49)

The task of semantic analysis is usually assigned to philosophers, but on occasion scientists take on this responsibility.

Kagan (2007, p. 5)

The purpose of this chapter is to show how hurt feelings are avoided not only by humans, but also by the scientific and professional literature. This avoidance is either straightforward – hurt feelings are not mentioned – or indirect – as when a host of circumlocutions are used to avoid dealing with these feelings directly. However, an important distinction should be made from the outset: There is a difference between avoidance and neglect. Avoidance means denying, repressing, and suppressing hurt feelings. Neglect means being aware of those feelings but ignoring them by denying their importance. Neglect is another expression of avoidance.

With the advent of recent important publications (Barrett, Mesquita, Ochsner, & Gross, 2007; Coen & Allen, 2007; Reisenzein & Doring, 2009), relying on this distinction between feelings on the receptive side and emotions on the expressive side and adding a critical semantic analysis (such as performed in this chapter) might seem like beating a dead horse. However, equating and lumping together feelings with emotions without distinguishing between these two *separate* processes (L'Abate, 2009b) is an equation that is still persistently strong in the extant emotion literature. It must be shown that such an equation is misleading conceptually, unnecessary empirically, and superfluous practically.

HURT FEELINGS: THE FUNDAMENTAL BUT
NEGLECTED AFFECTS

Should there be any doubt about the pervasive absence of the term "hurt feelings" in the scientific psychological literature, a simple check of subject indexes of most emotion-related treatises as well as psychological textbooks in developmental, social, and personality psychology will suffice (Baumeister & Vohs, 2004; Coan & Allen, 2007; Gross, 2007; Lewis, Haviland-Jones, Barrett, 2008). The term "hurt feelings" or its equivalents will not be found. If and when generic terms such as "distress" or "negative feelings" are used frequently in these and other emotion-related texts, seldom will they be defined or appear in subject indexes. Furthermore, what is the difference between "unwanted emotions" (Campbell-Sills & Barlow, 2007, p. 545), "intense emotions" (Campbell-Sills & Barlow, 2007, p. 549), and "negative emotions"? Are sadness or depression unwanted, intense, or negative? (Bonanno, Goorin, & Coifman, 2008). Here is where value judgments and faulty equations about feelings lead into a veritable semantic Tower of Babel and an empirical trap.

The topic of hurt feelings is usually avoided by the scientific and professional literature, echoing arguments already proffered by Leary and Springer (2001). This topic has not been included in psychological theories or evidence about feelings and emotions. Instead, indirect terms such as "distress," "negative feelings," "social pain," or "emotional disturbances" have been and are frequently used to indicate the presence of underlying disturbing, painful, and traumatic conditions. These indirect constructs are used often without defining or including them in subject indexes. If and when such constructs are defined operationally, they either are measured inconsistently, with different metrics, or are described by models that cannot be verified directly.

This chapter, therefore, will show how hurt feelings are avoided in the scientific literature (L'Abate, 2009b) and will present a tripartite model that can locate hurt feelings as an underlying determinant of anger, sadness, and fear.

A Semantic Phenomenological Approach

Before considering in greater detail how affective feelings develop, emerge, and grow into emotions, it is important from a semantic phenomenological viewpoint to consider five major conceptual errors that have influenced and still plague the study of affective feelings and expressed emotions: (1)

refusing openly to consider and use the term hurt feelings; (2) equating feelings with emotions; (3) giving a judgmental valence to feelings; (4) considering emotions before feelings; and (5) using "distress" or similar terms that consist of undefined and unspecified affective feelings below and underneath the level of basic "core" feelings, such as social pain, upset, and "negative feelings" (Barrett & Russell, 1999). This critical semantic phenomenological approach does eventually lead back to an operational definition of hurt feelings amenable to empirically replicable verification.

Direct Aversion to the Term Hurt Feelings

Jerome Kagan, above and beyond a critical review of the emotion literature (2007), expressed a negative opinion about hurt feelings (personal communication, May 28, 2008). In spite of Kagan's possibly relevant and reasonably well-taken objections, the thesis that hurtful feelings lie at the basis of our experience, but have been avoided in the extant scientific and professional literatures, is expanded here.

Equating Feelings with Emotions

Most of the past literature on feelings and emotions blends and equates feelings as emotions without differentiating one process from the other. Feelings and emotions are viewed as being one and the same process: Emotions are understood to include affects, moods, and feelings, all under same label, an error I have pointed out repeatedly in the past (L'Abate, 1986, 1997, 2005, 2009b). This conceptually faulty equation has lead to further theoretical confusion and empirical dead ends (Abramowitz, Whiteside, Lynam, & Kalsy, 2003), where "negative affect" is defined by diagnosis of depression and anxiety disorders, sadness, and anger, or by inferred but undefined "emotional distress in general."

Affective feelings usually have been inferred and interpreted from expressed emotions or from self-reports and are not visible unless or until they are elicited (L'Abate, 1997, 2005, 2008a, 2009b). At best, some sources have differentiated feelings as "affects" (Watson, 2000) or as "emotional experience and subjective well being"(Saarni, 1999). At the receptive side, as also represented by receptive language functions, feelings have different cerebral and physiological correlates and determinants than expressed emotions and expressive language functions. The former are related to cerebral and physiological factors. The latter may be more likely determined by and related to cultural and socialization influences (Larsen, Berntson, Poehlmann, Ito, & Cacioppo, 2008; Shweder, Haidt, Horton, & Joseph, 2008; Stearns, 2008). That possibility means that there is a feedback loop from emotions to feelings according to the principles of equifinality and equipotentiality.

Recently, this faulty equation has been corrected by the work of Coan and Allen (2007), in which many contributors were able to separate the two processes conceptually and empirically, and by the work of Panksepp (2008), who argued about the fundamental importance of affective feelings as occurring before emotions. Nonetheless, this faulty equation is still present to this day in the relevant literature (Lewis, Haviland-Jones, & Barrett, 2008), in spite of a recent review issue focused on emotional experience as supposedly separate from its expression (Reisenzein & Doring, 2009) and a chapter on that topic (Barrett, Ochsner, & Gross, 2007).

Another misdirection in the literature on feelings and emotions is found in the way the topic is addressed. Usually feelings and emotions are combined and assigned the same importance without distinguishing between their separate functions and processes as far as their salience or developmental level are concerned (Lewis, Haviland-Jones, & Barrett 2008a). Consequently, no distinction or differentiation about their relative functions or salience can be made. The controversy about just how many feelings or how many emotions really exist – anywhere from five to fifteen or more at the expressive side (Izard, 1979) – has resulted in the viewing of feelings as emotions linearly and equally on horizontal and vertical axes, as in circumplex models (Gray & Watson, 2007; Russell, 1980; Russell & Barrett, 1999; Widen & Russell, 2008).

Not all feelings and emotions are created equal. This is why we need a vertically hierarchical model to differentiate feelings on the receptive side before beginning to deal with their positive or negative expression as emotions on the output side (Figure 1.2). We assume, admit, and accept, even provisionally, that we cannot live and love without experiencing excitement, enthusiasm, and even ecstasy without inevitable losses, rejections, put-downs, and betrayals, that is, the hurts to joys ratio (Greenberg, 2008; L'Abate, 1997, 1999b; Vangelisti, 2009).

Plutchik and Kellerman's (1983) seminal work and Mascolo and Griffin (1998) questioned what emerges in emotional development. To answer that question, Saarni's (1999, 2008) comprehensive model of competent emotional socialization is partly built on the presence of seemingly developmentally progressive skills. Although the phrase "distressing circumstances" was used by Saarni (1999) in a chapter title and liberally in the text, the phrase was left undefined and did not appear in the subject index. Nonetheless, Saarni's skills model could become a starting point to evaluate whether hurt feelings in general develop progressively throughout the life cycle and whether and how they particularly vary or covary with gender and individual differences as well as with personality socialization and maturation (Harris, 1989; Lewis, Haviland-Jones, & Barrett 2008; Magai, 2008).

Value Judgments about Feelings

When feelings are considered separately from emotions, which does not happen very often, the emotion literature erroneously and misleadingly separates them into "negative" and "positive" feelings *or* emotions (Beach & Fincham, 1994; Kagan 2007; Russell & Carroll, 1999), or "negative affectivity" (Davila, Bradbury, & Fincham, 1998). This practice has been criticized repeatedly (L'Abate, 1997, 2005, 2009b). Usually anger and sadness have been included in this category without considering that the developmental trajectory of each feeling is completely different. Anger tends to lead toward externalizations and Axis II Cluster B personality disorders in the DSM-IV (American Psychiatric Association, 1994). Sadness tends to lead toward internalizations and Axis II Cluster C personality disorders (Fox & Calkins, 2000; Kring, 2008; L'Abate, 2006). Fear tends to lead toward Cluster A of Axis II and disorders of Axis I. Beach and Fincham (1994), for instance, defined negative affectivity in marriage as composed of distress (undefined), anger, and sadness, without considering that for anger, sadness, and fear, the developmental trajectories of these feelings lead to completely different outcomes.

Even without considering their different trajectories, it is misleading to include into an hedonic positive-negative dichotomy feelings that do not deserve such value judgment, especially when there are no validated criteria to make such distinctions (Kagan, 2007; L'Abate, 1997). Expressed emotions, on the other hand, may be divided into positive and negative, depending on their personal and relational impact.

Considering Emotions before Feelings

The two conceptual errors just cited lead to a third source of confusion – considering emotions before feelings, which is akin to putting the cart before the horse. Feelings, as "primitive affect," occur before their expression, not after emotions. Feelings need to occur before we can express them. However, that is usually not the case. Just to use one recent egregious example, Lewis (2008) considers "emotional expressions" with their development from page 310 to page 311. Emotional experiences and their development are considered from page 311 to page 314. This is not the only example that can be cited. If pressed, a complete list of such a practice can be found readily in the relevant literature (Frijda, 2007, pp. 82–83).

However, the reason for this sequence depends on what Lewis defines as emotional experiences:

> Emotional experiences as the interpretations and evaluations by individuals of their perceived situations, emotional states, and expressions. Emotional experiences require the individuals attend to their emotional states (i.e., changes in their neurophysiological behavior), as well as the situations in which the changes occur, the behaviors of others, and their own expressions. (p. 311)

Therefore, by Lewis adding completely cognitive and contextual aspects to affective feelings, these feelings, as he defines them, certainly do occur together with or after emotional expressions. On the other hand, if feelings refer to what he calls attending to "changes in neurophysiological behavior," then the latter definition of affective feelings as subjective inside-the-skin experiences locates them before their out-of-skin expression. Feelings in their primitive, sensory, and cerebral perception occur before their expression. Here is where the difference in localization needs to be understood. Emotional experiences according to Lewis's definition as cognitive appraisal certainly occur after feelings have been experienced, and when expressed as emotions, words are used to identify them. Feelings as sensations and perceptions of internal cerebral, muscular, and physiological changes occur according to the present formulation before they are expressed as emotions (L'Abate, 1986; Panksepp, 2008).

Using "Distress" as an Undefined and Unspecified Emotional State

The emotion literature uses "distress" without ever defining it. Many examples have been given as to how this term is used frequently and inconsistently in the emotion literature without even being defined, except in one out of a dozen instances (L'Abate, 2009b). When this term is used in a text, it is usually not cited in the subject index. However, what are the contents of that distress and at what level does it function? It is no wonder that Huston (2009) could not find support for an inadequately defined model of "emergent distress" to predict success or failure in marriage. When the term distress is used in marital conflicts (Papp, Goeke-Morey, & Cummings, 2007), for instance, we do not know whether that term denotes anger, disgust. sadness, fear, or anything else.

Even more important, in addition to frequent previous examples already cited (L'Abate, 2009b), it is important to trace historical considerations of distress in the three editions of an encyclopedic treatise about emotions (Lewis & Haviland-Jones, 1993, 2000; Lewis, Haviland-Jones, & Barrett,

2008). For instance, in the first edition (Lewis & Haviland-Jones, 1993), in the subject index distress was considered only once within the entry of sadness and included was in the text without any specification (Stearns, 1993). In the second edition (Lewis & Haviland-Jones, 2000), in the subject index distress received two entries, first as distress signals in infants (Fox & Colkins, 2000) and second within the context of sadness (Barr-Zisowitz, 2000). In both instances, distress was left undefined.

However, Barr-Zisowitz (2000, p. 618) raised an interesting, somewhat prophetic question about distress: "I am now arguing that what is biologically basic is distress, not sadness. Is there a way to explain the function of distress?" She went on to refer to grief and loss theorists who "felt that distress functions to help people become more aware of what they value, in part to motivate them to conserve what is important, and more importantly to maintain attachment to others." Barr-Zisowitz cited distress "as an explanation for the problem of human suffering" (p. 618), adding: "I am skeptical that it would be possible to operationalize such an hypothesis, through certainly it seems intuitively appealing" (p. 618).

In the third edition of Lewis, Haviland-Jones, and Barrett (2008), distress is cited eleven times in the subject index. However, in the text this term is either left undefined or it is used inconsistently, except for the work of Panksepp (2008). He clearly defined what he meant by "separation distress" and demonstrated its existence in rats. Otherwise, distress in infants (Lewis, 2008, pp. 308–309, 316) is listed, but in his model of development of "emotions" (not feelings) over the first three years of life, Lewis lists distress at the same level as contentment, joy, interest, and surprise over sadness, disgust, anger, and fear during the first years of life. However, he leaves distress undefined, a practice followed by many other contributors in the same volume (Lewis, Haviland-Jones, & Barrett 2008).

In an exception to the foregoing argument, this is not the case in the model proposed by Widen and Russell (2008; Figure 21.2, p. 349), where distress is defined by displeasure and high arousal; depression, as a polar opposite to distress, is defined as displeasure and low arousal. However, in this model distress is located at the same level of analysis as depression. Distress occurs at a different, more basic level of experience than depression, as shown by the research of Leary and his collaborators (Chapter 6, this volume).

In discussing the development of facial expressions, Camras and Fatani (2008) quote Oster (2005), who proposed that "pouting" in infants may reflect an effort at "distress regulation" rather than sadness, a label that fails to capture the more specific meaning and signal value of distress (p. 295).

Camras and Fatani (p. 295) argue that certain extreme emotional expressions may "reflect a more generalized distress reaction" that does not correspond to discrete emotional labels such as anger or sadness. Distress belongs to a different level of discourse and interpretation than anger, a conclusion highlighted by a model presented here and supported by Leary's work.

Whereas Hoffman (2008) proposed "global emphatic distress" (p. 444, 446), Bates, Goodnight, and Fite (2008) proposed "novelty distress" with two different patterns, one "under gentle maternal control" and the other as "predisposition to novelty distress" (p. 490). Minsky (2008, pp. 625–626) came close to hurt feelings by what he called "pain" as a physical or mental sensation that leads to conditions such as "hurting," "distress," and "suffering." Kring (2008), in her list of emotion-based symptoms related to DSM-IV-TR disorders (pp. 692–693), included "marked distress" for adjustment disorders. However, without a definition, it is impossible to determine what kind of distress she means and how it is related to adjustment disorders. Lemerise and Dodge (2008) reviewed theory and research on anger as a primary emotion or as differentiated from a "generalized distress state" (p. 730).

The most egregious uses of "negative affect" (Addis, 2008, p. 168) or "general distress" (Nolen-Hoeksema, 2008, p. 181) as underlying states to explain gender differences in depression, only serve to indicate the need to specify what these terms mean (L'Abate, 2009b). An even more relevant point, however, is made by Nolen-Hoeksema in her excellent summary of gender differences in depression. In asking what women do when they are "upset," that is, what they do in response to *amorphous negative affect* (p. 179, italics mine), she asserts that they tend to ruminate whereas men tend to act out negative affect by drinking, swearing, or, more positively, becoming involved in sport. Nolen-Hoeksema's use of the qualifying "amorphous" nature of negative feelings supports De Giacomo's et al. (2010) expansion of Pennebaker's A to D model. This means moving from an underlying analogic, amorphous, and undefined mass at the internal, receptive input side to a digital, verbal, nonverbal, or written expression of feelings on the output side. This mass, more often than not, is composed of hurt feelings that constitute the unconscious.

Apparently, the term distress has been taken for granted and accepted uncritically and inconsistently to describe whatever hurtful feelings might be considered as the essence of our experience and existence. Notable exceptions to this conclusion are found in (1) Baumeister, Zell, and Tice, (2007, p. 423), where distress is defined "as an umbrella term to refer to unpleasant, upsetting, or negative moods or emotions"; (2) Russell (1980), who placed distress at the other side of relaxation in a circumplex model;

and (3) frequently in Lewis, Haviland-Jones, & Feldman Barrett (2008, pp. 316, 349f, 446–447, 590f, 692–693t, 730).

As one can determine from this review, the distress construct remains undefined and inconsistently used in past references. It does not receive the attention it deserves, because in addition to being left undefined most of the time, it has not been accorded citation in subject indexes until lately, and it is left without a specific function or position in relation to other core feelings. This is why distress as hurt feelings belongs to a different underlying level of analysis and discourse below core feelings. By defining it operationally, it can be subjected to verification and expansion (Table 1.1), and even preventive and clinical applications (Chapter 12, this volume).

Additional Conceptual Errors May Lead to Questionable Research and Results

The foregoing semantic analysis is not complete by any means. We must consider the circumlocutions and misleading equations of hurt feelings with such other descriptors as: (1) negative emotions, (2) social pain, and (3) emotional disturbances.

Hurt Feelings as Negative Emotions

Negative feelings is another term that is left undefined and absent from subject indexes, even though it is frequently used in most emotion-related literature. The negative valence applied to feelings is most unfortunate because it groups completely different feelings with completely different developmental and relational outcomes, as shown, for instance, by Flannery, Montemayor, and Eberly's research (1994), and in Huston and Chorost's longitudinal study (1994). Such valence is an unnecessary moralistic value judgment that goes back to ethical and religious historical roots rather than being supported by empirical evidence – positive means "good," negative means "bad" (Kagan, 2007, p. 11).

Except for feelings being joyful (pleasant/pleasurable) or hurtful (unpleasant/not pleasurable), their expression as emotions does definitely need a positive-negative valence. This would be the case of DSM-IV (American Psychiatric Association, 1994) Axes I and II disorders, as noted by Kring (2008). A distinction between primary and secondary feelings may be a more appropriate and meaningful way to distinguish among feelings in terms of their different developmental outcomes, different cerebral localizations, and physiological factors (Damasio, 1994, 1999, 2003). Hurtful feelings in Table 1.1 would qualify as primary feelings. They relate to physical and emotional survival in flight, possibly as an avoidance of hurt feelings in Axis I and Axis II Clusters A and C personality disorders; they may also relate to fight, possibly in Cluster B personality disorders (Kring, 2008; Mullin & Hinshaw, 2007).

Higher-level feelings (Figure 1.2) would qualify as secondary, even tertiary or higher. Damasio (1994) indicated that cerebral locations of these two classes of feelings, primary and secondary, may differ, a finding corroborated also by others (Beer & Lombardo, 2007; Davidson, Fox, & Kalin, 2007; Larsen et al., 2008; LeDoux, 1998; LeDoux & Phelps, 2008; Ochsner & Gross, 2007). Niedenthal et al. (2006) did consider how feelings and emotions arise from the socialization process, including (pp. 299–300) how the genders experience and express what they call emotions differently (Blechman, 1990; Brody & Hall, 2008; Magai & McFadden, 1995).

Here is where the scholarly psychological literature on feelings and emotions shows its inconsistency and limitation (L'Abate, 1997, 1999, 2005, 2009b). In Niedenthal's et al. work (2006), for instance, undefined circumlocutions, such as distress (p. 55, 60), injury (p. 78), or even hurts (p. 99, 286) are cited but not defined or included in references or subject indexes. The same omission is found in another introductory text (Oatley & Jenkins, 1996), where distress, to these authors' credit, does appear in the subject index even if left undefined in the text.

Hurt Feelings as Social Pain

In a controversial article concerning the relationship between social and physical pain, MacDonald and Leary (2005) hypothesized that social exclusion is experienced as painful because reactions are mediated by aspects of the physical pain system. This overlap in social and physical pain may be due to an evolutionary development to aid social animals in responding to threats of exclusion. There is evidence showing that humans demonstrate convergence between the two types of pain in thought, emotion, and behavior. This convergence, that social and physical pain may share common physiological mechanisms, is demonstrated primarily through nonhuman animal research. This implication may allow exploration for a theory of social pain as related to rejection-elicited aggression and physical-pain disorders.

Panksepp (2005) commented on this possible overlap by citing substantial evidence that separation-distress (here called hurt feelings) in animal models may be related intimately to opioid-sensitive pain regulatory systems of the brain. However, the evidence that basic pain-affect mechanisms may be integral to feelings of defensive fear, anxiety, and aggression seems modest. Although anger and anxiety can be reduced by opiates, effects do not seem as robust and specific as those observed with low doses that may quell separation distress. The role of social pain may be larger for the affective underpinnings of jealousy, shame, and guilt (all variants of social exclusion and abandonment) than for fear and aggression. Interdisciplinary insights into these relationships might be facilitated by more forthright analyses of how affective states are created within the brain. These analyses will require a better dialogue between behavioral neuroscientists and psychologists interested in foundational psychoevolutionary issues.

Corr (2005) discussed the implications of MacDonald and Leary's hypothesis, in which their viewpoint was supported by a hierarchical defense system. Research findings may be better understood by a system of interacting neural modules, which may lead to state dissociations between affective states and by general modulatory influences on the entire defense system. This system may lead to trait associations (i.e., personality) between physical pain and emotional distress.

MacDonald and Leary (2005) replied to Panksepp's (2005) emphasis on social pain mechanisms by clarifying their positions on the topics of anger, the usefulness of rat models, the role of analgesic mechanisms, and basic motivational processes. In response to Corr's (2005) emphasis on physical defense mechanisms, MacDonald and Leary clarified their positions on the relation of social exclusion to fear, the value of the pain affect construct, and the nature of the social pain experience. Consideration of the roles of both social pain and defense mechanisms is essential to best understand human response to social exclusion.

Hurt Feelings as Emotional Disturbances

Berenbaum et al. (2003) presented a hierarchical model for a proposed taxonomy of emotional disturbances, defined as being "present when the emotion system operates in such a way that adaptation is impeded rather than promoted, resulting in undesirable consequences for the well-being of either the individual whose emotion system is in question or of others around the person" (p. 208).

Below the level of emotional disturbances, these authors allocated a second level comprising emotional value disturbances, emotional intensity/regulation disturbances, and disconnections. The third level of this model comprised emotional valence disturbances divided into unpleasant and pleasant; emotional intensity/regulation disturbances were divided into emotional hyperreactivity and hyporeactivity; disconnections were divided into affect and awareness. At a fourth level, predominantly unpleasant disturbances were divided into deficits in pleasant and excesses in unpleasant emotions. Predominantly pleasant emotions were divided into deficits of unpleasant in unpleasant and excesses in pleasant emotions. The fifth and final level included deficits in pleasant emotions that lead to happiness, tranquility, contentment, pride, and love/affection; excesses in unpleasant emotions lead either to distress, sadness, fear, anxiety, anger, and fear or to self-conscious shame, guilt, and embarrassment. Deficits in unpleasant emotions lead to fear, guilt, and shame, whereas excesses in pleasant emotions lead to happiness (euphoria), pride, love/affection, interest/curiosity. Using this hierarchical model, Berenbaum et al. illustrated the relationship between pleasant and unpleasant in emotional valence disturbances and emotional intensity/regulation disturbances, demonstrating the clinical utility of this taxonomy with four case descriptions.

Rottenberg and Gross (2003) in commenting on the this taxonomy, decried what had been the gist of previous criticisms (L'Abate, 1997, 2005, 2009b): "Unfortunately, for many years, considerable confusion has clouded the use of emotion-related constructs, with different investigators employing their own, often idiosyncratic definitions and operalizations of terms such as affect, emotion, and mood" (p. 228). A major issue addressed by Berenbaum et al. that merits highlighting is to offer a taxonomy that addresses both functional and dysfunctional aspects of emotions. Rottenberg and Gross (2003) then emphasized the importance of emotional generation and regulation to develop a more nuanced taxonomy of emotional disturbances grounded in a causal analysis of underlying processes. They proceeded to illustrate their points by drawing on recent studies of depression that would build a much-needed bridge between affective and clinical science.

Watson (2003) discussed potential problems with and limitations in Berenbaum's et al. taxonomy, such as lack of evidence to support the existence of predominantly pleasant disturbances in psychopathology. Emotional reactivity is confounded with valence, and it is unclear whether these two proposed types of disturbances actually provide independent information. Therefore, this taxonomy fails to model the behavioral substrate of emotions in a way that should supplant rather than supplement existing psychiatric classification.

Litz (2003) commented on Berenbaum's et al. taxonomy by emphasizing the distinction between emotional experience and expression problems, independent of diagnostic labels: "[I]t is unclear whether, at present, specific, functional emotional processing difficulties can be reliably and validly assessed," including trauma and posttraumatic stress disorder (PTSD) (p. 239).

These four terms, distress, negative emotions, social pain, and emotional disturbances, therefore are either left undefined, or if defined, are insufficient and inadequate to describe the internally subjective experience derived from abandonment, abuse, loss, criticism, discounting, or betrayal, among other aversive events (L'Abate, 1997). As Kagan indicated (2007, p. 9), there may be an "inadequacy of most language to capture the range of intensity and quality of frequent human experiences."

THE RELATIONSHIP BETWEEN FEELINGS AND EMOTIONS

What is the relationship between feelings and emotions? Can we say that hurt feelings always produce depression? What about acting out, externalizing Cluster B individuals with personality disorders who discharge and explode with minimal provocation? Can we predict what emotion can be related to which feeling? What about depressed, internalizing Cluster C personality disorders who keep their feelings inside without sharing them with anyone and who are at risk of committing suicide? At this point the answer is no. The best we can say is that the relationship between affective feelings and expressed emotions is nonlinear, even though we can make some predictions that a great deal of chronic anger, based on a great many unexpressed hurt feelings, very likely will lead toward Cluster B personality disorders and, in extremes, to murder. Sadness, based on great unexpressed hurt feelings, may very likely lead to Cluster C internalizing personality disorders with depression and, in extremes, to suicide (L'Abate, 1997, 2005). Fears, in their unexpressed extremes, may lead to psychopathology, as will be discussed in greater detail. These predictions are probable but not absolute. Other factors, including intensity and ratio of joyful to hurtful feelings, presence of rationality, degree and type of awareness, and perceived context need consideration and inclusion (Cusinato & L'Abate, 2012; L'Abate et al., 2010).

In expanding on the nonlinearity of affective feelings with expressed emotions, we must consider three possibilities:

1. *Equipotentiality*: One of the five core feelings may cause different expressed emotions; that is, not all anger will lead to murder any more than all sadness will lead to suicide. In considering the relationships between feelings and emotions, we must evaluate the extent and ratio

of hurtful to nonhurtful, pleasant, and joyful feelings experienced over prolonged periods of time, as processed through Rationality, expressed as Activity, corrected by Awareness, and occurring within a perceived proximal and distal Context, the ERAwC model (Cusinato & L'Abate, 2012; L'Abate, 1986, 2005; L'Abate et al., 2010).

2. *Equifinality*: Different feelings may cause the same emotion; a combination of anger, sadness, disgust may lead to complete avoidance of any emotional expression or could lead to a more proactive expression, again depending on the extent of how many joyful and pleasant experiences one has experienced in comparison to hurtful ones, how much reliance is present on Rationality, extent of positive or negative Activity, and extent of Awareness and of perceived internal and external Context (L'Abate, 2009a).

3. *Multicausality*: Different hurt feelings may cause a variety of emotions essentially producing a chaotic and unpredictable outcome in how these feelings will be expressed as emotions. This may cause a variety of unexpected negative outcomes, such as random murders, unprovoked attacks, seemingly unexpected suicides, and so forth. Another way to explain this possibility lies in the existence of a confused, undifferentiated mass of undefined and otherwise unexpressed hurt feelings mixed together without any avenue of expression except violence against others and/or self, such as extremely confusing and unpredictable nonverbal behaviors in expressed emotions, including murder or suicide, as will be elaborated.

Hurt Feelings as the Unconscious

What is called distress may be composed of an amorphous, ambiguous, analogic amalgam of undefined feelings that may constitute the unconscious (De Giacomo et al., 2010). If not elicited and expressed verbally, nonverbally, or in writing in functional relationships, this undefined analogic mass may linger inside the organism producing untold physical and emotional negative outcomes (Denollet, Nyklicek, & Vingerhoets, 2008; Myers, Burns, Derakshan, Elfant, et al. 2008). If avoided and unelicited, as usually happens in dysfunctional relationships, this amorphous mass consists of hurt feelings that instead constitute the so-called unconscious. This condition may vary along a dimension of unspoken or spoken experiences and memories, interacting with completely unconscious, quasi- or semiconscious, completely conscious but not expressed as in self-silencing (Jack, 1987, 1991, 2001; Jack & Dill, 1992), and completely conscious and spoken past hurts (Bargh, 2007: Barrett, Niedenthal, & Winkielman, 2005; Ohman,

2008). Aggression should be greater in the small-brained, not-so-intelligent species, as well as with children of lower intelligence. Language becomes possible through the use of contrived symbols (e.g., lexigrams in some primates). Even though there may not be speech, in some apes the ability to think and to problem-solve reduces the frequency and likelihood of aggression when apes interact with humans. As the brain becomes more elaborate, the interrelating of the labels becomes more likely and more complex. This is the essence of language – labels and their interrelating with others. Language as a public, interpersonal process rests on members of a species being able to agree about the referential basis for a signal. Then, semantics, syntax, and Ph.D.s become possible. By implication, aggression should be greater in the small-brained, not-so-intelligent species (Butler & Hodos, 2005; Rumbaugh & Gill, 1976; Rumbaugh & Washburn, 2003).

These seemingly minor semantic phenomenological differentiations have important implications for discovering the molecular, cellular, visceral, physiological-muscular, and cerebral bases of hurt feelings in their own rights, separate and independent of emotions (Panksepp, 2008). The major question raised by these differentiations lie in whether there can be emotions without feelings, a question that on the basis of the analyses conducted in this and previous writings may seem nonsensical. However, except for when we are dealing with unconscious hurt feelings, there may be a disconnect, if not a dissociation, between which feelings one may avoid and which emotions one may express without any awareness of their underlying bases, as, for instance, in histrionic personality disorders.

Another issue raised by the present formulation lies in the possibility that responses at one level of analysis may become stimuli at another level. For instance, either an internal stimulus or an external event may act as a trigger to elicit a given feeling. The feeling, therefore, becomes an emotional response to the internal stimulus or to the external event. However, feelings as responses are emotions that may in turn become stimuli when elicited at an intrapersonal level and experienced by someone else. Those responses could become stimuli for responses from others interpersonally. Those responses could go back to elicit new or more intense feelings that become emotions in a reflexive, never-ending chain of circular internal and relational processes (L'Abate, 1986, 1997, 2005).

TOWARD A HIERARCHICAL MODEL FOR HURT FEELINGS

If hurt feelings are at the bottom of our existence, and if they are not expressed and not offset by joyful and pleasurable feelings, then they will produce negative outcomes in how emotions are expressed outwardly. The fundamental uniqueness of hurt feelings is supported by its many pioneers (Chapter 6, this volume). Nonetheless, an additional model contained in Figure 2.1 is necessary. This tripartite model assumes that there are three extreme derivations from hurt feelings that lead developmentally into three separate negative trajectories: anger, sadness, and fear. Sometimes the term depression is used as synonymous and includes sadness, which mixes levels of discourse. Sadness is a feeling. Depression is a psychiatric label given to external, dysfunctional expressions of sadness.

In an important study furthermore, in trying to test key tenets of what they called a model of "specific emotions" of marital conflict on children, Crockenberg and Langrock (2001) illustrated how erroneous it is, conceptually and empirically, to lump together different emotions. Parents reporting about their marital conflict strategies were observed interacting with their six-year-old children and rated their children's behavioral adjustment. Children reported their emotional reactions to specific interparental conflicts. Results supported the specific emotions model; that is: *Children's behaviors mirrored the marital or parental behaviors of same-gender parents.* Indirect effects of marital aggression through parental behavior were detected, and marital and parental behaviors interacted to predict girls' externalizing. Girls' anger, sadness, and fear increased with fathers' marital aggression. Fear and anger by fear interaction predicted girls' internalizing. Fathers' marital aggression interacted with anger to predict externalizing and interacted with fear to predict internalizing in boys.

The foregoing research is highlighted because it is relevant to gender differences. The conclusion of children's behaviors mirroring marital or parental behaviors of same-gender parents is supported by the results of Weissman, Wickremaratne, and Nomura. Warner's et al. (2006) study that showed offspring of depressed parents constituted a high-risk group for psychiatric and medical problems, which begin early and continue through adulthood, which therefore warrants early detection of this disorder.

Consequently, the rest of this chapter is devoted to studies specifically related to the three feelings that derive from hurt feelings (Figure 2.1). However, there are studies where both anger, guilt, and sadness in marriage, such as the one by Guerrero, La Valley, and Ferinelli (2008), examined how expressions of those three feelings are related to marital (in)equity and satisfaction. Data from ninety-two couples demonstrated that feeling over-benefited was positively linked with guilt, whereas being under-benefited was positively associated with anger. For wives, being under-benefited was more positively associated with sadness. People who perceived equity

Hurt Feelings		
Anger	Sadness	Fear
Personality Disorders		Psychopathology
Externalizations	*Internalizations*	*Axis I**
Cluster B Axis II*	Cluster C	Cluster A
Oppositional	Shyness	Developmental
Defiant disorders	Shame	peculiarities
Conduct disorders	Guilt/remorse	Irregular socialization
Hostility	Phobias	Ruminations
Resentment	Anxieties/worries	Bipolar disorders
Envy	Depressions	Paranoias
Jealousy	Dissociations	Severe depressions
Antisocial		Schizophrenias
Personality disorders		
	Ultimate outcomes	
Murder	Suicide	Extended care

*Diagnostic and Statistical Manual for Mental Disorders-IV (2000).

FIGURE 2.1. A multilayered, tripartite model of hurt feelings and their major derivatives.

reported using more constructive, prosocial emotional expressions; under-benefited people reported using more destructive, antisocial emotional expression; and over-benefited people reported using both prosocial and antisocial emotional expressions. Both husbands and wives reported higher levels of marital satisfaction when they perceived themselves to be treated equitably or to be over-benefited as compared to under-benefited. Angry feelings and aggressive expressions of anger may mediate the relationship between under-benefiting inequity and marital satisfaction, and the way people express anger mediated the relationship between anger and marital satisfaction.

Anger

Anger is the major characteristic feeling of extreme, externalizing, impulsive, and antisocial, criminal, and aggressive personality disorders described by Cluster B in Axis II of the DSM-IV, and is defined by discharge, dysregulation, or dysinhibition of feelings in general and of hurt feelings in particular (Lemerise & Dodge, 2008; Mullin & Hinshaw, 2007; Patrick, 2007; Spielberger, Reheiser, & Syderman, 1995). In its extreme, anger would progressively lead to acting out, aggression, and finally, to murder. One characteristic of the extreme prototype of these disorders, psychopathic and sadistic personalities, lies in the relative absence of fears (Hare, Cooke, & Hart, 1999), a characteristic that is relevant to their presence in the other two derivations from Model 2.1: sadness and fear.

Anger in Children and Youth

Although preschool-age children are at risk for witnessing domestic violence, the majority of research has focused on children ages six to twelve years. Levendosky, Huth-Bocks, and Shapiro (2003) studied how children function in families experiencing domestic violence. Maternal report and behavioral observations of mother-child interactions were used to assess relationship quality. Participants consisted of 103 children and their mothers. The results fit the Model 2.1 well, but these researchers indicated that some of the correlations were not in the expected direction. Although depressed mothers struggled with parenting, other mothers appeared to be compensating for the violence by becoming more effective parents. Domestic violence negatively impacted children's behavior with their mothers but did not influence maternal report of problem behavior, suggesting that the impact of domestic violence begins very early and in the realm of relationships rather than in individual mental health.

Support for Figure 2.1 related to anger is found in the research of Levendosky, Leahy, Bogat, Davidson, and von Eye (2006), among many others. They examined whether maternal functioning mediated the relationship between domestic violence (DV) and infant externalizing behavior. Participants were 203 mother-infant dyads. Support was found for a partially mediated model in which maternal functioning mediated the relationship between current DV and infant externalizing behavior. Past DV was directly associated with infants' externalizing behavior. Of course, these results suggest the need for early intervention and prevention for families such as these at risk for violence.

Because anger in close relationships is not only a source of strain, but can also serve to further emotional competence, a questionnaire was constructed by von Salisch and Vogelgesang (2005) on nine strategies of anger regulation within a same-sex friendship (SAR). A factor analysis of the children's version resulted in four factors: (1) confrontation and harming; (2) distancing; (3) explanation and reappraisal; and (4) humor. A confirmatory factor analysis corroborated the compatibility of the factor structures of the children's and adolescents' version of the SAR by adding three more factors: (1) redirection of attention; (2) ignoring; and (3) self-blaming and reappraisal. Results of a five-year longitudinal study suggests that participants tended to use negotiation more frequently as adolescents than as children. Aggression and distancing strategies declined in adolescence. These results were discussed under the perspective that learning to manage conflicts of interest and anger without resorting to hostility (or avoidance) is a social task of friendship.

Externalization, found in most Cluster B personality disorders, is the outcome of anger and hostility derived from one's family of origin (Richmond & Stocker, 2006; Stocker & Richmond, 2007). Hussong, Wirth, Edwards, Curran, et al., (2007) examined heterogeneity in risk for externalizing symptoms in children of alcoholic parents, as it may inform the search for entry points into an antisocial pathway to alcoholism. These investigators tested whether the number of alcoholic parents in a family, the comorbid subtype of parental alcoholism, and the gender of the child predicted trajectories of externalizing symptoms over the early life course, as assessed in high-risk samples of children of alcoholic parents and matched controls. Through integrative analyses of two independent, longitudinal studies, Hussong et al., showed that children of either an antisocial alcoholic parent or two alcoholic parents were at greatest risk for externalizing symptoms. Moreover, children with a depressed alcoholic parent did not differ from those with an antisocial alcoholic parent in reported symptoms. These findings were generally consistent across mother, father, and adolescent reports of symptoms, child gender, and child age (ages two through seventeen). Multialcoholic and comorbid-alcoholic families thus convey a genetic susceptibility to dysregulation along with environments that both exacerbate this susceptibility and provide inadequate support to offset it.

The cumulative effect of maternal mental health disorders, substance use, and DV on risk of behavior problems in young children was examined by Whitaker, Orzol, and Kahn (2006). DV was present in at least one of three categories: (1) depressive or anxiety disorder; (2) substance use (smoking, binge drinking, and illicit drug use); and (3) domestic, emotional, and physical violence. The prevalence of child behavior problems increased with the number of categories (0, 1, 2, or 3) in which the mother reported a condition, respectively: (1) 7, 12, 17, and 19 percent for aggression; (2) 9, 14, 16, and 27 percent for anxious/depressed; and (3) 7, 12, 15, and 19 percent for inattention/hyperactivity. This graded risk persisted after adjustment for sociodemographic and prenatal factors and for paternal mental health and substance use.

Prospective measures of psychosocial risk factors as predictors of severe intimate-partner violence in a community sample of 610 young adults at risk for intergenerational transmission of depression were examined by Keenan-Miller, Hammen, and Brennan (2007a, 2007b). The hypothesized factors were youth history of depression by age fifteen and maternal history of depression. Youth functioning at age fifteen was tested as a mediator of these associations. Results showed that youth history of depression by age fifteen predicted victimization at age twenty. Severe violence perpetration was predicted by maternal depression history among women but not men. Youth social functioning was a partial mediator of both associations. These findings suggest that psychosocial factors observed in adolescence may contribute to the risk of experiencing severe partner violence during young adulthood.

Perhaps the seemingly contradictory results of the last two foregoing studies may be explained further by the results of a study by Tull, Jakupcak, McFadden, and Roemer (2007) who argued more to the point of presumed hurt feelings, even though they used the catch-all term of "heightened negative affect intensity." The tendency to evaluate emotions negatively may be associated with the development and maintenance of posttraumatic stress symptoms. However, the specific role of these vulnerabilities has yet to be explored. Thus, this study was conducted to examine the influence of negative affect intensity and the fear of emotions in posttraumatic symptom severity among 102 childhood interpersonal violence victims. Fear of emotion significantly predicted posttraumatic symptom severity above and beyond negative affect intensity and negative affect. These findings also suggest that posttraumatic outcomes may not be influenced by an underlying vulnerability of heightened negative affect intensity, but instead are affected by the extent to which emotional responses are negatively evaluated.

Mahoney, O'Donnelly, Boxer, and Lewis (2003) examined the interplay of marital and severe parental physical aggression, and their links to child behavior problems, in 232 families of clinic-referred adolescents. Combined reports from mothers and adolescents indicated that two thirds of adolescents exposed to marital aggression in the past year had also experienced parental aggression. Mothers and fathers who used and/or were victims of marital aggression were both more likely to direct aggression toward their adolescent. Mother and youth reports of marital aggression were tied to each party's report of greater externalizing problems and to youth reports of greater internalizing problems. Severe parental aggression uniquely predicted maternal report of both behavior problems, after controlling for marital aggression; the reverse was not true. Also, adolescents exposed to both types of family aggression did not display greater maladjustment than those subjected to only one type of family aggression.

This study, among others reviewed in this volume, also illustrates the conceptual and empirical error cited in the course of this chapter by combining under one catch-all term of "negative affectivity" terms with completely different developmental trajectories. We do not know how much anger, sadness, and fears may have contributed to the overall effect of this catch-all term.

The relationship between use of physical punishment of children, marital conflict, and individual adult hostility were examined longitudinally by Kanoy, Ulku-Steiner, Cox, and Burchinal (2003) among others (Deater-Deckard, Lansford, Dodge, Pettit, & Bates, 2003. Couples expecting their first child completed self-report scales of individual information during the prenatal period. The marital problem-solving situations were again assessed at two and five years following the child's birth. At the later points, discipline practices were assesses through interview. A climate of negativity, manifested through either high rates of individual hostility or marital conflict, predicted the use of more frequent and severe physical punishment of children at two and five years, even when parental educational level was controlled.

Anger in Adults
However, the ability to make precise distinctions among related personality constructs helps clarify theory and increases the utility of clinical assessment (L'Abate, van Eiden, Goldstein, & Rigamonti, in press). For instance, Smith, Fischer, Cyders, Annus, et al. (2007) evaluated the validity of distinctions among four personality-like traits in three studies relevant to Cluster B personality disorders; (1) sensation seeking; (2) lack of planning; (3) lack of persistence; and (4) urgency, acting rashly when *distressed* (italics mine). Factor analyses indicated that lack of planning and lack of persistence are two distinct facets of one broader trait, whereas urgency and sensation seeking are both very modestly related to each other and to the planning/persistence measures. These authors, after developing an interview assessment for each trait according to a multitrait, multimethod matrix, found clear convergent and discriminant validity among their constructs. Distinctions among them were useful. Traits accounted for different aspects of risky behavior. Sensation seeking appeared related to the frequency of engaging in risky behaviors, and urgency appeared related to problem levels of involvement in those behaviors.

This interpretation is supported by a study by Briere and Rickards (2007) about abuse and trauma exposure because it predicted identity problems, affect dysregulation, and relational disturbance of 620 individuals from the general population. Multivariate analyses indicated that maternal (but not paternal) emotional abuse was uniquely associated with elevations on all seven scales of the Inventory of Altered Self-Capacities (IASC): Interpersonal Conflicts, Idealization-Disillusionment, Abandonment Concerns, Identity Impairment, Susceptibility to Influence, Affect Dysregulation, and Tension Reduction Activities. Low paternal (but not maternal) emotional support did not significantly decrease the negative effects of maternal abuse. Sexual abuse was predictive of all IASC scales except for Interpersonal Conflicts and Identity Impairment. Non-interpersonal traumas and adult traumas were typically unrelated to IASC scales. Childhood emotional and sexual maltreatment – perhaps especially maternal emotional abuse – may be critical factors in the development of disturbed self-capacities.

Anger in Couples

Hostility may contribute to risk for disease through psychosocial vulnerability, including the erosion of the quality of close relationships. Baron, Glazer, Smith, Butner, Neadley-Moore et al. (2007) examined hostility, anger, concurrent ratings of the relationship, and change in marital adjustment over eighteen months in 122 married couples. These investigators found that wives' and husbands' hostility and anger were related to concurrent ratings of marital adjustment and conflict. In prospective analyses, wives' but not husbands' hostility and anger were related to change in marital adjustment. Hierarchical regression and statistical models about wives' anger was a unique predictor of both wives' and husbands' change in marital adjustment. The association between wives' anger and change in husbands' marital satisfaction was mediated by husbands' ratings of conflicts in the marriage. These results support the role of hostility and anger in the development of psychosocial vulnerability, but also suggest an asymmetry in the effects of wives' and husbands' trait anger and hostility on marital adjustment.

How can we reconcile the occurrence of violence with an underlying antecedent of depression? Figure 2.1 would predict a direct intergenerational transmission of violence through the mediation of anger rather than depression. However, Keenan-Miller's et al., study did not specify whether the gender of participants was only males, both men and women, or only women. Notice that fathers were not considered as predictors of severe intimate-partner violence. Consequently, we do not know whether fathers were evaluated about their propensity for violence. A more complex selfhood model (Chapter 13, this volume) would predict that depressed wives (as shown in various studies reported in this and other chapters) might usually marry hostile, angry husbands who would serve as direct models for their sons as perpetrators of violence toward their wives. Violent men, who represent the extreme in anger and hostility, predictably exhibit poor empathic accuracy when attempting to understand their female partner's thoughts and feelings (Clements, Holtzworth-Munroe, Schweile, & Ickes, 2007).

Physical aggression in at-risk couples significantly increased the likelihood of relationship dissolution, even after accounting for psychological aggression, prior relationship satisfaction, and relationship contextual factors (length of relationship, relationship type, and children in the household). Of the contextual factors, relationship type was predictive of relationship dissolution (Shortt, Capaldi, Kim, & Owen, 2006). However, both men and women may tend to report less abusive behavior and consequent injury than partners reported about them. In other words, perpetrators tend to minimize the intensity and frequency of aggressive acts, whereas victims may tend to maximize the same acts (O'Leary & Williams, 2006). Marital problems of former POWs are more related to PTSD than to captivity, which is also associated with decreased marital satisfaction, increased verbal aggression, and heightened sexual dissatisfaction among former POWs (Dekel & Solomon, 2006).

Slep and O'Leary (2009) explored whether and how men and women differ in their risk profiles if they are (1) not physically aggressive; (2) physically aggressive toward only their children or their partners; or (3) aggressive toward both children and their partners. Risk factors unrelated to the partner of parenting role (e. g., impulsivity) and specific to one of these roles (e.g., negative parenting attributions or negative partner attributions) were examined using profile analysis. Dually aggressive men and women had the highest overall risk across all types of risk factors; nonaggressive men and women had consistently low risk factors. Individuals who were aggressive toward only their partners or their children had distinct risk profiles, with highest levels of risk on the role-specific risk factors rather than on the role-related risk factors. These results suggest that theories of partner and parent aggression might gain precision if co-occurrence status were specifically taken into account.

Sanford (2005) investigated two types of attributions believed to predict anger in married couples. Wives' anger was expected to be predicted by event-dependent attributions, appraisals based on the unique aspects of one's current situations. Husbands' anger was expected to be predicted by schematic attributions, appraisals based on one's global sentiment in the relationship. Sanford found strong support for the expected gender differences, suggesting that wives are particularly attentive to the details of interpersonal interactions.

More specifically and to the point, Rogge, Bradbury, Hahlweg, Engl, and Thurmaier (2006) used measures of communication, hostility, and neuroticism taken from eighty-five couples from Germany before marriage to find whether these measures predict marital outcomes five years later. Hostility and neuroticism discriminated between couples who separated or divorced after five years and those who remained married, whereas communication discriminated between marriage-satisfied and marriage-dissatisfied couples. Only hostility and neuroticism predicted marital satisfaction at eighteen months, suggesting that these factors contribute to rapid, early declines in marital functioning. Rogge et al. (2006) concluded that poor communication alone cannot account for the full range of marital outcomes and that skill-based models of marriage can be strengthened by considering relatively rare exchanges between partners (e.g., aggression) and their enduring vulnerabilities (e.g., neuroticism).

All this information supports the view that hurt feelings underlie most if not all of anger and hostility. What other explanatory construct could be used instead?

Sadness

Sadness is the major characteristic feeling of depressed individuals whose major developmental trajectory is visible in internalizing Cluster C personality disorders (PDs) based on inhibition and restraint (Bonanno, Goorin, & Coifman, 2008; Campbell-Sils & Barlow, 2007; Hammen, 1991; Ohman, 2008; Pauli-Pott & Beckman, 2007; Rottenberg, 2007). This feeling in its extremes might lead to the actual act of killing oneself, concretely or functionally, as in the inability to function appropriately and adequately. There is evidence that depression during adolescence and early adulthood, following high school graduation, may be marked by deficits in interpersonal functioning. However, few studies have prospectively examined whether interpersonal difficulties are a risk factor for depression onset, so it is unclear whether these deficits in interpersonal functioning may be products or predictors of depression. Eberhart and Hammen (2006) aimed to clarify the direction of associations between interpersonal factors and depression by examining whether social factors longitudinally predicted onset of depression in a diverse sample of young women with no history of depression. Hierarchical regression analyses controlling for baseline depressive symptoms indicated that poorer family relationship quality and anxious attachment cognitions predicted onset of depressive episodes during a two-year period. Further, a wide range of interpersonal factors predicted depressive symptoms over six months, including poor peer and family relationship quality, difficulty being close to others, and difficulty depending on others, controlling for baseline depressive symptoms and college attendance. These results may provide evidence for the importance of an interpersonal perspective on vulnerability to depression.

Sadness in Children and Parents

Indeed, the more depressed parents were, the more the children showed negative affectivity and lack of effortful control (Pesonen, Raikkonen, Heinonen, Jarvenpaa, & Strandberg, 2006). Significant interactions with the parent's gender and between the spouse's depressive vulnerabilities were found by these investigators, highlighting the fact that child outcomes are dependent on family processes. All associations were independent of maternal and paternal depressive symptoms. Additionally, Leung and Slep (2006) investigated relations among parents' psychological difficulties (i.e., depressive symptoms, overt anger), dysfunctional attributions for child misbehavior, and inept discipline in a representative community sample of 451 mothers and 449 fathers. Depressive symptoms and anger were hypothesized to relate to discipline via their link with parents' attributions. Path analyses revealed the depressive symptoms predicted parent-centered causal attributions (i.e., stable, global, and dispositional), which in turn related to laxness. Depressive symptoms also predicted child-centered responsibility attributions (i.e., controllable, intentional, and negative), which in turn related to overactivity. Anger predicted overactivity directly. The patterns of relations were similar for fathers and mothers. The importance of addressing parents' psychological difficulties and dysfunctional attributions in interventions for families with disruptive children was highlighted by these findings.

Predictors of maternal depression trajectories were examined longitudinally by Poelmann, Schwichtenberg, Bolt, and Dilworth-Bart (2009) in families with an infant born preterm or at a low birth weight. A total of 181 mother-infant dyads enrolled in the study before the infants' neonatal intensive care unit (NICU) discharge. Maternal depressive symptoms were assessed at five time points, and contextual variables and infant risks were assessed at NICU discharge. Hierarchical linear models revealed that mothers who experienced more risk factors reported more depressive symptoms just before their infant's NICU discharge and showed less decline in depressive symptoms in the months immediately following the child's birth.

Although cumulative risks predicted depression trajectories, this effect appeared driven by maternal and family sociodemographic risks rather than infant risks. Addition of family support as a covariate in the multi-level models with a subsample of families revealed that social support and depression covaried across time. However, most of the findings regarding the association between risk and depression remained consistent, whereas the effects of maternal race and multiple birth were slightly attenuated.

Sadness in Women

Some depressed women have a history of antisocial behavior, but research into maternal depression has not ascertained whether this conclusion has implications for children of depressed mothers. Kim-Cohen, Caspi, Rutter, Tomas, et al. (2006) compared the developmental outcomes in caregiving environments provided by depressed mothers with or without an antisocial history. These investigators found that, compared with children of mothers with depression only, children of depressed and antisocial mothers had significantly higher levels of antisocial behavior and rates of DSM-IV conduct disorders, even when the number of symptoms and chronicity of maternal major depression was controlled. Children of depressed and anti-social mothers were at an elevated risk of experiencing multiple caregiving abuses, including physical maltreatment, high levels of maternal hostility, and exposure to domestic violence. Consequently, if one ignores the common co-occurrence of an antisocial history in depressed mothers, it may obscure significantly elevated risks in children's development for early-onset psychopathology.

Coyne, Thompson, and Palmer (2002) compared three groups of women – outpatients depressed, inpatient depressed, and community control – and their husbands on a range of variables including marital functioning and styles of coping with conflict. Outpatients depressed couples reported greater marital distress and more destructive and less constructive tactics for resolving conflict than did community control couples. They also were more likely to have been previously married and to express regrets about having married their current husbands. There were smaller and less consistent differences for couples with inpatient depressed spouses, although inpatient couples with younger wives were similar to outpatient depressed couples. Both groups of depressed women and their husbands reported fewer expressions of affection and more complaints about their marriage than did control couples. These results indicate how even though depression may originate in the individual it does have important effects on intimate relationships.

Sadness in Old Adults

The buffering function of parental and partner bonding in the relationship between negative life events and depressive symptoms at old age was examined by Kraaij and Garnefsky (2002). A community sample of 194 people aged sixty-five years and older was interviewed. In particular, the control dimension of both parental and partner bonding seems to be of importance in relation to elderly depression. More psychological control is related to higher depression scores, and low partner control seems to work as a protective mechanism when negative life events are faced. Developing prevention and intervention programs aimed at optimizing bonding relationships throughout life seems advisable.

Sadness in Personality Disorders

However, many impulsive, unexpected, and unpredictable acts could be traced to avoided (denied, repressed, or suppressed) hurt feelings. One example of how depression in Cluster C PDs can express itself above and beyond just sadness, can be found in the study by Lejoyeux, Arbaretaz, McLoughlin, and Ades (2002). They discovered how a great many PDs can be traced back to depression in a psychiatric institution, rather than in a jail, prison, or penitentiary, where "pure" Cluster B PDs are more likely to be found. Lejoyeux et al. assessed the frequency of impulse control disorders (ICDs) and their association with bulimia, compulsive buying, and suicide attempts in a population of thirty-one depressed inpatients with the Minnesota Impulsive Disorders Interview, Zuckerman Sensation-Seeking Scale, and Barratt's Impulsivity Rating Scale.

Among these participants, they found eighteen cases of intermittent explosive disorder, three cases of pathological gambling, four cases of keptomania, three cases of pyromania, and three cases of trichotillomania. Patients with co-occurring ICDs were significantly younger (mean age = 37.7 versus 42.8 years). Patients with kleptomania had a higher number of previous depressive episodes (5.7 versus 1.3). Patients with pyromania had a higher number of previous depressions (3.3 versus 1.3). Bipolar disorders, bulimia, and compulsive buying were much more frequent than with antisocial personality disorders (Cluster B) who had higher scores on motor impulsivity than the other patients.

Consequently, only pure internalizing disorder predicted suicidal ideation in addition to psychosocial variables, such as social support, family environment, negative life events, and problem-solving (Esposito & Clum, 2003). In spite of these mixed results, there is ample evidence to support the association between marital quality and depression (Davila, Karney, Hall, & Bradbury, 2003; Uebelacker & Whisman, 2006).

Sadness in Couples

Beach and O'Leary (1993) examined the ability of early and concurrent relationship satisfaction to predict newlyweds' level of depression. The sample consisted of 241 couples, all white, responding to advertisements for couples about to marry. Both spouses were assessed prior to marriage and at six and eighteen months after marriage. Marital relationship variables were found to be predictive of later depressive symptomatology for all spouses, but a chronically dysphoric subsample was found to be more reactive to changes in marital adjustment. These results were interpreted as support for the hypothesis that those who are chronically dysphoric are more vulnerable to stresses within the marital relationship. There was no evidence that the prospective effect of marriage on later symptoms was moderated by gender.

Fear

This feeling was already defined in Chapter 1 of this volume, but as Levitt and Dubner (2009, p. 8) viewed it in its outcome: "Fear sometimes distorts our thinking to the point where we become convinced that certain threats are so enormous as to be unstoppable." Chronic and intense fears are possibly at the bottom of most psychopathologies, leading to avoidance of close intimate relationships and to the development of internally deviant thoughts and ruminations, as in Cluster A of Axis II and in disorders described by Axis I in the DSM-IV. Cluster A personality disorders and Axis I severe psychopathologies represent the extreme outcomes of chronic fear with a concomitant inability to approach any kind of feeling, very likely not even fear because of the many criticisms, emotional overinvolvement, and lack of warmth received over a long period of time (Blanchard, Cohen, & Correno, 2007; Ciompi. 1998; Mueser, Bellack, Wade, Sayers, Tierney, and Haas, 1991).

Fear of rejection seems one of the most powerful types of fear (Feeney, 2009, pp. 317, 322; Kowalski, 2009, p. 472; Shaver, Mikulincer, Lavy, & Cassidy, 2009, pp. 105–106) and fear of loneliness (Metts, Braithwaite, & Fine, 2009, p. 345):

> [T]here is also the possibility that experience of excessive and enduring levels of hurt can promote physical and psychological withdrawal that eventually cease to function as an effective coping strategy. Dispositionally

sensitive or vulnerable individuals, for example, may be psychologically paralyzed both by the lingering pain of past hurts and the anticipation of future hurt to the point where they fail to maintain existing relationships and shy away from initiating new relationships. (p. 339)

Metts's et al. hypothesis was supported by DeWall, Baumeister, and Masicampo's (2009, p. 123), emphasizing that "emotional numbness" results from social exclusion and that this construct "may prove more useful than emotional distress" (p. 123). In addition to emotional numbness, DeWall et al. (2009) added "detachment" as one of the outcomes of social exclusion. The foregoing conclusions and finding may go a long way to trying to describe and perhaps understand the role of fear in the etiology of severe psychopathologies.

Among severe psychopathologies, of course, one must differentiate among schizophrenias, bipolar disorders, severe depression, and paranoias. Whereas very little if any emotionality might be seemingly shown in the first condition, a great deal of on-and-off emotionality is expressed in bipolar disorder (Johnson, Gruber, & Eisner, 2007), alternating between mania and depression. Emotionality, on the other hand, is continuously expressed in the paranoias, as the prototypical examples of fears, where fears of definite physical harm to the self from external and imagined adversaries and enemies are clearly and unambiguously expressed and externalized (Blaney, 1999).

Schizophrenias

Here is where Ohman and Ruck's four principles of fear may be relevant. Even though these researchers relate these principles to anxiety disorders, I beg to differ with them. I believe that chronic fear of feelings in general and especially fear of dealing with hurt feelings is at the bottom of the severe psychopathologies considered in this section. In spite of this disagreement, these principles bear including: (1) fear mobilizes the body; (2) fear can be conditioned and extinguished; (3) effective fear stimuli need not be consciously perceived; and (4) fear stimuli guide attention. As discussed in the next chapter, rather than fear being conditioned and extinguished, chronic fears could be present as emergents that are strongly avoided, especially in psychopathology, and are difficult to extinguish. The schizophrenic's inability to enjoy life could be conceived as just one expression of the fear and avoidance of dealing with hurtful feelings.

In making chronic, intense, and deeply unconscious fears basic to the development of psychopathology, one is aware of walking on the thin conceptual and empirical ice of evidence. This choice has been made on the basis of exclusion rather than inclusion. For instance, most PDs of Cluster B, where anger is the major feeling, are the least fearful of most personality disorders (Hare et al., 1999). In Cluster C, where sadness is the major feeling, worries, anxieties, and painful internalization of self-conscious feelings of guilt, shame, and remorse make up the clinical condition of depression. Fear, however, is not the major feeling state in that condition; rather, sadness is (Howland & Thase, 1999; Ingram, Scott, & Siegle, 1999).

Therefore, although there is ample evidence for anger being present in Cluster B and for sadness in Cluster C populations, the hypothesis that fears underlie psychopathology needs to be demonstrated more fully before stating it as a conclusion. Flack, Laird, Cavallaro, and Miller (1998, p. 319) differentiated between emotional expression and experience, and suggested that "flattened expressive behavior in schizophrenics may be a self-control strategy adopted to reduce the intensity of their emotional feelings. Such a 'strategy' is not, of course, adopted consciously, since self-perception processes usually take place outside of awareness." What are these intense "emotional feelings"? An additional possibility to the foregoing hypothesis is suggested by Ellgring and Smith (1998, p. 331): "The lack of expressive behavior [in schizophrenia] can thus be seen as an attempt to control internal affective bursts, or as an inability to produce the appropriate social expressions because of distraction from sensory overload."

We need, therefore, to identify the nature of "internal affective bursts" and of "sensory overloads." Underlying those bursts there may be a sensory overload of hurt feelings. Unfortunately, worry as the chronic fear of some dreadful, impending, and hurtful doom has not been differentiated, as far as I know, from rumination. How can these two processes be disentangled? Could worry be differentiated by different degrees, whereby a slight frequency and small intensity of worry could be related to anxiety and depression whereas a great deal of frequent and chronic worry, i.e., rumination, could be related to severe psychopathology (Brossshot & Thayer, 2006)?

Clearly, worry may be one way to blunt, avoid, and inhibit hurt feelings associated with generalized anxiety disorder, but not fear (Borkovic & Hu, 1990). Furthermore, what other conditions may be associated with one process or the other? This issue was evaluated by Hay, Fingerman, and Lefkowitz (2007), who studied the experience of worry in parent-child relationships within the context of neuroticism, importance of the relationship, and ambivalence.

This foregoing possibility was considered also by Morrison and Wells (2007). In their study of fifty-one patients with psychotic diagnoses, forty patients with anxiety disorders, and sixty nonpatients on measures of psychotic experiences, cognitive components of anxiety, and depression, they examined whether worry is associated with psychotic experiences, and whether worry would contribute significantly to emotional response independently of the intensity of psychotic experiences. Morrison and Wells (2007) found that dimensions of worry were associated with dimensions of delusional ideation and with psychotic experiences, whereas social worry predicted emotional responses over and above intensity of emotional experiences. Both clinical groups showed significantly higher levels of worry in comparison to nonpatients. These results indicate the need to differentiate between (1) realistic versus unrealistic, (2) occasional versus chronic, and (3) intense versus weak worry.

More specifically, Leitman, Loughead, Wolf, Ruparel, Kohler, Elliott, et al. (2008) argued that patients with schizophrenia have difficulty in decoding facial affect. Their study using event-related functional neuroimaging indicated that errors in fear detection in schizophrenia are associated with paradoxically higher activation in the amygdala and an associated network implicated in threat detection. Furthermore, this exaggerated activation to fearful faces correlated with severity of flat affect. These findings suggest that abnormal threat-detection processing may reflect disruptions between nodes that comprise the affective appraisal circuit. Leitman et al. examined connectivity within this network by determining the pattern of inter-correlations among brain regions (regions of interest) significantly activated during fear identification in both healthy controls and patients using a novel procedure called CORA-NOVA. This analysis tested differences in the interregional correlation strength between schizophrenia and healthy controls. Healthy participants' task activation was principally characterized by robust correlations between medial structures like thalamus (THA) and amygdala (AMY) and middle frontal (MF), inferior frontal (IF), and prefrontal cortical (PFC) regions. In contrast, schizophrenic patients displayed no significant correlations between the medial regions and either MF or IF. Further, patients had significantly higher correlations between occipital lingual gyrus and superior temporal gyrus than healthy participants. These between-group connectivity differences suggest that schizophrenia threat-detection impairment may stem from abnormal stimulus integration. Such abnormal integration may disrupt the evaluation of threat within frontocortical regions.

Hall, Whalley, McKirdy, Romaniuk, McGonigle, McIntosh, et al. (2008) argued that the amygdala plays a central role in detecting and responding to fear-related stimuli. A number of recent studies have reported decreased amygdala activation in schizophrenia to emotional stimuli (such as fearful faces) compared with matched neutral stimuli (such as neutral faces). These researchers investigated whether the apparent decrease in amygdala activation in schizophrenia could actually derive from increased amygdala activation to the neutral comparator stimuli. Nineteen patients with schizophrenia and twenty-four matched control participants viewed pictures of faces with either fearful or neutral facial expressions, and a baseline condition, during functional magnetic resonance imaging scanning. Hall et al. found that patients with schizophrenia showed a relative decrease in amygdala activation to fearful faces compared with neutral faces. However, this difference resulted from an increase in amygdala activation to the neutral faces in patients with schizophrenia, not from a decreased response to the fearful faces. Consequently, Hall et al. concluded that patients with schizophrenia show an increased response of the amygdala to neutral faces. This is sufficient to explain their apparent deficit in amygdala activation to fearful faces compared with neutral faces. The inappropriate activation of neural systems involved in fear to otherwise neutral stimuli may contribute to the development of psychotic symptoms in schizophrenia.

Forabosco, Ruch, and Nucera, (2009) argued that the fear of being laughed at brings to the fore the problematic side of an otherwise very positive aspect of human experience. In the streamline of investigations analyzing the presence and characteristics of what they called "gelotophobia," their study focused on psychiatric patients with diagnoses established according to the criteria of the DSM-IV TR (American Psychiatric Association, 2000). Based both on clinical and empirical observations, the main hypothesis advanced was that using the Geloph < 15> scale, participants with a psychiatric diagnosis would have higher mean scores than Normal Controls. An additional hypothesis was that intragroup differences were also expected among the various diagnostic categories. The main hypothesis was amply supported, and explanatory suggestions of the finding were proposed. Intragroup differences proved also to be significant. Patients with PDs and patients with schizophrenic disorders scored higher than Normal Controls and the other diagnostic groups. Also the number of years spent in psychiatric care resulted in being significantly associated with higher gelotophobia mean scores. From this study, a circular, interactive relationship was confirmed between laughter and mental health, which can alternatively be highly positive or deeply negative.

Bipolar Disorder
Papolos, Hennen, and Cockerham, (2005) argued that obsessive fear of harm, either fear of doing harm or fear of harm coming to self, may be

closely associated with aggressive behaviors in juvenile-onset bipolar disorder. These investigators analyzed parent-report data on the Yale-Brown Obsessive Compulsive Scale (YBOCS) and Overt Aggression Scale (OAS) for 1601 children and adolescents with a clinician-assigned diagnosis of bipolar disorder. The summing of six YBOCS items rated "often" or "very often or almost constant" yielded a biphasic distribution of scores. Median-split was used to define meaningful subgroups contrasting high versus low "fear-of-harm," which were then compared on parent-reported severe injury to self and others and on parent-reported suicide threats. Papolos et al. found that high fear of harm was strongly associated with parent-reported severe injury to self and others. For self-injury, the estimated risk ratio for high versus low fear-of-harm subgroups was 2.68 (95 percent confidence interval 1.87–3.86), indicating greater than doubling of risk associated with high fear of harm. For severe injury to others, the estimated risk ratio was 7.97 (95 percent confidence interval 4.19–15.2), suggesting a nearly eight-fold increased risk associated with high fear of harm. High fear-of-harm participants were reported to make serious suicide threats much more frequently than low fear-of-harm participants (odds ratio, estimated by ordinal logistic regression modeling methods, was 2.42 (95% CI 2.00 to 2.92; $z = 9.12$, $p < 0.001$).

Limitations were highlighted by the fact that child-report data was not obtained and clinician diagnosis was not validated via research interview. Nonetheless, this study does support the thesis that obsessive fears about harm to self or others in a sample of children with a clinician-assigned diagnosis of bipolar disorder were found to be positively related to increased behavioral aggression toward self and others, as well as to frequent suicide threats.

To validate the previous conclusion, Papolos, Mattis, Golshan, and Molay (2009) summarized their findings from the prior concordance study of affected sibling pairs with a community diagnosis of pediatric bipolar disorder (PBD); a behavioral phenotype termed Fear of Harm (FOH) was found to have one of the strongest concordance coefficients (rho) between probands and siblings, and the widest contrasts between the rho-estimates for the proband/sibling versus proband/comparison pairs (Papolos, Hennen, Cockerham, Lachman, 2007). In this study, Papolos et al. (2009) employed a strategy for identifying phenotypic subtypes – that is, phenotypic subtypes were matched according to symptom dimensions between sibling pairs who met screening criteria for a genetic linkage study of childhood-onset bipolar disorder using the Child Bipolar Questionnaire (CBQ). These investigators used the CBQ to further elucidate this behavioral phenotype of PBD. They hypothesized that (1) selective factors including parent-reported symptoms of mania and depression would be distinguishing features of impairment between groups defined by the magnitude of their score on a continuous measure of FOH, and (2) the high FOH group would have significantly greater levels of severity on course of illness variables. These measures included earlier age of onset of first psychiatric symptoms and first hospitalization and higher frequency of psychiatric hospitalizations, as well as degree of social impairment as determined by exposure to the juvenile justice system and school performance problems.

Their sample was composed of children with community diagnoses of bipolar disorder or at risk for the illness based on enriched family history with multiple first-degree relatives diagnosed with BPD (N = 5,335). Included were all participants who had N40 positively endorsed CBQ symptom items at frequencies of very often, almost always, and always. This group was divided randomly into two groups, the exploratory group (N = 2668) and the hypothesis testing (study) group (N = 2666). The exploratory group was used for the development of hypotheses, and the study group was used to test these hypotheses on a new set of data. All results reported here derive from the latter group. In subsequent analyses, Papolos et al. (2009) classified each child as having a high degree of FOH, low FOH, or no FOH by examining a subset of the sample for differences in age of onset of first psychiatric symptoms, course of illness, and measures of symptom severity. These groups were compared using the chi-square procedure for categorical data and the Analysis of Variance (ANOVA) with Scheffe pair-wise tests for continuous variables.

These investigators found that children representative of the FOH phenotype, when compared to children with PBD who lack this trait, had higher indices of severity of mania and depression, as well as other indices that reflect severity and course of illness. Trait factors were derived from a factor analysis of CBQ in a large population of children diagnosed with or at risk for PBD, and used to further elucidate trait features of children with FOH. Children with the FOH traits were also more likely to be defined by six CBQ factors; Sleep/Arousal, Harm to Self and Others, Territorial Aggression, Anxiety, Self-esteem, Psychosis/Parasomnias/Sweet Cravings/Obsessions (PPSO).

On the basis of these findings, Papolos et al. (2009) concluded that the FOH phenotype is a clinically homogeneous behavioral phenotype of PBD with early age of onset, severe manic and depressive symptoms, and significant social impairment that is strongly associated with six CBQ factors easily identified using the CBQ. Through the examination of dimensional features of PBD in an enriched sample of large size, these investigators were able to further refine a phenotype and identify clinical dimensions potentially linked to endophenotypic markers that may prove fruitful in differential diagnosis, treatment, and etiological studies of PBD.

Paranoias

In an early introduction to the topic, Ovesey (1962) argued that success phobias can be traced in both men and women to threatening childhood competitions with the father or with brothers. Aggression was seen as inherently hostile by these patients. The patients may be extremely ambitious as well as compulsive, emotionally rigid, self-referential, distrustful, wary, and detached. They may be neurotic or psychotic depending on whether the passive-submissive, compulsive, or the paranoid personality component outweighs both conditions. Psychotherapy must carefully evaluate their ego-strength, because the attempt to overcome the fear of success may lead to collapse. Setting lower goals may be necessary. For more severe cases, medication or even hospitalization may be indicated.

More specifically, Sarwer-Foner (1979) described the characteristics of individuals with social paranoia as those who direct their delusional beliefs at individuals or subgroups who are easily identifiable in a society (making them both a part of and separate from society). These differences are feared, hated, and perceived as dangerous. Several aspects of normal and pathological psychosexual development are summarized: Though the social paranoid individual is capable of entering into various social relationships, these relationships are distinguished by suspiciousness and an effort to control all situations; when psychopathological processes reach a particular height, a group is selected unconsciously, and all that is deemed undesirable in themselves is projected onto that group. The importance of understanding the mechanisms of social paranoia and realizing that some social paranoid individuals are capable of serious social harm is emphasized.

Menuck (1992) described an account of persecution by undercover government agents. Like the tale of persecution by New York Mafiosi and police told by the patient, the account sounded implausible and pathological. However, sometimes "paranoid" people do have real persecutors, and this possibility needs to be evaluated before reaching a definite diagnosis of paranoid personality or paranoid disorder. Kennedy, Kemp, and Dyer (1992) hypothesized that delusions and actions in fifteen patients (aged twenty-three to forty-five years) with delusional (paranoid) disorder would be congruent with an abnormal mood characterized by *fear* and *anger*. Informants and participants indicated a pervasive and persistent abnormality of mood (fear and defensive anger), with delusions and actions that were congruent with this mood during the offense and for more than a month before. Other behaviors, such as fleeing or barricading to avoid delusional persecutors, were also consistent with congruence of mood and delusions. In all participants, violent acts and mood were congruent, but in three participants the violent act was unrelated to delusions. Data suggest that moods of fear and anger in delusional disorder are not sufficiently recognized as part of the disorder.

Persons with high levels of paranoid ideation may be more sensitive to emotional stimuli, particularly "negative emotions," reflecting the operation of a paranoid schema. However, this finding has not been consistently supported and needs further study. Combs, Michael, and Penn (2006) examined the effects of paranoia on emotion perception as measured on a continuum. These investigators predicted that higher levels of paranoia should be associated with improved emotion-perception scores, with better recognition for negative emotions than positive. They found that persons with persecutory delusions had lower identification scores than the moderate and low subclinical groups. Anger was especially problematic for clinical participants. There were no differences for positive emotions among the three groups. Consequently, Combs et al. were forced to conclude that instead of an enhanced sensitivity for the recognition of emotional states, higher levels of paranoia were linked to a performance deficit on emotion perception tasks.

Russell, Reynaud, Kucharska-Pietura, Ecker, Benson, Zelaya, et al. (2007) concluded that abnormalities in social functioning are a significant feature of schizophrenia. One critical aspect of these abnormalities is the difficulty these individuals have with the recognition of facial emotions, particularly negative expressions such as fear. These investigators focused on fear perception and its relationship to the paranoid symptoms of schizophrenia, specifically how underlying limbic system structures (i.e. the amygdala) react when probed with dynamic fearful facial expressions. Seven paranoid and eight nonparanoid participants (all males) with a diagnosis of schizophrenia took part in a functional magnetic resonance imaging study (1.5T) examining neural responses to emerging fearful expressions contrasted with dissipating fearful expressions. Participants viewed emerging and dissipating expressions while completing a gender discrimination task. Their brain activation was compared to that of ten healthy male participants. Increased hippocampal activation was seen in the nonparanoid group, whereas abnormalities in the bilateral amygdalae were observed only in paranoid individuals. These patterns may represent trait-related hippocampal dysfunction, coupled with state-related (specifically paranoia) amygdala abnormalities.

Severe Depression

Warner, Wickramaratne, and Weissman (2008) argued that the overlap between anxiety and major depressive disorder (MDD), the increased risk for depression and anxiety in offspring of depressed parents, the sequence of onset with anxiety preceding MDD, and anxiety as a predictor of depression are well established. The specificity of anxiety disorders in these relationships is unclear. This study, using a longitudinal high-risk design, examined whether anxiety disorders associated with the emotions fear and anxiety mediate the association between parental and offspring depression. Two hundred twenty-four second-generation and 155 third-generation descendants at high and low risk for depression because of MDD in the first generation were interviewed over twenty years. Probit and Cox proportional hazard models were fitted with generation 2 (G2) or G3 depression as the outcome and parental MDD as the predictor. In G2 and G3, fear- (phobia or panic) and anxiety-related (overanxious or generalized anxiety disorder [GAD]) disorders were examined as potential mediators of increased risk for offspring depression due to parental MDD. In G2, fear-related disorders met criteria for mediating the association between parental MDD and offspring MDD, whereas anxiety-related disorders did not. These results were consistent, regardless of the analytic methods used. Further investigation of the mediating effect of fear-related disorders by age of onset of offspring MDD suggests that this mediating effect occurs primarily in adolescent onset MDD. The results for G3 appear to follow similar patterns. These findings support the separation of anxiety disorders into at least two distinct forms, particularly when examining their role in the etiology of depression.

DISCUSSION

Lara, Pinto, Akiskal, and Akiskal, (2006) argued that current formal psychiatric approaches to nosology are plagued by an unwieldy degree of heterogeneity with insufficient appreciation of the commonalities of emotional, personality, behavioral, and addictive disorders. These investigators addressed this challenge by building a spectrum model that integrates personality and temperament while avoiding some of its limitations. They specifically proposed that "fear" and "anger" traits – used in a broader connotation than in the conventional literature – provide an optimum basis for understanding how the spectra of anxiety, depressive, bipolar, ADHD, alcohol, substance-use and other impulse-control, and cluster B and C personality disorders arise and relate to one another. By erecting a bidimensional approach, Lara et al. attempted to resolve the paradox that apparently polar conditions (e.g., depression and mania, compulsivity and impulsivity, internalizing and externalizing disorders) can coexist without canceling one another. The combination of excessive or deficient fear and anger traits produced four main quadrants corresponding to the main temperament types of hyperthymic, depressive, cyclothymic, and labile individuals, which roughly correspond to bipolar I, unipolar depression, bipolar II, and ADHD respectively. Other affective temperaments resulting from excess or deficiency of only fear or anger include irritable, anxious, apathetic, and hyperactive. This model, however, did not consider schizophrenia. Nonetheless, these researchers proposed that "healthy" or euthymic individuals would have average or moderate fear and anger traits. They further proposed that family history, course, and comorbidity patterns can also be understood based on fear and anger traits. The implications of this newly derived model for clinical diagnosis of common psychiatric disorders, and for subtyping depression and anxiety as well as cognitive and behavioral styles, represented a heuristic attempt to build bridges between basic and clinical science.

One could conclude from these findings that worry may be implicated in psychotic experiences and that people with psychiatric diagnoses may possess high levels of worry to the point of rumination. Nonetheless, one would still question whether various degrees or types of worry would allow differentiation between worry as chronic fears in severe psychopathology from worry in anxiety and depression. Here is where the neurosciences and possibly imaging will allow us to make such a determination (McNally, 2007). Here is also where posttraumatic stress disorder as one type of extreme worry and anxiety may be differentiated from severe psychopathology (Ohman & Ruck, 2007).

An important issue that still needs consideration is the duration of hurts, where an important distinction must be made before making any prediction about how long hurt feelings will last. For instance, hurt feelings will stay and fester within the organism for as long as they remain unexpressed, producing the unconscious (De Giacomo et al., 2010). These feelings cease to exist once they are expressed appropriately. From this expressed-unexpressed dichotomy we can distinguish between *introjective* hurts (feeling sad, engaging in self-blame, and wondering what one did wrong) as in sadness and depression (Cluster C) and *retaliatory* hurts (yelling at, blaming, confronting, and feelings angry toward the offender, as in Cluster B). Consequently, introjective hurts are less likely to be expressed than retaliatory ones, whereas with the latter, the discharge of hurt feelings is direct and immediate.

In a longitudinal study lasting two months, May and Jones (2007) explored these types of hurt with fifty-one participants who were asked in a survey format to describe a recent hurtful incident and the subsequent various behavioral reactions, including hurt and forgiveness. Results suggested the stability and relative independence of the two types of hurt and the differential significance of predictor variables (for example, apology) for each type of hurt, both simultaneously and over time. These results, therefore, support not only the distinction between introjective and retaliatory hurt as they represent distinct reactions with different feelings (anger versus sadness) with differential interpersonal outcomes, but they support also the validity of the model presented in Figure 2.1.

As shown by Figure 2.1, developmentally, from hurt feelings flow a whole range of self/other destructive emotions, and within this range there exists a whole panoply of how these feelings are expressed outwardly and relationally as emotion, that is, actions and behaviors, verbal and nonverbal. One could argue about the simplistic nature of this model and question how it would account for, say, disgust. This argument becomes irrelevant once we consider disgust (Rozin, Haidt, & McCauley, 2008) as one type of immediate, reactive, short-lived fear, such as a temporary annoyance. Disgust, apparently, does not lead to any psychopathology, except perhaps at worst in obsessive-compulsive disorder (Berle & Phillips, 2006).

Furthermore, there is no question that there is an inevitable mixture of these three basic feelings that predict a greater variety of unpredictable outcomes, according to the three principles of equifinality, equipotentiality, and multicasuality enunciated earlier. That mixture complicates the model as well as a whole number of relational competence factors that must be taken into consideration. For instance, one would predict that anger and its projected outcomes of Model 2.1 in offspring may result from inconsistent and inadequate parenting in depressed mothers. This prediction seems supported by the results of two studies by Tenser, Murray, Vaughan, and Sacco (2006) with eighty-six depressed mothers of six- to ten-year-old children with a history of attention deficit hyperactive disorder, one of the possible antecedent of conduct disorders based on anger and immediate reactions to noxious events. Apparently depression begets anger, especially if gender factors enter into the picture.

Additionally, Miller and Pilkonis (2006) examined correlates and consequences of two constructs related to affective experience: Neuroticism is related to anxiety, and affective instability is related to anger, the former being strongly related to an anxious avoidant personality style whereas the latter is related to more externalizing personality style. Neuroticism predicted later symptoms, occupational impairment, and global dysfunction, whereas affective instability predicted romantic impairment. Therefore, these findings suggest that neuroticism and affective instability, which are considered core aspects of personality pathology, are related but distinct constructs with unique correlates and different predictive abilities. The results of this study were further supported by a study by Hettema, Neale, Myers. Prescott, et al. (2006), who asserted that anxiety and depressive disorders exhibit high levels of lifetime comorbidity with one another. These authors examined how genetic and environmental factors shared by the personality traits of neuroticism and seven internalizing (Cluster C) disorders may help explain this comorbidity. They found that genetic factors shared with neuroticism accounted for between one-third and one half of the genetic risk across internalizing disorders. Additionally, a neuroticism-independent genetic factor could be identified that significantly increased risk for major depression, generalized anxiety, and panic disorders.

The overall picture must include level of functioning as assessed by cognitive functioning and attribution of importance to self and others before any predictions can be made about developmental trajectories from these three sets of feelings.

CONCLUSION

Hurt feelings as subjectively salient sensations can be elicited by internal and external events to emerge normatively speaking as expressed emotions through rational appraisal and corrected through awareness. They occur within a perceived proximal or distal context. These feelings can be offset by joyful experiences in a ratio that needs further exploration. Through rationality and awareness, we may choose inwardly to approach or avoid certain feelings; we choose how we can, must, ought, should or want to express those feelings outwardly through anger, sadness, or fears. However, this choice might not always be ours if we are not aware of such feelings and what produced them.

3

The Origins of Hurt Feelings

Pleasure is always contingent on change and disappears with continuous satisfaction. Pain may persist under persisting adverse conditions.
Fridja (2007, p. 13)

Humans show an innate preference for positive affect over negative.
Ellgring & Smith (1998, p. 323)

All individuals, if they live enough years, experience the loss of a significant person.... The family's loss history provides a template for their present grieving and mourning.
Weiss (2000, p. 6)

The purpose of this chapter is to consider the emergence and transformation of feelings in general and of hurt feelings in particular as subjectively experienced affects processed and transformed into observably expressed emotions according to salience theory (Fuller, 1967; Kagan, 2007; Rumbaugh & Washburn, 2003) and hierarchical RCT (Cusinato & L'Abate, 2012; L'Abate, 2005, 2006, 2008, 2009a; L'Abate et al., 2010; L'Abate & Cusinato, 2007). More specifically, here I will consider hurt feelings in a manner that parallels Rumbaugh and Washburn's (2003) treatment of emergent responses and emergent problem-solving generated by processes initiated by salient events. Rumbaugh and Washburn (2003) have shown how in primates new, unexpected, and creative behaviors not previously thought of, taught, or even learned arise and emerge into newly creative behaviors without conditioning or reinforcement. Panksepp (2008), by the same token, has shown how animals, including rats, do indeed have affective feelings that can be elicited as they are elicited in human beings. L'Abate (2005) stressed the importance of emotionality from the very outset of RCT, as shown in Chapter 13 of this volume.

These emergent affective feelings are salient and lie dormant in the organism until or unless favorable proximal and distal contextual factors allow or encourage their emergence. Rumbaugh and Washburn (2003) focused their efforts and research on intelligent problem-solving and other cognitive functions, but did not focus as yet on the role of affective feelings in their emergence as emotions. Affective feelings, therefore, can be conceived as internally salient, passively receptive, subjectively experienced, psycho-physiological emergents elicited when specific internal or external conditions or stimuli arise. These feelings are transformed into expressed emotions once words are added or available to name such feelings (Barrett et al., 2007; Buchanan, 2007; Coan & Allen, 2007; Frijda, 2009; Lewis, 2008; Mascolo & Griffin, 1998; Panksepp, 2008; Saarni, 1999).

Emotions, on the other hand, are conceived as externally expressed modes of reacting and activities that are observable and, therefore, directly measurable through verbal, facial expressions, and physical movements (Coan & Allen, 2007; Frijda, 2008, p. 74; Rachorowski & Owren, 2008). Consequently, it is necessary to show how salience theory could be applied to the study and research of how affective feelings emerge as emotions. Affective feelings constitute that supposedly "irrational" mass that controls us in spite of our best "rational" intentions, oftentimes outside of our own awareness (Ariely, 2008; Travis & Aronson, 2007).

HOW DO FEELINGS EMERGE AS EMOTIONS?

A brief introductory answer to the title question consists of two processes: Affective feelings emerge as emotions according to *developmental, internally organismic factors interacting with externally relational processes with intimates in close, committed, interdependent, and prolonged relationships.* This answer brings us back to the old chicken-and-egg controversy. Aspects of relational competence both within organisms and in relationships with intimates are one and the same. There is no development without relationships, as there is no relationship without someone or something to nurture and help develop it. This answer will need conceptual and empirical expansion and support after the semantic phenomenological approach introduced in Chapter 2 of this volume showed at least four faulty conceptual views about feelings and emotions.

Salience Theory: Beyond Conditioning and Reinforcements

Salience theory (Fuller, 1967) derives from presumed genetic differences, as for instance, in breeding differences in dogs, where emergent responses according to their salience occur without any special training. Basing their version of salience theory from observations with primates, Rumbaugh and Washburn (2003) criticized previous explanations of new behavior learning occurring through either conditioning where feelings could be considered as respondents (pp. 38–41) or as operants (pp. 40–41) reinforced by external rewards. In either conditioning and or reinforcement theories, feelings in and of themselves may be strengthened but nothing else emerges; that is, neither new feelings, cognitions, problem-solving, or new emotions arise from either process (Frijda, 2008, p. 78; LeDoux & Phelps, 2008, pp. 160–164; Ohman, 2008, pp. 712–715). Neither conditioning nor reinforcements can account for the emergence of core or more complex feelings. Imitation may be the most likely candidate for such an emergence (L'Abate et al., 2010).

Historically, salience theory can be conceived as a third wave in learning theories after respondents and operants. Salience theory can account for novel feelings that cannot be accounted for by either conditioning or reinforcements. For instance, Rumbaugh and Washburn (2003) reported many examples where a special type of primate would show new and totally unexpected creative behaviors that had not been thought of, taught, or shown before. For instance, there were new problem-solving strategies "invented" by primates that were not present in their past behavioral repertoires.

Extending this position to humans, creativity is neither thought nor learned. It arises and emerges, like feelings do, into uncharted, unexpected expressions, as seen in play (L'Abate, 2009b) or in genius (Simonton, 2008). A special type of rare, relational creativity is present in superior intimate interactions according to hierarchical RCT (see Chapter 13, this volume; L'Abate, 2009c; L'Abate et al., 2010).

Rumbaugh and Washburn (2003) list the characteristics of emergents (p. 256) as follows: providing unanticipated surprises and novel response patterns and solutions to problems that have been formed covertly, unobtrusively, or silently. Emergents generally cannot be charted, with learning sets as a notable exception, affording new behaviors that have no specific reinforcement history by emphasizing a class of experiences entailing the syntheses of individually acquired experiences and responses. Consequently, emergents are not subject to specific stimulus control, as are respondents and operants, frequently reflecting rearing conditions or early experiences by being positively associated with brain complexity (per species and maturation).

Emergent feelings lie dormant at various levels of awareness ranging from completely unconscious, preconscious, semiconscious, completely conscious but unspoken (as in self-silencing), or conscious and spoken. Unconscious feelings may become conscious when elicited through talking or writing as well as through nonverbal means (L'Abate, 1997, 2008a, 2008b, 2009b). These feelings are salient but lie dormant at various levels of awareness, to be elicited under appropriate circumstances when there is a match between what is available inside and what is available outside the organism.

As the American Psychological Association Dictionary defines it, salience represents "a parameter of a stimulus that indexes its effectiveness" (p. 810). The salience hypothesis is a general theory of perception according to which highly salient stimuli (objects, people, meaning, etc.) will be perceived more readily than those stimulus events of low salience. Salience, consequently, may also be related to what Gibson (1982) called "affordances," which represent the multiple functions or usability of a stimulus event depending on its match with favorable contextual circumstances (Saarni, 2008).

In response to a query to compare affordances with emergents, Duane Rumbaugh (personal communication, October 2, 2009) responded that for Gibson (1982) the organism gets information from the environment and coordinates that information with its abilities – what it can and cannot do. Emergents embrace the Gestalt principles of perceptual organization of stimuli received from the external environment. Both incorporate past experiences as parameters as well. These are important dimensions of similarity between the two constructs of affordances and emergents. Gibson did not want to see affordances in a closet, apart from the rest of psychology. He opposed Stimulus-Response (S-R) models to account for them because they didn't work well. On this point, Rumbaugh and Washburn agreed, incorporating associative Stimulus-Response and Stimulus-Stimulus models but radically redefining reinforcement.

Notwithstanding these provisos, the authors of "Salience Theory" certainly look to emergents as keys to building a comprehensive psychology of behavior that runs from instincts through conditioning and on into cognition, social behavior, and intelligence. They addressed specifically how amalgams formed in all kinds of situations are then organized by the brain into templates that collectively form a knowledge base. That base then might service future behaviors by nominating more efficient ways of doing old/familiar things and addressing new challenges in new contexts – that is, emergents. Rumbaugh and Washburn postulated that it is in the process of trying to find the best fit between templates (both natural and arbitrary) that emergents are likely formed (Capitelli, Guerra, L'Abate, and Rumbaugh, 2009).

Rumbaugh and Washburn (2003) provided a more specific model for the formation of emergents that should be applicable to the definition of affordances. Affordances may be emergent (in that they are perceived, not conditioned), but not all emergents are affordances. Affordances are some perceived aspects of the environment that allow (or afford) the organism to engage in some action including problem solving. Although affordances are often salient, the two constructs are different. Salient stimuli, by definition, grab the organism's attention but do not necessarily provide an opportunity for some action. Likewise, stimuli with high affordances may be noticed but may not necessarily be salient, and therefore are not used for any action. Those high in affordance – low in salience stimuli may, however, become salient through the formation of amalgams combining a new salient stimulus with high-affordance stimuli.

A related concept of "ecological validity" was used by Egon Brunswick in the 1950s. Brunswick's ecological validity was the correspondence between proximal stimulation (e.g., a retinal image) and an external stimulus. As was the case with affordances, salient stimuli overlap imperfectly with ecologically valid proximal events. However, Brunswik's definition of ecological validity is quite different from the way the term is currently used, which vaguely relates to the extent that behaviors or experimental settings are presumably "relevant" to the natural habitat (rather tricky for humans!).

Salience, therefore, means experiences and events that capture attention due to past and attendant learning (Rumbaugh & Washburn, 2003, p. 261). Inherently weak stimuli can become highly salient because of other experiences or events that have been reliably associated with them, either contiguously in space or sequentially in time:

> Salience is a basic parameter of perceptual attention, learning and performance. Salience is perhaps the most powerful parameter of learning (p. 262).... Relatively subtle (nonsalient) cues may become salient if used as conditioned stimuli in classical conditioning.... Biological needs, as for food or water, can result in otherwise subtle cues becoming highly salient through association with events whereby these needs are met. (p. 262)

This view has been expanded (independently from Rumbaugh and Washburn and without reciprocal citation of each other's work) by

Kagan (2007). After criticizing inadequate models of conditioning in rats expanded on humans, Kagan (pp. 17, 32, 91–92, 101, 108), in addition to hedonic valence, introduces the construct of *salience* (pp. 97–103) (in spite of his seemingly equating feelings with emotions):

> The perceived salience, or intensity, of a feeling or emotion is a poten-tially useful feature in classifying emotions because alient feelings recruit attention, disrupt ongoing thoughts or behaviors, and are difficult to ignore. Salient feelings are often induced by events that are distinctive because they are physically intense, discrepant, or contain biologically prepared features (p. 97).... Although the salience of an emotional expe-rience is typically a function of the perceived intensity of the under lying feeling, it can refer to the effort associated with a behavioral component of the emotion....The salience of an emotion is always influenced by the unfamiliarity or unexpectedness of the incentive or the feeling it gener-ates. (p. 98)

We have here two different and independent sources that agree in sup-porting the salience of affective feelings. However, what is the relation-ship between hurtful and nonhurtful feelings? When hurtful feelings are approached, admitted into awareness, accepted as valid, and expressed and shared with loved ones or with professional helpers, either verbally or non-verbally, as in crying (Nelson, 2008) or in writing (Pennebaker, 1995), they tend to dissipate and disappear, even though they may remain in episodic memory (Watson, 2003). However, when these feelings are unexpressed and avoided (denied, repressed, or suppressed), here is where "emotional disturbances" may arise (Berenbaum et al., 2003).

Developmentally, an infant starts with experiencing feelings in a dichot-omous fashion: Feelings are either pleasant or unpleasant (Lewis, 2008). Caretakers can be either pleasant or unpleasant. There is no such a thing as a neutral caretaker or neutral experience. If there are neutral experiences, they would not leave any trace or memory in the organism. The infant either cries when experiencing pain or hunger, coldness, or wetness, or smiles and laughs when physical needs are taken care of (Chapman & Foot, 1976; Hendriks et al., 2008; Lutz, 1999; Nelson, 2008; Stearns, 1972). From this dichotomy over time develop more differentiated and complex feelings along very differentiated dimensions introduced in Figure 1.2 With physi-cal growth and with proper presence and positive nurturing from adults, infants learn how to express feelings in a much more differentiated manner according to what kind of cognitive and linguistic repertoire is present in their proximal context (Lewis, 2008; Saarni, 2008).

What happens when hurtful feelings occur when children do not have a large vocabulary that would allow them to talk and to express those feelings (Bachorowski & Owren, 2008; Campbell, 2002; Larsson, 2004)? Or if there is a vocabulary large enough to express these feelings, what happens when their expression is further punished and forbidden? Expressing feelings in general and hurt feelings in particular might be a taboo in many dysfunctional families. How many already mistreated children are abused further to the point of being killed because they continue crying after being physically abused or neglected? Criminal behavior may occur when adult perpetrators were abused before they had developed a vocabulary large and differentiated enough to become aware of their feelings, let alone express them, that is, within the first twelve to eighteen months of life (Belsky, Woodworth, & Crnic, 1996).

This hypothesis is strengthened by the finding that aggression measured by number of shots from an electric machine gun was significantly and negatively correlated with IQ scores in elementary school children (L'Abate, 2009c). It would not be surprising to discover that if such hurt feelings were elicited in inmates, whose major deficit may be verbal over relatively superior eye-hand motor performance, strong physical reactions could occur. This is why a signed Informed Consent Form (Appendix A) is necessary for professionals who want to explore these feelings in their patients, regardless of diagnosis.

Now that the emergence of feelings in general have been considered, we need to review in particular possible or presumptive causes that are antecedents if not causative of hurt feelings. This selective review will consider relevant research on this topic. Here possibly antecedent but presumably aversive causes of hurt feelings will be included by updating a now-outdated summary of the relevant literature (L'Abate, 1997).

THE CAUSES OF HURT FEELINGS

Exclusion, ostracism, and rejection are one of the most common antecedent causes of hurt feelings. Without exception, the consequences of exclusion on the targeted individual are negative. These reactions include negative mood, hurt feelings of isolation, and the loss of feelings of belonging, self-esteem, and meaningful existence. What has differed, however, has been the behavioral reactions to the exclusion. Several studies show evidence of behavioral supplication, and several studies show evidence of what appears to be the direct opposite pattern of behavioral reactions to exclusion. Clearly, we have an interesting conundrum: Does being excluded by others cause people to try to regain their exclusionary status, or does it cause antisocial behavior? Williams and Govan (2005) examined the current literature and derived hypotheses that suggest which of these behavioral reactions will occur. They summarized three studies that tend to support their predictions. It is important to underscore that presumed sources of hurt feelings could be based on the commission of an act or an omission, and it could be voluntary/intentional or involuntary/unintentional. It is relatively easy to document the former, but it is more difficult to document the latter.

Hurt Feelings and Parental Rejection

Of course, nothing is more hurtful than parental rejection during childhood. This shows itself in manifestations of depression both then and in young adulthood. Lefkowitz and Tesiny (1984) explored this relationship in three studies. In Study 1 participants were seen in two waves at respective ages of eight and nineteen years. In the first wave parents of these children were also interviewed with a child-rearing questionnaire that included a measure of rejection. In the second wave, participants, now nineteen years old, were administered the Minnesota Multiphasic Personality Inventory, of which the D scale served as a measure of depression. In Study 2, the contemporaneous relationship between maternal rejection and childhood depression was investigated. The identical measure of rejection used in the prospective study was administered to mothers, and four measures of depression – peer ratings, self-ratings, teacher's ratings, and mother ratings – were obtained for their children. Study 3 replicated the significant findings of the contemporaneous Study 2, showing an association between maternal rejection and depression. The long-term deleterious effects of "childhood abuse and household dysfunction" was well documented by the now classic Adverse Childhood Experiences study (Felitti, Anda, Nordenberg, Williamson, et al., 1998).

An exemplary study of how hurtful messages are perceived as a function of age and gender in children and their parents was conducted by Mills, Nazar, and Farrell (2002). Citing the work of two pioneer researchers on hurt feelings: Mark Leary and Anita Vangelisti (reviewed in Chapter 6 of this volume), Mills et al., had forty-eight children (twenty-eight girls and twenty boys) between seven and ten years of age and their mothers recall an instance when their feelings had been hurt by having them rate their emotions, make casual attributions, and describe their answers. Hurt feelings were typically caused by disciplinary encounters or messages of disregard that comprised a painful quality and other "negative emotions," such as guilt, fear, anger, shame, and irritation, among others. The more children and mothers reported feeling hurt, the more negative were their self-perceptions, the more they felt rejected, and (for children) the more feelings about the other person changed.

Hurt Feelings and Harsh Punishment

Another important genetically informed study of the association between harsh punishment and offspring behavioral problems (Lynch, Turkheimer, Slutske, D'Onofrio, Mendle, and Emory (2006) found that "Although corporal punishment per se did not have any significant negative childhood outcomes, harsher forms of physical punishment did appear to have specific and significant effects, supporting the position that [when] harsh physical punishment [reaches abusive proportions it] becomes a serious risk factor for children" (p. 190).

The foregoing results were expanded in a study by Erath, Bierman, and the Conduct Problem Prevention Group at the Pennsylvania State University (2006). These investigators explored whether there was a direct association between aggressive marital conflict and child aggressive-disruptive behavior at home and school in a cross-sectional sample of 360 kindergarten children. This research included also exploring mediated pathways linking aggressive marital conflict to maternal harsh punishment to child aggressive-disruptive behavior. Moderation analyses explored how the overall frequency of marital disagreement might buffer or exacerbate the impact of aggressive marital conflict on maternal harsh punishment and child aggressive-disruptive behavior. Hierarchical regressions revealed direct pathways linking aggressive marital conflict to child aggressive-disruptive behavior at home and school, and a partially mediated pathway linking aggressive marital conflict to child aggressive-disruptive behavior at home. Further analyses revealed that rates of marital disagreement moderated the association between aggressive marital conflict and child aggressive-disruptive behavior at home, with an attenuated association at high rates of marital disagreement as compared with low rates of marital disagreement. The controversial borderline between what constitutes legitimate limit setting and abuse by parents is still to be settled (Chang, Schwartz, Dodge, & McBride-Chang, 2003; Straus & Douglas, 2008).

In relation to physical punishment, Spitzberg (2009) produced a whole classification of violence based on the proviso (p. 216) that "the emotional state experience of hurt must be largely assumed rather than demonstrated," a proviso that applies to what is presented in this chapter, where hurt feelings are presumed to be produced by direct and indirect, aversive and negative origins. His classification (pp. 217–219) of "intimate violence" that influences healthy functioning is worthy of partial inclusion here: (1) *general*, and vague; (2) *affective*, as in many dysfunctionalities; (3) *cognitive*, as in volitional/rational quality of life; (4) *physical/physiological*, as in sleep and alimentary disorders; (5) *behavioral*, as in employment or daily routines; (6) *social*, as in strains and stresses in community and family relations; (7) *resources*, such as changes in economic and financial status; (8) spiritual, as in faith-based beliefs; (9) *societal*, as in crime and cultural stereotypes; and (10) level of *resilience* by developing stronger self-confidence and family ties.

Hurt Feelings and Emotional Unavailability

The other side of the punishment coin, producing hurt feelings indirectly, are parental emotional unavailability and inconsistent discipline. Sturge-Apple, Davies, and Cummings (2006), for instance, examined the nature of pathways between marital hostility and withdrawal, parental disagreements about child rearing issues, and subsequent changes in parental emotional unavailability and inconsistent discipline in a sample of 225 mothers, fathers, and six-year-old children. Results of autoregressive, structural equation models indicated that marital withdrawal and hostility were associated with increases in parental emotional unavailability over a one-year period, whereas marital hostility and withdrawal did not predict changes in parental inconsistency in discipline. Additional findings in this study supported the role of child-rearing disagreements as an intervening or mediating mechanism in links between specific types of marital conflict and parenting practices.

Hurt Feelings and Stressful Family Events

Winter, Davies, and Hightower (2006) examined associations among family discord, caregiver-communication quality about emotionally stressful family events, and child internal representations of family security in fifty preschool children and their primary caregivers. Consistent with risk and protective models (Sapolsky, 2007), findings indicated that children's representations were predicted by the interaction between family discord and caregiver-communication quality. Children exhibiting the highest level of secure representations of the family experienced a consistency between low levels of family discord and communications emphasizing family security. Conversely, incongruence between family experiences and communication, reflected in high levels of family discord and communications underscoring family security, was associated with the lowest level of child-secure representations. Apparently, child representations hinge on the fit between caregiver-communication quality and family experience.

Hurt Feelings and Couple Conflict

An interesting study about how it is possible to change positive and negative expectancies through structured conversations during marital conflict was conducted by Sanford (2006). In a sample of seventy-seven recently married couples, within-person variance in communications during conflict showed three types of appraisal were considered: (1) expectancies of partner understanding; (2) expectancies of partner *negative communication* (assuming hurt feelings); and (3) negative attributions about the partner. Couples were observed in four different conflict conversations completed during two assessment sessions. Appraisal were assessed prior to each conversation. Hierarchical linear modeling was used to analyze within-person effects. Changes from one conversation to the next in all three types of appraisal predicted corresponding within-person change in communication, with many effects larger for wives than for husbands. Results were strongest for expectancies of partner understanding. Expectancies predicted change in one's own behavior after controlling for the accuracy of the expectancy.

In a related study, Roloff, Soule, and Carey (2001) argued that although relational transgressions constitute a potential interpersonal threat, research suggests that some relationships survive them. However, few studies inform as to why individuals try to maintain these relationships, as well as the extent of the impact of their reasons on how they react to transgressions. Undergraduates involved in dating relationships were given the choice of either leaving or staying in a relationship with a transgressor due either to fear of losing a partner or to emotional involvement including cognitive and communication responses to a transgression. Their answers indicated that staying in such a relationship due to the fear of losing one's partner was associated with a variety of negative responses, whereas staying because of emotional involvement was related to positive reactions.

Given that this study was conducted with hypothetical rather than real transgressions, it would need replication with married couples who faced actual transgressions with their partners. Furthermore, these results support Higgins and Spiegel's (1998) thesis that we avoid pain in prevention and approach pleasure in promotion, a point expanded in Chapter 12. Apparently, emotional involvement is more rewarding than losing one's partner.

Hurt Feelings and Children's Behavior

How children behave or misbehave cannot always be laid at the feet of their parents. What happens when children misbehave and their wrongdoings hurt their parents? Scarnier, Schmader, and Lickel (2009) attempted to answer this question in by differentiating between shame and guilt as distinct emotional reactions that parents in the United States may experience in reaction to their children's misdeeds. In one study, these researchers asked ninety-three parents to write about their child's worst transgression. Their ratings of perceived public exposure and threat to their self-image predicted shame, whereas the degree to which they felt a lack of control over their child and believed the transgression harmed others predicted guilt. In a second study by Scarnier et al., when 123 mothers rated their reactions to an imagined wrongdoing, the presence of a critical observer tended to elevate shame but not guilt. Across both studies, guilt predicted adaptive parenting responses, whereas shame predicted maladaptive responses. These findings emphasize the implications that self-conscious feelings may have for family functioning.

Hurt Feelings and Peer Rejection

Although rejection by peers during childhood has been associated with many kinds of adjustment problems, relatively little is known about factors that increase children's vulnerability to peer rejection, according to Patterson, Vaden, and Kupersmidt, 1991), at least until the date of their publication. These investigators examined the relations of family background and recent life events to peer status among 949 elementary school children, focusing especially on rejected status. Peer status was assessed using sociometric methods and techniques for classification. Family background variables and life events were assessed by reports of the children's teachers (Study 1) and parents (Study 2). Results showed that children who came from certain family backgrounds and who experienced certain life events were rejected by their peers more often than other children. In particular, chronic background variables such as low income and acute life stresses such as parental separation or divorce contributed to the probability that a child would be rejected by peers. The probability of rejection by peers was greater for children subjected to relatively high levels of both chronic and acute life stresses.

Hurt Feelings and Childhood Sexual Abuse

Childhood sexual abuse (CSA) is associated with a wide range of negative outcomes. Senn, Carey, Vanable, Coury-Doninger, et al. (2006) investigated the relation between CSA and sexual risk behavior in 827 patients recruited from a sexually transmitted disease (STD) clinic. Overall, CSA was reported in 53 percent of women and 49 percent of men and was associated with greater sexual risk behavior, including more sexual partners, unprotected sex, and sex trading. Alcohol use for men and drug use for women mediated the relation between CSA and the number of sexual partners during the last three months; intimate partner violence mediated the relation between CSA and the number of episodes of unprotected sex in the past three months for women. These results document the prevalence of CSA among patients seeking care for an STD and can be used to tailor sexual-risk-reduction programs for individuals who were sexually abused as children.

Of course, the literature on the possible origins of presumed hurt feelings is staggering. To review it critically and responsibly would require more than a volume of its own. In the following section, there is a representative sample of references but not the actual summaries of these references. An effort was made in each category to select the most validated research studies on this topic from three peer-reviewed journals: the *Journal of Family Psychology*, *Journal of Social and Personal Relationships*, and *Personal Relationships*.

Because there are many other sources available, references listed represent only the illustrative tip of the iceberg for possible, presumed, or potential antecedents of hurt feelings. Some antecedents of hurts and categories not considered here might be considered in other chapters of this volume. Furthermore, none of the categories listed is independent of the others: Overlap among some categories may be undeniably present; incest could be included into the subcategory of sexual abuse. By the same token, abandonment could be conceived as a form of loss or betrayal. Not included in this representative sample are addictions, criminalities, and severe psychopathology considered in appropriate chapters of this volume.

Possible Antecedent Causes of Hurt Feelings

A definition of hurt feelings (Table 1.1) does not include the possible causes of those feelings. Consequently, only select references can be cited; a complete literature search would require more space than it is possible to include here.

Abuses
In addition to substance abuse (Harwood & L'Abate, 2010), here are different kinds of abuses, each having different long-term consequences:

PHYSICAL: (Mulvaney & Mebert, 2007); *sexual* (Pereda, Guilera, Forns, & Gomez-Benito, 2009); *verbal* abuse can be distinguished according to *Coercive Control* (Wilson, Jocic, & Daly, 2001); *criticism*, as in blame and shame (Corrigan, Watson, & Miller, 2006; Mills & Piotoski, 2009); *oppression and depression in women*, as in self-silencing (Jack, 1991); *oppression and racism* (Walsemann, Geraniums, & Gee, 2008); *deception* (Cole, 2001), *devaluation* (Weger, 2005); *incest* (Alexander & Schaeffer, 1994); and *teasing* (Mills & Piotroski, 2009).

AGGRESSION AND VIOLENCE: The research about this antecedent cause of hurt feelings is so vast that only more recent and relevant studies can be cited (Haden & Hojjat, 2006; Milardo, 1998; O'Leary & Slep, 2006; O'Leary & Williams, 2006; Pugliese & Tinsley, 2007; Shakelford, Goetz, Buss, Euler, & Hoier, 2005; Spitzberg, 2009; Taft, O'Farrell, Torres, Panuzio, Monson, Murphy, & Murphy, 2006; Taft, Vogt, Mechanic, & Resick, 2007).

BETRAYAL: (Fehr & Hamusymchuk, 2009; Haden & Hojjat, 2006; Harrison, 2009).

BULLYING: (Lento, 2006).

CONFLICT: (Adams, & Laursen, 2007; Kaczynski, Lindahl, Malik, & Laurenceau, 2006; Lindsey, Colwell, Frabutt, & MacKinnon-Lewis, 2006; Papp, Goeke-Morey, & Cummings, 2007; Papp, Kouros, & Cummings, 2009; Troy, Lewis-Smith & Laurenceau, 2006).

COUPLE/MARITAL BREAK-UP, DISSOLUTION, DISRUPTION, DIVORCE, OR SEPARATION: (Lansford, Malone, Castellino, Dodge, Pettit, & Bates, 2006; Sbarra & Emery, 2005; Terhell, van Groenouvan, & van Tilburg, 2004).

INFIDELITY: Hall & Fincham, 2009; Lenton & Bryan, 2005; Previti & Amato, 2004; Roloff, Soule, & Carey, 2001;

JEALOUSY: (Allan & Harrison, 2009; Buunk & Dijkstra, 2001; Edlund & Sagarin, 2009; Fleischmann, Spitzberg, Anderson, & Roesch, 2005; Guerrero, Trost, & Yoshimura, 2005).

LONELINESS: (Flora & Segrin, 2000; Pinquart, 2003; Rotenberg, 1998; Rottenberg, Shewchuk, & Kimberley, 2001).

LOSSES: (Drew, Heesacker, Frost, & Oelke, 2004; Field & Sundin, 2001; Golish & Powell, 2003; Guiaux, van Tilburg, & van Graenou, 2007).

SECRETS: (Finkenauer & Hazam, 2000; Selvini. 1997; Vangelisti & Caughlin, 1997).

PHYSICAL SICKNESS: (Benazon, Foster, & Coyne, 2006; Kuijer, Buunk, & Yrema, 2001; Manne, Norton, Ostroff, Winkel, Fox, & Grana, 2007).

TRANSGRESSIONS: (Boon & Holmes, 1999; Menzies-Toman & Lydon, 2005).

TURBULENCE: (Solomon & Knobloch, 2004).

CONCLUSION

Hurt feelings as subjectively experienced affects are salient and are or can be elicited under proper circumstances that allow their expression as emotions. Additionally, as can be readily seen from this narrowly selected and inexhuastive reference list, antecedents or sources of presumed hurt feelings are innumerable. There are overlaps among categories of causes likely because similar behaviors, both functional and dysfunctional, are identified with different terms using different criteria and methods of evaluation. Oftentimes, it is difficult if not impossible to clearly identify directly the presence of hurt feelings. For the rest of this volume, using the term "hurt feelings" means that they are *presumed* to be present but that no direct evidence for their existence can be given at this time, except for what is presented in Chapter 7.

4

The Developmental Socialization of Hurt Feelings

Development implies a process of internal growth, whereas socialization implies a process of emergence produced by the complex interaction of the organism with environmental influences (Saarni, 2008). We need both processes to understand how feelings in general and hurt feelings in particular originate. Development usually is evaluated according to ages and stages of the life cycle, whereas socialization is such a constant and continuous process that is difficult to conceptualize it according to levels of emotional, cognitive, and social functioning, including personality characteristics. Nonetheless, both processes are necessary because different individuals react differently to environmental influences and to hurt feelings. For instance, what could be hurtful at one age might not be longer hurtful either at a younger or older age or vice versa.

However, one cannot consider age as a criterion to evaluate the hurtfulness of a word or a deed. Malatesta-Magai (1991), for instance, proposed that socialization of affective expression constitutes a major item on the parental socialization agenda. That expression has a material individualizing impact on the development of personality, focusing on the role of social influences and addressing what and how socialization experiences may interact with innate dispositions. After a brief overview of the history of (laboratory-based) research on emotions, she presented a summary of some of the essential features of Silvan Tomkins's (1962, 1963) "affect theory." Unfortunately, there is no room to expand on that seminal theory. The bulk of Malatesta-Magai's discussion involves an analysis of three studies from her laboratory that can be interpreted within the framework of affect theory and that appear to support several of Tomkins's formulations; examples are drawn from emotional socialization research work with both normal and clinical participants: In normal and "at risk" infants, emotional exchange patterns of contempt and shame in affect socialization were found between depressed mothers and their four- to six-year-old children.

One must consider the emotional level reached by an individual according to how that individual was socialized (Camras & Fatani, 2008). One could be sixty years old and operate emotionally at the level of six year old, as would be the case of certain histrionic personality disorders (L'Abate et al., 2011) and there may be some six-year-old children who may be emotionally more mature than typical of their age. Hence, age in and of itself does not dictate the emotional level of an individual. One way to view development could refer to Jane Loevinger's "ego development" levels according to pre-conformist, conformist, and post-conformist progression. However, these three stages are not specific enough to explain development across the life cycle. Other models will be necessary (Novy, 1993). Erikson's stages of development may be another possible source of developmental integration. An easy way out from this conundrum would be to define development as individual experiences perceived internally whereas socialization is what an individual learns from external sources objectively. Unfortunately, as shown in Model 1.2, it is difficult if not impossible to disentangle one process from the other.

For the time being, even though possibly age related, the individual (L'Abate, 1994, p. 57), couple (p. 58), and family (p. 59) life cycles may be necessary but not sufficient to deal with this issue. Individually, there are seven stages of development: infancy (years one to four), childhood (five to eight), latency (nine to twelve), adolescence (thirteen to nineteen), early (twenty to thirty), middle (thirty-one to fifty), and late (fifty-one to sixty-five) adulthood, and retirement (sixty-six to death). Couple stages could be divided into courtship and marriage, childbearing and parenting, childbearing socialization, middle age and adolescence, and old age. The normative family life cycle considers couples, parenting, siblings, education, and occupation. Unfortunately, none of these life cycles focuses on emotional development, even though they represent a chronological framework within which one can embed emotional socialization across the life cycle. Particular patterns of social development, that is, socialization, may play an important role in predisposing certain individuals to become emotionally disordered, as summarized in Figure 2.1.

Affect regulation, that is, how feelings are expressed and shared in a relationship, is an important aspect of socialization (Bradbury & Fincham, 1989). For instance, Butner, Diamond, and Hicks (2007) examined two forms of affect regulation in forty-eight cohabiting heterosexual couples who provided daily ratings of positive and negative affect for twenty-one days. Coregulation was operationalized as covariation in partners' daily levels of affect and coupling of the rates of change in partner's affective cycles. Both forms of coregulation were detected, and both were moderated by attachment style. These results could be interpreted with respect to the timescales and time courses of each form of coregulation, suggesting that covariation may be more sensitive to discrete affective episodes unfolding during couples' shared time together, whereas coupling may be a longer term process in which partners manifest sensitivity to one another's overall patterns of affective fluctuation.

One cannot cover the developmental aspects of hurt feelings in particular without considering how feelings are socialized in general, because hurt feelings are one aspect of how those feelings are socialized. Here the work of Harris, Lewis, Saarni, and Izard is relevant to developmental aspects of how hurt feelings will be reviewed generally. Their implications for how those feelings may reduce the strength of the immune system, are demonstrated by Pennebaker (2001) and many others who replicated his research. As in previous and chapters to follow, one will accept circumlocutions and unspecified generalities such as "distress" or "negative affect" to locate relevant work.

FOUR MODELS OF EMOTION DEVELOPMENT AND SOCIALIZATION

Lewis (2008, p. 316) proposed a model of emotion development in the first three years of life, which consists of three primary emotions: contentment leading to joy, interest leading to surprise, and distress leading to sadness and disgust or to anger and fear during the first six months. During the second half of the second year, as these three primary emotions evolve into consciousness, and as self-referential behavior, these processes become linked to embarrassment, with further expansions as either envy or empathy. From two-and-a half to three years, there is acquisition and retention of standards and rules, with further refinement of embarrassment leading to pride, shame, and guilt. If one were to change distress to hurt feelings, then this formulation would tend to support Model 2.1, wherein hurt feelings lie at the bottom of anger, sadness, and fears.

Harris (2008) discussed "children's developing awareness and understanding of emotions" (p. 320), as they themselves feel how emotions are expressed by other people. To evaluate how children understand feelings and emotions in themselves and others, Harris and his collaborators (Pons, Harris, & de Rosnay, 2004) developed and validated (p. 326) a Test of Emotion Comprehension (TEC) composed of : (1) recognizing facial expressions of emotions; (2) understanding situational causes; (3) understanding the effect of external reminders on emotion; (4) understanding the link between desire and emotion; (5) understanding the link between belief and emotion: (6) understanding the potential discrepancy between *felt* and *expressed* emotion (hurrah!); (7) understanding guilt; (8) understanding the regulation of emotion; and (9) understanding mixed or ambivalent emotions. Administration of this test in a variety of studies allowed Harris to reach firm conclusions about "children's ability to understand and predict their own emotions" in ways that allows them to make decisions on what course of action to take.... [C]hildren's insight into their emotional lives does not simply enable them to foresee the inevitable; it allows them to look into the future and to make choices about what their own emotional life should be like. In that respect, children's understanding of emotion enables them to alter their experience of emotion" (p. 329).

Saarni's (1999, 2008) skills development model includes (1) awareness of one's own emotions; (2) ability to discern and understand others' emotions; (3) ability to use the vocabulary of emotional expression; (4) capacity for empathic involvement; (5) ability to differentiate internal subjective emotional experience from external emotional expression; (6) capacity for adaptive coping with aversive emotions and distressing circumstances; (7) awareness of emotional communication within relationships; and (8) capacity for emotional self-efficacy.

A fourth model of emotional experiences, called Differential Emotions Theory (DET), is included here (Izard, Libero, Putman, and Haynes (1993, 847–849), even though it focuses on relations between emotions and personality traits, a topic outside the realm of interest here. Nonetheless, some of its general background dimensions are relevant to the developmental origins of hurt feelings: (1) Each of the basic emotions (experiences?) has unique motivational properties; (2) emotion experiences and expressions (finally a separation between the two processes!) show continuity and stability; (3) emotions have activation thresholds, and each individual has a characteristic threshold for each emotion; (4) each emotion tends to form stable links to certain other emotions; (5) each emotion tends to become linked to particular thoughts or memories to form affective-cognitive structures; and (6) an emotion experience is characterized by a particular action tendency that provides a natural bridge to behavior. From these dimensions, a Differential Emotions Scale was constructed, based mostly on how participants feel about a variety of joyful and hurtful experiences.

These experiences included both subjective and objective external events, as well as personality traits, which confuses, as in most other cases, levels of discourse from internal feelings to external events.

Changes within an individual's personal network may reflect either non-deliberative endings, such as loss, or objective choice of social partners. Lang (2000) explored to what extent perceptions of limited future time are associated with deliberate endings of social relationships and active maximization of intrinsic benefits in one's personal network. In a longitudinal follow-up study, Lang twice assessed the personal networks of 206 adults aged between seventy and one hundred three years within a four-year time interval. Change of personal networks and change within social relationships were explored in association with age cohort, extraversion, and subjective nearness to death. Most changes within personal networks occurred in less close relationships, whereas close emotional relationships proved stable. More than half of discontinued relationships were ended for deliberate reasons. Within ongoing social relationships, emotional closeness after four years was improved when social partners were family members and emotional supporters (e.g., confidants). When older adults felt close to death, emotional closeness with others decreased, except within relationships with family members and with social companions. These findings suggest that individuals actively shape the compositions of their personal networks in order to maximize the availability of intrinsic and extrinsic benefits from others.

RESEARCH ABOUT DEVELOPMENTAL SOCIALIZATION OF FEELINGS

Before becoming more specific about each of three major feelings, anger, sadness, and fears as postulated in Model 2.1, one study shows what happens when anxiety and anger were elicited and lumped together under the construct of "negative affectivity" (Wolfe, Finch, Saylor, Blount, Pallmeyer, & Carek, 1987). These feelings were elicited through self-report from 102 children and adolescents hospitalized in an inpatient psychiatric facility and ranging in age from six and a half to sixteen years (mean age = 11.7). The measure used to evaluate these three emotions was the Child Behavior Checklist-Teacher Report Form. The resulting matrix produced significant correlations between scales of anxiety and depression, and correlated significantly with the Internalizing Scales Scores of the Checklist but not with self-report of Externalizing Scales, supporting the position that anger may belong to externalizations rather than internalizations. These results partially support Model 2.1, which divides anger from sadness and both emotions from fears.

Therefore, the rest of this chapter should be considered as an extension of the Model presented in Figure 2.1 in this volume, because only the developmental socialization of three basic feelings will be reviewed: anger, sadness, and fears over the life cycle. All three feelings stem from unexpressed hurt feelings. Because very little has been written about the developmental socialization of hurt feelings, except indirectly in many chapters of Vangelisti's (2009) pioneering volume, the developmental socialization of these basic three feelings will be traced.

A study based in part on Vangelisti's research results and interpretations, which will be reviewed in Chapter 6 of this volume, was conducted by Young (2004), who examined factors that influence participants' appraisals of hurt-evoking messages. Specifically, Young examined three types of appraisals individuals make about a comment that hurt their feelings: the extent to which it reflects *concern*, provides *comfort*, or offers *help*. Results revealed that both distal (e.g., relational satisfaction and closeness) and proximal factors (e.g., message intensity and message hurtfulness) influenced participants' appraisals of hurtful statements. Interestingly, the only variable that was consistently a significant predictor of each type of appraisal was message intensity, supporting the importance of this dimension as one of the three gate keepers for hurt feelings presented in Chapter 1. How a message was stated was pivotal in shaping participants' its appraisal. Given the importance of investigating how people navigate relational transgressions, the findings of Young's study shed light on factors that may help promote less negative interpretations of hurtful communication in personal relationships.

Developmental Socialization of Anger

In most cases anger is expressed with aggression. Anger, therefore, is assumed to be at the bottom of aggression or correlated with it. Unfortunately, many investigators study feelings and emotions at different levels of discourse. For instance, Guerrero, La Valley, and Farinelli (2008) investigated processes of experiencing and expressing anger and sadness, which belong together as basic feelings at one level, and guilt, which operates at a subjectively different level than anger or sadness (Model 1.3).

Anger in Childhood and Youth

Lemerise and Dodge's review (2008) concluded that since the publication of the first and second editions of their volume (Lewis & Haviland, 1993; Lewis & Haviland-Jones, 2000), research on emotions has grown to the point where emotion is a major focus in the sixth edition of the *Handbook of Child Psychology* (Eisenberg, 2006). These authors trace the normative development of anger in infants and children, with the thesis that anger develops and comes to be regulated in the context of transactions with the social environment. Also, individual differences in abilities/capacities and developmental changes contribute to this transaction and shed light on important processes. The literature they reviewed includes studies on infants' and children's expression of anger; their reactions to and appraisal of anger; their regulation of and/or coping with anger in themselves and others; and their understanding of anger, including display rules. Lemerise and Dodge also considered socialization processes relevant to anger as well as both adaptive and maladaptive aspects of anger and angry interactions.

Del Vecchio and O'Leary (2006) found that aggression is stable as early as two years of age and predicts many negative adult outcomes. Although longitudinal predictors of child aggression have been identified, information is lacking regarding the proximal precursors of toddlers' aggression. Observing fifty-four mother-child dyads for thirty minutes allowed them to categorize toddlers as aggressive or nonaggressive based on whether they exhibited aggression toward their mothers within the interaction. Most toddlers in both groups escalated from mild to more severe forms of misbehavior. Mothers of aggressive toddlers displayed more lax and overreactive discipline when addressing misbehaviors that preceded aggression than mothers of nonaggressive toddlers. Mothers of aggressive toddlers either ignored or attended neutrally or positively to the aggression.

Awong, Grusec, and Sorenson (2008) assessed teenage working-class mothers, shortly after the birth of their infants, on their attitudes toward the need for deference to family authority (respect-based control) and anger. Their children's internalizing and externalizing problems and self-esteem were assessed approximately twelve years later. High respect-based control was linked to higher levels of externalizing problems in boys, regardless of level of maternal anger. Mothers who were low in anger and high in respect-based control had children who exhibited higher levels of self-esteem. Respect-based control predicted inconsistent rule enforcement, but not harsh parenting or lack of warmth. Arguments are made for distinguishing among various forms of control (e.g., authoritarian, psychological, behavioral, and respect-based) as well as the affective context in which they are administered in order to achieve an adequate understanding of the socialization process.

Anger in Young Adults

The link between anger, social skills, and psychological symptoms was investigated by Conger, Conger, Edmondson, Tescher et al. (2003) in a college population. Seven hundred nine students were administered the State Trait Anger Expression Inventory, the Anger Inventory, the Social Problem Solving Inventory, the Social Skills Inventory, and a series of questions about the degree to which anger affected their lives. Symptomatology was measured by the Brief Symptom Inventory and served as the criterion measure for a series of multiple regression analyses. Results indicated that both anger and social factors related to measures of psychological "distress" (undefined). Implications of the relationship between anger, social skills, and psychological symptoms were discussed in terms of research and assessment of individuals who may suffer from anger problems.

Developmental Socialization of Sadness

This section reviews selected studies that relate to sadness through depression or other affective disorders of Axis II Cluster B of the DSM-IV, such as anxiety.

Sadness in Children and Youth

In a pioneer study, Sandler and Joffe (1965), for instance, investigated depression in childhood by examining case materials of one hundred children of all ages treated psychoanalytically at the Hampstead Child Therapy Clinic. This examination revealed a pattern of depressive reaction to a wide range of internal and external precipitating circumstances. A combination of the following interrelated clinical features were found: (1) looking sad, unhappy, or depressed; (2) showing withdrawal, boredom, and discontent; (3) communicating a sense of feeling rejected or unloved; and (5) a general tendency to regress to oral passivity, insomnia, and other sleep disturbances, with autoerotic or other visibly repetitive activities, such as daydreaming, thumb-sucking, obsessional rituals, and so forth. These investigators attributed these reactions to a pervasive feeling of helplessness and loss in obtaining appropriate acceptance, nurturance, and rewarding intimate relationships.

Rotenberg, Mars, and Crick (1987) asked twenty-four children from grades one, three, five, and seven to describe situations in which they were sad and assessed the causes, intensity, motives, and consequences of their sadness. Data show that sadness was caused by harm in the majority of incidents. There was a shift with age in the nature of the harmful causes of sadness. Consistent with expectation, the younger participants tended to report a lower intensity of sadness than did older participants. There was an increase with age in participants' identification of their motives for sadness, particularly in the viewpoint motive. The most and least frequent of consequences of participants' sadness were passive nonexpressive and verbal expression of feelings, respectively. There was a decrease with age in participants' redirective behavior as a consequence of sadness.

Depressive symptoms in a sample of 515 male and female elementary and middle school children ages seven to eleven were evaluated from their parents' reports according to whether they had been subjected to combined and cumulative effects of supportive-positive versus harsh-negative parenting practices (Dallaire, Pineda, Ashley, Cole, Ciesla, et al. (2006). Results from structural equation modeling indicated that both practices were nearly orthogonal dimensions of parenting and both related to children's depressive symptoms. Supportive-positive parenting did not moderate the relation between harsh-negative parenting and children's depressive symptoms.

Blumberg and Izard (1985, 1986) studied depression in ten- and eleven-year-old children and found that these children were like depressed adults in that they reported experiencing a pattern of emotions including sadness, anger, self-directed hostility, and shame. They tended to explain negative events in terms of internal, stable, and global causes. The similarity between depressed children and depressed adults on indexes of emotion experiences, attribution style, and intellectual performance was greater for girls than for boys. Measures of emotion experiences accounted for 78.1 percent and 46.1 percent of the variance in girls' and boys' depression scores respectively, after the variance accounted for by attribution style was partialed out. In another analysis of children and teachers completing inventories assessing children's emotions, anxiety level, and depression level, Blumberg and Izard (1986) found distinct patterns of emotion variables involved in anxiety and depression, supporting Izard's (1979) differential theory of emotions.

Teachman and Allen (2007) argued that little is known about how to predict which individuals with known temperament vulnerabilities will develop social anxiety problems. Adolescents (N = 185) were followed from age thirteen to eighteen to evaluate psychosocial, prospective predictors of social anxiety symptoms and fears of negative evaluation (FNE), after accounting for preexisting social withdrawal symptoms. Results from structural equation modeling suggested that lack of perceived social acceptance predicts subsequent explicit social anxiety and FNE, whereas the emotional intensity of close peer interactions predicts subsequent implicit FNE, indicating the importance of peer interaction in the development of social anxiety and the value of measuring both implicit and explicit FNE. Even better would be to study each of these emotions separately from each other.

Sadness in Adults

In examining the association between unipolar depression with immature dependence and self-criticism, Mongrain and Leather (2006) administered a battery of tests to a sample of 158 graduate students with a diagnosed history of depression. Approximately, twenty months later, 102 students were reached for an assessment of new depressive onsets. Self-criticism and neuroticism were uniquely associated with a past history of depression, whereas self-criticism and immature dependence interacted in predicting past occurrences of depression. Self-criticism was increasingly associated with past depressive episodes as level of immature dependence increased. The interaction of immature dependence and self-criticism was also evident in predicting future occurrence of depression after controlling statistically for the effects of current symptoms, neuroticism, certain Axis II diagnoses, and number of previous depressive episodes. This interactive effect suggests that individuals with high levels of both self-criticism and immature dependence are particularly prone to depressive episodes.

Sadness in Psychiatric Patients

Brinkman and Overholser (1994) examined whether adolescent male psychiatric patients were less likely than comparable female inpatients to communicate their feelings of distress on direct and indirect measures, such as the Rorschach, the Minnesota Multiphasic Personality Inventory, and other measures of emotional distress. These investigators found that in general male and female participants reported highly similar levels and patterns of distress, whether direct or indirect measures were used. Although direct measures showed evidence of convergent validity, indirect measures were largely uncorrelated with each other and with direct measures, suggesting that assessment of emotional distress in both male and female adolescent inpatients is best facilitated by the use of direct measures. Of course, if the construct of distress is not specified operationally, it will be difficult if not impossible to evaluate it properly.

Jolly, Dyck, Kramer, and Wherry (1994) found it difficult to discriminate between anxiety and depression "*because of strong reliance on the construct of negative affect*" (p. 551; italics mine). Consequently, measures of both affect and cognitions are needed to discriminate effectively between the two disorders. Participants in this research were 159 psychiatric outpatients who completed the Positive and Negative Affect Schedule and the Cognition Checklist, as well as the Symptom Checklist 90 – Revised, the Beck Depression Inventory, and the Beck Anxiety Inventory. Results indicated that the incorporation of both affect and cognition increased the ability to discriminate between anxiety and depression. "*Negative affect was significantly correlated with a variety of disorders, indicating its poor discriminatory value*" (p. 552; italics mine). As participants became increasingly anxious, their cognitions were more like those of a depressed individual. From these results, could one conclude that anxiety might be a more benign level of depression?

Gamble, Talbot, Duberstein, Conner, et al. (2006) examined neuroticism's role in the association between childhood sexual abuse and severity of depressive symptoms in a sample of 105 psychiatric patients fifty years of age and older diagnosed with major depressive disorder. As hypothesized, men and women who reported histories of childhood sexual abuse had more severe depressive symptoms than those without abuse histories. Further, neuroticism partially accounted for the association between severe childhood sexual abuse and depressive symptom severity. Self-consciousness, a facet of neuroticism conceptually related to shame, also partially accounted for that relationship, suggesting that neuroticism may be one way in which childhood sexual abuse contributes to depressive symptoms in later life.

De Raedt, Schacht, Frank, and De Honwer (2006) attacked an issue relevant to the Selfhood Model[11] in RCT (Chapter 13 of this volume). According to these investigators, the cognitive behavioral model of depression holds that negative cognitions, especially self-esteem, relate to the self and have etiological importance for the development, maintenance, and relapse of depression. This model has been confirmed by research using questionnaires. Recent research using the Implicit Association Test, however, showed positive implicit self-esteem in formerly depressed participants, even after negative mood induction. These results are not in line with cognitive theory of depression. Because this could be an artifact of the specific procedure that was used, De Raedt et al. (2006) investigated implicit self-esteem of currently depressed participants and healthy controls using three different experimental measures: (1) Implicit Association Test; (2) Name Letter Preference Test; and (3) Extrinsic Affective Simon Task. Results of the three experiments are unequivocally indicative of positive implicit self-esteem in currently depressed patients. However, what exactly do these indirect measures really assess? A possible answer to this question will be given in Chapter 13.

Finally, an important meta-analytic review about the relationship between depression and immune system functioning (Herbert & Cohen, 1993) found that the presence of clinical depression was associated with decreases in all measures of lymphocyte functioning, an important and broad-spectrum measure of immune system competence. Moreover, these associations were robust and moderate to large size effects. The effect of depression on cellular immunity was significantly stronger among older and inpatient populations, who would be less immune to environmental influences.

Sadness in Old Age

Kraaij and Garnefski (2002) examined the buffering function of parental and partner bonding in the relationship between negative life events and depressive symptoms interviewing a community sample of 194 seniors sixty-five years and older. In particular, the control dimension of both parental and partner bonding seems important in relation to elderly depression. More psychological control is related to higher depression scores, whereas low partner control seems to work as a protective mechanism when negative life events are faced. Both researchers concluded that developing prevention and intervention programs aiming at optimizing bonding relationships throughout life seems advisable. These results show that negative late-life events can be offset by a lifetime of caring (Blieszner, 2006), emotional support (Lawrence, Bunde, Barry, Brock, Sullivan, Pasch, White, Dowd, & Adams, 2008; Shrout, Herman, & Bolger, 2006), and intimacy (Gore, Cross, & Morris, 2006; Weinberger, Hofstein, & Whitbourne, 2008).

Sadness and Gender Differences

Fivush and Buckner (2000) explored the ways in which sadness comes to be understood and expressed differently by females and males. Just as different cultures develop different "emotion scripts" that modulate the understanding of emotional experience, these scholars argued that women and men come to understand and integrate emotional experience into their lives in different ways as a result of participating in gender-differentiated activities and interactions.

Developmental Socialization of Fear

Fear develops early in life and does not develop in an interpersonal vacuum.

Fear in Childhood and Youth

Banks (2000) considered in general the development of social competence, popularity, and friendships/relationships, isolation, rejection, group formation, and the development of fears in childhood and adolescence. Broad theoretical considerations were provided to aid the conceptualization of selected issues to indicate the need for a better understanding of the developmental socialization of fears. More specifically, Ohman (2008) proposed a model of "fast, unconscious mechanisms in the generation of fear" (p. 709), differentiating between fears and anxiety thus:

> Fear and anxiety are obviously overlapping aversive activated states centered on threat. They both involve *intense negative feelings* (italics mine) and strong bodily manifestations. Subjectively, however, they take somewhat different forms. Fear denotes dread of impending disaster and an intense urge to defend oneself, primarily by getting out of the situation. Clinical anxiety, on the other hand, has been described as an ineffable and unpleasant feeling of foreboding. (p. 710)

This scholar went on to discuss the important role of unconscious processes in anxiety and fear and their neurobiology, a role explicated by Quirck (2007), who, however, did not include anxiety in his review. This position supports a view of anxiety as belonging within the realm of sadness and depression rather than belonging with fears. Anxiety and fear may be two separate feelings etiologically and developmentally separate from anger (Figure 2.1).

Kendler, Gardner, Annas, and Lichtenstein (2008), operating on an assumption that common fears change over developmental stages, studied whether genetic and environmental risk factors for fears are partly shared across fears and partly fear-specific. The nature of the changes in common and fear-specific genetic and environmental risk factors over time is unknown. Self-reported fears were obtained at ages thirteen to fourteen, sixteen to seventeen, and nineteen to twenty from 2,404 twins in the Swedish Twin Study of Child and Adolescent Development. Eighteen individual items formed four fear factors: animal, blood-injury, situational, and social. The best-fit model had no quantitative or qualitative gender effects or shared environmental effects, but included a strong common factor with a stable cross-time structure, with highest loadings on situational and lowest loadings on social fears. New common and fear-specific genetic risk factors emerged over developmental stages. With increasing age, genetic effects declined in overall importance and became more fear-specific. Cross-time continuity in specific genetic effects was highest for animal and lowest for social fears. Social fears had a "burst" of specific genetic effects in late adolescence. Individually specific environmental factors impacted both on the general fear factor and on specific fears. Compared to genetic effects, the impact of the unique environment was more time-specific. Consequently, genetic (developmental) and environmental (socialization) risk factors for individual fears are partly mediated through a common fear factor and are partly fear-specific in their effect. The developmental pattern of these risk factors is complex and dynamic, with new common and specific genetic effects arising in late adolescence and early adulthood.

CONCLUSION

We cannot yet study directly the developmental socialization of hurt feelings. We can only presume their existence from circumstances and situations that we assume to be hurtful. The only evidence that will satisfy this requirement of direct study will consist of empirical manipulation of hurtful variables, such as rejection, and from imaging on how our organism reacts to such circumstances.

5

Hurt Feelings in the Family

Although the family is a central, enduring, and taken-for-granted social institution, it is also one of the most variable, contested, debated, and analyzed by scholars, policy-makers, special interest groups, and family members alike.

Bielby, 1999 (p. 391)

The concept of family *qua* family, dear to most researchers and theorists, no longer exists as conceived in the past. As Hofferth and Casper (2007) demonstrated, only one-fourth of all domiciles in United States qualify as families, defined traditionally by two legally married adults with children born from that particular bond. Three-fourths of most domiciles today include unmarried singles, single mothers or fathers with children, married couples with no children, remarried couples with children from two previous marriages, same-sex couples with no children or with children from previous marriages, grandparents raising grandchildren, cohabiting couples, or single parents living with another partner and not remarried, among many other possibilities.

That is why, given such a tenuous standing in the scholarly community, the construct of intimate relationships was chosen instead, as characterized by closeness, commitment, interdependence, and duration (Burleson, 1995; L'Abate, 2005). These characteristics are found more often in friends than in some families (Fehr & Harasymchuk, 2009). The term family will be used here provisionally, with an understanding of its relative and limited nature: people living under the same roof linked by emotional, financial, legal, practical, and friendship bonds that go beyond what has existed in the past. The family, caretakers, partners, or friends are the gymnasia where we learn how to experience and express feelings in general and hurt feelings in particular (Cummings, Davies, & Campbell, 2000; Jacob, 1987; Kaslow, 1996; L'Abate, 1997).

Family environments may range from relationships where hurt feelings are kept inside and never disclosed with anyone to relationships where hurt feelings are expressed immediately and freely. This freedom allows hurt feelings to dissipate and eventually disappear over time without leaving any traces in the unconscious, especially if there are sufficient number of joyful experiences to offset them.

A BRIEF HISTORICAL BACKGROUND

It is important to trace the overall importance of feelings and emotions in past treaties and secondary references about the family and family psychopathology. Jacob's (1987) treatise, for instance, did not include feelings or emotions in its index. However, one chapter was devoted to depression (Coyne, Kahn, & Gotlib, 1987), a second to alcoholism and family interaction (Jacob & Seilhamer, 1987), a third to coercion and neglect in two major classes of childhood behavior disorders (conduct and dependency) (Wahler & Dumas, 1987), and a fourth to a behavior-genetic perspective (Pogue-Geile & Rose, 1987). More specifically, a volume devoted to affective disorders in the family (Clarkin, Haas, & Glick, 1988) had no entry about either feelings or emotions in its subject index.

In the fourth edition of a widely known sociological treatise on the family (Handel & Whitchurch, 1994), there was no entry for feelings, but the term "emotion" was mentioned five times (pp. 45, 314, 403, 459, 610) in various chapters. In a now classic and extremely comprehensive treatise on family psychopathology (Kaslow, 1996), feelings were not mentioned, but three references were found about emotions: a first one on emotional disposition in schema-focused personality diagnosis (Young & Gluhosky, 1996, pp. 313–315), the second on expressed emotions (EE; Denton, 1996, p. 38), and the third on EE and culture (Koss-Chioino & Canive, 1996, pp. 147–148). In L'Abate's (1997) treatise there was no mention of feelings, but there was information about EE in schizophrenia (Nicholson, 1997).

In a more recent treatise (Cummings, Davies, & Campbell, 2000), an entire excellent chapter is devoted to supporting the relationship between marital conflict and distress and psychopathology in children (p. 252); that is, the child's emotional security hypothesis, where aggression and violence (p. 262–263), nonverbal conflict or the silent treatment (p. 263), emotion regulation (p. 280), regulation of exposure to family affect (p. 281), and the family emotional climate (p. 290–291) are considered in detail, but with no specification about any distinct feelings, except parental depression.

Neglect of feelings and emotions in the family by standard psychological texts was corrected by Blechman's edited work (1990b) with outstanding, but now outdated, contributions. Expanding on these chapters would take more space than one can use for secondary references. The field of feelings and emotion has grown considerably since Blechman's pioneering contribution, which should be remembered as the first step in the right direction, even though hurt feelings were not yet even remotely considered.

What can be concluded from this brief survey about feelings and emotions in the family? One safely concludes that feelings and emotions were not given a great deal of attention in past secondary references about families, let alone hurt feelings. This shortcoming, however, did provide a clear rationale for devoting greater specific attention to this topic in primary references.

RESEARCH ON HURT FEELINGS IN THE FAMILY

Thompson and Meyer's (2007) chapter on socialization of emotion regulation in the family is so comprehensive that an attempt to expand on it would be unnecessary. These scholars introduce the topic thus:

> As any parent knows, infants are born with only the most rudimentary capacities to manage their arousal, and they depend on caregivers for soothing distress, controlling excitements, allowing fears, and even managing joyful pleasure. (p. 249)

After defining emotion regulation and its individual differences through direct interventions, parental evaluations of children's emotions are related to the family life's emotional climate. A great many of children's emotion representations depend on parental modeling and parent-child conversations that may vary in quality from constructive to destructive, depending on the nature of the parent-child relationship.

Whereas most of Thompson and Meyer's references came from child development journals, selected references cited will come mostly from three journals: the *Journal of Family Psychology, Personal Relationships*, and the *Journal of Social and Personal Relationships*, with the exception of Gottman, Katz, and Hooven's (1997) often cited pioneering research. Gottman et al., (1997) contributed monumentally to how feelings and emotions are communicated within families and how these communications impinge longitudinally on a child's development.

Gottman et al. (1997) described results of a three-year study of fifty-six parents and their children at ages five and eight based on extensive interviews, physiological measures, and observations of husband-wife, parent-child, and child-peer interactions; they focused especially on how anger and sadness were expressed. Unfortunately, other important variables, such as the influence of siblings, parent-child attachment, and children's concepts of emotions, could not be included given the already-wide scope of this study.

However, that research is not free from critical considerations from the viewpoint of hurt feelings. In the first place, Gottman et al. (1997) implied that a family's emotional style is a different and perhaps broader construct than various dimensions of parenting style. How family members think about feelings and emotions (meta-emotion) is linked directly to how they will transmit them to their children. In the second place, from the viewpoint of a dichotomy of communal/expressive versus agentic/instrumental relationships made in the first chapter of this volume (Bakan, 1968), Gottman's et al. contribution would distinguish between feelings and emotions as representing in the communal rather than in the agentic aspect of family relationships. In the third place, how parenting is intermixed with feelings and emotions is the independent variable to consider when assessing a child's emotional self-regulation. This intermingling between feelings on one hand and actions on the other needs to be included into the awareness of parents. That intermingling pervades affect regulation, peer relations, academic performance, as well as physical health (Stegge & Tervogt, 2007). In terms of the two separate processes between feelings and emotion already discussed, one could locate feelings in communal aspects of family relationships whereas emotions could be located in the agentic aspects.

One interesting conclusion that speaks to the topic of gender differences (considered in Chapter 8) deals with the husband's willingness and ability to accept the wife's lead in influencing and socializing him on the importance of feelings and emotions. That supposed willingness, stereotypically, at least in the American culture, may have been inadequate in the man. Emotional compatibility between parents, therefore, is the crucial variable that will determine how parents will operate as a team rather than as two separate individuals.

How do these observations and results relate to the importance of hurt feelings in families? By focusing on anger and sadness as "negative emotions," it seems that these investigators did not study these feelings, but rather studied the expressions of these feelings. To put it bluntly, they did not reach to the bottom of our existence, but remained solely at the outward expressions of these feelings as emotions. This conclusion in no way is meant to detract from their important and detailed research contribution. Their methodology in studying meta-emotions was so sophisticated and complex, that it might be difficult to replicate.

More recently, Mills and Piotrowski (2009) provided a comprehensive, integrated social information-processing and cognitive structural perspective on hurt feelings in the family, encompassing acts of commission and omission as part of this perspective. These scholars included a process similar to the information-processing ERAAwC model introduced briefly in Chapter 1 of this volume, expanded somewhat in Chapter 13 of this volume, and detailed in future publications (Cusinato & L'Abate, 2012; L'Abate et al., 2010). Mills and Piotrowski's (2009) dynamic process consists of five steps: encoding (E), interpreting (R), clarifying goals (R), accessing possible responses (A), and selecting a response (AW) (p. 261). Included in this process is the inevitable *repetitive reactivity* (RR) that permeates most family relationships (p. 262). The latter characteristic of RR, mentioned also by Waring (reviewed in Chapter 6 of this volume), needs underscoring because it is a style of responding in Model[9] in RCT (Chapter 13 of this volume).

Mills and Piotrowski (2009) divided their chapter into one section on parent-child relationships, including: (1) children's online processing of hurtful interactions with parents, such as psychological aggression, teasing, perceived sibling favoritism, the presence of feelings like shame, anger, and alienation; and (2) parents' online reactive processing of hurtful interactions with children, such as perceiving, appraising, and responding to hurtful child acts in ways that could become either hurtful or reparative. A second section of Mills and Piotrowski's chapter was devoted to the perception and appraisal of hurtful sibling interactions, such as physical and relational aggression, teasing, and tattling. A third section of this chapter was devoted to perceptions and appraisal of hurtful triadic interactions involving siblings and parents that include rivalry, parental responses to sibling aggression and conflict. A fourth section included an organizing framework (p. 277; figure 13.1) that starts with hurtful acts and sensitivity to hurt proceeding to perceptions, appraisal, and responses to hurt feelings. These processes are based on beliefs and dispositions that involve explanatory style, emotional dispositions, and scripts leading to developmental outcomes such as more functional mental health.

In a fourth section on future research, Mills and Piotrowski emphasized the need to learn more about the process of parental shaming to children's proneness to shame, sibling bullying, benign neglect, and maladjustment. It will be difficult to go above and beyond the detailed comprehensiveness of Mills and Piotrowski's chapter, and an attempt will be not made to even match it by organizing research in a different outline.

Whatever highly selected, representative research and studies are included here do not represent by any means an exhaustive review of the literature. Only studies about *presumed* hurt feelings will be included as exemplary of how those feelings may occur in the family. We are assuming that many aversive conditions included in the following should be conducive to hurt feelings in parents and offspring. However, unless specified, most conditions seem very likely to produce hurt feelings, directly or indirectly.

HURT FEELINGS IN PARTNERS AS A COUPLE

Presumably, hurt feelings are more likely to be found in couple and marital conflict. Using two very different sets of survey data, Holman and Jarvis (2003) investigated Gottman's (1999) observational findings regarding couple-conflict types on the basis of a 5:1 ratio of positive to negative interactional processes. These include regulated versus nonregulated, and even more specifically, validating, volatile, and conflict-avoiding couples. These negative processes were due mostly to what Gottman called the "Four Horsemen of the Apocalypse": criticism, contempt, defensiveness, and withdrawal or stonewalling. Holman and Jarvis hypothesized that defensible couple-conflict types could be established using survey data based on an individual's perception of the style he or she used in couple-conflict situations. Furthermore, Holman and Jarvis hypothesized that membership type would be related to relationship quality indicators, such as satisfaction, stability, communication processes, and affect regulation. Their results showed that survey data can reliably produce couple-conflict types similar to Gottman's. Additionally, these investigators found that, on satisfaction, stability, positive communication, and soothing, hostile couple-conflict types had the lowest mean scores and validating couple-conflict types had the highest mean scores. The types related in the opposite manner to negative communication, the Four Horsemen, and flooding of emotions. The other couple-conflict mean scores – volatile and avoiding – were almost always between the extreme means of the hostile and validating couple-conflict types.

The most relevant aspect of this research linked to hurt feeling involves the 5:1 ratio of positive to negative interactions between couples. This ratio brings us back to Chapter 1, where it was considered in regard to joys and hurts. When the former are greater than the latter, there is functionality. When the latter are greater than the former, there is dysfunctionality

Consequently, Gottman's (1999) ratio, as supported by Holman and Jarvis's results, may be an appropriate beginning quantification of the relationship between joys and hurts. It may take up to six joyful events to offset one hurtful event, as detailed in Model[10] of RCT in Chapter 13.

Even though cognitions rather than feelings were not studied in the following study (Langhinrichsen-Rohling, Heyman, Schlee, & O'Leary, 1997), it is reported here for its relevance to both positive and negative cognitions assessed in a sample of recently married childless couples (328 husbands and 331 wives), who were involved in nondistressed, distressed, and husband to wife (H-to-W) aggressive marriages. As predicted, maritally distressed couples held more negative cognitions about parenthood than did nondistressed spouses. Spouses in H-to-W aggressive marriages expected parenthood to be a more unpredictable and difficult job than spouses in marriages not marked by H-to-W aggression. Wives also reported more fears that having a child would result in a loss of freedom than their husbands. No distress, H-to-W aggressive level, or gender differences were obtained for pre-parenthood cognitions. Wives' but not husbands' positive and negative pre-parenthood cognitions at six month of marriage were able to predict parenthood status at thirty months of marriage.

Another study of 102 self-selected, middle-class couples with at least one child under five years of age completed questionnaires about the impact of division of labor, including "emotional work," on levels of depressive symptoms (Strazdins, Scannel, & Galligan, 1997). Women's depressive symptoms were predicted by emotional work, as well as by appraisal of conflict between a division of labor that would suit themselves and a division of labor that would be best for the family. Men's depressive symptoms were predicted by their spouse's disagreement with their estimate of how much housework they performed. Depressive symptoms for both men and women were associated with discrepancies between premarital expectations and the current division of labor. Focus on division of labor, especially *sharing* of emotional work, was recommended for treating depression.

Prager and Buhrmester (1998) conducted two studies to explore the following questions: (1) Does intimacy, within the context of a couple relationship, contribute to individual need fulfillment? (2) Does self-disclosure have beneficial effects on need fulfillment without being accompanied by intimacy's others dimensions, that is, positive affective tone and partner listening and understanding? (3) Does intimacy's impact on need fulfillment mediate its relationship with physical and psychological well-being? The researchers found that, indeed, relational intimacy, assessed globally and as a characteristics of the couples' daily interactions, is positively associated with individual need fulfillment. If and when self-disclosure was present, it may soften the effects of negative interactions on need fulfillment. Additionally, intimacy's relationship to psychological well-being is most likely accounted for by its effects on individual need fulfillment. Couples in which the wife was either clinically depressed or nondepressed participated in a videotaped problem-solving interaction and completed a battery of self-report measures of mood, family life, and perceptions of the marital interaction. Depressed wives tended to perceive their family life to be more negative than did nondepressed wives. Depressed wives also became increasingly negative in their verbal behavior over the course of the interaction. Depressed couples perceived the marital interaction to be more hostile, less friendly, and more dominated by their partners than did nondepressed couples. Only depressed couples appeared to be more immediately more reactive to their spouses' behaviors in the interactions (McCabe & Gotlib, 1993).

Hurt Feelings and Marital Discord

Sher and Baucom (1993) explored differences in communication and perception of communication among three types of married couples: distressed with wife depressed, distressed only, and nondepressed-nondistressed. These investigators found that depression within the context of a distressed marriage is related to (1) more negative communication both toward and from the depressed person; and (2) spouses' lower comprehension of each other's messages. Among the nondistressed couples, the more negative their communication, the more maritally satisfied they were, suggesting that negative communication might be used constructively by nondistressed couples, whereas negative communication might be detrimental to distressed couples.

Beach, Katz, Kim, and Brody (2003) argued that evidence suggests marital discord is related to depressive symptoms in married couples. In this study, investigators explored the potential gender-related differences in the prospective effect of marital discord on depression. One hundred sixty-six spouses from randomly sampled married couples with adolescent children provided reports of their marital quality and depressive symptoms at baseline and one year later. Results revealed that Time I marital quality was associated with Time 2 depressive symptoms, with the magnitude of this effect being similar for both husbands and wives, and spouses' own marital quality at Time 1 predicted their partners' Time 2 depressive symptoms net of other predictions in the model.

Hurt Feelings and Online Infidelity

Even though infidelity is considered in other chapters of this volume, a recent development since the advent of the Internet is online infidelity, defined as when a partner spends more time with a computer than with a partner. Henline, Lamke, and Howard (2007), for instance, examined the similarities, differences, and potential linkages between perceptions of online infidelity and traditional infidelity using a sample of 123 individuals in committed relationships. Participants nominated both sexually and emotionally based behaviors as unfaithful and expressed greater distress in response to hypothetical emotional, as compared to sexual, online infidelity. Unlike traditional infidelity, men generally were no more upset by sexual online infidelity than were women. Both men and women believed that emotional and sexual online infidelity were likely to co-occur. A face-to-face meeting was perceived to be more likely following emotional, as compared to sexual, online infidelity, and men were viewed as more likely than women to engage in sexual intercourse, given a face-to-face meeting with the online contact.

Hurt Feelings and Relationship Breakup

Variables most highly associated with distress at the time of a breakup might be nonmutuality in alternatives (i.e., partner having more interest in alternatives), commitment, satisfaction, greater effort in relationship initiation, being "left" by the other, and a fearful attachment style (Sprecher, Felmlee, Metts, Fehr, & Vanni, 1998). Developmentally, rather than structurally, several models of relationship dissolution imply a sequence of steps or stages for which there might exist a cultural script. Previous research has identified a script for first dates. Battaglia, Richard, Datteri, and Lord (1998) attempted to identify a relationship dissolution script by asking men and women to list the steps that typically occur when a couple breaks up. An analysis of 1,480 responses indicated a sixteen-step ordered script based on approach-avoidance theories of conflict and relevant relationship dissolution theories.

Cohen, Klein, and O'Leary (2007) examined the effects of marital dissolution on two potential outcomes, relapse into and recovery from major depression, within a sample that explicitly faced the recurring risk of depression. Among participants who were depressed at the time of marital dissolution, Cox proportional hazard models revealed a five-fold increased probability of recovering from major depression for participants who experienced a separation/divorce relative to participants who did not experience separation/divorce. Among participants who were remitted/recovered at the time of marital dissolution, analyses did not reveal a significant probability of relapsing into a major depression following a separation/divorce. These findings suggested that among individuals with a history of major depression and marital stressors, experiencing a separation/divorce may function to alleviate rather than precipitate depression.

HURT FEELINGS IN PARTNERS AS PARENTS

Wierson, Armstead, Forehand, Thomas, and Fauber (1990) wondered whether there would be differences between a mother or a father in viewing parent-adolescent conflict as a common dimension in most families during the teenage years. Mothers reported a less positive relationship, a greater number of conflicts, and more intense discussions of conflicts with their adolescents. This finding indicates that this variable is the primary difference between mothers and fathers (Crockenberg & Langrock, 2001).

Eisenberg, Losoya, Fabes, Guthrie, Reiser, Murphy, Shepard, and Padgett (2001), for instance, reviewed parental influences on the emotion regulation of their children's feelings. Thompson (1998), in commenting on previous publications of Eisenberg and her coworkers concerning parental socialization of children's emotions, noted that the social-relational foundations of self-referent emotions makes them highly relevant to an analysis of the development of emotional competence. It is less clear, however, whether the modes of parental socialization profiled by Eisenberg et al. have comparable consequences for the development of self-referent emotions as they do for basic emotions like fear, anger, and sadness. He concluded that thoughtful empirical exploration of these questions that recognize the intimate connections between the growth of emotional competence and the development of conscience, self-understanding, and relationships is likely to significantly advance developmental emotions theory. His conclusions may be supported by the work of Curran, Hazen, Jacobvitz, and Sasaki (2006).

Hurt Feelings and Sadness

In addition to sadness, it is important to see how sadness in marriage might be related to marital hostility and depression in spouses' depressive symptoms. Proux, Buehler, and Helms (2009) examined the moderating roles of marital warmth and recent life events in the association between observed marital hostility and changes in spouses' depressive symptoms over three years in 416 couples. These investigators found that husbands' marital hostility was significantly related to increases in wives' depressive symptoms, whereas husbands' and wives' warmth moderated the association between husbands' hostility and increases in wives' depressive symptoms, which was stronger under conditions of lower levels than under conditions of higher levels of husbands' warmth. The same pattern was found for wives' warmth. Regarding life events, the association between wives' hostility and increases in husbands' depressive symptoms was stronger for couples with more recent life events than for couples with fewer recent life events.

Hurt Feelings and Parent Gender

Parenting as a mediator of association between marital and child adjustment and parent gender was examined as a moderator of associations among marital, parental, and child functioning in 226 families with a school-age child (146 boys). Kaczynski, Lindahl, Laurenceau, and Malik (2006) found that parenting fully mediated associations between marital conflict and child internalizing and externalizing behaviors. Parent gender did not moderate associations when data from the full sample or families with girls only were evaluated. Parent gender did moderate associations when families with boys were evaluated, with the association between marital conflict and parenting stronger for fathers than for mothers. A trend suggested that fathers' parenting may be more strongly related to internalizing behavior, whereas mothers' parenting may be more strongly related to externalizing behavior in boys. After all, maternal negative thoughts and feelings associated with authoritarianism in individualistic but not collectivist groups may be more detrimental to children's self-esteem than is authoritarianism in and of itself (Rudy & Grusec, 2006).

THE FAMILY AS A UNIT OF INTERACTING PERSONALITIES

Even though the purpose of this work is to concentrate on hurt feelings at the receptive input side of experience rather than on the output expression of those feelings as emotions, there is no question that the family furnishes the first and more important setting for experiencing feelings and for their expression as emotions (Cleary & Katz, 2008; Katz & Windecker-Nelson, 2006), especially anger, sadness, and fears (Figure 2.1 of this volume). There may be gender differences with mothers "coaching philosophy of sadness and fathers' emotion-coaching behaviors." In spite of this possible gender difference, which may need replication, the overall conclusion is that "mothers' attitudes and behaviors may work together to shape children's emotional development" (Cleary & Katz, 2008, p. 11). If their conclusions are reliable and valid, then they would suggest that mothers might be more responsible than fathers on how feelings are experienced, as in sadness, and fathers might be more responsible for how feelings are expressed outwardly.

For example, Teicher, Samson, Polcari, and McGreenery (2006) argued that childhood maltreatment is an important psychiatric risk factor, whereas past research has focused primarily on the effects of physical and sexual abuse or witnessing domestic violence. These authors maintained that parental verbal aggression has received little attention as a specific form of abuse, and they delineated the impact of parental verbal aggression, witnessing domestic violence, physical abuse, and sexual abuse. They found that verbal aggression was associated with moderate to large effects, comparable to those associated with witnessing domestic violence or nonfamilial sexual abuse, and larger than those associated with familial physical abuse. Exposure to multiple forms of maltreatment had an effect size that was often greater than the component sum. Combined exposure to verbal abuse and witnessing domestic violence apparently may have a greater negative effect on some measures than exposure to familial sexual abuse.

Hurt Feelings and Marital Conflict in the Family

A series of studies (Cummings, Davies, & Simpson, 1994; Cummings, Goeke-Morey, Papp, & Dukewich, 2002; Fincham, 1994; Fincham, Crych, & Osborne, 1994; Kirzmann & Emery, 1994), with their causes, consequences, or correlates (Rutter, 1994), showed the relationship between marital conflict and child maladjustment. However, this association is not linear. Other factors, such as coping, may mediate such a relationship (Cummings, Davies, & Simpson, 1994; Kitzmann & Emery, 1994). What happens when children are subjected to the other side of the conflict coin? Toddlers (at ages twelve, eighteen, twenty-four, and thirty-six months) and their parents participated in a longitudinal observational study of children's responses to constructive marital disputes (Easterbrooks, Cummings, & Emde, 1994). Even though there was temporal stability in couples' interactions over time, that stability did not extend to individual child behavior. Children with more difficult temperaments were more reactive, highlighting the importance of a balance between positive and interfering behaviors of toddlers during constructive family disputes.

A representative study more specifically relevant to hurt feelings (Lindahl, Clements, & Markman, 1997) assessed longitudinally whether couples' disregulated "negative affect" and diminished affective quality before parenthood is predictive of conflict in family relationships five years later when data were collected on parent-child and family interactions. Husbands' prechild marital behavior and couples' prechild negative escalation were predictive of husbands' conflict and triangularization of the child into marital conflict. Family level functioning (e.g., coalition formation) was predicted by prechild negative escalation. Parenting was not predicted by prechild marital functioning, but was related to current marital functioning.

These findings provide support for how couples regulate negative affect early on in marriage and set the tone for future interactions involving parents and their child. This study also illustrates the fallacy (discussed at length in Chapter 2 of this volume) of lumping together as "negative affect" feelings with different proximal and distal consequences, because one cannot discern from the foregoing methodology and results which of the three "negative" affects was more negatively effective than the other two.

A similar study was conducted by Owen and Cox (1997), whose results supported the prediction that chronic marital conflict interferes with sensitive, involved parenting and thereby predicts insecurity in the attachment relationship, particularly for fathers. Chronic marital conflict presents the infant with experiences of frightened and frightening parents and diminishes behavior options to alleviate accompanying "distress." As predicted, disorganized attachment behavior with mother and father was explained by chronic marital conflict and not mediated by parental ego development or sensitive parenting.

The two foregoing studies were followed up by a study of children's responses to verbal and physical conflict between adult-adult, mother-girl, and mother-boy dyads. Seven- to nine-year-old children viewed videotaped arguments and were interviewed afterward. In comparison with children from low-conflict homes, children from high-conflict homes perceived the actors engaged in both interadult and mother-child disputes as more angry, and reported feeling more fearful during those arguments. These results support the sensitization hypothesis that children from conflictual homes may become habituated to conflict; it also indicates, however, that parental marital conflict exacerbates children's perceptions of conflict and fear when responding to interadult as well as to mother-child conflict.

Marital conflict may not only effect offspring negatively, but it may also influence how children relate with their peers. Lindsey, McKinnon-Lewis, Campbell, Frabutt, & Lamb, 2002), for instance, examined the role of mother-son emotional reciprocity in connections between marital conflict and the quality of boys' peer relationships. Parents from eighty-four intact families with preadolescent boys reported on their level of conflict in their marital relationship. Observations of mother-son interactions were coded for emotional reciprocity, and assessment of boys' peer relationships were obtained from both teachers and classmates. These investigators found that marital conflict affected boys' social competence indirectly through its effect on the emotions expressed between mother and son. These findings support the proposal that emotional processes play an important role in connections between marital conflict and children's peer relationships, and suggest that family emotional expressiveness deserves greater attention in both research and intervention.

Hurt Feelings and Family Conflicts

As the studies reviewed thus far tend to show, up-to-date research suggests that the family plays a significant role in the development and perpetuation of feelings and emotions. If that is the case, then feelings in families might predict whether a depression relapse will occur in its members. Slesnick and Waldron (1997), for instance, examined videotaped interactions of parents with a depressed adolescent and of control parents and youth during a conflictual problem-solving task. In comparison with parents of nondepressed adolescents, parents of depressed adolescents engaged in higher rates of inconsistent and contradictory communication in which aversive content was linked with positive affective content. Adolescent depressed content led to greater suppression of parent content in nondepressed than in depressed families. This finding could support the conclusion that dysfunctional family communication may be associated with the development and maintenance of depression in the adolescent.

Arguing that there may be a gap between methodological approaches to study links between marital conflict and children, Cummings, Goeke-Morey, Papp, and Dukewch (2002) trained fifty-two couples to complete home dairy reports on everyday marital conflicts and children's responses. Parental negative emotionality and destructive conflict tactics related to children's insecure emotional and behavioral responses. Parental positive emotionality and constructive conflict tactics were linked with children's secure emotional responding. When parents' emotions and tactics were considered in the same model, negative emotionality was more consistently related to children's negative reactions than were destructive conflict tactics, whereas constructive conflict tactics were more consistently related to children's positive reactions than parents' positive emotionality. Differences in children's responding as a function of specific parental negative emotions (lumped together as anger, sadness, and fear) and parental gender were identified. This is an error that according to the present formulation should be corrected in future research, because each of those three feelings produces completely different developmental outcomes (Figure 2.1).

Children are aware of their parents' conflicts much earlier than we may have thought. McDonald and Grych (2006), for instance, investigated two questions pertinent to understanding developmental aspects of children's appraisals of their parents' conflict: (1) Do seven- to nine-year-old children make reliable distinctions between their perceptions of conflict and their appraisals of threat and self-blame? (2) Do threat and blame appraisals mediate the association between exposure to interparental conflict and adjustment problems in this age group? Factor analyses of a new version of the Children's Perceptions of Interparental Conflict Scale designed for younger children showed that 179 seven- to nine-year-old children distinguished properties of conflict in their appraisals of it. Moreover, as predicted by the cognitive-contextual framework, threat and self-blame appraisals mediated the link between conflict and internalizing but not externalizing problems. This study provides compelling evidence that appraisals of interparental conflict can be reliably measured at relatively young ages and suggests that perception of threat and self-blame function similarly in seven- to nine-year-olds as they do in older children.

However, not all conflict is "necessarily detrimental" (Adams & Laursen, 2007). Negative qualities of parent-adolescent and friend relationships were linked to adjustment problems (aggression, anxiety and depression, delinquency, and withdrawal). Positive qualities of parent-adolescent relationships were linked to school grades and adjustment problems. Nonlinear associations between conflict and adolescent outcomes were moderated by negative qualities of relationships such that increases in conflict from low to moderate levels were linked to (1) higher school grades for adolescents in better-quality, but not poorer-quality, relationships, and (2) greater delinquency and withdrawal for adolescents in poorer-quality, but not better-quality, relationships.

More specifically, partner-to-mother aggression might be positively associated with child reports of externalizing problems at lower, but not higher, levels of maternal warmth (Skopp, McDonald, Jouriles, & Rosenfield, 2007). Similarly, partner-to-mother aggression was positively associated with mother reports of girls', but not boys', externalizing problems at lower, but not higher, levels of maternal warmth. On the other hand, the moderating effects of partner warmth were in the opposite direction and present only in child-reported externalizing problems. Increased levels of partner-to-mother aggression related positively to child-reported externalizing problems when partners were higher, but not lower, in warmth.

Hurt Feelings and Addictions

Duncan, Duncan, and Hops (1996) investigated developmental trends in adolescent, parent, and older-sibling substance use across a three-year period as well as the predictive effect of these trends on adolescent substance use two years later. Participants were 101 adolescents (50 boys and 51 girls) who were an average of 12.34 years old at the first assessment, their parents, and an older sibling. These researchers found that although parents and siblings contribute to the level of adolescent substance use, only siblings appear to contribute to adolescents' subsequent substance-use development. The adolescents' developmental trajectory was the best predictor of later use, but siblings contributed to later use indirectly through their influence on adolescents' substance-use development. This use, as in the case of many addicts, could be one way to medicate oneself and avoid dealing with hurt feelings, as is the case in many psychopathologies reviewed thus far in this volume.

Addictive behavior could be seen as an attempt to medicate oneself from unacceptable, unexpressed, and inexpressible hurt feelings, which may be expressed either through internalizing these feelings in depression or externalizing them through addictive behavior. Tafa and Baiocco (2009), for instance, examined how adolescent and parental perceptions of family system characteristics predict adolescent addictive behavior patterns. These investigators sampled 252 families by administering to them questionnaires measuring family functioning (FACES III) and addictive behavior (Shorter Promise Questionnaire). The results provided support for the assumption that family system characteristics could predict adolescent addictive behavior, despite using a normative sample and taking nonclinical families into consideration. These characteristics consist of (1) weak emotional bonds (low cohesion); (2) incapacity to change their power structure; (3) role relationships; and (4) relationship rules in response to situational and developmental stress.

Ragarajan and Kelly (2006) examined the role of perceptions of family environment and family communication as mediators of the effects of parental alcoholism on the self-esteem of adult children of alcoholics. Participants (N = 227) completed self-reports of parental alcoholism, family environment, family communication patterns (FCP), and self-esteem. Results indicated a negative relationship between the seriousness of both maternal and paternal alcoholism and self-esteem. Paternal and maternal alcoholism were related to the two dimensions of family environment, family stressors and parental disregard, although the effect for paternal alcoholism was larger. The relationship between maternal alcoholism and offspring self-esteem was partially mediated by parental disregard, whereas the relationship between parental alcoholism and self-esteem was mediated by parental disregard and perceptions of a conversation-orientation.

Hurt Feelings and Parental Divorce

Zill, Morrison, and Coiro (1993) investigated whether effects of parental divorce were evident in young adulthood. Among eighteen- to twenty-two-year-olds from disrupted families, 65 percent had poor relationships with their fathers and 30 percent with their mothers, 25 percent had dropped out of school, and 40 percent had received psychological help. Even after controlling for demographic and socioeconomic differences, youth from disrupted families were twice as likely to exhibit these problems as youths from nondisrupted families. A significant effect of divorce on mother-child relationships was evident in adulthood, whereas none was found in adolescence. Youth experiencing disruption before six years of age showed poorer relationships with their fathers than those experiencing disruption later in childhood. Overall, remarriage did not have a protective effect, but there were indications of amelioration among those who experienced early disruption.

Hurt Feelings and Emotionality

In a study representative of many others, which cannot all be reviewed here, Margolin, Christensen, and John (1996) compared thirty-eight distressed and thirty-eight nondistressed families on two interaction processes: the continuance of tensions involving some family members and the spillover of tensions from one family subsystem to another. One parent reported perceptions of family tensions and satisfaction ratings each day for two weeks. Sequential analyses revealed that distressed, compared with nondistressed, families experienced (1) greater continuance of tensions, particularly tensions that occurred the following day during the same time period; and (2) more spillover, particularly between marital and child-related tensions. Correlations with daily satisfaction ratings indicated that marital dissatisfaction in distressed families is highly related to the occurrence of marital tensions. These findings support the importance of examining daily events and multiple family subsystems in order to understand family distress.

Parental emotionality expanded to offspring is deemed to be the glue that links parents with their children (L'Abate, 2005). For instance, one-year-old infants (N = 62) were observed in free play and teaching sessions with their parents in order to examine parents' emotional availability and the infants' emotional competence (Volling, McElwain, Notaro, & Herrera, 2002). Mothers were more emotionally available than fathers, and infants exhibited more effortful attention with mothers than with fathers. Similar relations between parental emotional availability and infant emotional competence were found for mother-infant and father-infant dyads. Change in parental emotional availability covaried with change in infant emotional competence. Individual differences in parental emotional availability and infant emotional competence were more consistent across contexts than across parents. Infant effortful attention at twelve months was a mediator between maternal emotional availability at twelve months and toddler situational compliance at sixteen months.

Wong, McElwain, and Halberstadt (2009) examined parental beliefs about children's negative emotions (unspecified), parent-reported marital conflict/ambivalence, and child negative emotionality and gender as predictors of mothers' and fathers' reported reactions to their kindergarten children's negative emotions and self-expressiveness in the family (N = 55 two-parent families). Models predicting parents' nonsupportive reactions and negative expressiveness were significant. For both mothers and fathers, more accepting beliefs about their children's negative emotions were associated with more negative expressiveness. Furthermore, interactions between child negative emotionality and parental resources (e.g., marital conflict/ambivalence, accepting beliefs) emerged for fathers' nonsupportive reactions and mothers' negative expressiveness. In some instances, child gender acted as a moderator such that parental beliefs about emotions and the emotion socialization outcomes emerged when child and parent gender were concordant.

Presumed Hurt Feelings and Punishment

Even more to the point, Trickett (1993) examined the development of twenty-nine school-aged physically abused children between four and eleven years as well as the child-rearing beliefs and practices of the abusive parents, compared to a control group of nonabusive parents matched on age, race, gender, and socioeconomic status. A multimethod approach was used to evaluate these families. This researcher found that abused children had poorer cognitive maturity, interpersonal problem-solving skills, and social competence, and had many more behavior problems than the comparison children. In some instances, aspects of the child-rearing context were stronger predictors of the children's development than was abuse-group membership.

Lynch, Turkheimer, Slutske, D'Onofrio, Mendle, and Emery (2006) argued that conclusions about the effects of harsh parenting on children have been limited by research designs that cannot control for genetic or shared environmental confounds. These investigators used a sample of children of twins and a hierarchical linear modeling statistical approach to analyze the consequences of varying levels of punishment while controlling for many confounding influences. The sample 887 twin pairs and 2,554 children came from the Australian Twin Registry. Although corporal punishment per se did not have significant association with negative childhood outcomes, harsher forms of physical punishment did appear to have specific and significant effects. The observed associations between harsh physical punishment and negative outcomes in children survived a relatively rigorous test of its casual status, increasing the authors' conviction that harsh physical punishment is a serious risk factor for children.

Erath, Bierman, and the Conduct Problems Prevention Research Group (2006) explored in a cross-sectional study direct associations between aggressive marital conflict and child aggressive-disruptive behavior at home and school in 360 kindergarten children. In addition, mediated pathways linking aggressive marital conflict to maternal harsh punishment to child aggressive-disruptive behavior was examined. Moderation analyses explored how the overall frequency of marital disagreement might buffer or exacerbate the impact of aggressive marital conflict on maternal harsh punishment and child aggressive-disruptive behavior. Hierarchical regressions revealed direct pathways linking aggressive marital conflict to child aggressive-disruptive behavior at home and school and a partially mediate pathway linking aggressive marital conflict to child aggressive-disruptive behavior at home. Further analyses revealed that rates of marital disagreement moderated the association between aggressive marital conflict and child aggressive-disruptive behavior at home, with an attenuated association at high rates of marital disagreement as compared with low rates of marital disagreement.

What happens when inconsistent discipline is paired with emotional unavailability, the double whammy? Sturge-Apple, Davies, and Cummings (2006) examined the nature of pathways between marital hostility and withdrawal, parental disagreements about child-rearing issues, and subsequent changes in parental unavailability and inconsistent discipline in a sample of 225 mothers, fathers, and six-year-old children. Results of auto-aggressive, structural equation models indicated that marital withdrawal and hostility were associated with increases in parental emotional unavailability over the one-year period, whereas marital hostility and withdrawal did not predict changes in parental inconsistency in discipline. Additional findings supported the role of child-rearing disagreements as an intervening or mediating mechanism in links between specific types of marital conflict and parenting practices.

Hurt Feelings and Sibling Relationships

Graham-Bermann, Cutler, Litzenberger, and Schwartz (1994) investigated in two studies young adults' recollections of high levels of conflict and violence with a sibling during childhood and adolescence and compared the experiences of four groups: (1) those who were violence perpetrators; (2) violence victims; (3) those with reciprocal violence; and (4) a control group. Of college students in the first study, 28 percent reported high levels of conflict or violence with a sibling. Female participants and those who were the younger sibling experienced more conflict and violence than did male participants and older siblings. In the second study, association of conflict and violence with emotional adjustment revealed that female participants had more negative emotional outcomes than did male participants. A positive association was also found among severe violence in the parental and sibling dyad.

Hurt Feelings and Family Resilience

The interaction of individual and environmental characteristics over time in children from maltreating families would predict long-term damage in children raised under abusive and neglectful home conditions. On the other hand, there are so-called resilient children who are able to grow above and beyond those negative circumstances when they are able to rely on supportive influences in the extended family and in the wider community, and when they are able to determine to be different, if not the opposite, from abusive parents (Herrenkohl, Herrenkohl, & Egolf, 1994). This interesting phenomenon can be explained in part with Model[8] of RCT dealing with identity differentiation in Chapter 13 of this volume.

CONCLUSION

Intimate relationships model, reinforce, weaken, encourage, and discourage the expression of feelings in general and of hurt feelings in particular – those very feelings that these relationships willy-nilly produce. Whether these intimate relationships involve parents and children or all the many variations on the theme of "family," no matter what we call it, it is in intimate relationships that we learn how to experience feelings and how and whether to express them as emotions, positively or negatively, constructively or destructively.

PART TWO

THE SCIENTIFIC BASES OF HURT FEELINGS

This section contains information and research about the empirical bases of hurt feelings.

6

The Discovery of Hurt Feelings: The Pioneers

> Mace's (1976) arguments concerning the love-anger cycle in marriage are
> criticized on philosophical (theoretical) and technical (clinical) grounds.
> Underneath the smoke screen of anger there is the fire of hurt feelings.
> Dealing with these feelings decreases the expression of anger and helps
> the couple reach "real" intimacy: the sharing of hurt feelings. Victories
> we can share with anybody. Anybody is willing to share victories with us.
> Hurt feelings, on the other hand, belong within the marriage.
>
> L'Abate (1977, p. 13)

This admittedly self-serving introductory quote is reprinted to proffer a
chronological timeline to the study of hurt feelings. This quote was followed
up by a specific study by Frey, Holley, and L'Abate (1979), who found that
couples liked a sharing-of-hurts scenario better than two other scenarios.
Because I cannot think of any other way to organize pioneers about the
study of hurt feelings except chronologically, this is the way pioneers in the
study of hurt feelings will be presented within and among themselves.

EDWARD M. WARING

This Canadian physician/psychiatrist wrote about "intimacy" rather
than specifically on hurt feelings. Nonetheless, his contribution is worth
inclusion as a pioneering study of intimacy, if not hurt feelings (Waring,
McElrath, Mitchell, & Derry, 1981). He has been ignored by the emotion and intimacy literature, even though his work deserves relevant
coverage. For example, in a whole series of studies summarized herein,
Waring, Tillman, Frelick, and Russell (1980), in an open-ended format, questioned fifty adults in the general population regarding their
concepts of intimacy. A second random sample of twenty-four couples

from the general population and twenty-four clinical couples received a standardized interview in which concepts of intimacy were systematically rated to develop an operational definition of the dimensions of intimacy.

Waring and Russell (1980) found that patients with chronic physical symptoms of obscure etiology who were referred to a psychiatric consultation service demonstrated characteristic differences in their marital adjustment and family structure when compared with nonpatient controls. Although marital adjustment, as perceived by patient and spouse, was similar to that of nonpatient couples, where absence of conflict was demonstrated, marriages of patients were characterized by specific incompatibilities in intimacy, socializing, and initiative. The family structure also demonstrated a preoccupation with relationships within the family, with resultant isolation from extrafamiliar social contacts, and a lack of problem-solving ability. These observations suggested that the level of intimacy in a marriage may be a predisposing vulnerability risk factor in the sickness role assumed by at least some hospitalized patients. Finally, this study suggested that marital assessment may have value in the evaluation of patients with chronic physical complaints of obscure etiology.

Self-disclosure was identified as a fundamental aspect of intimacy in interpersonal relationships and marriage (Waring, 1980). Dimensions of intimacy in marriage (Waring, McElrath, Lefcoe, & Weisz, 1981) defined operationally produced eight components: (1) affection; (2) expressiveness; (3) compatibility; (4) cohesion and commitment to marriage; (5) sexuality; (6) conflict resolution; (7) autonomy; and (8) identity. Perceptions of one's parents' levels of intimacy were thought to influence respondents' own interpersonal relationships. Couples with marital maladjustment and/or psychiatric illness were less aware of aspects of their marriage that influence intimacy, suggesting that self-disclosure and parental interpersonal intimacy may be fundamental factors in marital adjustment that merit further research.

Waring (1981) gave credit to quite a few writers who, up to the date of that publication, emphasized the nature of intimacy and the lack thereof in psychiatric populations, defining intimacy as "a multifaceted interpersonal dimension that describes the quality of a marital relationship at a point in time." In addition to these components of intimacy, Waring added the requirement of cognitive self-disclosure using cognitive family therapy as one way to help family members become more intimate, as described in a case history.

Waring and Chelune (1983) examined the relationship between the qualitative aspects of marital intimacy among twenty couples and a quantitative microanalysis of their self-disclosing behavior. Two interview segments and their combinations were scored for basic parameters of self-disclosure using the Self-Disclosure Coding System (SDCS). These scores served as predictor variables for each of twelve intimacy dimensions derived from the standardized Victoria Hospital Intimacy Interview in stepwise multiple regression analyses. Resulting multiple R's ranged from .36 for Sexuality in segment I to .85 for Identity in segment II. Analysis of the couples' self-disclosures across segments I and II yielded multiple R's from .44 to .85, with the intimacy dimensions of Expressiveness, Compatibility, Behavior, and Identity showing the highest correlates. These results suggested that although self-disclosure and intimacy are not synonymous, self-disclosure behavior is a major determinant of various aspects of marital intimacy and accounts for more than 50 percent of the variance in at least four dimensions.

Waring followed up this definition and previous studies by constructing the Waring Intimacy Questionnaire (1984b), which was specifically developed to measure the quality and quantity of marital intimacy, and which mirrored the eight items just listed. Reliability and validity were high enough to recommend further study (Waring & Chelune, 1983).

Waring (1984a) evaluated his theory of family psychopathology, which suggested that in families where one member suffers from nonpsychotic emotional illness, an affective dysfunctional potential in the parental interpersonal relationship will be demonstrated. This deficiency of marital intimacy results in a pattern of *obligatory repetition* that is specific for nonpsychotic emotional illness. He reported the results of a pilot study with 102 patients with nonpsychotic emotional illness and their spouses that demonstrated that deficiencies of marital intimacy were significantly associated with family patterns of chaos and enmeshment. Deficiencies in the family environment dimension of personal growth were also associated with lack of intimacy.

Implications of this work about the relationship of intimacy to various models of RCT will be discussed in Chapter 13.

JAMES W. PENNEBAKER

The monumental contribution of James W. Pennebaker to the study of trauma, by now globally known as the "Pennebaker Paradigm," is also well known as "expressive writing." It has been so often replicated and repeatedly reviewed over the years (Esterling, L'Abate, Murray, & Pennebaker, 1999; Kacewicz, Slatcher, & Pennebaker, 2007; Lepore & Smyth, 2002; Pennebaker, 2001) that it would be impossible to cite and include in this volume all the research that has stemmed from his now-classic work (Pennebaker & Beall, 1986), published the same year, incidentally, in which I published a workbook with six exercises on intimacy containing three exercises focused on sharing hurts (L'Abate, 1986). His A to D model, expanded by De Giacomo et al. (2010) and mentioned in Chapter 2 of this volume, is another example of the geniality and originality of Pennebaker's work.

Basically, this paradigm consists of asking participants to write about heretofore undisclosed traumas for fifteen to twenty minutes a day for four consecutive days. Pennebaker and Beall (1986) found that undergraduates who completed this assignment, in comparison to a control group that wrote about banal topics, showed improved immune system functions and a significantly lower frequency of visits to the medical services of the university. This study has been replicated around the world with functional and dysfunctional, medically sick participants with varying results, but with sufficiently satisfactory results to warrant continued studies. Nonetheless, more recent studies using a paradigm relevant to prevention and treatment of traumas are summarized in De Giacomo's et al. work (2010).

Perhaps the summary of one recent publication (Hughes, Uhlmann, & Pennebaker, 2004) may capture the flavor of Pennebaker's contribution. Hughes at al., argued that when individuals talk or think about upsetting experiences, different coping and defensive processes are invoked from one minute to the next. A central assumption of this study is that some coping strategies are more biologically activated than others.

A new methodology developed by Pennebaker himself was introduced, which links production of natural written language with autonomic activity on a word-by-word or phrase-by-phrase basis. Using this technique with a sample of twenty-four participants who wrote about traumatic experiences, it was found that certain text dimensions are highly related to skin conductance level (SCL) but not to heart rate. In general, participants' SCLs increased when expressing negative emotions and when using denial and passive voice. SCLs were more likely to drop when participants used positive emotion words and self-references, especially at the conclusion of sentences or thought units. These results and its methodology, of course, have important implications for understanding psychological defenses and physical health. Preventive and therapeutic implications of this paradigm will be covered in Chapters 11 and 12 of this volume.

ANITA L. VANGELISTI

Feeling hurt, by its nature, is a social phenomenon.
(Vangelisti, 1994b, p. 53)

I owe this volume to Vangelisti's using my original writings about hurt feelings. When I eventually called to congratulate her on her work (and even citing my work!), in the early 2000s, she told me that she thought that after so much time had elapsed since 1977, I would surely be dead! Her request to write an epilogue chapter for her handbook (L'Abate, 2009a) started the process of discovering that I had amassed a great deal of information about feelings, emotions, and, of course, hurt feelings.

Vangelisti started her work on hurt feelings in a paper presented in 1989, eventually published in 1994, which described the social interactions that can be defined as hurtful; she presented evidence that distinguishes socially elicited feelings of hurt from other emotions on the basis of attributions (internal, external, interpersonal, relational, stable/unstable, and global/specific). She then proceeded to present a typology (a first!) of hurtful messages, including accusations, evaluations, directives, advice, expressions of desire, informing, questions, threats, jokes, and lies. Lastly, factors that influence the impact of hurtful messages on relationships were examined. Therefore, this paper/chapter was an introduction; subsequent series of studies have built on her findings published therein (Vangelisti, 2001, 2007; Vengelisti & Hampel, 2010; Vangelisti, Mcguire, Alexander, & Clark, 2007).

The year 1998 represents a watershed achievement for Vangelisti, when she published two different research studies. In the first publication (Vangelisti & Crumley, 1998), two studies tested the assumption that relational contexts affect the way people react to messages that hurt their feelings. In the first, the range of responses people have to hurtful message was explored, and underlying dimensions reflecting the responses were identified. Participants' reactions were characterized by three broad dimensions: (1) active responses (e.g., attacking the other, defending the self, asking for an explanation); (2) acquiescent responses (e.g., crying, apologizing); and (3) invulnerable responses (e.g., ignoring the message, laughing). Analyses indicated that people who felt extremely hurt tended to react more often by acquiescing than those who were least hurt. Also, those who felt relatively low impact of hurt on their relationships responded more often with invulnerability than those who felt the impact was high.

In the second study, the association of people's reactions to hurt and the quality of their relationship with the person who hurt them was examined, as was the influence of particular types of relationships (e.g., those between family members or romantic partners) on individuals' responses to hurt. Among other findings, relational satisfaction was positively associated with active verbal responses and negatively correlated both with the degree of experienced hurt and the perceived impact of the hurtful message on the relationship. Further, hurtful messages from family members tended to elicit greater feelings of hurt than those from other people – regardless of the closeness, similarity, amount of contact, or level of satisfaction reported by participants. By comparison, messages from romantic partners had greater effect on participants' relationships than did those from individuals involved in family or nonfamily/nonromantic relationships.

Vangelisti and Sprague (1998) explored the idea that "Guilt and hurt are two emotions that are often closely linked" (p. 123). The defining characteristics of guilt and hurt vary around the following dimensions: (1) individual versus interpersonal; (2) temporary versus enduring; (3) intentional versus unintentional; (4) prosocial versus antisocial; and (5) rational versus irrational. Guilt and hurt are elicited by making others feel guilty and using words that hurt. The results and findings from these 1998 studies were followed up by Vangelisti and Young (2000, p. 393), who attempted to answer the following question: "Why is it that some hurtful messages have a greater impact on relationships then others?"

Past theorists suggested that the way people interpret another individual's negative behavior can influence how close or distant they feel from that person as well as the emotions they experience. In a first study, Vangelisti and Young examined how judgments of intent affect individuals' tendency to distance themselves from someone who hurt them and how such judgments impact people's experience of hurt. Results indicated that the people who judged something an individual said to them as intentionally hurtful felt the comment had more of a distancing effect on their relationship with the individual than did those who perceived the message as being unintentionally hurtful. Furthermore, those who viewed the comment as intentionally hurtful tended to be less satisfied with the relationship they had with the person who hurt them and felt less close to the person than did those who saw it as unintentional. Findings also revealed that people's perceptions of messages that they saw as unintentionally hurtful varied in theoretically important ways.

To follow up on the notion that there are qualities of messages viewed as unintentionally hurtful that contribute to relational distancing and hurt feelings, a second study indicated that the perception of messages as part of an ongoing patterns of hurtful communication – as relatively frequent and as part of a general tendency to hurt others – was associated with relational distancing. Also, people's tendency to feel disregarded by the individual who hurt them was linked with relational distancing and hurt feelings.

On an expansion of previous research, Vangelisti, Young, Carpenter-Theune, and Alexander (2005) evaluated previous findings that people's explanations for their hurt feelings can influence how they feel and how they respond to others. Although events and behaviors that elicit hurt have been examined, individuals' beliefs about what made them feel hurt had not been explored. Vangelisti et al. (2005) investigated the causes that people associate with their hurt feelings. First, participants' explanations for why a specific interaction hurt their feelings were examined; then, underlying dimensions characterizing people's explanations for hurt were identified and associations with theoretically relevant outcomes assessed. Results yielded eight factors characterizing perceived causes of hurt feelings. Relational satisfaction and self-esteem were linked to reasons people felt hurt. Individuals' perceptions about the causes of their hurt feelings were also associated with the intensity of their feelings, their responses to being hurt, and their tendency to distance themselves from the person who hurt them.

Theoretical, clinical, and empirical implications of Vangelisti's findings, as well as the findings of the two pioneers to be reviewed next, have been discussed in full by Vangelisti (2007 , 2009b) and Vangelisti and Beck (2007).

MARK R. LEARY

Because covering all the research performed by Leary and his collaborators could fill the rest of this chapter, I must limit myself to presenting a few illustrative examples of his work. What is now considered the first, most important, and most quoted classical study on hurt feelings was published in a mainstream "power" journal. This study bestowed legitimacy to the scientific study of hurt feelings in psychology, Leary, Springer, Negel, Ansell, and Evans (1998) asked 164 participants to recount situations in which their feelings had been hurt (victim account) or in which they had hurt another person's feelings (perpetrator account) and then to complete a questionnaire. Content analysis of the answers given by respondents' ratings of hurt feelings yielded seven categories of feelings that were roughly similar to those developed conceptually rather than empirically by L'Abate (1997): (1) active dissociation (explicit rejection, ostracism, or abandonment); (2) passive dissociation (being ignored, being excluded from others' activities, and other instances of implicit rejection); (3) criticism; (4) betrayal; (5) teasing; (6) feeling unappreciated, used, or taken for granted; and (7) unclassified.

Hurt feelings, therefore, were precipitated by events that connoted relational devaluation, and the victims' distress correlated strongly with feelings of rejection. Victims were typically hurt by people whom they knew well, suggesting that familiarity or closeness played an important role in the creation of hurt feelings. Analyses of the subjective experience revealed that hurt feelings are characterized by *"undifferentiated negative affect"* (italics mine), which is often accompanied by emotions such as anxiety and hostility. Victims' responses to a hurtful event were related to their attributions for perpetrators' actions, and hurtful episodes typically had negative repercussions for the relationships between perpetrators and victims.

Leary's concept of relational devaluation is relevant to Coyne's (1976) interpersonal model of depression that asserts that devaluation and rejection by relationship partners may exacerbate depressive symptoms as well as to the Selfhood Model[11] of RCT (Cusinato & L'Abate, 2012; L'Abate, 2005; L'Abate et al., 2010). Katz, Beach, and Joiner (1998) tested this assertion empirically by investigating theoretically based moderators of this effect: reassurance seeking and self-esteem level in women. Male partners completed a measure of devaluation of the woman. Partner devaluation was not associated with increased emotional distress for women across the entire sample. However, significant moderating effects of both reassurance seeking and self-esteem were found. Partner devaluation predicted increased emotional distress among women who reported high levels of reassurance seeking and low levels of self-esteem.

Snapp and Leary (2001) operated on the assumption that people's feelings are hurt more frequently by those whom they know well rather than by strangers or acquaintances. However, thus far this assumption has been based on retrospective accounts of hurtful events. Snapp and Leary instead examined the moderating effect of familiarity on hurt feelings among people who have recently become acquainted. Participants experienced either a relatively low or high degree of familiarity with a confederate. Afterward, the confederate chose to listen primarily to them or to another participant as they talked about themselves. Results showed that participants were significantly more hurt when they were ignored by a confederate who barely knew them than by a confederate who was more familiar with them. Effects of being ignored showed a similar pattern on a measure of self-esteem.

Buckley, Winkel, and Leary (2004), in two experiments, examined the effects of various levels and sequences of acceptance and rejection on emotion, ratings of self and others, and behavior. In experiment 1, participants who differed in agreeableness received one of five levels of acceptance and rejection feedback, believing that they either would or would not interact with a person who accepted or rejected them. In experiment 2, participants who differed in rejection sensitivity received one of four patterns of feedback over time, reflecting constant acceptance, increasing acceptance, increasing rejection, or constant rejection. In both experiments, rejection elicited greater anger, sadness, and hurt feelings than acceptance, as well as an increased tendency to aggress toward the rejector. In general, more extreme rejection did not lead to stronger reactions than mild rejection, but increasing rejection evoked more negative reactions than constant rejection. Agreeableness and rejection-sensitivity scores predicted participants' responses but did not moderate the effects of interpersonal acceptance and rejection.

Leary's extremely important research has been summarized in one chapter (Leary & Leder, 2009), in which these writers attempted to answer the crucial question about what kind of emotion hurt is, as it has not been included in previous classifications of basic feelings, such as anger, fear, joy, sadness, disgust, and surprise, that are understood as not reducible to more fundamental states. Two studies compared three conceptual models of hurt feelings: (1) an emotion blended by basic feelings; (2) a common negative affect that is shared by all negative emotions; and (3) an emotion that is distinct and unique and that cannot be accounted for by the two previous models, a model that supports L'Abate's work (1977, 1986, 1994, 1997, 1999; 2005), and Leary's et al. (1998) original research. The results of a first study were "consistent with the notion that hurt is a distinct emotional experience, albeit one that also shares features with other negative emotions" (pp. 18), including sadness, shakiness, and sluggishness.

In a second study, "the degree to which hurt feelings included unique and shared contributions of other negative emotions in addition to *hurt* per se" (p. 21) was examined.

A summary of both studies is worth reporting *in toto* because they are relevant to the tripartite model reported in Figure 2.1 and to the *raison d'etre* for this volume:

> Taken together these two studies show that the reliable variance of self-reported hurt feelings is attributable to (a) undifferentiated negative affect that is common to all negative emotions, (b) small contributions of specific discrete emotions, such as sadness and guilt, and, importantly, (c) the unique experience of feeling hurt. It appears that all negative emotions, including hurt feelings, share a common core of negative affect that contributes to the unpleasantness of the experience (p. 21).... *Our data*

suggest that there are reasons to consider hurt as a discrete emotional experience that cannot be reduced entirely to one or more other emotions or to blends of other emotions.... feeling hurt includes a distinct subjective quality that is unique to being hurt. (pp. 22, italics mine)

After this conclusion, Leary and Leder (2009) went on to answer the question of the fundamental cause of hurt feelings, producing relevant research studies that support a relational devaluation hypothesis already formulated in the original Leary et al. (1998) study. Additionally, studies consistently find that hurt is typically accompanied by one or more other emotions, particularly sadness and anger: "We have the sense that the subjective experience of hurt feelings is more diffuse and less phenomenologically distinct than other common emotions, possibly because hurt involves a larger component of core negative affect than other negative emotions" (p. 30).

Leary and Leder's conclusion is further elaborated by Fitness and Walburton (2009), whose research "demonstrates that hurt is intimately intertwined with cognition: with perceptions, appraisals, expectations, and beliefs. It is our hope that over the coming years we will achieve a deeper understanding of this primal, excruciating, yet indispensable emotion. After all, hurt is what makes us human" (p. 47). Leary and Leder's results and conclusion tend to support the validity of the tripartite model of Figure 2.1. Hurt feelings are experienced at a different level than anger, sadness, and fear. Together with joys, they are at the base of most feelings (Figure 1.2). In answer to my question of whether he knew of any research concerning a direct relationship between hurt feelings and fears, he (Mark Leary, personal communication, Oct 23, 2009) wrote:

The way that I think about the link is that rejection episodes are multifaceted, so people may engage in a number of discrete appraisals that influence their emotions. So, when a rejection also involves features that might threaten one's well-being, hurt feelings will be accompanied by fears of various kinds. But if a person does not make any cognitive appraisals involving possible threats, fear will not be involved. So, the logic is the same as with sadness and anger – what other appraisals are present? In most lab studies of hurt feelings, there is no real threat, so we tend not to find anxiety or fear. But I assume that some real-life rejections do include fears (of physical harm, financial loss, disconnections with family members and others, or whatever). I don't know of any research on this, but that's my guess.

From this response, it looks like we shall have to wait for further evidence in the neurosciences to learn more about this possible relationship between fears and hurt feelings and how fear is different from anger and sadness, as already discussed in Chapter 2.

JUDITH A. FEENEY

Whereas most of the research by Vangelisti and Leary was conducted with individuals who were mostly undergraduates under contrived, hypothetical, and experimental conditions, Feeney broke this mold, as Waring did originally, by eventually studying hurt feelings in real couples (Feeney, 2004). Basing her study on previous research by Leary and Vangelisti, she assumed that hurt feelings can have powerful effects on individual and relational outcomes. Feeney examined Leary's et al. (1998) original typology of hurtful events in couple relationships, together with integrative models predicting ongoing effects on victims and their relationships. Participants were 224 students from introductory and third-year psychology classes who completed open-ended and structured questionnaires concerning an event in which a partner had hurt their feelings.

By tailoring Leary's et al. (1998) typology to the context of romantic relationships, five categories of hurtful events were proposed: active dissociation, passive dissociation, criticism, infidelity, and deception. Analyses assessing similarities and differences among those categories confirmed the utility of that typology. Structural equation modeling showed that longer-term effects on the victim were predicted by relationship anxiety and by the victim's immediate reactions to the event (negative emotions and self-perceptions; feelings of rejection and powerlessness). In contrast, ongoing effects on the relationship were predicated by avoidance, the victim's attributions and perceptions of offender remorse, and the victim's own behavior. These results highlight the utility of an integrated approach to hurt, incorporating emotional, cognitive, and behavioral responses, and dimensions of attachment security.

In a follow-up, Feeney (2005) focused on perceptions of the appraisals and emotions involved in hurtful events in couple relationships. In a first study, she tested the broad proposition that hurt feelings are elicited by relational transgressions that generally imply relational devaluation and that evoke a sense of personal injury by threatening positive mental models of self and/or others. Participants (N = 224) provided retrospective accounts of an experience of being hurt by a romantic partner. These accounts, together with expert judges' ratings, showed that the most hurtful events involved relational transgressions that signal both relational devaluation and threat to positive mental models; however, relational devaluation was relatively unimportant in explaining the hurt associated with partners' distrust. A sense of injury emerged as the dominant theme in open-ended accounts of emotional reactions; however, other negative reactions were also featured and were related to the type of event reported. The emotion terms generated in the first study were used as stimuli for a second study in a word-sorting task. The results of this study confirmed that many of the terms were perceived specifically as injury related and shed further light on the link between appraisals and emotions.

Feeney and Hill (2006) addressed the issue of different perceptions between victims and perpetrators relevant to couple relationships by having dating and married couples complete questionnaires and structured diaries. In the questionnaires, victims and perpetrators gave retrospective accounts of the same events. Participants were first asked to think (individually) of hurtful events that had occurred in their relationship during the past year; a research assistant then facilitated a brief couple discussion in which partners jointly selected one male-perpetrated and one female-perpetrated event. Thus, each couple described one event in which the woman was the victim and one in which the man was the victim. Participants gave open-ended accounts of each event, which were scored for such variables as to the extent to which the reporter highlighted or downplayed the severity of the event. Participants also completed rating scales assessing attributions, perceptions of offender remorse, and perceptions of long-term effects on the victim and the relationship, variables similar to those employed in Feeney's (2004) study. In the diary component, participants were asked to report up to five events as a victim and five events as a perpetrator. The gist of this important study is that offenders or perpetrators "are more likely to even fail to report an event as hurtful if the victim's hurt is less severe, or if the issue is not discussed openly. Further, offenders may 'miss' events that occur in an ongoing argument, or do not involve overtly hurtful actions" (p. 329).

In the introduction to her chapter, Feeney (2009) answered the question "Why study hurt in couple relationships?" by stating that "These relationships are fundamental to the structure of society, and play a unique role in meeting individuals' needs for comfort, companionship, support and security.... couple bonds are communal ... and voluntary in nature" (p. 313). In attempting to answer a second question, "What events do couples find hurtful?" Feeney summarized the central feature of hurtful evens in terms of Vangelisti's work involving relational transgressions and threatening the attachment bond (p. 316). Additionally, Feeney answered the same question by reviewing typologies of hurtful events already addressed, including the results of her previous studies about different perceptions that victims and perpetrators have of hurtful events. That is, perhaps victims may tend to exaggerate the hurtfulness of an event whereas perpetrators may tend to downplay it, a conclusion further discussed in Chapter 13 of this volume.

MARK H. THELEN

This chapter would not be complete without including the contribution of Mark H. Thelen, who is responsible for a Fear-of-Intimacy Scale (FIS; Doi & Thelen, 1993). Citing Waring's work, Discountner and Thelen (1991) in two independent studies showed the FIS to be a reliable and valid measure of individuals' anxiety about close dating relationships correlating positively with a loneliness measure and negatively with self-disclosure, social intimacy, and social desirability measures. Participants' FIS scores were significantly related to self-report data (e.g., participants with higher scores reported briefer relationships) and positively related to therapists' ratings about their clients' fear of intimacy. These investigators also found that androgynous participants had less fear of intimacy than masculine and undifferentiated ones.

Doi and Thelen (1993) replicated and extended the first study by administering the FIS to a middle-aged sample, using many of the same measures that Discountner and Thelen (1991) used previously with college students, adding, however, measures of adult attachment as potential correlates of fear of intimacy. Data were obtained from 171 participants (83 men and 88 women, age range thirty-five to fifty-five years), who, in addition to completing a battery of questionnaires already mentioned, were asked to give biographical information. The FIS showed high internal consistency, and evidence supporting its construct validity was replicated with several measures. For instance, significant correlations were found between the FIS and measures of self-disclosure, loneliness, and relationship satisfaction. After controlling for trait anxiety, several significant associations between the FIS and other measures were upheld, and a few unpredicted associations became nonsignificant. Thelen then proceeded to validate and extend the validity of the FIS with an adolescent population (Sherman & Thelen, 1996) and with a lesbian (N = 40) and gay male (N = 57) population (Greenfield & Thelen, 1997).

As with primarily heterosexual populations, fear of intimacy was shown to be negatively related to self-disclosure, comfort with emotional closeness, and relationship satisfaction; the FIS was positively related to loneliness and trait anxiety. In addition, fear of intimacy was significantly related to measures of adult attachment style. Overall, in the studies just reported, the FIS was shown to be a valid, reliable, and useful measure of fear of intimacy with lesbians and gay men. Perhaps, further evaluation of the link between the pursuit of intimacy goals and satisfaction in close same-sex friendships can be obtained from the results of the research by Sanderson, Rahm, and Beigbeder (2005).

What is most relevant to the FIS, which was apparently not mentioned by Thelen, relates to its face-validity; that is, most items in this scale are related to hurt feelings, a topic discussed at greater length by Firestone and Calett (1999) and Vangelisti and Beck (2007). Surprisingly enough, they did not mention Thelen's work, nor did he mention theirs.

CONCLUSION

As with any selection of literature, there may be other competent and competitive contributors who may feel their work was left out of this chapter, although they would inevitably be cited in this volume if they made a significant contribution to hurt feelings. If by not including them in this chapter I hurt their feelings, I apologize profusely.

7

Biological Processes Underlying Hurt Feelings: With Special Attention to Neural Mechanisms

LIN XIAO, DANA SMITH, ANTOINE BECHARA
AND LUCIANO L'ABATE

The purpose of this chapter is to consider briefly the biological foundations of hurt feelings according to the model in Figure1.1 of this volume. This model emphasizes the circularity of how emotionality is based on various physical levels from the bottom up and from the top down, following principles of equipotentiality and equifinality found in reductionism and interactionism (Buck, 1999; Ochsner & Gross, 2007, pp. 88–89). Simply put, what comes up and emerges upwardly as emotionality from felt feelings becomes emotions when appraised and expressed outwardly, verbally, non-verbally, and in writing. Once experienced inside as feelings and expressed outside as emotions, emotions move downward to the bottom, affecting the organism at molecular and higher levels of functioning – cellular, visceral-muscular, and cerebral – as influenced by attitudes, emotions, and relationships (Hafen, Karren, Frandsen, & Smith, 1996; Stockdale, 2009).

An attempt will be made to include as many levels of Figure 1.1 as there is conceptual and empirical evidence to support them. Within that model, however, we need to include emotionality within a larger context of personality functioning at the various levels included in Figure 1.1.

There is no one way to summarize in one single chapter all that is known about the biological bases of hurt feelings (Kolb & Whishaw, 1985). Consequently, only selective evidence that relates to feelings and emotions, and especially hurt feelings, will be summarized.

MOLECULAR LEVEL

This level is included in a recent scholarly review that Canli (2008) considered as constituting "molecular psychology" of personality. He, as well as Hariri and Forbes (2007), argued that the molecular level includes genetic DNA that underlies personality traits, including (1) endophenotypes for extraversion (one possible characteristic of Cluster B PDs) and neuroticism (one possible characteristic for Cluster C PDs); (2) emotional attention and inattentional biases, as shown in neuroticism; and (3) interactions of genotypes and life stresses. Canli focused on extraversion and neuroticism because these tendencies are linked to individual differences in cognitive processes, especially the processing of "valenced stimuli" (p. 313). He suggested that attentional bias is especially linked to neuroticism in response to negative word and face stimuli based on the emotional Stroop task. On this instrument, highly anxious participants, for instance, show an interference effect (slower reaction times) when processing anxiety-related words, as compared to low-anxiety participants (p. 316). Conli also reviewed research with the emotional Stroop task that identified the Anterior Cingulate Cortex as a region that is most sensitive to the emotional meaning of words (p. 317) and, within that region, especially the subgenual area (p. 318).

I cannot give full justice to Conli's or Hariri and Forbes's reviews, because some of their findings are consistent with what has been found in greater detail in the latter part of this chapter dedicated to neural mechanisms. Nonetheless, it is relevant to include what Canli (p. 323) concluded at the end of his chapter: "But in the excitement of using cutting edge molecular biology and neuroimaging techniques to better understand the biological basis of personality, it is critical not to forget the *top-down perspective of psychology.*" (italics mine).

In reviewing behavioral genetic and personality traits, and to support Canli's conclusion, Krueger and Johnson (2008) summarized postulates based on well-established research findings. These findings included (1) personality results from both genetic and environmental influences that derive from: (1) evidence from self-reports of twins, (2) evidence beyond self-reports of twins including (3) adoption studies and (4) the possibility that the genetic structure of personality may closely resemble the phenotypic structure of personality. Personality stability over time is attributable more to genetic than to environmental influences and to measures of environmental influence that may partly be genetically influenced. Much of the genetic effect of these measures is shared with personality, and most environmental influences on personality are nonshared. Unfortunately, the meaning of this finding remains elusive.

From these three postulates Krueger and Johnson (2008) derived three additional propositions: (1) Genetic and environmental influences on personality interact; (2) personality is linked to outcomes through correlational and interactive processes; and (3) finding main effects of specific genes on personality has been difficult.

From these postulates and propositions, Krueger and Johnson (2008) asked two broad questions to frame future research on behavioral genetics: "Do we need to find specific genes and specific environmental effects in order to understand many personality processes?" and "What can we learn from pondering the link between quantitative and molecular genetic research?" This section could not be completed without mentioning the critical importance of nonneuronal glia cells in controlling neurons and influencing many cerebral regions and their functions in complex ways that cannot be expanded here for reasons of space (Fields, 2009).

CELLULAR LEVEL

This level includes the brain *in toto* above and beyond the molecular level (Beer & Lombardo, 2007; Davidson, Fox, & Kalin, 2007; Ledoux & Phelps, 2008). Within the brain, the amygdala serves as an emotional computer that allows the processing of fear as an emotional stimulus through the sensory thalamus and cortex, with the amygdala mediating emotional responses (Quirk, 2007). After considering in detail fear acquisition and regulation, Ledoux and Phelps proffered the hypothesis that: "the mechanism of consciousness is the same for emotional and non-emotional subjective states, and that what distinguishes these states is the brain system that consciousness is aware of at the time" (p. 171). After reviewing evidence to support their hypothesis, these investigators proposed a model of how the brain consciously experiences emotional stimuli, moving from sensory processing to long-term memory, both semantic and episodic converging on working memory, which allows emotional processing that leads to emotional responses both central and peripheral. Clearly, this model is important because it integrates reception of emotional stimuli through the sensory system, connecting them to memory and leading them to their expression as emotions. Sadly, there is not more space to expand on the implications of this model for its relationship to Figure 1.1.

In addition to the brain, feelings and emotions are processed through the peripheral autonomic and somatic nervous system and the central nervous system (Larsen, Berntson, Poehlmann, Ito, & Cacioppo, 2008), which are basic to the vocal (Bachorowski & Owren, 2008) and facial expression of emotion (Matsumoto, Keltner, Schiota, O'Sullivan, & Frank, 2008). These are areas that should be expanded on, but can be only cited in passing, in spite of their importance. Additionally, one cannot deny the importance of the olfactory system in the reception of emotional information (Haviland-Jones & Wilson, 2008).

All of the foregoing research could not have been gathered without the use of neuroimaging technology, which has been responsible for most of the biological breakthroughs in the last generation (Wager, Barrett, Bliss-Moreau, Lindquist, Duncan, Kober, Joseph, Davidson, & Mize, 2009). It is on the basis of this technique that those researchers found "selectivity for pleasant experience in midline brainstem, hypothalamic, and ventromedial frontal regions, and selectivity for negative experience in distinct brainstem (PAG), insular, striatal, and orbital cortical regions" (p. 261).

Any receptor that responds to bodily stimuli related to feelings and especially hurt feelings is fundamental to their embodiment in interoceptive awareness, more specifically: "[N]eural substrates responsible for subjective awareness of y(our) emotional state are based on the neural representation of y(our) physiological state.... anterior insula and the anterior cingulate cortices are conjointly activated during all human emotions." (Craig, 2008, p. 272). This researcher proceeded to present an important anatomical model of subjective awareness of feelings, agency, and time based on the relationship between awareness and the anterior insula, including Von Economo neurons. Craig contributed to the functional anatomy of the ascending interoceptive pathway and functional imaging of temperature sensation as an example of a homeostatic emotion. He concluded that "human emotional awareness [is] lateralized to the anterior insula and ACC on the right fore-brain.... physiological evidence has accumulated indicating that the left and right halves of the human forebrain are differentially associated with particular emotions and affective traits" (p. 284).

This conclusion will be expanded shortly. However, it is relevant at this juncture, to cite Greenfield's (2000) argument about the importance of feelings as a subjective experience versus emotions as observable behavior as originally proposed by LeDoux (1998), because he did not distinguish then between feelings and emotions, at least at that time of publication:

> I am going to try and convince you that at the end of the spectrum of pure emotion – the type of sensation experienced during road rage, a crime of passion, an orgasm, or at a rave – can best be viewed as the core of our mental states when, as when we are infants, feeling is not greatly tempered with individual differences, with cultural or private meaning, or, most important of all, with the self. *Feelings just are*. (Greefield, 2000, p. 21; italics mine)

Hemispheric Dominance

The main reason for including hemispheric dominance here lies in its relationship to gender differences in how emotionality is experienced and expressed (see Chapter 8 of this volume). Emotional asymmetry in the right forebrain mentioned by Craig (2008, pp. 284–285) finds its historical background in an exhaustive but by now possibly outdated review of asymmetrical, left-brain-right-brain differences by Iaccino (1993). He summarized from the extant research available at that time, when imaging was not yet widely available, the different cognitive styles associated with cerebral hemispheric dominance. Supposedly, the left hemisphere is mainly responsible for the following functions: verbal, sequential/temporal, analytic, and rational, as represented by Western thought. The right hemisphere is mainly responsible for the following functions: nonverbal, visuospatial, simultaneous gestalt, synthetic, and intuitive, as represented by Eastern thought. Hence, one could tentatively conclude that the right hemisphere is relatively more responsible for the experience of feelings whereas the left hemisphere is more responsible for logical appraisal and language, that is, naming particular feelings. If one does not have words for hurt feelings, for instance, it would be difficult if not impossible to appraise them and name them accordingly. Even if one does have words for those feelings, one may not be allowed to utter them, as possible in abusive and neglectful intimate relationships (De Giacomo et al., 2010).

Developmentally, the right hemisphere is the first to grow within the first year of life, followed by the growing relative influence of the left hemisphere. This sequence is in line with my contention that the infant is first born in a world of space defined by a dimension of approach-avoidance, which is followed by the world of time defined by a dimension of discharge-delay, as discussed in Chapter 13 of this volume (L'Abate, 2005; L'Abate et al., 2010).

The simplistic dichotomy of specific hemisphere functions was also considered by Iaccino, who concluded, "Results from many of these measures [with normal participants] tend to indicate that [in] the traditional verbal-nonverbal distinction between hemispheres.... the right hemisphere plays a very important role in the perception of speech-related stimuli" (p. 136). On the other hand, Iaccino did review research that supported the role of gender differences in hemisphere lateralization, especially verbal bilateralization (p. 154). In spite of its outdatedness, I would still recommend Iaccino's now classical contribution as a beginning point for the study of brain asymmetries, as updated by Festa and Lazar (2009) and Mendoza and Foundas (2008).

Additionally, Hopkins, Russell, Cantalupo, Freeman, and Schapiro (2005) found that primates, like humans, tend to be right-handed 70 percent of the time, unless they feel threatened or are angry. Even more to the point, Papadatou-Pastou and Martin (2008) in their analysis of 144 handedness and brain laterality studies accounting for almost two million participants, found that men are about 2 percent more likely to be left-handed than women, 12 percent versus 10 percent respectively. However, in highly masculine countries like Japan and Mexico, these investigators found an even higher correlation between men and left-handedness. These cultural differences, however, are trumped by the possibility that left-handed and ambidextrous individuals may have a larger corpus callosums than right-handed people, which may explain gender differences in brain development. Controversially, testosterone may accelerate right hemisphere growth, which encourages left-handedness. Eventually, if left-handedness were to be linked to shorter longevity, this may be one possible link to different mortality rates in men than in women, as discussed in Chapter 8 of this volume.

VISCERAL-MUSCULAR LEVELS

This level includes temperament because it involves an individual's emotionality as shown by speed and strength of response, which include both visceral and muscular organismic components. This characteristic is evaluated by how fast (discharge) or how slow (delay) an individual responds to neutral or emotional stimuli. Clark and Watson (2008), for instance, considered temperament within the context of the Big Three, Big Four, and Big Five Factors within a hierarchical framework. In this structure, extraversion and neuroticism are supraordinate factors, with extraversion comprised by more specific facets, such as assertiveness, gregariousness, cheerfulness, and energy. At a lower level, there are factors of negative emotionality and disinhibition. The latter factor breaks into disagreeable and unconscious disinhibition. Clark and Watson focused on the Five Factors model consisting of traits such as neuroticism, extraversion, conscientiousness, agreeableness, and openness to experience.

This model has directed their thinking, and many researchers have linked these factors to their neurobiological substrates and particularly affective experiences *"because temperament has long been considered to have an emotional basis"* (p. 267; italics mine). Within this framework, Clark and Watson included social behavior, daily rhythms and sleep, substance abuse, and spirituality, work and achievement. Additionally, these investigators reviewed various levels of stability in those traits and the relationship of temperament to psychopathology.

It is unfortunate that no more space can be devoted to a more detailed and thorough review of the biological foundations of feelings and emotions, except to note that up to the present writing, the discrimination of hurt feelings has not and will not occur specifically as long as abstract concepts of social pain or negative affectivity are not defined operationally. Perhaps the next section will make up for whatever deficits were present in the previous pages.

NEURAL MECHANISMS OF REGULATION ABOUT HURT FEELINGS AND "NEGATIVE EMOTIONS"

Correspondence about this section should be sent to: Lin Xiao, Ph.D., Department of Psychology, Brain and Creativity Institute, University of Southern California, Los Angeles, CA 90089–2520, USA. E-mail: linxiao@usc. edu. Studies described in this Section on Neural Mechanisms for Hurt Feelings and Emotion Regulation were supported by NIDA grant R01 DA023051.

Emotions and feelings play a crucial role in adaption, decision making, and social interaction in our daily life (Ekman, 1993; Tooby & Cosmides, 1990). Although people dedicate much time and effort to do things that make them feel happy and loved, their feelings are often hurt by a wide variety of interpersonal events, such as social exclusion, social loss, public deprecation, and stinging criticism. Because other affective states such as distress, upset, and anguish often go along with hurt feelings, some researchers also use the term *social pain* to refer to such specific emotion reactions (MacDonald & Leary, 2005). Studies show that social pain and physical pain both activate the threat-defense system and share common physiological changes designed to prepare an organism for urgent action, such as increased heart rate, increased blood clotting factors, and analgesia (Panksepp, 1998a, 1998b; Gray & McNaughton, 2000). Indeed, we often speak about the experience of feeling hurt in terms of "broken hearts." Many studies also show that the ability to self-regulate these negative emotions enhances psychological, social, and physical health outcomes, and loss of such capacity confers risk toward psychopathology and emotional disorders, such as anxiety states, cycles of depression, and mania (Abelson, Liberzon, Young, & Khan, 2005; Gross 2002, 2007).

In recent years, there has been a growing interest in, and a genuine effort to understand, the neural underpinnings of emotions and feelings. This section will review both lesion and functional imaging studies, and will outline current knowledge about the neuroanatomical systems underlying emotion and feelings as well as the essential role these neural systems play in negative emotions and hurt feelings.

DEFINITIONS OF EMOTIONS AND FEELINGS

Some authors argue that emotions and feelings should not be used interchangeably (see L'Abate, 1997, 2005, and Chapters 1 and 2 of this volume). They can be differentiated conceptually and neuroanatomically. According to Damasio (1994, 1999, 2003), there is an important distinction between emotions and feelings. The specific object or event that predictably causes an emotion is designated as an "emotionally-competent stimulus." The responses toward the body proper enacted in a body state involve physiological modifications. These modifications range from changes in internal milieu and viscera, which may not be perceptible to an external observer (e.g., endocrine release, heart rate, smooth muscle contraction) to changes in the musculo-skeletal system that may be obvious to an external observer (e.g., posture, facial expression, specific behaviors such as freezing, flight or fight, and so on). The ensembles of these enacted responses in the body proper and in the brain constitute an emotion.

Responses aimed at the brain lead to (1) the central nervous system release of certain neurotransmitters (e.g., dopamine, serotonin, acetylcholine, noradrenaline), (2) an active modification of the state of somatosensory maps such as those of the insular cortex, and (3) a modification of the transmission of signals from body to somatosensory regions. The ensemble of signals as mapped in somatosensory regions of the brain itself provide the essential indigents for what is ultimately perceived as a feeling, a phenomenon perceptible to the individual in whom they are enacted. Thus emotions are what an outside observer can see, or at least can measure. Feelings are what the individual senses or subjectively experiences.

THE NEUROANATOMY OF EMOTIONS AND FEELINGS

After the initial debate of the James-Lang versus Cannon-Bard theories of emotion, the neuroanatomist James Papez demonstrated that emotion is not a function of any specific brain center. Rather, emotion is a function of neural circuitry that involves several brain structures interconnected through several neural pathways. The subsequent work of Paul McLean provided further elaboration on the original Papez circuit by adding the prefrontal cortex, parahippocampal gyrus, amygdala, and several other subcortical and brainstem structures. The culmination of all this work resulted in what has become known as the "limbic system."

Damasio's description of the neural systems that subserve emotions and feelings (Damasio, 1999, 2003) is consistent and overlaps considerably with the neuroanatomy of the limbic system as described originally. The functional anatomy of this system includes the following: An emotion begins with appraisal of an emotionally competent object. An emotionally competent object is basically the object of one's emotion. Emotion may be induced in two different ways: (1) an impulsive or automatic way, which we have referred to as *primary induction*; and (2) a reflective or thoughtful way, which we have referred to as *secondary induction* (Bechara, Damasio, & Damasio, 2003). *Primary inducers* are stimuli or entities that are innate or learned to be pleasurable or aversive; once they are present in the immediate environment, they automatically, quickly, and obligatorily elicit an emotional response. Death of a loved one in the immediate environment is an example of a primary inducer. After a somatic state has been triggered by a primary inducer and experienced at least once, a pattern for this somatic state is formed. The subsequent presentation of a stimulus will evoke memories about a specific primary inducer. The entities generated by the recall of a personal or hypothetical emotional event, that is, "thoughts" and "memories" of the death of a loved one are called *secondary inducers*. Secondary inducers are brought to working memory slowly and gradually begin to elicit an emotional response, and they are presumed to reactivate the pattern of somatic states belonging to a specific primary inducer. For example, recalling or imagining the experience of death of a loved one reactivates the pattern of somatic states belonging to the actual previous encounter of death of a loved one.

Therefore, emotional objects can be present in the immediate environment or recalled from memory. In neural terms, images related to the emotional object are represented in one or more of the brain's sensory processing systems. Regardless of the duration of this representation, signals related to the presence of that object are made available to a number of emotion-triggering sites elsewhere in the brain. Some of these emotion-triggering sites are the amygdala and the ventromedial/orbitofrontal prefrontal cortex (VMPC/OFC). Evidence suggests that there may be some difference in the way the amygdala and the orbitofrontal cortex process emotional information. The amygdala is engaged more in the triggering of emotions when an emotional object is present in the environment, that is, the amygdala is a critical substrate in the neural system necessary for triggering somatic states from primary inducers. By contrast, the VMPC/OFC is more important when the emotional object is recalled from memory, that is, the VMPC/OFC is a critical substrate in the neural system necessary for triggering somatic states from secondary inducers, although it can be involved in the emotions triggered by some primary inducers as well. However, the general function of the two structures is the same, that is, to trigger emotional responses from emotionally competent stimuli.

To create an emotional state, the activity in triggering sites must be propagated to execution sites by means of neural connections. The emotion execution sites are visceral motor structures that include the hypothalamus, the basal forebrain, and some nuclei in the brainstem tegmentum. Feelings, on the other hand, result from neural patterns that represent changes in the body's response to an emotional object. Signals from body states are relayed back to the brain, and the representation of these body states are formed at the level of visceral sensory nuclei in the brainstem. Representations of these body signals also form at the level of the insular cortex and lateral somatosensory cortices (SII and SI areas). Most likely the presentation of body signals at the level of brainstem does not give rise to conscious feelings, as we know them, but the reception of these signals at the level of the cortex does so. The anterior insular cortex, especially on the right side, plays a special role in mapping visceral states and in bringing interoceptive signals to conscious perception (Craig 2002; Damasio, 1999). Anterior cingulate cortex is also involved in translating the visceral states into subjective feeling and self-awareness (Craig, 2002).

Recent studies also indicate that social pain or hurt feelings share some common neural systems mentioned earlier for processing and regulating emotions and feelings (MacDonald & Jensen-Campbell, 2011). We will review these studies in the next section.

NEURAL SUBSTRATES OF PROCESSING NEGATIVE EMOTIONS AND HURT FEELINGS

A range of brain activities are observed in the processing and regulation of negative emotions and hurt feelings, which include the amygdala, basal ganglia, insular cortex, anterior cingulate cortex, and prefrontal cortex, all regions that constitute the main emotional brain circuits.

Amygdala

Evidence suggests that the amygdala is a critical substrate in the neural system necessary for the triggering of emotional states from primary inducers.

It couples the features of primary inducers, which can be processed subliminally via the thalamus, or explicitly via early sensory and high-order association cortices, with the representations (conscious and nonconscious) of the emotional state (i.e., the feeling) associated with the inducers. This emotional state is evoked via effector structures such as hypothalamus and autonomic brainstem nuclei, which produce changes in the internal milieu and visceral structures, along with other effector structures such as ventral striatum, periaqueductal gray (PAG), and other brainstem nuclei, which produce changes in facial expression and specific approach or withdrawal behaviors.

Several lines of studies support this notion. Monkeys with mesial temporal lesions that include the amygdala have an increased tendency to approach "emotionally competent" stimuli – snakes, for example – suggesting that objects of fear can no longer evoke a state of fear (Aggleton, 1992; Kluver & Bucy 1939; Zola-Morgan, Squire, Alvarez-Royo, & Clower, 1991). In humans, studies have shown that patients with bilateral amygdala lesions have reduced, but have not completely blocked, autonomic reactivity to aversive loud sounds (Bechara, Damasio, Damasio, & Lee, 1999). Amygdala lesions in humans have also been shown to reduce autonomic reactivity to a variety of stressful stimuli (Lee, Arena, Meador, Smith, et al., 1988; Lee, Bechara, Adolphs, Arena, et al., 1998).

The amygdala is involved in a wide variety of aversive emotional processes. Clinical observations of patients with amygdala damage (especially when the damage is bilateral) reveal that these patients express one form of emotional lopsidedness: Negative emotions such as anger and fear are less frequent and less intense in comparison to positive emotions (Damasio, 1999). Many laboratory experiments have also established problems in these patients with processing emotional information, especially in relation to fear (Adolphs, Tranel, Damasio, & Damasio, 1995; Adolphs, Tranel, & Damasio, 1998; Labar, Ledoux, Spencer, & Phelps, 1995; Phelps, Labar, Anderson, O'Conner, et al., 1998). Functional magnetic imaging (fMRI) studies have also shown that the amygdala has consistently been implicated in responding to threatening stimuli and in general fear processing (Bishop, Duncan, & Lawrence, 2004; Dolan, Morris, & de Gelder, 2001; Morris, Frith, Perrett, Rowland, et al., 1996).

Studies also suggest that the amygdala is implicated in detecting social danger (Amaral, 2002; Panksepp, 1998a). fMRI studies show that facial fear and anger have consistently been associated with amygdala activity (Glascher, Tuscher, Weiller, & Buchel, 2004; Morris, Friston, Buchel, Frith, et al., 1998; Phan, Wager, Taylor, & Liberzon, 2002), even when facial expressions are processed without conscious awareness. Oxytocin, a neurotransmitter implicated in promoting attachment and bonding, potently reduces activation of the amygdala and reduces coupling of the amygdala to brainstem regions' reactivity to interpersonal threats in humans (Domes, Heinrichs, Glascher, Buchel, et al., 2007; Kirsch, Esslinger, Chen, Mier, et al., 2005). Juvenile primates with bilateral amygdala lesions, unlike control and hippocampus-lesioned infants, did not preferentially seek proximity to their mother, nor did they produce distress vocalizations (Bauman, Lavenex, Mason, Capitanio, et al., 2004). One recent fMRI study examined the neural correlates of three cardinal symptoms of acute grief (grief occurring within three months of a loss), and suggested that the amygdala mediates affective and attentional reactivity to reminders of a decreased attachment, including attentional bias and sadness (Freed, Yanagihara, Hirsch, & Mann, 2009).

The Insular Cortex

The insula has been divided into various subregions based on both anatomical connectivity and cytoarchitectonic features (Chikama, McFarland, Amaral, & Haber, 1997; Mufson & Mesulam, 1982; Mesulam & Mufson 1982a, 1982b; Stefanacci & Amaral, 2000). The more posterior, granular regions of the insula, which receive inputs from the thalamus in addition to parietal, occipital, and temporal association cortices, have been ascribed a role in somatosensory, vestibular, and motor integration. The more anterior, agranular regions, which have reciprocal connections to "limbic" regions, such as the anterior cingulate cortex, the ventromedial prefrontal cortex, the amygdala, and the ventral striatum, have been ascribed a role in the integration of autonomic and visceral information into emotional and motivational functions.

The emergence of affective and social neuroscience has accumulated evidence implicating the insular cortex, particularly its most anterior portion. It has been suggested that the anterior insula plays a key role in translating the raw physiological signals that are the hallmark of a somatic state into what one subjectively experiences as a feeling of desire, anticipation, or urge (Bechara & Damasio, 2005; Damasio, 1994). There are several lines of studies supporting this notion. Studies show that enhanced anterior insular activity is observed during high physiological arousal and during declarative awareness of changes in bodily states (Critchley, 2005). Both the activity and structure of the right anterior insula are related to the ability to detect one's heartbeat (Critchley, Wiens, Rotshrein, Ohman, et al., 2004). Evidence also shows that the insula is implicated in food craving (Pelchat, Johnson, Chan,

Valdez, et al., 2004). Recent evidence also shows that strokes that damage the insula tend to literally wipe out the urge to smoke in individuals previously addicted to cigarette smoking (Naqvi, Rudrauf, Damasio, & Bechara, 2007). Similarly, other studies report changes in activity in the insular and somatosensory cortices in association with "high" or euphoric experience of acute doses of drugs (Verdejo-Garcia & Bechara, 2009).

The insular activity reflects the subjective intensity of both one's own and others' emotional experiences, for example, when one experiences visceral pain and negative affective experience such as distress and disgust (Aziz, Schnitzler, & Enck, 2000; Cechetto & Saper 1987; Lane, Reiman, Ahern, Schwartz, et al., 1997; Phillips, Young, Senior, Brammer, et al., 1997; Phan, Wager, Taylor, & Liberzon, 2002; Wicker, Keysers, Plailly, Royet, et al., 2003) or when one empathizes with others who are in these emotional states (Singer, Seymour, O'Doherty, Kaube, et al., 2004; Jabbi, Swart, & Keysers, 2007; Saarela, Hlushchuk, Williams, Schurmann, et al., 2007). One recent fMRI study has shown that greater insular activity was related to greater self-reported distress in the experience of social rejection (Masten, Eisenberger, Borofsky, Pfiefer, et al., 2009).

The Orbitofrontal/Anterior Cingulate Cortex

The orbitofrontal region of the prefrontal cortex includes the rectus gyrus and orbital gyrus, which constitute the inferior surface of the frontal lobes lying immediately above the orbitofrontal cortex, but they extend into neighboring cortex and involve differently sized sectors of the ventromedial prefrontal (VM) region. The VM region includes the medial and varying sectors of the lateral orbitofrontal cortex and the anterior cingulate cortex (ACC), thus encompassing Brodmann's areas (BA) 25, lower 24, 32, and medial aspect of 11, 12, and 10, and the white matter subjacent to all of these areas. The VMPC is thus a relatively large and heterogeneous area.

The VMPC encompasses different regions that have also been identified in functional imaging studies. The VMPC includes the medial prefrontal area identified as being deactivated by a broad range of cognitive tasks that require focused attention, reflecting a high level of resting activity that is suspended during goal-directed behavior (Raichle, MacLeod, Snyder, Powers, et al., 2001). Other investigators have argued that the VMPC encompasses the medial orbitofrontal area, in which activity is consistently related to the "reward value" of hedonically positive stimuli (Kringelbach & Rolls 2004). In addition, the VMPC includes the subgenual cingulate cortex, an area that has been implicated through functional imaging studies in the pathogenesis of mood disorders (Drevets, Price, Simpson, Todd, et al., 1997). It remains to be seen whether these seemingly distinct functions reflect the operation of a single brain area that can be called the VMPC, or instead are due to separate mental processes mediated by three functionally distinct areas encompassed by the VMPC.

The evidence suggests that the VM region is a critical substrate in the neural system necessary for triggering emotional states from secondary inducers. It serves as a convergence-divergence zone, in which neuron ensembles can couple (1) a certain category of event based on memory records in high-order association cortices to (2) the effector structures that execute the emotional response, and to (3) the neural patterns related to the nonconscious (e.g., in the PBN) or conscious (e.g., in the insular/SII, SI, posterior cingulated cortices) feeling of the emotional state. In other words, the VMPC couples knowledge of secondary inducer events to emotional state patterns related to "what is feels like" to be in a given situation. Indeed, several studies have reported increased right ventral prefrontal cortex (RVPFC) activity when thinking about, labeling, or evaluating affective stimuli, particularly when thinking about negative stimuli (Cunningham, Johnson, Gatenby, Gore, et al., 2003; Lieberman, Jarcho, Berman, Naliboff, et al., 2004).

Nauta (1971) and then Neafsey (1990) proposed that the ventral prefrontal cortex represents a distinct visceromotor output region. Price and colleagues (Ongur & Price 2000) later refined this concept, synthesizing the previous anatomic literature on the prefrontal cortex with their own anatomical studies in macaques. In their conception, the ventral prefrontal cortex (a region they term "the orbitomedial prefrontal cortex") is composed of functionally distinct orbital and medial networks. The orbital network is essentially a sensory input area that receives afferents from late sensory cortices for vision, audition, olfaction, taste, and visceral sensation, and has reciprocal connections with the dorsolateral prefrontal cortex. The medial network is essentially a visceromotor output area that sends projections to subcortical structures that are involved in emotional and motivational processes, such as the amygdala and the nucleus accumbens, as well as regions of the brainstem and hypothalamus that directly govern the state of the viscera. In between the orbital and medial networks lies a transitional zone that is interconnected with both the orbital and medial networks that may function to transfer information between those networks. According to this scheme, the VMPC, as we define it, corresponds largely to the medial and intermediate networks, areas that are largely concerned with translating highly processed sensory inputs into visceromotor output.

Much of the early evidence for the role of the VMPC in the control of visceral functions came from studies examining the cardiorespiratory effects of stimulation in this area in cats and macaques, but further support for the role of the VMPC in visceral motor functions also comes from lesion studies. Early studies in humans (Luria, Pribram et al. 1964) examined the effects of relatively large lesions of the frontal lobes on visceral functions. Our own laboratory has performed studies examining the effects of lesions in an array of cortical areas on visceral responses (Tranel and Damasio, 1994). These studies demonstrated that a number of cortical regions, including the VMPC and the right inferior parietal cortex, are necessary for the generation of visceral responses to sensory stimuli. These studies also showed that the role of the VMPC in governing visceral responses is specific to stimuli with emotional or social content.

Other examples also come from the research on neural substrates of social and physical pain. Evidence shows that social pain, especially the separation from or the loss of close others, seems to share the same neural pathways that are associated with physical pain (Eisenberger, 2006; MacDonald & Jensen-Campbell, 2011; Macdonald & Leary, 2005). Evidence shows that the VMPC that encompasses the ACC plays a key role in the physical-social pain overlap. In an fMRI study investigating the neural correlates of social exclusion, participants played a virtual ball-tossing game; they were initially included playing with two others but later excluded from the game (Eisenberger, Lieberman, & Williams, 2003). The RVPFC, dorsal ACC, the insula, and the periaqueductal gray matter in the brainstem were found to be active in response to such social exclusion (Eisenberger, Lieberman et al. 2003). Moreover, the magnitude of dorsal ACC activity correlated strongly with self-reports of social distress felt during the exclusion episode, and right RVPFC activity was negatively correlated with participants' self-reported distress (Eisenberger, Lieberman, & Williams, 2003). Similarly, acute grief after the loss of an unborn child was closely related to the activation of the physical pain network encompassing the cingulate gyrus, the inferior frontal gyrus, the thalamus, and the brainstem (Kersting, Ohrmann, Pedersen, Kroker, et al., 2009).

In another fMRI study in adolescents, these authors found the neural circuitry associated with feelings of distress when being excluded by peers is similar to that which has been found among adults experiencing social exclusion (Masten, Eisenberger, Borofsky, Pfiefer, et al., 2009). Although dorsal ACC has been found to be related to the distress experienced during social exclusion, subgenual ACC was found to correlate with higher reports of distress following social exclusion in adolescents (Masten,

Eisenberger, Borofsky, Pfiefer, et al., 2009). One study demonstrates that the dorsal ACC is sensitive to expectancy violations independent of social rejection, whereas ventral ACC responds specifically to social feedback (Somerville, Heatherton, & Kelley, 2006). Therefore, it is possible that adolescents are more sensitive to social feedback during peer rejection, whereas adults respond more to violations of the expectation of social inclusion. Interestingly, in one recent fMRI study, when participants received emotionally supportive text messages during the social exclusion in the virtual ball-tossing game, these individuals exhibited greater attenuation of social pain and lower ventral ACC activity (Onoda, Okamoto, Nakashima, Nittono, et al., 2009).

NEURAL MECHANISMS OF EMOTIONAL CONTROL

There are many instances of emotional disturbances that follow lesions to neural structures thought to be critical for the expression of emotions and the subjective experience of feelings, as outlined earlier. Some patients have difficulties inhibiting or controlling the expression of the emotions under certain circumstances. One example is rage reactions, violence, and aggression. It is proposed that poor ability to control emotions, such as anger and aggression, is the results of an imbalance between two neural subsystems underlying emotions and feelings: (1) an *impulsive* amygdala-dependent system for triggering emotional responses from primary inducers, and (2) a *reflective*, prefrontal cortex dependent system for triggering emotional responses from secondary inducers. Evolutionarily, aggression and violence may serve an adaptive role for survival: These behaviors ensure the capture of prey, intimidate others, protect food resources, and so on. In animals, this mechanism is basic and crucial for survival, and the amygdala seems critical for facilitating aggressive behaviors. Humans also retain these basic mechanisms of aggression, which can be easily triggered via amygdala mechanisms. However, through socialization, humans learn to inhibit and control these tendencies to become angry and aggressive. When neural systems critical for expression and/or control of these mechanisms become impaired, then disturbances in the ability to regulate and control emotions emerge.

More specifically, exposure to primary inducers triggers emotional responses via the amygdala system that are fast, automatic, and obligatory, that is, very quickly, without much thought and effort. These amygdala-mediated responses are short lived and habituate very quickly. On the other hand, secondary inducers trigger somatic states via the VMPC/OFC from perceived or recalled mental images, when the amygdala is engaged in emotional situations requiring a rapid response; that is, as "low-order" emotional reactions arise from relatively automatic processes, the VMPC/OFC is engaged in emotional situations driven by thoughts and reflection. Once this initial amygdala emotional response is over, "high-order" emotional reactions begin to arise from relatively more controlled, higher-order processes involved in thinking, reasoning, and consciousness. Unlike the amygdala response, which is sudden and habituates quickly, the VMPC/OFC response is deliberate, slow, and lasts for a long time.

Thus the prefrontal cortex, especially the VMPC/OFC, helps to predict the emotion of the future, thereby forecasting the consequences of one's own actions. Initially, the reflective system is poorly developed, and our behavior is perhaps dictated by our impulsive system – that is, children tend to behave in a manner where they do what they feel like doing whenever the urge strikes, without much thought about the future. However, through learning and socialization, they learn to constrain many emotions, desires, and behaviors that conflict with social rules and lead to negative consequences. This is the first sign of the development of willpower and an example of how the reflective system gains control over the impulsive system. Thus difficulties in controlling one's emotions arise (1) when the reflective system is damaged, in which case the impulsive system loses its restraint. Indeed, this is what happens when areas of the VMPC/OFC are damaged, as described in the case of Phineas Gage, who became impatient of restraint or advice when it conflicted with his desires; (2) the loss of emotional control also arises when the impulsive (amygdala) system becomes abnormally strong.

This disturbance or poor ability to control emotions as a result of imbalanced activity within impulsive and reflective neural systems is not restricted to anger and aggression, but seems to apply to other situations, such as the ability to control social distress or social pain. We will review these studies in the next section.

NEURAL SUBSTRATES IN THE REGULATION OF NEGATIVE
EMOTIONS AND HURT FEELINGS

To cope with negative emotions and hurt feelings, individuals employ a wide variety of emotion-regulatory strategies, including affect labeling, appraisal, suppression, and distraction. Recent fMRI research has begun to offer insight into how both common and distinct neural systems support various forms of emotion-regulatory strategies.

Putting feelings into words (affect labeling) has long been thought to be one of the best strategies to manage negative emotional experiences and to benefit mental and physical health (Pennebaker, 1997; Hemenover, 2003). Recent neuroimaging studies have investigated the neural substrates by which putting feelings into words may help to regulate negative emotions. These studies indicate that affect labeling of a negative emotional image results in less amygdala activity and greater activity in the RVPFC, which suggests that putting feelings into words may activate RVPFC and dampen the response of the amygdala (Hariri, Bookheimer, & Mazziotta, 2000; Cunningham, Johnson, Gatenby, Gore, et al., 2003; Nomura, Iidaka, Kakehi, Tsukiura, et al. 2003). One recent fMRI study has suggested a possible neurocognitive pathway for this process (Lieberman, Eisenberger, Crockett, Tom, et al. 2007). The results of this study indicate that affect labeling, compared to other ways of encoding, produced diminished response to negative emotional images in the amygdala and other limbic regions. Moreover, affect labeling was associated with increased activity in the RVPFC, and the magnitude of RVPFC activity was inversely correlated with the magnitude of amygdala activity during affect labeling. This inverse relationship between the amygdala and RVPFC was mediated by changes in medial PFC activity. These findings suggest that affect labeling may diminish negative emotional activity via a pathway from RVPFC to medial PFC to the amygdala.

Another efficient strategy for emotion regulation is reappraisal of highly negative scenes, which involves reinterpreting the meaning of affective stimuli in ways that alter their emotional impact (Beck, Rush, Shaw, & Emery, 1979). In laboratory studies, reappraisal has been shown to be successful in decreasing negative emotional responses, as measured by self-reports of negative affect and peripheral physiological measures of arousal (Gross, 1998; Ohira, Nomura, Ichikawa, Isowa, et al., 2006). In one recent fMRI study, the authors examined both up- and down-regulation of emotional responses using reappraisal strategies by simultaneously recording self-report, peripheral physiological (startle eye-blink and skin conductance response, SCR), and brain activation data (Eippert, Veit, Weiskopf, Erb, et al., 2007). They found that up-regulation was also associated with amplified SCR, indicating an increased level of arousal, and startle potentiation in successful regulators, indicating an increased negative affective state. Amygdala activity was increased and decreased in the up-regulation and down-regulation trails, respectively. Trial-by-trial rating of regulation success correlated positively with activity in the amygdala during up-regulation and the OFC during down-regulation. Other fMRI studies consistently demonstrate that reappraisal leads to greater decreases in negative affect and to greater decreases in the amygdala activity, and such decrease concurs with increased activation in the prefrontal cortex such as the ACC, the dorsolateral PFC, and the OFC (Beauregard, Levesque, & Bourgouin, 2001; Ochsner, Bunge, Gross, & Gabrieli, 2002; Ochsner, Ray, Cooper, Robertson, et al., 2004). Children showed similar patterns of neural activity during emotion reappraisal, although a greater number of prefrontal loci of activation were involved compared with adults (Levesque, Joanette, Mensour, Beaudoin, et al., 2004).

Different prefrontal cortex activity during appraisal might be due to different strategies subjects used in the experiment. Evidence shows different appraisal strategies might recruit particular prefrontal systems that modulate the amygdala activity: Self-focused reappraisal, which modified the personal relevance for a given image, recruited medial PFC, whereas situation-focused reappraisal, which reinterpreted the action and outcomes for a given image, recruited lateral PFC (Ochsner, Ray, Cooper, Robertson, et al., 2004). One other study shows that the strength of amygdala coupling with the OFC and dorsal medial PFC predicts the extent of alleviation of negative affect following reappraisal (Banks, Eddy, Angstadt, Nathan, et al., 2007). The strength between amygdala and the PFC might also reflect the individual differences in reappraisal use. Indeed, the participants with higher reported use of reappraisal in everyday life were more likely to engage in spontaneous reappraisal and also showed greater decrease in amygdala activity and increase in PFC activity during the processing of negative emotional facial expressions (Drabant, McRae, Manucj, Hariri, et al., 2009).

Other strategies shown to be effective for reducing negative emotions include suppression and distraction. Compared to appraisal, which modulates emotional response tendencies early on before they give rise to full-fledged responses, suppression modulates the emotional responses later on once these responses have arisen. Suppression produced decreased expressive behavior (e.g., facial expressions, verbal utterances, gestures). Compared to reappraisal, which resulted in early (0–4.5s) PFC response and subsequent late (10.5–15s) reduction in amygdala and insula responses, suppression produced late (10.5–15s) PFC responses but sustained elevated responses in the amygdala and insula (Goldin, Mcrae, Ramel, & Gross, 2008). The increased amygdala and insula responses are consistent with increased sympathetic activation to the cardiovascular system while watching emotionally evocative films reported in previous studies (Gross & Levenson, 1997). The significant increased activity in the PFC at late component may reflect increasing efforts to counter neural input from the amygdala and insula conveying ongoing emotional salience of the negative film (Goldin, McRae, Ramel, & Gross, 2008). During emotional regulation, in addition to altering the way we interpret the meaning of a stimulus (reappraisal), we can also alter the way we attend to a stimulus (distraction). Relative to reappraisal, distraction led to greater decreases in amygdala activation and to greater increases in activation in PFC and parietal regions (McRae, Hughes, Chopra, Gabrieli, et al., 2009). Taken together, these studies suggest that although various emotion-regulation strategies all engage the areas of the reflective PFC-system and the impulsive amygdala system, the exact neural mechanisms leading to greater decreases in negative affect may depend on the regulatory goal and strategy employed.

In concluding this section on neural mechanisms, we are mindful that social pain including negative emotions and hurt feelings are normal occurrences in response to social exclusion, rejection, or loss in all individuals. The capacity to successfully down-regulate social pain has implications for well-being in daily life. On the other hand, dysfunction of processing and regulating social pain can be found in many psychiatric conditions (e.g., anxiety, depression, and posttraumatic stress disorder), which are associated with hyperactivity in the impulsive amygdala system (Herpertz, Dietrich, Wenning, Krings, et al., 2001; Rauch, Whalen, et al., 2000; Sheline, Barch, et al., 2001) in combination with lack of inhibition in the reflective PFC-system (Anand, Li, Wang, Wu, et al., 2005; Ray, Ochsner, Cooper, Robertson, et al., 2005; Rauch, Whalen, Shin, McInerney, et al., 2000; Yamasue, Iwanami, Hirayasu, Yamada, et al., 2004). Therefore, underlying the neural mechanisms of processing and regulating negative emotions and hurt feelings holds promise for successful intervention or treatment of mood and anxiety disorders.

CONCLUSION

This chapter has illustrated how the original distinction made in previous chapters of this volume – experiencing feelings versus expressing emotions – finds biological evidence in the location of hurt feelings in the dorsal anterior cingular cortex. It has further demonstrated how feelings and emotionality interact with environmental effects. Although this interaction between feelings and environmental effects could not be reviewed in greater detail in this chapter, previous and following chapters in this volume are dedicated to these proximal and distal influences.

8

Gender and Individual Differences in Hurt Feelings

"In the last decade, thanks to unexpected but incredibly progressive advances in technology in psychology, psychiatry, and neurology, a great deal of information has been gathered around gender differences"
(L'Abate, 2011c, p. 167).

This chapter will consider gender differences first and individual differences second in how genders deal with emotionality in general and with the presumed presence of hurt feelings in particular. The specific condition considered in this chapter within the context of emotionality is *presumed* hurt feelings because this construct might not be specifically addressed in the studies reviewed here (Brody & Hall, 2008; Burleson, 1997).

This chapter pays attention also to the wider cultural context of gender differences within the somewhat idealistic but relevant arguments made by Eisler (2009). She proposed going beyond the simplistic and overused dichotomy between capitalist versus socialist economies by presenting new dimensions between *power-oriented* and *partnership-oriented* economies. In the former, men dominate women at the expense of women and children, whereas in the latter, men and women are considered as coequals for the benefit of children, as in Scandinavian countries. The United States, for example, among others, represents a dominator-capitalist economy in which men hierarchically assume positions of power over subordinate women. China and Russia represent dominator-socialistic economies in which men are still at the top of the hierarchy at the expense of women and children.

Gender differences are fairly prominent in prosocial behavior, which consists of behaviors that are beneficial to others, including helping, sharing, comforting, guiding, rescuing, and defending others (Eagly, 2009, p. 644; Maccoby, & Jacklin, 1974). Although women and men may be similar in

engaging in extensive prosocial behavior, they are different in their empha-
ses on particular classes of these behaviors. Women engage in prosocial
behaviors that are more communal and relational, whereas men engage
in behaviors that are more agentic, collectively oriented, and power and
strength intensive. These gender differences match widely shared gender-
role beliefs. The origins of these beliefs lie in the division of labor, which
reflects a biosocial interaction between male and female physical attributes
and the social structure. The effects of gender roles on behavior are mediated by hormonal processes, social expectations, handedness, and individual
dispositions (Cohan, Booth, & Granger, 2003; Ehrhardt, 1985; Papadatou-
Pastou, Martin, Munafò, & Jones, 2008). For instance, women may be more
sensitive to painful stimuli and events than men are. Female hormones,
weaker pain inhibition in women than in men, the ways in which hurtful
events are experienced, as well as social factors may explain some, but not
all, gender differences (Campbell, France, Robinson, Logan, et al., 2008;
Diatchenko, Nackley, Tchivileva, Shabalina, et al., 2007; Nielsen, Staud, &
Price, 2009).

How about gender differences in the criminal justice system? There are
approximately 200,000 women in U.S. prisons and jails and 950,000 on
parole, whereas there are roughly two million men in U.S. prisons and jails,
with the latter increasing by 45 percent in the last ten years and with women's
percentage increasing by 81 percent. Approximately 74 percent of women
have been diagnosed with mental health problems compared with 59 percent
of men. In state prisons, 75 percent of women meet criteria for substance
abuse problems, and 68 percent had past physical and sexual abuse; most
are poor, undereducated, unskilled, single mothers whose paths to crime are
usually marked by abuse, poverty, and addiction (Clark, 2009).

However, why is it that women often report more problems in their
romantic relationships than do men? One explanation in the literature
is that women may have different standards they consider important for
relationships than their male counterparts, and as a consequence, women
may be less likely to have their standards met. A second explanation is that
although women and men may differ in the importance they attribute to
various standards, the experiences they have in their romantic relationships may lead women to believe their standards are not fulfilled as often
as men's.

Vangelisti and Daly (1997) offered preliminary tests of the two rival
explanations and found greater support for the latter. Analyses of two composite measures and more detailed factor-based measures generally indicated that the standards held by women and men involved in heterosexual

romantic relationships were rated similar in importance. Women, however, tended to note that their standards were less fully met than did men. Further, compared to men, women reported a greater discrepancy between the importance they associated with various standards and the extent to which the standards were fulfilled in the context of their relationship. Even though not dealing with emotionality, the ability of the two different theoretical models evaluated by Vangelisti and Daly (1997), to predict and explain these findings, are relevant to the more specific issue of gender differences in emotionality.

Participating in interviews may have the potential to change beliefs about dating relationships. Changes in beliefs could vary as a function of how much participants think and talk about their relationships. Surra, Curran, and Williams (2009) evaluated the validity of those conclusions by interviewing 464 participants randomly selected from households in a large southwestern U.S. city. The governing hypotheses were that participants should have positive effects on beliefs when thinking or talking is high and negative effects when thinking and talking is low. As predicted, talking moderates the association between participations, and conflict and thinking moderates the effects of participation on satisfaction and friendship-based love. Results, however, differed for men and women. Under conditions of low talk and high thinking, participation has negative effect:

> One explanation is that women who think a lot about their relationships to begin with may begin to ruminate in unproductive ways about them as the result of participation.... Women ruminate more than men do, passively focusing on symptoms, causes, and consequences of their distress.... obsessive thought, which may be more characteristic of some women, may be deleterious. (p. 18)

Male and female speech has been observed to differ in their form, topic, content, and use (Hass, 1979). Early writers were largely introspective in their analyses; more recent work has begun to provide empirical evidence. Men may be more loquacious and directive; they use more nonstandard forms, talk more about sports, money, and business, and more frequently refer to time, space quantity, destructive action, perceptual attributes, physical movements, and objects. Women, are often more supportive, polite, and expressive, talk more about home and family, and use more words implying feeling, evaluation, interpretation, and psychological state. A comprehensive theory of "gender-select" must include information about linguistic features under a multiplicity of conditions (Hass, 1979). Whether these gender differences will hold up in the last thirty years since publication of that review remains to be seen.

One important factor about gender difference refers to how cross- and same-gender friendships define and express intimacy (Monsour, 1992). Participants assigned an average of two meanings to the term "intimacy," although the number of meanings ranged from one to five. There were substantial similarities in the meanings of intimacy in both types of friendship, as well as some gender differences. For instance, five of the seven most frequently mentioned definitions of intimacy were specified by both cross- and same-gender friends: self-disclosure, emotional expressiveness, unconditional support, physical contact, and trust. One of the remaining two meanings of intimacy, that is, sexual contact, was mentioned by cross- but not by same-gender friends. Sharing activities was given as a definition of intimacy by 9 percent of men in same-gender friendships and 4 percent by the women in cross-gender friendships. Within cross-gender friendships, emotional expressiveness and sexual contact were specified as meanings of intimacy by a higher percentage of men than women, whereas physical contact was specified by a greater percentage of women in those relationships.

GENDER DIFFERENCES IN CHILDREN AND YOUTH

Developmentally, there are relatively few studies concerning affect-regulation in children (Clark, 1994). Franko, Powers, Zuroff, and Moskowitz (1985), for instance, interviewed thirty-two children aged six to eleven concerning their responses to distressing situations. Results indicated that these children possessed expectancies for coping with both sadness and anger. Coping strategies were predominantly behavioral, verbalized, and self-oriented: The most common was to engage in a distracting activity. Strategies employed with parents differed from those used with peers, and girls reported higher proportions of sadness-inducing events than did boys, who described relatively more events that elicited anger than did girls. Hence, these results tend to support the view that anger may be more likely present in men and sadness more likely to be present in women.

Stereotypically, many studies have demonstrated that boys are more aggressive than girls and that emotion-regulation difficulties are associated with problematic behaviors (Conway, 2005; Feder, Levant, & Dean, 2007). However, Conway argued that recent findings indicate that gender differences in aggressive behaviors disappear when assessments are broadened to include relational aggression – behaviors designed to harm the relationship goals of others by spreading rumors, gossiping, and eliciting peer rejection of others. Moreover, although difficulties regulating emotions have been reported for physically aggressive children, little research has examined these processes in relationally aggressive children. Investigation into the association between emotion regulation and relational aggression is a critical direction for future research on the etiology and prevention of mental health problems, especially in girls.

Although not related specifically to feelings and emotions, the study by Clark (1994) further developed the theory of gender differences by asking fourth, sixth, eighth, and tenth graders to indicate whether the person they most wanted to talk with was male or female in eight hypothetical situations involving different communicative objectives. As expected, younger children preferred a same-gender partner, but by eighth grade more cross-gender preferences emerged, particularly when wanting to pass time or feel included. Boys were generally preferred for telling jokes and stories. By eighth grade, female partners were preferred when the participant wanted to be cheered up or needed advice in persuading or explicating a complicated idea.

Gender cleavage, the segregation of the sexes, is a powerful phenomenon affecting socialization during childhood, but its developmental trajectory is far from clear, according to Smith, Davidson, and Ball (2001). They used sociometric responses by 299 boys and girls in grades three to six from a group preference record to investigate age-related variations and gender differences in cleavage. Moreno's (1953) developmental model of gender cleavage was examined in the light of sociocultural changes as well as advances in the theory and measurement of gender cleavage. Gender differences were found in same-gender preference, with older elementary school girls showing greater same-gender preference than boys of the same age. However, this finding plus the absence of gender differences in cross-gender evaluations, did not support more recent developmental accounts of gender cleavage. Linear trend analyses contradicted Moreno's (1953) basic concept of increasing same-gender preference between grades three and six. Whereas same-gender acceptance and rejection were relatively similar regardless of grade level, cross-gender acceptance was higher in lower grades and the reverse was true for rejection. Furthermore, weaker gender cleavage effects in rejection data than in acceptance data suggested that strong same-sex liking does not infer equally robust cross-gender dislike. Gender cleavage appears to be relative rather than absolute. A more complex model could incorporate gender differences as well as rejection evaluation.

Hussong (2000) examined gender differences in the structural and mean levels of two adolescent friendship qualities (intimacy and peer control). Structural gender differences were identified when the indicators of friendship quality differed for boys and girls. Mean gender differences were noted when boys and girls differed in the frequency of expressing the friendship quality. Characteristics of same-sex sex friendships were surveyed in 230 male and 221 female high school students. Structural gender differences were supported such that (1) companionship was more strongly indicated than by intimacy in boys than in girls, and (2) overt behavioral control was more strongly indicated by peer control in girls than in boys. Mean gender differences replicated previous findings: Girls reported more frequent intimate behaviors than did boys, whereas boys reported more frequent peer control than did girls. These findings suggest that structural and mean gender differences can be independent of one another. The presence of such differences has implications for developing appropriate measures of a variety of psychological constructs for both genders. However, there is little doubt that developmental exposure to marital conflict over time and gender are important factors in determining why some children appraise their parents' disputes negatively (Richmond & Stocker, 2006).

GENDER DIFFERENCES IN YOUNG ADULTS

Rather than embed gender characteristics within emotionality and presumed hurt feelings, it might be helpful, for a change, to introduce and provide an overall, positive context concerning gender and personality differences in conceptions of love. Fehr and Broughton (2001), for instance, presented three studies that tested predictions derived from interpersonal theory regarding the relations among gender, personality, and conceptions of love. These investigators predicted that women would conceptualize love in terms of its nurturant varieties, namely, companionate kinds of love, whereas men would conceptualize love in terms of non-nurturant varieties, namely, passionate kinds of love. Only the latter prediction received consistent support. Both women and men held a companionate conception of love, with the exception that women assigned higher ratings to friendship and sisterly love than men.

Regarding personality, it was predicted that high nurturance traits (e.g., warm, agreeable) would be associated with a companionate conception of love whereas low-nurturance traits (e.g., cold-hearted) would be associated with a passionate conception of love. The results supported these predictions. Consequently, it appears that women's and men's conceptions of love may be more similar than has been assumed. Two robust interpersonal dimensions of dominance and nurturance hold considerable promise for integrating the literature on personality and gender differences in perceptions of love. Both dimensions of love and dominance are found, perhaps using synonymous terms, such as communal and agentic among others, in two-factor models reviewed in L'Abate (2009b) and in L'Abate et al. (2010). Men tend to emphasize physical attractiveness more than women for dating, sexual intercourse, and serious relationships, whereas humor seems to interact with attractiveness, particularly more in men than in women (Lundy, Tan, & Cunningham, 1998).

More specifically, Hodgson and Fischer (1979) examined gender differences in processes of identity and intimacy development among college youth in fifty men and fifty women; they administered measures of identity, intimacy status, and self-esteem. Men were found to focus on intrapersonal aspects of identity and intimacy status as well as self-esteem. Women were found to focus on interpersonal aspects. The pursuit of various identity development pathways affected self-esteem differentially for both genders. More women than men were found to be intimate, and the achievement of intimacy seemed more closely related to identity in men than in women. These early findings are generally supported by the evidence reported in this chapter and elsewhere in this volume. However, all these studies deal with (1) hypothetical and imaginary situations and (2) undergraduates who are not as yet facing losses and hurt feelings that increase as a function of age. Therefore, the presence of hurt feelings would be more "real" in actual couples and families.

This "reality" was evaluated by Gaines, Rugg, Zemore, Armm, et al. (1999). They examined patterns of interpersonal resource exchange (drawing from resource exchange theory of Foa and Foa, 1974), along with the influences of gender-related personality traits (i.e., agency and communion) on participants' interpersonal resources (i.e., affection and respect) among seventy-nine brother-sister pairs (mean age = 19.94, standard deviation = 8.38 years). Consistent with prediction for a normative sample, brothers' and sisters' (as self-reported) exchanges of both affection and respect were positive and significant. Also consistent with predictions, communication was a positive and significant predictor of respectful behavior among sisters. However, contrary to the original hypotheses, communion did not achieve or even approach significance as a predictor of respectful behavior among brothers, nor did communion achieve or approach significance as a predictor of affectionate behavior among sisters and brothers.

Schmookler and Bursik (2007) examined gender and gender role differentiation in the valuing of monogamy using a sample of emerging adults currently in heterosexual dating relationships. Monogamy attitudes were measured on four dimensions: (1) valuing emotional monogamy; (2) valuing sexual monogamy; (3) perceptions of monogamy as relationship enhancing; and (4) perceptions of monogamy as a sacrifice. Gender differences emerged, with women valuing both emotional and sexual monogamy more strongly than men. Whereas both men and women viewed monogamy as relationship enhancing, men were more likely to view monogamy as a sacrifice. Individuals with gender roles defined by communal traits valued monogamy more highly. Each of the monogamy dimensions was significantly correlated with reported relationship satisfaction. These findings could be interpreted from evolutionary and social constructionist perspectives.

GENDER DIFFERENCES IN ADULTS

A discussion of gender differences in *presumed* hurt feelings would not be complete without inclusion of the classical study by Schmitt et al. (2003) about the dismissing style of adult romantic attachment as part of a survey study of 17,804 people from sixty-two cultural regions. Contrary to research findings previously reported in Western cultures, these investigators found that men were not significantly more dismissing than women across all cultural regions. Gender differences in dismissing romantic attachment were evident in most cultures, but were typically only small to moderate in magnitude. Looking across cultures, the degree of gender differentiation in dismissing romantic attachment was predictably associated with sociocultural indicators. Generally, these associations supported evolutionary theories of romantic attachment, with smaller gender differences evident in cultures with high-stress and high-fertility reproductive environments. Social-role theories of human sexuality received less support: More progressive sex-role ideologies and national gender equality indexes were not cross-culturally linked as expected to smaller gender differences in dismissing romantic attachment.

Reis and Franks (1994) found that compared to men, women reported being more anxious and depressed, less hostile, and in poorer subjective health, including greater dietary fat, relatively greater body mass, and more visits to a medical center (the largest r^2 for gender was .017). These differences, however raise questions about issues of *awareness*: Are women more aware of these and other factors than men because of their monthly confrontation with their periods? Given such an awareness, are women more willing to disclose factors that men would not be willing to admit and disclose because of their possibly narrower awareness than women?

Self-Disclosure

A meta-analysis of 205 studies involving 23,702 participants was conducted by Dindia and Allen (1992) to determine whether there are gender differences in self-disclosure. Across these studies, women disclosed slightly more than men ($d = .18$). This effect size was not homogeneous across studies. Several moderator variables were found. Gender of target and interaction effects of the relationship to target and measure of self-disclosure moderated the effect of gender on self-disclosure. Gender differences in self-disclosure were significantly greater to female and same-gender partners than to opposite-gender or male partners. When the target was a relationship with the discloser (i.e., friend, parent, or spouse), women disclosed more than men regardless of whether self-disclosure was measured by self-report or observation. When the target was a stranger, men reported that they disclosed similarly to women. However, studies using observational measures of self-disclosure found that women disclosed more than men.

Preengagement Cohabitation and Marital Commitment

Rhoades, Stanley, and Markman (2006) longitudinally examined 197 couples' dedication (interpersonal commitment) levels on the basis of their premarital cohabitation history. Findings suggested that men who cohabited with their spouse before engagement were less dedicated than men who cohabited only after engagement or not at all before marriage. Furthermore, these husbands were less dedicated to their wives than their wives were to them. Such asymmetries were apparent before marriage and through the early years of marriage. Relationship adjustment and religiousness were related to dedication but did not account for these findings. These findings suggest that couples considering cohabitation before engagement could benefit from discussions about commitment and expectations before marriage.

Division of Labor and Work Setting

Before considering gender differences in emotionality, however, we may need to consider how caregiving as an action rather than a feeling is influenced by how people combine attention to gender and to emotional and instrumental availability. Here we need to consider both the number and type of tasks allocated among various family members (Lawrence, Goodnow, Woods, and Karantzas, 2002), as required by Hass's early review (1979). Gender can represent evident biological differences and less evident cultural influences, but what happens when the genders are subjected to perceived workplace support? Bansal, Monnier, Hobfoil, and Stone (2000) explored the influence of anger and depressive mood on the receipt of perceived workplace social support and perceived workplace resources among 121 postal workers over a period of three months. These investigators theorized that "emotional distress" would result in perceptions of decreased social support and workplace resources for women but not for men. This hypothesis was partially supported. Interaction effects revealed that whereas women perceived losing support and resources when experiencing depression and anger respectively, these emotions had only negative consequences for men. These findings suggest that emotions are more closely linked to perceptions of social support and workplace resources for women than for men.

Femininity and Masculinity

In her sections on gender and emotion work, gendered division of labor, and parenting, mothering, and fathering, Bielby (1999) commented:

> The social constructs of masculinity and femininity are integral to every aspect of the social organization of biological sex, and the symbolic display of gender in domestic settings is one of the most deep-seated of cultural expectations (p. 393).... [T]he emotion work that is done in family contexts has a unique relationship to responsibility and obligation. (p. 394)

The traditional division of labor in partners has important implications on how partners are going to assume changed roles and identities in the parenting arena in accordance with different feelings and expectations that have changed over the last two generations (Vescio, Schlenker, & Lenes, 2010).

Anastasi (1985) originally considered sex-role orientations within the framework of the overlap between affective-cognitive processes and their interactions with then fashionable constructs of masculinity and femininity intersecting with dimensions of self-assertiveness and expressiveness. Although now probably outdated, her conclusion is worth quoting;

> Most men and women exhibit a fair number of gender-congruent characteristics, but the particular assortment varies from one man or woman to the next. This conclusion suggests, in turn, that extant theories of

sex-role development are vastly oversimplified. Most of these theories imply that at each developmental period, gender-related qualities, attitudes, and behaviors emerge and are sustained as a total package, as it were, attributable to a common, monolithic set of processes. (p. 77)

These concerns were expanded by the contributions by Taylor-Spence (1985, p. 100), who considered briefly the fear of femininity in women, and in Eccles's chapter (1985, p. 126) concerning fear of success in women.

Sanfilippo (1993) examined the relations of masculinity, femininity, and gender with various depressive experiences in a sample of normal men and women. Results indicated that greater masculinity generally was associated with lower levels of different depressive experiences in men and women. Greater femininity was related to advantageous outcomes for various depressive experiences in a relatively weaker and gender-specific fashion, but was also associated with greater anaclitic depression in men and women. The variable of gender alone was either weakly related or unrelated altogether to various depressive experiences, suggesting that culturally defined gender-role characteristics may be more important than gender with respect to different aspects of depressive experiences in normal young adults.

Arguing that higher testosterone levels are related to assertiveness and dominance, given the relevance of those behavioral correlates to spouses' daily transactions, Cohan, Booth, and Granger (2003) explored the links between testosterone levels and marital interaction among ninety-two newlywed couples. Marital problem-solving and social support transactions were assessed, and saliva was collected and assayed for testosterone. Whether marital behavior was related to husbands' and wives' testosterone levels was examined. The link between spouses' testosterone and their behavior was contingent on the partner's testosterone levels. Husbands exhibited more adaptive problem-solving behaviors and social support provision when husbands versus wives were concordant for lower testosterone levels. In contrast, wives exhibited more adaptive social support provision when spouses had discordant testosterone levels such that wives had higher levels and husbands had lower levels. These findings illustrate also the descending equifinality effects of behavior and relationship of physiological functions, as illustrated by Figure 1.1.

Femininity may predict positive relationship outcomes over and above attachment styles and significant-other concept measures. Significant-other concepts mediated this relationship. Consequently, femininity (regardless of gender) in both men and women contributes to positive, clear, and significant-other concepts that directly influence relationship quality

(Steiner-Pappalardo & Gurung, 2002). However, women low in stereotyped masculinity and in relationships of shorter duration may be particularly likely to show increased depressive symptoms during weeks when they experience poorer relationship functioning than usual (Whitton, Stanley, Markman, & Baucom, 2008).

Hurt Feelings and Dominance/Submission

The traditional stereotype of male dominance and female passivity, especially in the area of sexuality, might be slowly giving way to increased equality in these roles (Kiefer & Sanchez, 2007), including achievement (Eccles, 1985). For both genders, apparently sexual passivity predicts poor sexual functioning and satisfaction. In one study, Kiefer and Sanchez (2007) found that endorsement of traditional sexual roles of male dominance and female passivity related to greater sexual passivity among college-aged heterosexual women but less passivity for college-aged heterosexual men. For both young men and women, greater sexual passivity predicted less overall sexual satisfaction. These results were replicated in a second study among sexually experienced adults recruited via the Internet. Autonomy mediated these relationships, which persisted when controlling for multiple potential confounds.

According to Snyder, Kirkpatrick, and Barrett (2008), previous research has led to a widely accepted conclusion that heterosexual women prefer mates who are high on *dominance*. These researchers designed three experiments to distinguish dominance from prestige and examined contextual factors that might challenge such a conclusion. College women at two U.S. universities evaluated hypothetical potential mates described in written vignettes. Participants in study 1 preferred a high-prestige to a high-dominance mate. With dominance and prestige manipulated independently in study 2, participants preferred high to low prestige but also preferred low to high dominance. Participants in study 3 preferred high to low dominance, but only when displayed in the context of an athletic competition, and in ratings of attractiveness and desirability as a short- versus long-term mate.

Hurt Feelings, Rejection, and Depression

The relationship between rejection and depression was evaluated by Thompson and Berenbaum (2009) in the context of college students' relationships with their parents. Female undergraduates (N = 183) provided self-reports of how rejected they felt by their parents, and parents provided self-reports of how rejecting they were of their daughters. In father-daughter dyads, it was found that fathers' reports of rejection moderated the relation of women's reports of rejection and depression. In mother-daughter dyads, these researchers found that daughters' reports of rejection, but not mothers' reports of rejection, was associated with depression. These findings suggest that relationship factors may be critical for understanding depression, and that the role of rejection in depression can only be understood by taking into account the nature of the relationship (Fivush, & Buckner, 2000).

Hurt Feelings and Violence

Milardo (1998) examined the acceptability of two forms of common couple violence according to a continuum of severity, according to violence being enacted equally by both genders, that is, gender symmetry. This form needs to be differentiated from what Milardo called "patriarchal terrorism," which often includes frequent and systematic violence enacted by men in the control and domination of women. Contrary to expectations of gender symmetry, 83 percent of undergraduate women indicated that they would be at least somewhat likely to hit their partner in any one situation compared to 53 percent of the men. Men were also more likely to report expecting to be hit (70 percent) than women (50 percent). These results were replicated in a second study with one exception: that women, in most instances, expected to be beaten. Motivations for hitting seemed to differ for men and women, but in both genders, anger or confusion, seemed to be the underlying feelings.

Although decreased relationship satisfaction may increase use of violence for both men and women, the increased quality of alternative relationships may also increase use of violence in men (Gaertner & Foshed, 1999). These findings could be consistent with the idea that whereas relationship duration simply makes partners more accessible to one another, commitment may promote cooperative strategies for conflict resolution that may vary with gender. Furthermore, mate-retention behaviors may be designed to solve several adaptive problems, such as deterring a partner's infidelity and preventing defection from the mating relationship. Even though many mate-retention behaviors may appear to be innocuous romantic gestures (e.g., displaying resources, giving flowers), some of these behaviors may be harbingers of violence (Shackelford, Goetz, Buss, Euler, & Hoier, 2005). Across two studies, as predicted, these investigators found that men's use of a particular mate-retention behaviors were related positively to woman-directed violence. In a third study, Shackelford et al., results corroborated those of the first two studies, with particular male mate-retention behaviors predicting violence against romantic partners.

Taft, O'Farrell, Torres, Panunzio, Monson, Murphy, and Murphy (2006) examined the correlates of psychological aggression (i.e., verbal abuse), victimization, and perpetration among a community sample of 145 heterosexual couples. For both women and men, psychological aggression victimization (PAV) was associated with greater psychological distress, anxiety, and physical health symptoms beyond the effects of physical aggression. PAV was also uniquely associated with higher levels of depression for women. Trait anger and poor relationship adjustment were the strongest correlates of psychological aggression perpetration (PAP) across genders. Childhood father-to-child and father-to-mother aggressions were associated with PAP for men only, suggesting possible distinct etiologies across genders. These results highlight the importance of further developments of models for psychological aggression for both women and men.

In addition to mate-retention behaviors, however, one must also go back to how violent men themselves explain, or better, excuse their violence with their partners (Wood, 2004): (1) *justifications*: "She disrespected me as a man," "A man has the right to control his woman," or "She provokes me"; (2) *dissociations*: "I am not an abusive type," "My violence was limited," or "Abusers do not limit their abuse"; and (3) *remorse*: "I regret that I abused her." Wood's conclusion about these explanations merit quoting: "Also, the themes that emerged from participants were informed by conflicting, although not wholly independent, codes of manhood that circulate in U.S. cultural life" (p.555).

Although other gender-difference factors, beyond violence, include gun availability, violence-mediated media influence, family and caretaker factors, and effects of teasing and bullying. Feder, Levant, and Dean (2007) highlighted new thinking on the potential relationship between boys' traditional masculine socialization experiences and violence. In this new perspective, traditional masculine socialization estranges and isolates many boys from their genuine inner lives and vital connections to others, which is theorized to heighten their risk of engaging in acts of violence. These authors identify school and community programs that may be helpful in counteracting damaging socialization experiences and supporting boys' healthier emotional and psychological development. Approaches that mental health professionals can use to deal with this vital issue will be discussed in Chapters 12 and 13 of this volume.

Self-Reports of Emotions

Eaton and Funder (2001) derived measurements of three basic affective phenomena – valence of emotion, intraindividual variability, and rate of change – from self-reports of emotion gathered from 123 participants (63 women, 55 men) sampled four times daily over eight days. Self-reports and acquaintances' descriptions of personality were also obtained. The three emotion variables were nonsignificantly interconnected and yielded different personality correlates. Valence of emotions positively correlated with extraversion, intraindividual variability with repression, and rate of change with fearfulness and hostility toward others, but not all results were consistent across gender. These investigators suggested that future research pay increased attention to patterns of emotional change over time and to the relations between gender and emotional experience.

Street, Gradus, Stafford, and Kelly (2007) examined gender differences in experiences of sexual harassment during military service and the negative mental health symptoms associated with these experiences. Female (N = 2, 319) and male (N = 1,627) former reservists were surveyed about sexual harassment during their military service and current mental health symptoms. As expected, women reported higher frequency of sexual harassment. Further, women had increased odds of experiencing all subtypes of sexual harassment. Being female conferred the greatest risk for experiencing the most serious forms of harassment. For both men and women, sexual harassment was associated with more negative current mental health. However, at higher levels of harassment, association with some negative mental health symptoms were stronger for men than for women. Although preliminary, these results suggest that although women are harassed more frequently than men, clinicians must increase their awareness of the potential for sexual harassment among men in order to provide the best possible care to all victims of harassment.

Hurt Feelings and Language Comprehension

In an interesting review relevant to gender differences and hurt feelings, Glenberg, Webster, Mouilso, Havas, and Lindeman (2009) argued that language comprehension requires a simulation that uses neural systems involved in perception, action, and emotion. A review of the literature as well as new experimental evidence support five predictions derived from this framework: (1) Being in an emotional state congruent with sentence content facilitates sentence comprehension; (2) because women are more reactive to sad events and men are more reactive to angry events, women understand sentences about sad events with greater facility than men, and men understand sentences about angry events with greater facility than women; (3) because it takes time to shift from one emotion (feeling?) to another, reading a sad sentence slows the reading of a happy sentence more for women than men, whereas reading an angry sentence slows the reading of a happy sentence more for men than for women; (4) because sad states motivate affiliative actions and angry states motivate aggressive action, gender and emotional content of sentences interact with the response mode; and (5) because emotion simulation requires particular action systems, adapting these action systems will affect comprehension of sentences with emotional content congruent with the adapted action system. These conclusions have important implications for the study of feelings in general, hurt feelings in particular, language, emotion, and gender differences.

Gender Differences in Jealousy

Previous research has shown that in men jealousy is evoked more by a rival's status-related characteristics than in women, whereas in women jealousy is evoked more by a rival's physical attractiveness than in men, according to Buunk and Dijkstra (2004), who examined whether the occurrence of this gender difference depends on the type of infidelity one's partner engages in – that is, emotional or sexual infidelity – and whether these types of jealousy evoke different emotional responses. These investigators used hypothetical jealousy situations with a mixed-factor design consisting of 2 (participant gender, male versus female) x 2 (rival physical attractiveness, high versus low) x 2 (type of infidelity, sexual versus emotional). Participants were 151 heterosexual undergraduates (75 women and 76 men). The stimulus materials were previously used and pretested facial photographs administered with questions about their attractiveness. Jealousy evoked by emotional infidelity was found to be primarily characterized by feelings of threat, and jealousy after sexual infidelity was found to be primarily characterized by feelings of betrayal and anger. Following emotional infidelity, in men, a rival's dominance was an important factor, whereas in women, a rival's physical attractiveness evoked feelings of threat but not feelings of anger and betrayal. In contrast, after sexual infidelity, in men but not in women, a rival's physical attractiveness evoked feelings of betrayal and anger but not anxiety or suspicion.

In a further expansion of sexual versus emotional infidelity, Becker, Sagarin, Guadagno, Millevoi, and Nicastle (2004) assessed whether previously reported gender differences in jealousy could be accounted for by other related emotions. Participants (223 undergraduates) were presented with hypothetical scenarios involving both a sexual and emotional infidelity, then they were asked how jealous, angry, hurt, and disgusted they would be. Results replicated gender differences in response to sexual and emotional infidelity, demonstrating that it is robust when continuous measures are used, and confirm that it is unique to jealousy. Gender differences did not emerge for anger, hurt, or disgust. Instead, sexual infidelity elicited greater anger and disgust but less hurt than emotional infidelity for both men and women. These results also suggest that it is the jealous response to an emotional infidelity that best discriminates women from men, and that both women and those participants in a serious, committed relationship reported significantly greater intensity in their emotional reactions, as compared to men and those not in a committed relationship.

Cann and Baucom (2004) examined differences in responses to relationship infidelity when the infidelity involved a former romantic partner as opposed to a new rival. Participants indicated for either sexual or emotional infidelity whether they would be more upset if their partner were involved with a former partner or with a new person, and whether they would be forgiving in either situation. Men and women undergraduates saw the former partner as a greater threat when the infidelity was sexual. However, for emotional infidelity, only women selected the former partner more frequently. Ratings of the degree of distress and likelihood of forgiveness followed a similar pattern. For women, measures of relationship commitment were related to distress and forgiveness. For men, these measures were related to forgiveness only. Gender differences in distress may be related to differences between men and women in beliefs about the importance of commitment.

Sagarin and Guadagno (2004) argued that research on gender differences in jealousy using continuous measures sometimes reveals that women report more intense jealousy than men in response to both sexual and emotional infidelity. These investigators performed two studies to test whether these differences might have stemmed from sex differences in the interpretation of the upper anchor of jealousy scales (e.g., "extremely jealous"). In study 1, women and men undergraduates offered different types of exemplars when describing situations in which they felt jealous. A significantly greater proportion of women than men reported feeling extreme jealousy in the context of romantic relationships. Additional results demonstrated that women and men confuse the term "jealousy" and "envy," although this confusion cannot account for the sex differences in the context of extreme jealousy. Study 2 demonstrated that the sex differences in the intensity of reported jealousy disappeared if the upper anchor of the scale is modified to include specific contextual information (i.e., "as jealous as you could feel in a romantic relationship").

Arguing that most studies examining gender differences in jealousy using continuous measures have produced inconsistent findings, Edlund and Sagarin (2009), to explain these inconsistencies, critically evaluated the criterion used to test sex differences in jealousy. They demonstrated that the Participant Gender x Infidelity type interaction was the only relevant effect. Using a U.S.-based sample of 1,082 (480 men and 601 women), the gender difference was investigated using fourteen continuous-measure response formats. This format revealed a highly significant gender difference ($p < .001$, $g = .300$) despite the gender difference being nonsignificant in nine of fourteen formats. These results highlight the danger of falling prey to the belief in the law of small numbers, as manifested in this debate as the erroneous interpretation of individual nonsignificant results as refuting the theory.

Gender Differences in Loneliness

Earlier studies of loneliness seemed to have obtained confusing results about gender differences, at least until Tornstam's (1992) publication. Tornstam at that time attributed such confusing results to the fact that many earlier studies used very limited and special samples. In his study of 2,795 representative Swedes fifteen to eighty years of age, Tornstam found that there certainly was a gender difference in loneliness, but that this difference was restricted to married individuals between twenty and forty-five years of age. Several possible explanations for this finding were evaluated, among them the assumption that women more willingly tend to accept their loneliness. This explanation was refuted by the fact that the gender difference in loneliness was not general but restricted to a certain group of married participants. Other hypotheses about the perceived causes of the observed gender differences in loneliness were related to assumptions of women having higher expectations for intimacy in a relationship and women having lower self-esteem. Even if gender differences were shown to exist in these respects, they do not explain the observed gender differences in loneliness; neither did differences in the social networks of men and women. These results, however, cannot rule out the remaining explanation: that the gender differences in loneliness may be due not to social-psychological factors, but to a more basic difference in which men and women react to the stresses and strains of a relationship.

Rotenberg and Kmill (1992) administered the UCLA Loneliness Scale to 96 male and 179 female undergraduates to identify individuals who represented prototypically lonely or nonlonely ones. Consistent with a social stigma view of loneliness, participants attributed lower psychosocial functioning to and were less accepting of the lonely than the nonlonely person. These results provided evidence for the prevailing perception of the lonely person as a negative stereotype and the social tendency to reject her or him. Women attributed lower psychosocial functioning to the lonely person than did men. In contrast to other findings, individuals did not attribute lower psychosocial functioning to, nor were less accepting of, the lonely person when identified as a male rather than a female. Lonely individuals seemed less accepting of the nonlonely person than were nonlonely individuals. This latter finding was attributed to the negative effects of upward social comparison and was regarded as a factor that would maintain loneliness.

Loneliness may well be associated with depression, at least in dating relationships (Segrin, Powell, Givertz, & Brackin, 2003). However, the chances of being alone and perhaps lonely increase with increasing age, where the presence of hurt feelings is more likely. Pinquart (2003), for instance, investigated predictors of loneliness in married, widowed, and never-married older adults. Contacts with adult children, siblings, friends, and neighbors showed a stronger negative relationship with loneliness in unmarried than in married adults. However, divorced and widowed adults were more likely to profit from contact with adult children, whereas never-married and childless and unmarried participants profited most from contacts with siblings, friends, and neighbors. A better functional status was associated with less loneliness in divorced, widowed, and never-married adults, but not in married adults. Furthermore, unmarried men showed higher levels of loneliness than unmarried women, whereas only small gender differences in loneliness were found in married participants. Gender differences in the loneliness of divorced and never-married adults were eliminated by controlling for gender differences in contacts with children, siblings, and friends. However, widowers were lonelier than widows even after controlling for gender differences in these contacts.

Above and beyond gender differences in loneliness, this condition should be also studied as a personal characteristic, as it is in the section devoted to this topic. Most studies reported here, with some exceptions, were performed with undergraduates and consisted of hypothetical or contrived questions or situations. Results, therefore, need to be taken with a grain of salt before generalizing them to the real world of actual relationships, as in partners, families, and patients. What happens when gender differences are observed in a naturally occurring barroom? Graham, Tremblay, Wells, Pernanen, et al. (2006), for instance, wanted to use the constructs of harm and intent to quantify the severity of aggression in the real-world setting of bars/clubs. They wanted to describe the range of aggressive behaviors and their relationship to harm and intent, and examine gender differences in the form and severity of aggression. Systematic observations were conducted by trained observers on 1,334 nights in 118 bars/clubs. Observers documented a range of aggressive acts by 1,754 patrons in 1,052 incidents, with many forms of aggression occurring at more than one harm and intent level. Women used different forms of aggression, inflicted less harm, and were more likely to have defensive intent compared to men.

Gender Differences in Partners

Griffin (1993) argued that negative-affect expression during marital interaction is the most consistent and powerful discriminator of marital quality. This expression may be also influenced by gender. He examined how covariates differentially influence, by gender, the "transitioning out" of negative affect during marital interaction. Self-reports of negative affect were gathered in real time from nineteen couples immediately after a positive and a negative interaction. Event history analysis was used to determine covariate influence on the negative-affect hazard rate. Results indicated substantial gender differences. Wives were influenced by marital satisfaction, communication orientation, education, and previous duration of negative affect, whereas husbands were influenced only by education. For husbands, evidence was found suggesting that some covariate effects were moderated by time already spent in the negative state.

Marital discord and depressive symptomatology have repeatedly been found to be associated but little is known about the variables that influence this relationship (Christian, O'Leary, & Vivian, 1994). Data were collected from 139 couples seeking marital therapy, and analyses were conducted separately by gender. For wives, lower problem-solving ability, physical aggression by the partner, and monogamous beliefs predicted depressive symptomatology after the variance due to marital discord was removed in regression analyses. In addition to these predictors, less spouse-specific assertiveness, unemployment, and monogamous belief were associated with depressive symptomatology for women after the variance due to marital discord was removed in partial correlation analyses. For men, lower problem-solving ability added to the prediction of depressive symptomatology.

It is important, however, to distinguish among various relationship involvement levels in mate selection (Buunk, Dijkstra, Fetchenhauer, & Kenrick, 2002), namely, marriage, serious relationship, falling in love, casual sex, and sexual fantasies among individuals of twenty, thirty, forty, fifty, and sixty years of age. Consistent with an evolutionary perspective, men preferred mates who were higher in physical attractiveness than themselves, whereas women preferred mates who were higher in income, education, self-confidence, intelligence, dominance, and social position than themselves. The lower the level of relationship involvement, the lower were the preferred levels of education, physical attractiveness, and, particularly for men, preferred intelligence in comparison to oneself. For sexual fantasies, men and women preferred mates who were higher in physical attractiveness than those they preferred for real partners.

Psychological distress and marital quality were assessed with 128 male and 49 congestive-heart-failure (CHF) patients and their spouses. Hopkins Symptom Check List-25 scores were in the distressed range for 57 percent of patients and 40 percent of spouses (Rohrbaugh, Cranford, Shohan, Nicklas, et al., 2002). This role difference was greater for men than for women and a gender difference (more distress in women than in men) was greater for spouses than for patients. The patient's distress, but not the spouse's, reflected the severity of the patient's illness, and distress for both partners correlated negatively with ratings of marital quality. Female-patient couples reported better relationship quality than male-patient couples, however, and a mediation analysis indicated that the gender difference in spouse distress could be explained by marital quality. These results highlight the contextual nature of CHF distress and suggest the role differences in distress vary by gender. Note also the undefined usage of the term "distress."

Sanford's (2005) original finding that wives are event dependent and husbands are more globally schematic needs additional explication and replication, because it may help explain why women tend toward depression more often than men, even though differences in selfhood propensities go a long way toward explaining such differences (see Chapter 13 of this volume). Matjasko and Feldman (2006) added to this possible differentiation by investigating how intrinsic work motivation, work hours, and taking time for self influenced the interplay between the emotional climates of home and work, given the salience of work in our society. These authors examined day-to-day emotional transmission between work and home (spillover) for 143 families using the experience sampling method and interview data from the Sloan Center's 500 Family Study. Intrinsic work motivation, work hours, and taking time for self were used as predictors of spillover. There was evidence of emotional transmission from work to home for mothers' happiness, anger, and anxiety as well as for father's anxiety. Also, fathers scoring higher on intrinsic work motivation tended to report greater overall anxiety at home after the workday. Anxiety from work was less likely to spill over to the home when fathers reported working longer hours. The authors felt that these finding have practical implications for improving worker productivity and the well-being of two-working-parent families.

Relationship satisfaction and sexual activity seemed governed by hassles and problems experienced within the marital dyad, which are in turn related to stress arising from outside the dyad (Bodenmann, Ledermann, & Bradbury, 2007). According to those authors, associations between external stress and relationship functioning are stronger for daily hassles then for critical life events. Higher levels of daily stress seem to predict less sexual activity for martially dissatisfied women and more sexual activity for martially dissatisfied men. Self-reports of stress may covary with self-reported indexes of satisfaction and sexuality, suggesting that contextual influences may be broadly influential in intimate relationships.

Two main questions about gender differences in conflict-management behaviors were studied by Hojjat (2000): (1) How do men and women perceive their own and their partner's conflict-management behaviors? (2) Is there a relationship between relationship satisfaction and self-partner congruence of perceptions? Consistent with past literature, the findings of this study indicated that women perceived themselves as significantly more negative-active in their conflict behaviors than men, whereas men perceived themselves as significantly more positive-passive in their conflict-management interactions compared with women. Women showed a greater understanding of their partner's conflict-management strategies; their perceptions of men as being more positive-passive, compared with women, were in accord with men's self-perceptions and with independent judges' ratings of men's conflict behaviors. In addition, consistent with women's self-ratings, independent judges evaluated women's conflict behaviors as significantly more negative-active when compared with men. There was also a positive association between understanding of partner's conflict-management strategies and satisfaction.

Attempting to integrate various strands in gender differences in couples, Pasley, Kerpelman, and Guilbert (2001) proposed a model that posits incongruencies between spouses in gender beliefs, expectations, and behaviors that affect marital instability through negative marital interactions, causing identity disruptions and resulting in distancing, marital instability, and, in some cases, divorce. On the other hand, there may be behavior genetic bases about the origins of gender differences in marital quality. Spotts, Prescott, and Kendler (2006), for instance, added to the literature on this topic by looking for genetic and environmental sources for variations in marital quality. Their first aim was to replicate previous findings of genetic and nonshared environmental influences on marital quality. The second aim was to explore the etiology of gender differences in marital quality. The Virginia Adult Twin Study of psychiatric and substance abuse disorder sample of twin men and women was used. Both genetic and environmental factors were again found to influence marital quality. Findings also suggested small differences between men and women in the levels of genetic and environmental influence on variance in marital quality. Men's reports of marital warmth and conflict were influenced by the same genetic factors, but women's reports of marital warmth and conflict were influenced by different genetic factors.

Gender Differences in Social Support

Even though the topic of social support (SS) will be reviewed in greater detail in Chapter 11 of this volume, Pasch, Bradbury, and Davila (1997) argued that most prior research (up to the date of their publication) on SS examined perceptions of support, failing to capture fully the helping behaviors that partners exchange while interacting. These investigators observed sixty newly married couples each engaged in two ten-minute interactions, with one spouse (the helper) responding while the partner (the helpee) discussed a personal characteristic or problem that he or she wanted to change with a reversal of roles afterward. Helper and helpee behaviors were coded and examined in relation to gender and negative affectivity, which have been linked in prior research to perceptions of support. Husbands and wives did not differ in helper behavior, but wives displayed more negative helpee behavior than husbands. Helper and helpee behavior covaried with negative affectivity in expected directions, and helper behavior covaried with the partner's negative affectivity. Finally, analysis of negative reciprocity sequences showed that, as helpers, husbands were more likely to reciprocate negative behavior and to have their negative behavior reciprocated to the extent that they were high on negative affectivity. The investigators emphasized the value of observational data in understanding social support in marriage (rather than in contrived or short-lived relationships), issues that will be reviewed in greater detail in Chapter 11 of this volume. This excellent study, however, shows what happens when a poorly defined term such as "negative affectivity" is used without distinguishing between anger, sadness, or fear.

A study that supports the principle of equifinality introduced in Chapter 1 of this volume (Whisman & Uebelacker, 2010) shows how marital distress may affect physical health through the metabolic syndrome in wives but not in husbands. Nonetheless, the results of this study are relevant to gender differences in emotionality and raise questions about what kind of physiological and cerebral processes occur that produce such differences.

Gender Differences in Families

Stresses in the parenting role, as shown by the foregoing studies, have been found to be related to family functioning. However, most research in this area has been conducted with clinical samples and has not compared parenting stress of mothers and fathers. Deater-Deckard and Scarr (1996) studied 589 married couples with young children (twelve to sixty month old) who completed the Parenting Stress Index Short Form (PSI-SF) and measures of child-rearing behavior and attitudes, social support, and child behavior. The validity of the PSI-SF and the theory behind its development was tested, but results were mixed. Small effect sizes were found for mothers and fathers, and these were moderated by child age and marital happiness. Stress may well be a normal and natural consequence of parenting.

Recent research has established a pattern of impairment and *distress* (a term left undefined) associated with the symptoms of DSM-IV Axis II disorders; for instance, personality disorders that occur more commonly among men are associated with more social and occupational impairment, but with less personal distress than personality disorders occurring more commonly among women. Howell and Watson (2005), for instance, examined whether a similar pattern exists for the DSM-IV Axis I disorders. Lay judges (N = 206) rated the social impairment, occupational impairment, and personal distress associated with the symptoms of six male-typed and six female-typed Axis I disorders. Impairment and distress were associated with male-typed and female-typed Axis I disorders in the same manner as personality disorders. Reasons for the emphasis on social and occupational impairment among male-typed disorders and distress among female-typed disorders can be found in the socialization process that may tend to produce greater externalization processes in men and greater internalization processes in women (Vescio et al., 2010).

Reeb and Conger (2009) used perspective longitudinal data from a community sample of 451 families to assess the unique contribution of parental depressive symptoms to adolescent functioning. Results indicated that paternal depressive symptoms were significantly related to subsequent depressive symptoms in adolescent offspring; this association remained significant after controlling for previous adolescent depressive symptoms, maternal depressive symptoms, gender, and family demographic variables. Adolescent gender and perception of father-adolescent relationship closeness moderated this association such that paternal depressive symptoms were positively associated with adolescent depressive symptoms for girls whose relations with fathers lacked closeness. These findings add to a growing literature on the interpersonal mechanisms through which depression runs in families, highlighting the need for future investigations of paternal mental health, adolescent gender, and intrafamily-relationships quality in relation to adolescent development and personality.

Nelson, O'Brien, Blankson, Calkins, and Keane (2009) examined relations between four sources of family stress (marital dissatisfaction, home chaos, parental depressive symptoms, and job-role dissatisfaction) and the emotion socialization practice of mothers' and fathers' responses to children's negative emotions. Participants included 101 couples and seven-year-old children. Dyadic analyses were conducted using the Actor-Partner Inter-dependence Model, and relations were tested in terms of the spill-over, crossover, and compensatory hypotheses about the relation between home- and work-setting stresses. Results suggested that measures of family stress relate to supportive and non-supportive parental responses, though many of these relations differ by parent gender, supporting parental gender differences originally found by Kerig, Cowan, and Cowan (1993). All three theoretical hypotheses were supported depending, however, on the nature of the family stressor examined. One specific conclusion reached by Nelson et al. is worth quoting:

> These findings suggest that family stress is associated with how parents socialize their children's emotions. The more family stress parents experience, the less supportive and non-supportive are their techniques to teach children about emotions.... The parent gender differences found in this study are consistent with previous research that has suggested that mothers and fathers show emotional support for their children in different ways, with mothers showing their support during times of child distress. (2009, p. 677)

Gender Differences and Health

In order to create a single measure that simultaneously evaluates emotion-, problem-, and relationship-focused coping, Badr (2004) performed an exploratory factor analysis on Coyne and Smith's (1994) Relationship-Focused Coping Scale and Carver's (1997) Brief COPE, using data collected from 182 married couples. In ninety couples, both spouses were healthy; in ninety-two couples, one spouse had a chronic illness. Results yielded an abridged twenty-three-item, six-factor measure. Using the new measure, a series of repeated analyses of variance were conducted to determine whether coping styles vary by gender and health. Results showed husbands and wives differ in their use of active engagement, approach coping, and protective buffering depending on whether they were healthy or ill. Hierarchical linear modeling showed couples who were more congruent in their use of active engagement and more complementary in their use of protective buffering and avoidance coping reported greater marital adjustment. Although husbands and wives may employ different coping strategies, these results highlight the importance of examining the ways in which spouses cope *together* in the face of a shared stressor.

Gender Differences in Personality Disorders

Why should we look at gender differences in personality disorders? Because each type of disorder deals in different ways with hurt feelings. These disorders include Axis II, Cluster A schizotypal, Cluster B externalizing, and Cluster C internalizing disorders already considered in Chapter 2 (Model 2.1). King and Terrance (2006), for instance, argued that personality disorder trait predictors of the quality and duration of close personal relationships have been rarely examined in the personal relationship literature. These investigators examined links between Acquaintance Description Form (ADF-F2) friendship qualities and Millon Clinical Multiaxial Inventory (MCMI-II) personality disorder attributes in 363 college students. Passive-aggressive, avoidant, schizotypal, sadistic-aggressive, antisocial, borderline, and self-defeating features were most closely associated with friendship insecurity. Participants exhibiting passive-aggressive, self-defeating, and borderline features tended to view their closest friendship as being more strongly influenced by external forces. Passive-aggressive scores and personal maintenance difficulty were positively related. Histrionic traits were associated with descriptions of the closest friend as affirming and useful in utilitarian value. Gender differences were minimal in the prediction of relationship qualities using the MCMI-II personality disorder dimensions. Consequently, we need to look at gender differences between the two major types of personality disorders, Cluster B and Cluster C.

Gender Differences in Externalization Disorders

Using data from more than one thousand male and female twins participating in the Minnesota Twin Family study, Hicks, Blonigen, Kramer, Krueger et al. (2007) examined developmental change, gender differences, and genetic and environmental contributions to the symptom levels of four externalizing disorders from ages seventeen to twenty-four: (1) adult antisocial behavior; (2) alcohol dependence; (3) nicotine dependence; and (4) drug dependence. Both men and women increased in symptoms for each externalizing disorder, with men increasing at a greater rate than women, such that a modest gender gap at age seventeen widened to a large one at age twenty-four. Additionally, a mean-level gender difference on a latent externalizing factor could account for the mean-level gender difference for individual disorders. Biometric analyses revealed increasing genetic variation and heritability for men, but a trend toward decreasing genetic variation in increasing environmental effects for women. These results illustrate the importance of gender and developmental context for symptom expression and the utility of structural models to integrate general trends and disorder-specific characteristics.

Traditional conceptualizations of psychopathy highlighted the importance of affective features as they relate to social deviance; however, according to Rogstad and Rogers (2008), little empirical research has actually investigated the specific roles of emotion and emotion processing with respect to antisocial conduct. Antisocial personality disorder (APD) prevalent in forensic populations is commonly associated with psychopathy, despite the notable omission of such core affective features in its diagnosis. These investigators reviewed the empirical literature on the contribution of emotion to psychopathy and APD, highlighting in particular research on emotion processing and various facets of emotional expression, including empathy and alexithymia. Research findings "have almost exclusively focused on male offenders"(Rogstad & Rogers, 2008, p. 1474). Emotion-processing deficits relate to an inability to learn from positive feedback, with empathy being relatively more pronounced in women than in men, and alexithymia being relatively more pronounced in men than in women.

Forouzan and Cooke (2005) found evidence of gender differences in the core characteristics of psychopathic traits (p. 768): (1) differential expressions of psychopathic behavior; (2) differences in interpersonal characteristics; (3) different psychological motivations underpinning indicators of psychopathy; and (4) potential bias in the assessment of psychopathy according to social norms. These two brief paragraphs do not give full attention to Rogstad and Rogers's (2008) review, which deserves greater attention than can be allotted here.

How do these gender differences relate to how hurt feelings are felt and expressed as a function of severe dysfunctionalities and personality disorders? One explanation is given from the Selfhood Model[11] of RCT (Chapter 13 of this volume).

Gender Differences in Internalization Disorders

Substantial evidence indicates that women are more likely to develop anxiety disorders than men (McLean & Anderson, 2009). Women's greater vulnerability to anxiety disorders can be partly understood by examining gender differences in the etiological factors known to contribute to anxiety. McLean and Anderson (2009) examined evidence for gender differences across a broad range of relevant factors, including biological influences, temperamental factors, stress and trauma, and cognitive and environmental factors. Gender differences are observed with increasing consistency as the scope of analysis broadens to molar levels of functioning. Socialization processes cultivate and promote processes related to anxiety and moderate gender differences across levels of analysis.

How about gender differences in the prevalence of somatic versus pure depression? Using data from the Epidemiologic Catchment Area (ECA), in an attempt to replicate the findings of the National Comorbidity Survey that the prevalence of depression associated with somatic symptoms is much higher among women than men, Silverstein (2002) reanalyzed data from the ECA study. He divided participants into those who met criteria for major depression and exhibited appetite and sleep disturbances and fatigue (somatic depression) and those who met depression criteria but did not exhibit all of those somatic symptoms (pure depression). This reanalysis revealed that the prevalence of somatic depression but not pure depression was much higher among women than men. Somatic depression was associated with high rates of pain: Among women, it was associated with high rates of anxiety disorders and chronic dysphoria. It was concluded that the gender difference in depression may result from a difference in a specific type of depression-anxious somatic depression.

As already noted, Nolen-Hoeksema (1987, 1995), in her response styles theory (RST) proposed that gender differences about women having higher rates of depression than men lies in women being more apt to ruminate when confronted with negative mood whereas men engage in distracting activities. Besides rumination, distraction may be another way to cope with depressive mood. However, significant and stable effect sizes for gender differences were found only among adolescents; the effects of distraction were not stable enough to consider except with caution (Rood, Roelofs, Bogels, Nolen-Hoeksema, & Schouten, 2009). Nonetheless, Armey, Fresco, Moore, Mennin, et al. (2009) were able to break down rumination into two factors: brooding and pondering. Whether these two factors are related to "worry" needs to be ascertained further.

How does self-focused attention relate to "negative affect"? Mor and Winquist (2002) synthesized 226 effect sizes reflecting the relation between self-focused attention and negative affect (depression, anxiety, and negative mood). Their results demonstrated the multifaceted nature of self-focused attention and, apparently, elucidate major controversies in the field of gender differences. Overall, self-focus was associated with negative affect, but several moderators qualified this relationship. Self-focus and negative affect were more strongly related in clinical- and female-dominated samples. Rumination yielded stronger effect sizes than nonruminative self-focus. Self-focus on positive self-aspects and following a positive event were related to lower negative affect. More important, an interaction between foci of self-attention and form of negative affect was found. Private self-focus was more strongly associated with depression and generalized anxiety, whereas public self-focus was more strongly associated with social anxiety.

Even though RST may be one way to describe gender differences, this is not the only way. These differences could be described and perhaps explained according to a Selfhood Model[11] in RCT. This Model[11] (L'Abate, 1994, 1997, 2005, 2009b; Cusinato & L'Abate, 2012; L'Abate et al., 2010) predicts equal gender ratios in functionality (selfulness) and in dysfunctionality (no-self). However, it predicts unequal gender ratios between selfless and selfish individuals to the point that selflessness would be found more frequently in depressed women (Cluster C of Axis II) than in men, whereas selfishness would be found predominantly more in men who tend to act out impulsively (Cluster B of Axis II), as discussed in Chapter 13 of this volume. Furthermore, Model 2.1 would predict the same kind of gender differences for developmental disorders from anger in externalization disorders and for sadness in internalization disorders.

Consequently, according to the Selfhood Model introduced earlier, rumination and distraction, if valid constructs present in depression, are processes deriving from how women attribute more importance to others than to self, that is, selflessness. Worry and distraction are the outcome of negative views about oneself as hurt individuals rather than other causes. Furthermore, there may be differences between ruminations as temporary worries in sadness and rumination as a continuous, ever-present process in fear and psychopathology. A study about attachment, rumination, and postrelationship adjustment (Saffrey & Ehrenerg, 2007) may shed some light on the nature of rumination relevant to the differentiation between normal worry on one hand and abnormal rumination on the other hand. Worry, supposedly, occurs before the fact, whereas rumination occurs after the fact. Temporally, these two processes are different. How is rumination different from fear? According to Saffrey and Ehenberg, the latter is a feeling, the former is a cognitive process, which they found after they assessed rumination generally (brooding, regret, and reflection) and specifically concerning an ended relationship (relationship preoccupation and romantic regret) in 231 young adults who had been involved in a romantic relationship that was (1) of at least three month duration or longer and (2) had ended in the last twelve months since participation in this study.

At the general level, brooding and regret were associated with more negative adjustment, whereas reflection was associated with more positive adjustment; rumination largely mediated the association between attachment anxiety and adjustment. This study illustrates how important it is to dismantle and deconstruct such a complex process as rumination, which includes emotional and cognitive processes, to differentiate it from other feelings and to evaluate whether this process is a direct outcome of sadness, fear, or a mixture of both feelings. A longitudinal study with projections about their developmental trajectory would be in order. The General Rumination Scale and items derived from a principal component analysis of brooding and reflection (Saffrey & Ehrenberg, 2007, p. 368) may help in this deconstruction of rumination, as found also from the results of Armey, Fresco, Moore, Mennin's, et al. (2009) study mentioned earlier. Rumination was found to be composed of two factors, brooding and pondering, which are cognitive processes, not feelings.

Addis (2008) presented four conceptual frameworks for understanding the role of gender in the way men experience, express, and respond to depression because (1) most gender-difference frameworks are often limited by the absence of relevant theory to guide research; (2) the masked research framework assumes that depression in men can be hidden by substance abuse and other externalizing problems; (3) the masculine depression framework assumes that gender norms affect the presentation of depression and create a phenotypic variant of the disorder; and (4) the gendered responding framework assumes that gender norms affect how different men respond to *negative affect* in general. Addis (2008, p.164) concludes his discussion of pros and cons about these four frameworks thus:

> Theoretically, men who adhere more strongly to norms of emotional control and self-reliance should engage in more avoidant responses to a wide range of distressing emotions and should be more likely to keep their distress private. These same men should have a greater likelihood of exhibiting an array of externalizing symptoms. Such hypotheses are central to both the masculine depression and the gendered responding frameworks and have not be evaluated empirically.

In a commentary to Addis's article, Safford (2008) added that the study of gender issues in men is an interesting, relatively new area of focus in depression research. It is exciting to anticipate the continued development of the gender frameworks described by Addis (2008) as they are more thoroughly investigated. Given the high comorbidity rate in depression and the wealth of research on risk factors for depression, it is important that researchers who enter these arenas remember (1) not to limit their explorations of gender in men to only depression, and (2) not to focus their study of risk factors for depression in men too exclusively on gender issues.

In a second commentary to Addis's article, Mahalik (2008) presented a fifth bio-psychosocial framework to previous frameworks that heretofore focused mainly on social norms. In a third commentary to Addis's article, Nolen-Hoeksema (2008) argued that depression in men is a critical topic but unfortunately there has been more rhetoric than research on the nature, extent, and treatment of depression in men. Most of the models of depression in men are based on a medical model view of the "big D" depression. Addis's gendered responding framework provides an innovative perspective on depression in men that has important implications for theories, research, and clinical interventions. Additional support for Addis's model is provided from existing studies on substance abuse as a response to *negative affect* and gender differences in rumination, and from new results that Nolen-Hoesema presented in her article.

Some of her results are worth summarizing here: (1) Men are more likely than women to respond to "amorphous negative affect" by drinking alcohol or smoking; (2) women scored higher than men on expressiveness (i.e., communality), whereas men scored higher than women in instrumentality (i.e., agency); (3) social norms condone different types of emotion for men versus women: Anger is more acceptable for men to express and experience, whereas sadness is more acceptable for women to experience and express. Furthermore, epidemiological studies of generalized anxiety disorder report that women account for two-thirds of those affected (Weisberg, 2009).

Gender Differences and Psychopathology

The relationship between gender differences and psychopathology were fairly well summarized by Yonkers and Gurguis:

> Several psychiatric disorders show distinctive gender-related patterns of morbidity.... [I]llnesses such as alcoholism and antisocial personality disorder, as currently defined, are more often found in men, whereas women are at increased risk for eating disorders, mood disorders, and some anxiety disorders....Anxiety disorders are especially prevalent in women. Current evidence suggests that [in] some anxiety disorders, such as agoraphobia and PTSD, the course of illness is longer for women, whereas men may have longer periods of illness and greater morbidity when they develop Obsessive-Compulsive Disorder (OCD). Symptom profiles are similar for men and women for panic disorder, phobias, and PTSD, but they may vary for OCD. (1995, p. 126)

More specifically, in eating disorders the ratio of women to men is 10:1 (Bekker & Spoor, 2008). In addition to gender differences in sleep patterns (Sloan and Shapiro, 1995), Toner (1995) focused on gender differences in three somatoform disorders: irritable bowel syndrome (IBS), chronic fatigue syndrome (CFS), and (3) fibromyalgia syndrome (FMS). He found that "are all more prevalent in women than in men ... [but] these rates may be affected by gender differences in help-seeking behaviors and diagnostician bias" (p. 288).

Gender Differences in Alcohol Use

Although prevalence rates for alcohol use and related disorders differ widely between adult men and women, male and female adolescents do not exhibit the same disparity in alcohol consumption (Schulte, Ramo, & Brown, 2009). Previous research and reviews do not address the emergence of differences in drinking patterns that occur during late adolescence. Therefore, Schulte et al. (2009) presented a developmental perspective for understanding how various risk and protective factors associated with problematic drinking affect diverging alcohol trajectories in youth moving toward young adult-hood. These authors examined factors associated with risk for developing an alcohol use disorder in adolescent girls and boys separately. Certain biological (i.e., genetic risk for neurological abnormalities associated with P300 brainwave amplitudes) and psychosocial factors (i.e., impact of posi-tive drinking expectancies, personality characteristics, and deviance prone-ness) appear to impact boys and girls similarly. In contrast, physiological and social changes particular to adolescence appear to differentially affect boys and girls as they transition into adulthood. Specifically, boys begin to manifest a constellation of factors that place them at greater risk for dis-ruptive drinking: low response to alcohol, later maturation in brain struc-tures and executive function, greater estimates of perceived peer alcohol use, and socialization into traditional gender roles. On an individual level, interventions that may challenge media-driven stereotypes of gender roles while simultaneously reinforcing personal values are suggested as a way to strengthen adolescent autonomy in terms of healthy drinking decisions. Moreover, parents and schools must improve consistency in rules and con-sequences regarding teen drinking across gender to avoid mixed messages about acceptable alcohol use for boys and girls.

Gender Differences in Drug Abuse

Sometimes hurt feelings are so painful to the point that the individual feels there is no other resource available to stop the pain except drugs. Drugs appear as one way to medicate, mitigate, and even hide the pain of hurt feelings. Unfortunately, that is not the case. Over the years, the National Institute of Drug Abuse (2009) has made a major research commitment to identify and understand differences in the ways women and men – or girls and boys – are first exposed to drugs, the differences in their risks of abuse and addiction, and the effectiveness of drug treatment to reduce dangers and improve outcomes. Men and women tend to use different drugs, and the effects of drugs are different for men and women. Some treatment approaches are also more successful for women than for men. Women are more likely than men to become addicted to or dependent on sedatives and drugs designed to treat anxiety and sleeplessness, and less likely than men to abuse alcohol and marijuana. Women and men are equally likely to become addicted to nicotine, yet women typically smoke cigarettes with lower nicotine content than those smoked by men, smoke fewer cigarettes per day, and inhale less deeply than men. Overall, however, women are less successful than men in quitting smoking and have higher relapse rates after they quit. Nicotine replacement therapy – gum or patch – seems to work better for men than for women. Among cases that progress to a diagnosis of AIDS, drug abuse accounts for a greater percentage of cases among women than among men. In all, drug abuse is nearly twice as likely to be directly or indirectly associated with AIDS in women (66 percent) than in men (34 percent).

INDIVIDUAL DIFFERENCES

Individual differences are considered when there are no longer gender differences present as a personality characteristic (John & Gross, 2007). The nature of a personal relationship depends in part on the characteristics of the participating individuals. Yet the relations between individual characteristics and relationships are complex because (1) there are difficulties in specifying the dimensions along which individuals differ; (2) the characteristics that an individual displays vary with the situation; (3) relationships have properties of their own that result from interaction between participants; and (4) the mechanisms whereby individual characteristics affect relationships are diverse (Auhagen & Hinde, 1997). Individual characteristics of individual participants high on agreeableness and rejection sensitivity, for instance, react to messages matching their own individual characteristics (Buckley, Winkel, and Leary, 2004).

Although associations between marital conflict and children's adjustment problems are well established, as shown in various chapters of this volume, less is known about developmental individual differences that can have an impact on these relationships. El-Sheikh and Whitson (2006), for instance, examined longitudinal relations between marital conflict and children's adjustment using a community sample of elementary-school-age children and young adolescents by assessing the role of children's vagal regulation in moderating the conflict-child problems link. The vagal system is an index of parasympathetic nervous system functioning and may underlie individual differences in emotion regulation (El-Sheikh & Whitson, 2006, p. 31). Elevated marital conflict was predictive of negative child outcomes, and greater vagal suppression to simulated arguments was protective against internalizing problems associated with marital conflict. These findings tend to support the importance of a bio-psychosocial perspective and illustrate that child vagal regulation can contribute to the aggregation or amelioration of risk for maladjustment in the context of exposure to marital conflict.

Optimism-Pessimism

This is an important dimension that is very relevant to the ratio of joyful and hurtful experiences, because optimism has beneficial effects on physical and mental health whereas pessimism has negative effects on both physical and mental health (Scheier & Carter, 1992). As important as this dimension is, space limits do not allow for further discussion.

Lie Telling

Lie tellers in intimate relationships often claim their lies were told to protect their partner. However, based on several converging theories (e.g., motivated reasoning, cognitive dissonance), Kaplar and Gordon (2004) expected lie receivers to interpret lie tellers' motives less altruistically. These investigators also made predictions regarding other variables in which they expected lie tellers' and lie receivers' perceptions to differ (e.g., justification for the lie and responses to the lie, lie tellers' guilt, the temporal and situational context of the lies, or perceptions of causality and blame). Participants wrote two autobiographical narratives, one from the perspective of lie teller and the other from the perspective of lie receiver. Participants also completed questionnaire items that mirrored coding dimensions used in the content analyses of the narratives. As predicted, the same participants, when occupying the lie teller role as opposed to lie receiver, viewed their lies as more altruistically motivated, guilt inducing, spontaneous, justified by the features of the situation, and provoked by the lie receiver. When studying and evaluating lies, different potential explanations for perspective differences and the need for multiple perspectives arise, which lead to the potential understanding of perspective differences in aiding in conflict resolution.

Given the importance of lying in the elicitation of hurt feelings, the study of Ennis, Vrij, and Chance (2008) explored individuals' reported frequency of lying to strangers and close friends as a function of (1) type of lie told (self-centered, other-centered, and altruistic); and (2) attachment style in social relationships. One hundred university students (average age = 23.09, SD = 5.36) completed self-report questionnaires concerning telling lies to a friend who could be either a best friend (N = 52) or a romantic partner (N = 48). Results revealed that frequency and nature of lies told to strangers differ from those told to close friends. Attachment-related anxiety was positively associated with frequency of lying to strangers and best friends, whereas attachment avoidance primarily related to deception toward one's romantic partner.

Emotionality in Personality

The personalities of both partners are very likely associated with the qualities of their romantic relationship. Donnellan, Assad, Robins, and Conger (2007) extended that literature by examining whether or not reports of negative relationship interactions mediate the effects of personality traits on judgments of relationship satisfaction and quality. Participants were 337 couples who completed a comprehensive personality questionnaire and several scales measuring relationship behaviors and satisfaction. Negative and Communal Positive Emotionality were related to both self- and partner reports of relationship satisfaction. These associations were substantially mediated by negative relationship interactions. These results indicate how it is nearly impossible to disentangle personality from interpersonal factors in romantic dyadic relationships (Gaines, 2007).

Another important study to assess to what degree emotional factors in personality account for associations between marital quality and parenting and mediates genetic contributions to these relationships was conducted by Ganiban, Ulbricht, Spotts, Lichtenstein, et al. (2009). Participants included 318 men and 544 same-sex twin women pairs from the Twin and Offspring Study in Sweden. All twins completed self-report measures of marital quality and emotional personality factors (anxiousness, aggression, and sociability). Composite measures of parent negativity and warmth were derived from the twins and their adolescent children's ratings of the twins' disciplinary styles and the emotional tone of the parent-child relationship. Observational ratings of marital quality and parenting were also obtained for a subset of twins. Personality characteristics explained 33 to 42 percent of the covariance between observed marital quality and parenting. These results indicate that personality significantly contributes to associations between marital quality and parenting and that personality is an important path through which genetic factors contribute to family relationships.

A third study that related personality factors, such as novelty seeking and harm avoidance, to family functioning in dating-relationship quality was performed by Fischer, Fitzpatrick, and Cleveland (2007). The first pathway extended from family dysfunction to dating-relationship quality via novelty seeking and excessive drinking. The second pathway extended from family dysfunction to relationship quality via harm avoidance and interpersonal competence. Results obtained from undergraduate men (N = 64) and women (N = 105) who completed relevant questionnaires strongly supported the first pathway, including the systems principle of equifinality (considered in Chapter 1 of this volume). There were significant associations between adjacent variables in the path model, and the presence of both pathways in the tested model provided a good fit to the data. The second pathway, based on the systems principle of interdependence, was not supported when cross-pathway links were included in the tested model. Unfortunately, this study was not specifically oriented toward emotionality. However, it serves as a support for inclusion within the principle that we approach novelty/pleasure and avoid harm/hurt.

Extraversion, Social Support, and Negativity

Cutrona, Hessling, and Suhr (1997) examined the influence of extraversion and negative affectivity on support interactions among one hundred married couples observed in two ten-minute interactions designed to elicit supportive behaviors. Extraverted support providers gave more support to their spouse than did introverts. Reciprocity in the exchange of support behaviors was also observed. The amount of support given by the individual in the first interaction predicted the amount of support provided by him or her during the second interaction. Negative affectivity was negatively correlated with ratings of interaction supportiveness, even when controlling for the number of supportive and negative behaviors received from the spouse. Extraverts showed higher sensitivity to emotional support behaviors than introverts. The same level of emotional support behaviors from the spouse led to higher ratings of interaction supportiveness among those high on extraversion than among those low on extraversion. The results highlight the importance of integrative models of support that consider characteristics of the individual and his or her social environment.

Demand/Withdraw

Demand/withdraw is a pattern in which one spouse nags or complains while the other spouse avoids or withdraws. Given the fact that demand/withdraw has been repeatedly linked to marital discord, it is important to understand why couples engage in such a seemingly dissatisfying conflict pattern (Caughlin & Vangelisti, 2000). Although several scholars have suggested that power differences between men and women lead to demand/withdraw, the research conducted by Caughlin and Vangelisti focused on a different explanation: that individual differences are important contributors to demand/withdraw communication. In particular, two models connecting individual differences to demand/ withdraw were examined. The first self-influence model suggests that individuals' attributes primarily affect their own communication behavior. The second relational influence model posits that individuals' characteristics affect the extent to which the couple (i.e., both partners) engages in demand/withdraw. Results from this study supported both models, indicating that individual differences do contribute to demand/withdraw by interacting with the specific nature of the couple relationship itself.

Loneliness as a Personality Characteristic

If loneliness inclines people to a general hostility toward others and to a disparaging style of social interaction, then that style should appear in studies of lonely people interacting with their friends as well as observing other persons they do not know. Duck, Pond, and Leatham (1994) conducted a study with four features: (1) lonely and nonlonely persons' evaluation of (2) their own and other people's conversations with friends, using (3) both free evaluation and videotape-prompted evaluation (4) both immediately after an interaction and six weeks later. Lonely persons did not consistently evaluate their or others' conversations negatively, though they tended to rate communication quality lower. They did, however, draw negative global conclusions about their own relationships, especially after reviewing a videotape of their interaction six weeks later. The authors conjectured that lonely people may be negative about interactions when they focus on their own communication performance, and that they also have characteristic ways of evaluating and generalizing from their interactions that feed into general patterns of dissatisfaction with their own social performance in relationships as a whole.

Although this study did not give any information about gender differences, it did add results that could be relevant to future studies of loneliness and gender differences. For instance, Flora and Segrin (2000) examined the association of relationship development, relational satisfaction, and loneliness in one hundred participants in a current romantic relationship and one hundred participants in a recently broken-off romantic relationship. From their results, Flora and Segrin traced loneliness to relational satisfaction based on four variables: (1) we-ness/separateness; (2) glorifying the struggle of being together and apart; (3) relational disappointment; and (4) developmental trajectory. Unfortunately, the gender distribution of this study was very discrepant, with a woman to man ratio of nearly 3:1. Nonetheless, after repeated analyses, these researchers failed to find any gender differences.

In what specific relational context does loneliness arise? Feeney (2006) assessed the implications of parental attachment security and parental conflict behavior for offspring's relational adjustment (attachment security, loneliness, and relationship satisfaction). Further, reports of parental conflict behavior were obtained from both parents and offspring, addressing questions regarding agreement between reporters and the origin and extent of discrepant perceptions. Results revealed consistent patterns of conflict behavior and moderate agreement between reporters. However, offspring reported parental conflict behavior more negatively than parents, especially when offspring or parents were anxious about relationships. Parental attachment security had direct association with offspring's relationship anxiety, whereas associations between parental attachment and offspring's loneliness and discomfort with closeness were mediated by parental conflict behavior, which in turn was also associated with offspring's relationship satisfaction. These results are relevant to the mechanisms of intergenerational transmission of relationship difficulties discussed in Chapter 13 of this volume.

In old age loneliness could be seen as a social failure subject to causal, introspective search: Why am I lonely? Why do I lack friends? According to attribution theory, answers to these questions can influence emotions, motivation, and behaviors. Newall, Chipperfield, Clifton, Perry, and Swift (2009) examined the relationships between various affiliative causal beliefs (i.e., beliefs about loneliness and friendship development), social participation, and loneliness among older adults (seventy-two or more years). Cross-sectional and longitudinal (more than five years) results endorsed internal factors more strongly. Controllable causal beliefs (i.e., believing that making friends depends on effort) related to greater social participation. Moreover, greater social participation related to less loneliness. External/uncontrollable causal beliefs predicted greater loneliness. In fully addressing loneliness, it may be important to focus on people's causal beliefs.

Repressive Coping Style

This style is found in individuals who are rigidly invested in believing that they virtually never worry about "negative affect" by coping in ways that potentiate a number of important physical diseases (Diamond, Hicks, & Otter-Henderson, 2006). Weinberger (1990) summarized a great deal of literature relating repressive coping style to three physiological disorders: cardiovascular disease, cancer, and asthma. Prototypic repressors have been defined as individuals who maximally value rationality and self-control and attempt to maintain extensive cognitive control over their feelings and impulses. Most research has defined repressors operationally according to low scores on anxiety measures and high scores on measures of defensiveness.

Another way to define the same personality characteristic would be low in subjective awareness of "distress" and very high in self-restraint by suppressing anger, not considering others, and avoiding responsibility for their own actions. Essentially, these individuals are "distress deniers." In spite of these strong denials, repressors react physiologically to stressful tasks as if they were as upset or even more upset than participants who report high levels of conscious distress. As Weinberger indicated, evidence is quite convincing that repressors' preoccupation with avoiding awareness of "negative emotions" interferes with effective coping and is associated with heightened reactivity in a variety of physiological subsystems.

Repressors tend to avoid a range of negative affects, including anxiety, sadness, and anger, specific emotions (read "feelings") that trigger distinct patterns of physiological changes. Anger, rather than anxiety, tends to produce particularly toxic physiological consequences; these found in coronary-prone personalities, such as Type A, and cause high levels of heart rate and blood pressure reactivity and a tendency toward hypertension, as well as high levels of LDL-cholesterol, a major contributor to atherosclerosis, perhaps because of extreme inhibition of aggressive impulses. Pervasive over-control of anger and hostility seems at the bottom of this personality type. Extreme suppression of anger may mediate a link to abnormal cell growth according to an equifinality principle.

Weinberger (1990) also maintained that repressive coping style is associated with the development and progression of various types of cancer. For instance, cancer patients who openly express their angry feelings seem to have longer survival rates. By the same token, bronchial asthma as well as aches and pains of unknown origin seem present in young boys. Importantly, repressive style and asthma seemed to correlate with highly interconnected, conflict-avoidant families, where expressions of hostile feelings are deemed unacceptable. Therefore, anger and hostility, rather than anxiety, seem involved in the association between repressive styles and bronchial constriction in asthmatics, but there is sufficient reliable empirical data to conclude that extreme repressive control of anger and aggression can take a significant toll on one's body through a number of different physiological pathways.

From a seemingly intrapsychic viewpoint implied in repressive coping style, a more benign, relational definition of "communal coping" (Lyons, Mickelson, Sullivan, & Coyne, 1998, p. 579) would view this construct as a cooperative, problem-solving process salient in dealing with both individual and collective stressors, and involving appraisal of stressors as effecting both partners in a relationship or even family members.

CONCLUSION

Gender and individual differences about presumed hurt feelings tend to support the position that those feelings are relationally experienced. These feelings are not experienced in a vacuum, but they are learned in the gymnasium of close, committed, interdependent, and prolonged intimate relationships. Gender differences not only influence individual differences but may either improve or exacerbate them, depending on their positive or negative valence.

9

Cultural Differences in Hurt Feelings

> Most research on hurt feelings has been conducted in Western cultures, with relatively little attention paid to the ways in which the experience and expression of hurt feelings might vary cross-culturally.
> Kowalski, 2009 (p. 457)

Contributions about cultural factors included already in Vangelisti's (2009b) *Handbook* and especially in Kowalski's (2009) chapter will not be included here to avoid any duplication and overlap between this and those publications. There are clearly cultural differences in relationship beliefs across countries as they relate to how emotionality is experienced and expressed (Brase, Caprar, & Voracek, 2004; Goodwin & Gaines, 2004; Mesquita & Albert, 2007; Shweder, Haidt, Horton, & Joseph, 2008). Here is where Bakan's (1968) dichotomy of communal versus agentic relationships is worth mentioning. As Spiegel (1971) indicated, there are cultures in the Mediterranean basin, such as Greece, Italy, Portugal, and Spain, that place more value on being together communally in expressive conversation than on relating agentically or instrumentally, such as in United States and other industrialized countries.

In this chapter, only cross-cultural differences will be included if they are relevant to hurt feelings either directly or indirectly. Results from studies inside a single country without cross-cultural comparisons will not be included unless they are specifically related to hurt feelings. Furthermore, there may be genetic differences in how pain is experienced. For instance, there may be physiological differences between African Americans and white Americans in how much physical pain may be experienced and endured (Campbell, France, Robinson, Logan, et al., 2008; Diatchenko, Nackley, Tchivileva, Shabalina, & Maixner, 2007; Nielsen, Staud, & Price, 2009). How these possible differences in physical pain apply to how hurt feelings are experienced, expressed, and shared culturally will be the subject of this chapter.

Hurt Feelings and Friendships

A study by Adams and Plaut (2003), for instance, seems to support Bakan's and Spiegel's original differentiation, which considers how different constructions of the self and social reality influence the experience of relationship. Reflecting the relational interdependence of West African worlds, Adams and Plaut hypothesized and observed that Ghanaian participants were significantly more likely than U.S. participants ($N = 50$ in each group) to advocate caution toward friends and to emphasize practical assistance in friendship. Reflecting the atomistic independence of North African worlds, these authors hypothesized and observed that U.S. participants were significantly more likely than Ghanaian participants to indicate a large friendship network, to emphasize companionship, particularly relative to Ghanaian women, and to emphasize emotional support, particularly relative to Ghanaian nonstudents. These results may suggest that friendship is not a universal form; instead, it takes different forms in different cultural worlds.

Indeed, emotional support is a central feature around which white middle-class adults organize their same-gender friendships. Samter, Whaley, Mortenson, and Burleson (1997) examined whether emotional support is accorded the same significance in the friendships of Asian and African Americans. Participants included 199 students (60 European American men and women, 80 Asian American men and women, and 59 African American men and women attending either a state or private university in California. Each participant completed three different questionnaires designed to assess perceptions of (1) the importance of comforting skill in same-gender friendship; (2) the significance of emotion-focused versus problem-focused goals in a situation requiring emotional support; and (3) the sensitivity and effectiveness of various comforting strategies. Several significant differences due to ethnicity were found in participants' perceptions of emotional support and its attendant behaviors. These and related findings have implications for the conduct of same-gender friendships among individuals from different ethnic backgrounds.

Hurt Feelings and Toddlers' Self-regulation

Feldman, Mashala, and Alony (2006) examined pathways to children's self-regulation in two cultures representing individualistic and collectivistic orientations. Family interactions were observed in one hundred Israeli and sixty-two Palestinian couples and their firstborn child at five months and in a problem-solving task at thirty-three months. Patterns of gaze, affect, proximity, touch, and parental teaching strategies were coded. Child self-regulation was observed in childcare locations. Among Israeli families, interactions involved face-to-face exchange, social gaze, object focus, and active touch in infancy and indirect parental assistance to toddlers. Among Palestinian families, interactions consisted of continuous contact, neutral affect, reduced negative emotionality, and concrete assistance. Levels of self-regulation were comparable and were predicted by culture-specific patterns. Social gaze, touch, and indirect teaching were found to predict self-regulation among Israeli toddlers; contact and concrete assistance were predictors among Palestinians. Apparently, early relational patterns mirror cultural philosophies on the self and differentially support self-regulation at the transition from family to the larger social context.

Hurt Feelings and Bereavement

However, by now the fear and avoidance of painful internal experiences in dysfunctional relationships is pretty well established, at least in the English-speaking world, but we need to demonstrate the universality of such experience. Bonanno, Papa, Lalande, Zhang, et al., (2005), for instance, measured grief processing and deliberate grief avoidance in their relationship to adjustment at four and eighteen months after bereavement for two types of losses (spouse, child) in two cultures (the People's Republic of China and the United States). Three hypotheses were compared about grief work: traditional, conditional, and grief processing as a form of rumination absent among resilient individuals. Although cultural differences in grief processing and avoidance were observed, the factor structure of measures proved invariant across cultures. Consistent with grief work as rumination hypothesis, both grief processing and deliberate grief avoidance predicted poor long-term adjustment in U.S. participants. Furthermore, initial grief processing predicted later grief processing in both cultures. However, among the participants in China, neither grief processing nor deliberate avoidance evidenced clear psychological consequences.

A subsequent analysis of the same information by Pressman and Bonanno (2007) gave further details to the process of grieving in China and the United States. Participants reported significantly less frequent grief processing with friends than with family or when alone, with a more pronounced difference at the second wave (after eighteen months since the loss) of data collection. Interactions of culture and lost relationship type were also observed.

Hurt Feelings and Positive/Negative Interactions

Akiyama, Antonucci, Takahashi, and Langfahl (2003) examined age differences in positive and negative interactions in close relationships in 3,139 individuals (aged thirteen to ninety-two years) residing in the United States and Japan. Participants completed interviews concerning positive and negative interactions, familiarity, and frequency of contact with parents, spouse, child, and best friend of the same gender, as well as sensitivity to others, understanding, compassion, and eagerness to soothe hurt feelings. Results showed that participants in both countries reported that negative interactions decreased with age concerning all close relationships excepting spousal ones. No relationship was observed between familiarity and the age-related decline in negative relationships, whereas contact frequency accounted for the relationships with participants' child in the United States and with participants' mother, father, and child in Japan.

Hurt Feelings and Depression

Abe (2004) examined the relative-importance of self-esteem, family cohesion, and support from friends in predicting depressed mood and anxiety in Japanese and American college students. Contrary to expectations, self-esteem was the strongest predictor of emotional distress in both groups of students. Nevertheless, consistent with predictions derived from Marcus and Kitayana's (1991) theory of self-construals, family cohesion accounted for a significantly larger percentage of the variance in predicting emotional distress in Japan and in the United States. In both countries, the relations between support from friends and the measures of emotional distress were entirely mediated by self-esteem. However, among Japanese students, family cohesion accounted for additional significant variance in predicting measures of emotional distress, even after controlling for self-esteem.

Hurt Feelings in Individualism-Collectivism

To extend existing research about the effects of culture and self-construal on reports of accommodating dilemmas in dating relationships, Yum (2004) collected data from members of three different cultures: the U.S. mainland, Hawaii, and South Korea. Using a four-factor self-construal model (bicultural, marginal, independent, and interdependent), two hypotheses were posited: (1) Members of collectivistic cultures tend to enact accommodation (loyalty, voice) more and nonaccommodation (neglect) less than do individualistic counterparts; and (2) bicultural self-construal is more strongly and consistently associated with accommodation than are the other three self-construal types. These hypotheses received support. Collectivism-individualism was related consistently with the type of accommodation, and the four self-construal types also displayed a reliable pattern of associations with accommodation and nonaccommodations. Post hoc assessments revealed that the four-factor model predicted self-reported accommodation better than the two-factor model used in previous research. Small effect sizes in the present study, however, suggest that other factors (e.g., industrialization) may have a considerable bearing on responses to accommodative dilemmas.

Even though Yum's research does not relate particularly to hurt feelings, it is included here because it furnishes a wider background to studies included in this chapter and because its four-partite classification of self-construals may relate to the Selfhood Model[11], expanded in Chapter 13 of this volume. More specifically, Marshall (2008) examined emotional intimacy in European Canadians' and Chinese Canadians' dating relationships in two studies. Cultural differences in gender-role ideology and individualism-collectivism were hypothesized to differentially contribute to self-disclosure and responsiveness, and in turn, intimacy. Study 1 revealed that Chinese Canadians' lower intimacy relative to European Canadians was mediated by their greater gender-role traditionalism, but not by their individualism or collectivism. Study 2 further linked greater gender-role traditionalism to lower self-disclosure, and in turn, lower intimacy. Results also revealed that Chinese Canadians' lower intimacy mediated their lower relationship satisfaction and higher rates of relationship termination in study 1, but that Chinese Canadians were not any more likely to terminate their relationship in study 2.

Hurt Feelings and Demand-Withdraw in Marriage

Rehman and Holtzworth-Munroe (2006) used cross-cultural methodology to examine the demand-withdraw pattern of marital communication. In Western countries, women usually make more demands, whereas men are more likely to withdraw. However, the recently advanced marital structure hypothesis suggests that this pattern can be altered by gender roles and beliefs, particularly in traditional marriages. To test this hypothesis, these authors conducted an observational study of marital communication across very different cultures, with varying levels of patriarchy (ie., fifty white American couples, fifty-two Pakistani couples in Pakistan, and forty-eight Pakistani couples in America). Across cultures, demand-withdraw communication was related to marital distress, extending previous findings to new groups. However, the findings challenge the notion that demanding and withdrawing behaviors are inherently male and female. Rather, the results point to the relevance of contextual factors, specifically gender-power differences and acculturation, in understanding the demand-withdraw marital interaction pattern. Therapists working with foreign or immigrant couples must consider the cross-cultural generalizability of existing theories of marital communication.

Hurt Feelings and Conflict

Bodenmann, Kaiser, Hahlweg, and Fehm-Wolfsdorf (1998) used a Communication Patterns Questionnaire to assess marital communication level on three scales: (1) mutual constructive communication; (2) mutual avoidance of communication; and (3) demand-withdrawal. The questionnaire was found as reliable and valid in a German and Swiss sample as it was found to be in American samples. In both studies, communication avoidance and withdrawal were negatively associated with relationship satisfaction.

Hurt Feelings and Distress

Mak, Chen, Lam, and You (2009) explored the cultural mechanisms underlying the psychological distress experienced among Hong Kong and mainland Chinese, Chinese Americans, and European Americans by examining the role of face concern through a series of studies with college students and community samples. Face concern refers to one's preoccupation over maintaining or enhancing one's social position and worth that have been earned through the fulfillment of specific social roles. Study 1 confirmed the single-factor structure of face concern among Chinese Americans and European Americans. Face concern was significantly and positively related to distress above and beyond age, gender, and ethnicity. Study 2 deconstructed face concern into a two-factor model among Hong Kong and Mainland Chinese university students (self-face and other-face) with discriminant predictive power. In study 3, the two-factor model of face concern was further supported in community samples of Hong Kong and Mainland Chinese.

Self-face was found to be positively associated with distress. These findings highlight the importance of attending to specific cultural dynamics of face concern, especially in the mental health professions.

Hurt Feelings and Infidelity

Different adaptive problems faced by men and women over evolutionary history led evolutionary psychologists to hypothesize and discover gender differences in jealousy as a function of infidelity type. An alternative hypothesis proposes that beliefs about the conditional probabilities of sexual and emotional infidelity account for those gender differences. Buss, Shackelford, Kirkpatrick, Choe, et al. (1999) tested these hypotheses in four studies. Study 1 tested the hypotheses in an American sample (N = 1,122) by rendering the two types of infidelity mutually exclusive. Study 2 tested the hypotheses in an American sample (N = 234) by asking participants to identify which aspect of infidelity was more upsetting when both types occurred, and by using regression to identify the unique contribution of gender and beliefs. Study 3 replicated study 2 in a Korean sample (N = 190). Study 4 replicated study 2 in a Japanese sample (N = 316). Across all four studies, the evolutionary hypothesis, but not the belief hypothesis, accounted for gender differences in jealousy when the types of infidelity had been rendered mutually exclusive: (1) gender differences in which aspect of infidelity was more upsetting when both occurred; (2) significant variance attributable to gender, after controlling for belief; (3) gender-differentiated patterns of beliefs; and (4) cross-cultural prevalence of these gender differences.

Hurt Feelings and Jealousy

Prior research on gender differences in relationship jealousy and on reactions to third-party rivals have been conducted primarily in the United States, Central Europe, and Asia (earlier in this chapter). As these effects vary in magnitude across culture, it is important to investigate both how these patterns differ across a wider range of cultures and the key mediating cultural variables. Brase, Caprar, and Voracek (2004) obtained the reactions of 114 English and 202 Romanian participants to hypothetical relational infidelity situations and to various traits that a mate rival could possess. In both samples, males were much more upset than females by sexual infidelity, as compared with emotional infidelity, but this effect was much smaller for the Romanian sample. In line with evolutionary predictions, men were more upset by a rival who had better financial prospects, greater status and prestige, and was physically stronger, whereas women were more upset by a rival with a more attractive body and face. Additionally, unpredicted gender differences in the evaluation of rival traits were also found. Finally, different correlations were found (both across cultures and genders) between reported reactions to infidelities and to specific male rival traits.

Hurt Feelings in Divorce and Stress

Drawing on earlier models of stress and divorce, Bodenmann, Charviz, Bradbury, Bertoni, et al. (2007), in a retrospective study, investigated how divorced individuals appraise the role of stress in their divorce. Data from divorced individuals (N = 662) from Germany, Italy, and Switzerland suggested that low commitment and deficits in interpersonal competencies (communication, problem solving, coping) are more likely than stress to be perceived as reasons for divorce. However, when considering everyday stresses, participants reported trivial daily events to be one of the main reasons contributing to their decision to divorce. Although general stress level did not influence individuals' decision to divorce, most participants considered the accumulation of daily stresses as a central trigger for the divorce. In all three countries, the two major factors that seemed to predict divorce were commitment and interpersonal competencies. These two factors should be replicated in English-speaking countries to see whether the same results can be obtained as those in the three European countries considered in this research.

Hurt Feelings and Loneliness

According to Goodwin, Cook, and Yung (2001), studies about loneliness and life satisfaction have rarely assessed the role of culture in moderating the relationship between those variables. Those investigators examined the relationship between loneliness and life satisfaction using data from three nonstudent samples collected from Italian, Anglo-Canadian, and Chinese Canadian populations. A total of 206 participants completed the Revised UCLA Loneliness Scale (Russell, Peplau, & Cutrona, 1980) and the Satisfaction with Life Scale (Diener, Emmons, Larsen, & Griffin, 1985). Two contrasting hypotheses were compared: first, a "postmodern" hypothesis, predicting that the relationship between life satisfaction and loneliness would be stronger in the individualistic sample of Anglo-Canadians, and a second, "relational" hypothesis predicting this association to be strongest in the collectivist, Chinese Canadian sample. Findings demonstrated that culture has a small but significant impact on the relationship between loneliness and life satisfaction, and, consistent with the relational hypothesis, the relationship between the two concepts was strongest among the Chinese Canadian and weakest among the Anglo-Canadian participants. These results may be due to the strong expectations of social cohesion in collectivistic societies.

Comparing loneliness in older adults in Italy and the Netherlands, van Tilburg, Gierveld, Lecchini, and Marsiglia (1998) felt that the former are lonelier on the average than in the latter country. Loneliness may be more prevalent in European regions where living alone is rarest and where community bonds are strongest. The inverse macro-level association, an increasing proportion of lonely older people and a decreasing proportion of older people who live alone from northern to southern Europe, could not be explained by differences in individual social integration. The results from a survey conducted by van Tilburg et al. showed that fewer older people lived alone in Tuscany, Italy, than in the Netherlands, which may indicate that the Dutch might be less integrated. As regards their participation in social organizations and personal networks, however, Tuscan older adults seemed to be less integrated, indicating that regional differences in loneliness may be based on differences in social integration.

Hurt Feelings and Self-Disclosure

The reactions of Polish university students about norms governing self-disclosure as a function of degree of friendship and discloser's gender were assessed by Verlega and Stepien (1977). In the first study, most American norms governing reactions to self-disclosure to friends and strangers were replicated. Disclosure of personal information to a stranger was disapproved, whereas disclosure to a friend was approved. Somewhat different from the American data, Polish students disapproved of nondisclosure to a friend but not to a stranger. In a second study, American norms governing self-disclosure to males and females were not replicated. Polish students did not judge disclosure by males and females differently. These results seem to reflect different attitudes about gender roles governing self-disclosure by American versus Polish participants.

Hurt Feelings and Forgiveness

Hui and Bond (2009b) proposed that following a transgression, as a victim's perceived face loss increased, the victim would show: (1) less forgiveness toward the perpetrator; (2) increased motivation to retaliate; and (3) reduced desire to maintain a damaged relationship. Moreover, an independent self-construal was hypothesized to strengthen these associations. Results from Hong Kong Chinese and American university students revealed that greater face loss directly reduced forgiveness. For Hong Kong Chinese, face loss also indirectly lowered forgiveness through retaliatory and relationship-maintenance motivations. Self-construals, however, did not account for such cultural-specific findings. These investigators focused on how attributions for the face loss cross-culturally shaped the offended party's response to relationship transgression. This topic will be covered in greater detail in Chapter 11.

CONCLUSION

Most of these studies included in this chapter indicate how important it is to include cultural factors in our understanding of hurt feelings, whether they are called "distress" or "intimacy," or "negative interactions." A more likely hypothesis, derived from the results of Chapter 7, would suggest that the biological foundations for hurt feelings are universal as far as the subjective experience of hurt feelings. However, how hurt feelings are expressed as emotions is influenced by culture as well as by gender and individual differences, as already discussed in Chapter 8.

10

The Psychopathology of Hurt Feelings: Influences on Physical and Mental Health

[A] catastrophic illness does one of two things. It either makes you bitter
or makes you grateful. It made me grateful, especially for my family and
my friends and colleagues.

> (Marguita Lister as quoted by Eisenberg, 2009).

The purpose of this chapter is to show that the whole organism will suffer when presumed hurt feelings are produced by repeated, traumatic, aversive, painful, or objectively or negatively perceived circumstances or events. Even more specifically, presumed hurt feelings per se do not produce personal and relational dysfunctionalities. The avoidance of expressing them and the lower ratio of sharing joyful and pleasant experiences to hurt feelings is what causes those internal and relational dysfunctionalities. However, there is a growing concern in the United States about avoidable, unjust differences in health associated with sociodemographic characteristics, such as socioeconomic status (SES) and race/ethnicity. This concern has sparked research to identify how disparities develop and how they can be reduced. Studies that show that disparities occur at all levels of SES, not simply at the very bottom, suggest that psychosocial factors play an important role (Geronimus, Colen, Shochet, Ingber, & James, 2006; Geronimus, Hicken, Keene, & Bound, 2006). Therefore, this chapter will consider how presumed hurt feelings are present and influential in physical illness, in severe psychopathology (Axis I of the DSM-V), and in personality disorders (Axis II of the DSM-V), as well as in the population at large. These feelings constitute, therefore, the so-called unconscious (Bargh et al. 2008; De Giacomo et al., 2010).

The responsibility to survey the many complex mind-body relationships was rendered much easier by the important contribution of Stockdale (2009). She reviewed resources and bibliographic references that complemented an interesting, easy-to-read, vignette-based account, which combined humor and joy with serious scholarship in dealing with such severe disease as cancer. This book would be valuable to laypersons as well as to serious professionals in search of research-based information, and is also a pleasure to read. Within the context of body-mind relationships, there is also a great deal of research on many medically unexplained symptoms, which deserves much more attention than can be allotted here. That research could be traced to the possible presence of deeply unconscious hurt feelings (Brown, 2007; Deary, Chalder, & Sharpe, 2007; De Giacomo et al., 2010; Eminson, 2007; Iversen, Chalder, & Wessely, 2007; Rief & Broadbent, 2007; Roelofs & Spinhoven, 2007).

Past experimental research has examined the determinants of illness-related cognitive appraisals and their importance in the determination and maintenance of illness. Within the context of Lazarus and Folkman's (1984) stress and coping model, Croyle (1992) reviewed and discussed research support and extended that model. Cognitive determinants of illness-related behavior seemed to best account for by Leventhal, Nerenz, and Steele's (1984) self-regulation theory of illness behavior. One might refer to Stockdale's (2009) work for an update of theory and research about this topic.

AVOIDANCE OF HURT FEELINGS IN HUMAN BEINGS

The thesis of this work is that in functional relationships hurt feelings would dissipate and disappear when: (1) these feelings are disclosed, expressed, and shared verbally, nonverbally, and in writing with loved ones, family, and friends; and (2) joys offset hurts, perhaps in a ratio of five or six to one (Gottman, 1999). In dysfunctional relationships, on the other hand, hurt feelings are avoided through avoidance (denial, repression, and suppression), whereby they remain and fester inside the organism to constitute and become part of the so-called unconscious, negatively affecting individual and relational functioning (De Giacomo et al., 2010; Firestone & Firestone, 2004; L'Abate, 2005). For instance, there is a pathological avoidance of conflict in anorexia nervosa (Latzer & Gaber, 1998), perhaps due to the inability to accept, acknowledge, express, and share hurt feelings in the family, as well as in alexithymia (Ahrens & Deffner, 1986; Cusinato & L'Abate, 2012) and anedonia (Nicholson, 1997).

Further evidence for this argument can be found in pioneering research about grief avoidance by Bonanno, Papa, Lalande, and Zhang (2005), in Roemer, Salter, Raffa, and Orsillo's (2005) work on avoidance of internal experience on generalized anxiety disorder, and in other sources already included in previous writings (L'Abate, 2009b). This process, therefore, follows the generally accepted and established principle of our approaching pleasure and avoiding pain, respectively labeled promotion and prevention in regulatory focus theory (Higgins & Spiegel, 2004). Promotion means approaching helpful people, activities, and tasks. Prevention means avoiding aversive people, activities, and tasks. It takes more effort to avoid hurt feelings than to approach them. As simple as this statement may seem, approaching hurt feelings is not as easy or simple as it may seem at first blush.

Avoidance of pain may be fully mediated by thought suppression between negative affect intensity/reactivity and borderline personality disorder features, as well as partially mediated by the relationship between this disorder and perceived parental criticism (Cheavens, Rosenthal, Daughters, Nowak, et al., 2005). That investigation, among many others, supported the position that hurt feelings derive from past abandonments, abuses, criticisms, losses, and rejections discussed fully in previous chapters of this volume (L'Abate, 1997, 2005). Of course, there may be gender differences in such avoidance (as discussed in Chapter 8 of this volume). Hurt feelings, therefore, dissipate in functional relationships, where they can be approached, admitted, disclosed, and shared with loved ones, and where there is an ample reservoir of joyful and happy events and feelings to offset hurt feelings. In dysfunctional relationships, hurt feelings are avoided, denied, suppressed, or repressed and as a result tend to stay and fester (L'Abate, 1999, 2005, 2009b).

As anonymous Reviewer A mentioned, there are "Victims" and "Perpetrators" in how hurt feelings are experienced. The former "generally describe hurtful events in much more negative terms than do Perpetrators... reflecting self-serving biases on the part of both parties." Given the importance of this point, I would go one step above and beyond what Reviewer A had in mind: Hurt feelings are produced, received, expressed, and processed in what has been called the pathogenic Drama Triangle, Model[14] of RCT (see Chapter 13 of this volume).

It is difficult if not impossible to disentangle physical from mental health and their social context (Ertel, Glymour, & Berkman, 2009). This separation will occur with full cognizance of the interrelatedness between both types of health, where the presumed presence of hurt feelings is very likely to exist.

HURT FEELINGS IN PHYSICAL SICKNESS

Most treatises on feelings and emotions consistently link them with physical health, but not with mental health (Braithwaite, Fincham, & Lambert,

2009; Consedine, 2008; Diefenbach et al., 2008; Shaver, 1984; Stockdale, 2009). Only a few representative sources can be cited, even though this field would require much greater space than can be granted here. Lazarus and Lazarus (1994) identified psychosomatic disorders, cancer, and hypertension as some of the physical expressions of unexpressed feelings. The issue here lies in identifying which feelings are linked to physical health. Mayne (2001) questioned the validity of the simplistic equation: Positive emotions equals good health and negative emotions equals poor health (p. 375). He emphasized the importance of individual differences and the influence of age, gender, and marital status as variables that may have direct effects on health.

The immune system and human psychoneuroimmunology include the many routes through which psychological factors and, within this context, hurt feelings influence immune functions – how a stressor's duration may influence the changes observed, individual differences variables, the ability of interventions to modulate immune functions, and the health consequences of psychosocially mediate immune dysregulation. The importance of *negative affect* and supportive personal relationships must be considered because immune dysregulation may be one core mechanism for a spectrum of conditions associated with aging, including cardiovascular disease, osteoporosis, arthritis, Type 2 diabetes, certain cancers, and frailty and functional decline: production of proinflammatory cytokines that influence these and other conditions that can be stimulated directly by *negative emotions* and indirectly by prolonged infection (Kiecolt-Glaser, McGuire, Robles, & Glasser, 2002).

Neuroticism is also highly associated with physical disorders in the United States. Drawing from data in the National Comorbidity Survey, Goodwin, Cox, Brian, and Clara (2006), for instance, found that indeed neuroticism was associated with significantly elevated rates of a wide range of physical disorders, such as arthritis, diabetes, kidney/liver disease, stomach/gall-bladder problems, and ulcer. Much of this association appears to be partially mediated by comorbid mental disorders, yet the association between the disorders persisted even after adjusting for differences in demographic characteristics and comorbid mental disorders.

How an individual's health and well-being are related to intimacy and social support (SS) has been noted by Reis and Franks (1994). They intended to (1) establish whether intimacy and SS were related to mental and physical health in a large, representative community sample and (2) determine whether intimacy (measured by Schaefer and Olson's PAIR scale) and SS make unique contributions to predicting health. Both hypotheses were pursued in an attempt to develop a model of the relation between these processes. Results strongly supported the initial hypothesis that intimacy and SS were both related to health status. These investigators also found that the effects of intimacy on well-being were mediated by SS, but that the effects of SS were not mediated by intimacy. Consequently, Reis and Franks (1994) concluded that the health-promoting benefits of intimacy most likely occur because intimate relationships are very likely to engender higher levels of SS.

Watson (2000, p. 270), however, identified general and specific positive and negative affect with health complaints. Generally, positive affect was negatively correlated with health complaints, whereas negative affect was positively correlated. Specifically, fear, sadness, guilt, and hostility were positively correlated with health complaints. Watson also presented personality characteristics as being positively correlated with visits to a health center (p. 283). He concluded his review chapter with the following statement:

> The data are complex and inconsistent. It is noteworthy, however, that all three models (about the relationship between emotionality and health) have received some support in the literature. It is clear, therefore, that none of these models – by itself – is able to offer a complete explanation for the findings in this area. Future investigators must strive to integrate them into a more comprehensive scheme that better captures the complex links between *negative emotionality* and health. (p. 292; italics mine)

Could we substitute hurt feelings for Watson's negative emotionality? If we were to include all the feelings listed in Table 1.1, perhaps we may obtain more consistent and relevant results as to their effects on specific physical conditions and overall psychological functioning rather than grouping them in one construct called "expressed emotions." Both aging processes and psychological stress affect the immune system: Each process can dysregulate immune functions with a substantial impact on physical health (Graham, Christian, & Kiecolt-Graser, 2006). Worse, the effects of stress and age are interactive. Psychological stress can both mimic and exacerbate the effects of aging, with older adults often showing greater immunological impairment to stress than younger adults. In addition, stressful experiences very early in life can alter the responsiveness of the nervous and immune systems. Graham et al. reviewed the unique impact of aging and stress on immune functions, followed by evidence of interactions between age and stress. Further, these authors suggested that prenatal or early life stress may increase the likelihood of maladaptive immune responses to stress in later life. An understanding of the interactive effects of age and stress is critical to efforts to determine underlying mechanisms, clarify the directionality of effects, and develop effective interventions in early and late life. This understanding is provided in part by Uchino (2006; Chapter 11 of this volume).

Physicians as human beings are not immune to hurt feelings. Hareli, Karnieli-Miller, Hernoni, and Eidelman (2007) explored the emotional effect of the injury experienced by physicians as a consequence of a patient's termination of their relationship. These investigators distributed a vignette using different scenarios describing a patient who switched to another doctor to 119 family physicians, who answered an open question asking of situations that elicited negative emotions. The results indicated that termination of a relationship by a high status patient and/or after a long duration is more emotionally hurtful that termination by a lower status patient after a brief relationship. The results of the open question provided an additional insight into the emotional impact of the doctor's hurt feelings on the doctor-patient relationship. Too many terminations of this kind may have long-term effects on the physician's functioning and the onset of possible burnout.

HURT FEELINGS AND PHYSICAL ILLNESS

Specific illnesses will be included here with the already-stated assumption that most references relate to *presumed* rather than *actual* hurt feelings.

Hurt Feelings and Alexithymia

Bertholz, Artiges, Van de Moortele, Poline, et al. (2002) searched for differential regional activation in response to emotional stimuli in participants with alexithymia, the inability to be aware and express feelings of any kind. Two groups of eight men each were selected from 437 healthy participants on the basis of high or low scores on the twenty-item Toronto Alexithymia Scale. Using functional magnetic resonance imaging, these investigators compared the two groups for their regional cerebral activation in response to pictures with validated positive and negative arousal capabilities. Men with alexithymia demonstrated less cerebral activation in the left mediofrontal-paracingulate cortex in response to highly negative stimuli and more activation in the anterior cingulated and mediofrontal cortex, as well as middle frontal gyrus in response to highly positive stimuli than men without alexithymia. These findings provide direct evidence that alexithymia, a personality trait playing a role in affect regulation, is linked with differences in anterior cingulate and mediofrontal activity during the processing of emotional stimuli.

Hurt Feelings, AIDS, and HIV

AIDS and HIV do not occur in a vacuum (Elwood, 2002; Haas, 2002; Harvey & Wenzel, 2002). They occur within the context of personal and social relationships (Greene, Frey, & Derlega, 2002). Four major themes highlight such a conclusion: (1) the changing nature of HIV and AIDS from relatively short- to long-term, chronic illnesses; (2) the importance of personal and social relationships for those living with these illnesses; (3) the effects of these illnesses on the personal and social relationships of minorities and women in particular; and (4) the continuing stigma and coping with stigma that permeate the lives of those living with HIV and/or AIDS.

Because reviewing the research on these illnesses would occupy more space than can be allotted, I shall limit myself to consider relevant studies available in one single issue of the *Journal of Social and Personal Relationships* (2002).

Hurt Feelings and Cancer

Even though emotional expression and cognitive efforts to adapt to cancer have been linked to better psychological adjustment, little is still known about the relation between linguistic indicators of emotional and cognitive coping efforts and corresponding self-report measures of related constructs. For instance, Owen, Giese-Davis, Cordova, Kronenwetter, et al. (2006) sought to evaluate the interrelationships between self-reports of emotional suppression and linguistic indicators of emotional and cognitive coping efforts in those living with cancer. Although this study was conducted with individuals, one cannot conceive of this disease occurring in a relational vacuum. Nonetheless, this study was included in this section because of its originality and potential contribution to research and treatment of cancer. Owen et al. found that self-reports of emotional suppression were associated with more rather than less distress. Although linguistic indicators of both emotional expression and cognitive processing were generally uncorrelated with self-report measures of emotional suppression and mood disturbance, a significant intcraction was observed between emotional suppression and use of cognitive words on mood disturbance. Among those participants using higher levels of emotional suppression, increasing use of cognitive words was associated with greater levels of mood disturbance.

Children and Youth: A meta-analysis of the influence of pediatric cancer on parent and family functioning (Pai, Greenley, Lewandosky, Drotar, et al., 2007) found that mothers and fathers of children newly diagnosed with cancer reported significantly greater distress than comparison samples with mothers reporting greater distress than fathers up to twelve months post diagnosis. These mothers also reported higher levels of family conflict than mothers of healthy children.

Kasak, Christakis, Alderfer, and Coiro (1994) investigated adjustment in ten- to fifteen-year-old long-term survivors of childhood cancer and their parents (N = 59) at two points one year apart. Behavioral concerns, parental distress, anxiety, hopelessness, SS, and family functioning were assessed. Gender and the presence of learning problems were also examined. The data indicated levels of adjustment that were near normative levels. However, gender differences were found, with male adolescents reporting low levels of anxiety and hopelessness. Those survivors with learning difficulties appeared particularly vulnerable with respect to long-term adjustment.

Robinson, Gerhardt, Vannata, and Noll (2009), for instance, examined family predictors of distress among survivors of childhood cancer and comparison peers during the transition to emerging adulthood. Children with cancer (N = 55) comparison peers (N = 60) and parents completed measures of distress, family environment, social support, and demographic characteristics during initial treatment, as well as follow-up measures of young adult distress and demographic characteristics soon after participants turned eighteen years old. Severity of initial treatment and late effects were rated by health-care providers for participants with cancer. For all participants, mother and father report of initial parent distress was associated with their report of young adult distress at follow-up. Young adult gender moderated this association. For survivors of childhood cancer, severity of initial treatment and late effects also moderated the association between parent and young adult distress. Improving parent distress may help reduce child distress in general. For survivors specifically, ameliorating the impact of initial treatment and long-term physical problems may be beneficial.

Couples: Kuijer, Buunk, and Ybema (2001) examined to what extent couples facing cancer (N = 55) and healthy couples (N = 74) perceived various distributions of give-and-take to be just or fair when occurring within a relationship of a cancer patient and his or her partner. Participants read one of three versions of a bogus interview with a couple facing cancer. In these scenarios, both partners were either equally well off in terms of give-and-take or one partner was better off than the other. In general, participants judged the equitable situation to be the fairest. Thus, even in a situation in which one partner of a couple has cancer, people generally judge a relationship in which both partners mutually support each other to be the fairest. Only in extreme situations (i.e., if the patient were in a bad condition) did participants regard a distribution according to need fairer than a distribution according to equity. Couples facing cancer and healthy couples did not differ in their judgments. In addition, regarding emotional responses to the scenarios, consistent with equity theory, participants expected to feel more guilty in an overbenefited situation. In contrast to equity theory, however, participants did not expect to feel especially angry or sad in an underbenefited situation.

Helgeson, Novak, Lepre, and Eton (2004) measured perceptions of wives' attempts to encourage appropriate health behavior among men with prostate cancer, a phenomenon known as "social control." These investigators examined social control for health-enhancing behaviors (e.g., exercise), health-restorative behaviors (e.g., sleep), and health-compromising behaviors (e.g., smoking). They interviewed eighty married men with prostate cancer shortly after treatment and two and eight months later. Social control was distinct from social support and social conflict. There was no evidence that spouse social control was effective in producing positive changes in health behavior. In fact, health-restorative and health-compromising social controls were associated with poor health behavior. There were no relations between social control and changes in health behavior over time. Spouse social control was associated with greater psychological distress, especially health-restorative and health-compromising social control. There was some evidence that social control undermined personal control beliefs over time. Future research should consider examining differences in the way that social control is conveyed, so that we might better understand its relations to health behavior and well-being.

Protective buffering is defined as hiding worries, denying concerns, and yielding to one's partner in order to avoid disagreement and reduce one's partner upset and burden (Manne, Norton, Ostroff, Winkel, et al., 2007). These authors hypothesized that protective buffering would result in more distress among patients (N = 235) diagnosed with early-stage breast cancer and in their partners reporting higher relationship satisfaction than among patients and partners reporting lower levels of relationship satisfaction. Even though this hypothesis was found valid for patients with higher relationship satisfaction, buffering did not predict distress among patients rating their relationships as less satisfactory. Partner relationship satisfaction also moderated the association between patients' buffering and partner distress. Therefore, it appears that under certain conditions, protective buffering may have detrimental effects.

Families: Analysis of a corpus of family phone calls reveals how family members routinely address uncertain issues when attempting to understand cancer diagnosis, treatment, and prognosis (Beach & Good, 2004). A large collection of moments were overviewed and organized by Beach and Good into three prominent social activities: (1) biomedical reporting about anonymous medical staff; (2) references to physicians in anticipation of explanations; and (3) assessing the care provided by physicians and medical staff. Specific attention was drawn to how reporting included lay depictions about lack of knowledge, ambiguities associated with the passage of time, and emergent troubles with pain and medication. These instances make clear how family cancer journeys are interactively organized events, composed of distinct communication practices for raising and resolving illness dilemmas.

Alverfer, Navsaria, and Kasak (2009) investigated family functioning and relationships between family functioning and posttraumatic stress disorder (PTSD) in 144 adolescent survivors of childhood cancer one to twelve years post cancer treatment (M = 5.3 months). To assess family functioning, their parents completed the Family Assessment Devise (FAD), and to assess PTSD, adolescents were administered a structured diagnostic interview. Nearly half (47 percent) of the adolescents, one-fourth (25 percent) of mothers, and one-third (30 percent) of fathers reported poor family functioning, exceeding the clinical cutoff on four or more FAD subscales. Families in which the cancer survivor had PTSD (8 percent of the sample) had poorer functioning than other families in the areas of problem solving, affective responsiveness, and affective involvement. Three-fourths of the adolescents with PTSD came from families with categorically poor family functioning. A surprisingly high rate of poor family functioning was reported in these families of adolescent cancer survivors. Adolescents with PTSD were more than five times as likely to emerge from a poorly functioning family compared with a well-functioning one. The results of this study provide evidence that family functioning is related to cancer-related posttraumatic reactions in adolescent survivors.

Cancer and Social Support: Knowledge about how social support (SS) operates under specific circumstances lags behind the amount of research on the relationship between SS and well-being (Komproe, Rijken, Ros, Winnubst, et al., 1997). Therefore, those investigators set out to study the mechanisms through which SS influences psychological well-being under stressful circumstances. Komproe at al. (1997) distinguished between perceived available support and received support in evaluating a hypothetical model specifying the direct and indirect effects of support on depression of recently diagnosed breast cancer patients. Results showed that available support has direct beneficial effects on depression and received support has indirect effects via appraisal and coping. Moreover, dependent on the type of support and coping strategy, other effects of available and received support were found.

Using a retrospective design, Ptacek, Pierce, Dodge, and Ptacek (1997) assessed several aspects of SS, such as perceived support, received support, satisfaction with received support, and support seeking in ninety-five spouses of cancer survivors. Goals of this investigation were to (1) describe in detail the differences between husbands and wives on these support dimension, and (2) explore whether the relation between support and adjustment was different for husbands as compared to wives. Whereas husbands and wives were generally similar in their general perceptions of available support and in the amount of support they reported seeking, consistent with these investigators' hypothesis, compared to husbands of breast cancer victims, wives of prostate cancer victims reported receiving more support and being more satisfied with the support they received. Measures of SS predicted husbands' reports of marital satisfaction and adjustment, but not wives' reports. Gender differences in their support-adjustment links were not attributable to differences in age or in the time between completing treatment and participating in the study. The gender differences observed in the present study could be interpreted as highlighting the need for theory development to account for the complex mechanisms underlying links between supportive transactions and marital satisfaction and adjustment.

Hurt Feelings and Cardiovascular Reactivity

Stress related to relationship events has been a strong predictor of cardiovascular reactivity (Coyne, Rohrbaugh, Shoham, Sonnega, et al., 2001). A four-phase laboratory study (Kim, 2006) used a multinested design to examine variations in diastolic blood pressure (DBP) and rate-pressure product as a function of stress appraisal using thirty-three college-aged dating couples. Individual participants filled out questionnaires designed to assess (1) the length of their relationships (couple-level factor) and (2) gender and attachment styles (individual-level factors); they then (3) watched a film clip depicting relationship distress and (4) discussed relationship problems; they then received instructions for relaxation. Individuals' self-reported stress and *negative affect* levels (experimental phase-level factors),

DPB, SBP, and PR were also measured at each study phase. Hierarchical linear modeling analyses revealed that relationships with longer duration were associated with higher levels of DBP and RPP as perceived stress levels increased. Also, as perceived stress levels increased, men or individuals high in the anxiety dimension of attachment showed higher DBP and RPP reactivity, whereas individuals high in the avoidance dimension of attachment showed lower RPP reactivity. These findings imply that under relationship stress, individuals high in avoidance or anxiety dimensions of attachment may be vulnerable to a range of physical symptoms, such as cardiovascular disease or hypertension.

Hurt Feelings and Myocardial Infarction

Coyne and Smith (1991, 1994) examined perceived self-efficacy in men six months after a myocardial infarction. Patient efficacy was positively correlated with their degree of dependence on their wives and to the men's activity engaging their wives but their doing less protective buffering. Patient efficacy was also related to their wives being more efficacious and doing more protective buffering but being less overprotective. The asymmetry in patient and wife contribution to patient efficacy is noteworthy, given previous findings that wives' protective buffering is associated with greater distress in them.

Hurt Feelings and Chronic Constructive Airway Disease

Couples in which one spouse has chronic obstructive airway disease face great distress and change over the life course (Unger, Jacobs, & Cannon, 1996). Couples experience multiple losses and feelings of anxiety, depression, and hopelessness, usually beginning in mid-life and continuing into older age. Unger et al. (1996) explored two sources of SS from family and friends as resources for coping with illness. The relation of family's and friends' received and provided support with marital satisfaction and the effects of sex and length of marriage were studied. Results indicated that the association between support and marital satisfaction was moderated by the couple's length of marriage, the gender of patients and spouses, and the degree of congruency between husbands' and wives' evaluation of their marital satisfaction. Support acted as a stress buffer in regard to marital satisfaction only for male spouses and male patients.

Hurt Feelings and Spina Bifida

Jandasek, Holmbeck, DeLucia, Zebracki, et al. (2009) investigated change in family processes, including conflict, cohesion, and stress, across the adolescent transition, comparing the developmental trajectories of youth with and without spina bifida. Unfortunately, this study did not evaluate emotional factors directly. However, it is included here to serve as a benchmark for future research about emotionality in this severe physical condition that likely may effect families adversely. Individual growth curves modeling procedures were utilized to describe the developmental course of family processes across four waves of data collection, from ages nine to fifteen years, and to test whether illness status (spina bifida) versus matched comparison group ($N = 68$ for both groups at Time 1) would significantly predict individual variability in family processes. Potential moderators (child gender, socioeconomic status, and child verbal ability) of the association between illness status and family functioning were also examined. Differences were found between the trajectories of family processes for families of youth with and without spina bifida. For families of youth with spina bifida, changes in family conflict and cohesion may be less dramatic than or inconsistent with what is expected during typical adolescence. Families of youth with spina bifida from low SES homes appear to demonstrate resilience in terms of family stress.

Hurt Feelings, Physical Health, and Trauma

Research traditionally has focused on the development of individual symptoms in those who experienced trauma directly but has overlooked the interpersonal impact of trauma. Goff, Crow, Reisbig, and Hamilton (2007) reported data from forty-five U.S. Army veterans who recently returned from Iraq or Afghanistan and their partners/spouses. Past war traumas produced increased sleep problems, dissociation, and severe sexual problems in the soldiers, significantly predicting lower marital/relationship satisfaction for soldiers and partners. These results indicate how individual trauma symptoms negatively impact relationship satisfaction in military couples in which the husband has been exposed to war trauma. Physical health symptoms in women ($N = 388$) are also associated with intimate partner aggression (Taft, Vogt, Mechanic, & Resik, 2007). These authors found PTSD symptoms, such as anger/irritability, to fully mediate such an association.

Hurt Feelings and Stroke

Clark and Stephens (1996) examined the perceptions that fifty-five older married patients had about themselves and about the motivations of their caregiving spouses when they judged their spouses' actions to be helpful and when they judged them to be unhelpful. These investigators also examined how these perceptions were related to patients' well-being (depression, positive affect, marital satisfaction). Patients had more negative perceptions of themselves and of their spouses when they judged the actions to be unhelpful. The hypothesis that perceptions about unhelpful actions would be more strongly related to patients' well-being than would perceptions about helpful actions was only partially supported. Perceptions about unhelpful actions were related to patient's depression, but perceptions about helpful actions were related to positive affect. Both kinds of perceptions were related to marital satisfaction. These findings began to explicate the complex relation between perceived helpfulness of actions and well-being.

Hurt Feelings and Social Support in Physical Sickness

Throughout the lifespan, the everyday interactions among family members have the potential to have a tremendous impact on individuals' construction of health, talk about health, participation in health-care systems, enactment of healthy or unhealthy behaviors, and health *status*. (Bylund & Duck, 2004, p. 5)

In line with the findings by Graham et al. (2006) reported earlier, Hill, Stein, Keenan, and Wakschlag (2006) examined the association between positive and negative aspects of childrearing history and current parenting as well as the moderating effects of current stress on seventy mother-child dyads. These investigators found modest support for a direct association between positive childrearing experiences and more positive current parenting. Stress moderated the associations between both positive and negative childrearing experiences and current parenting: Stress exacerbated the negative effects of high-conflict histories whereas positive histories protected against the effects of current stress. These results highlight the importance of studying the influence of early experience on parenting within the context of current life stresses.

Although this topic will be covered in Chapter 11, it is relevant to include this link here when we are dealing with physical illness, where support, especially in spouses, is paramount to a successful recovery (Fekete, Stephens, Druly, & Greene, 2006; Franks, Stephens, Rook, Franklin, et al.,

2006). Masters, Stillman, and Spielman (2007), for example, examined low-back-pain patients' (N = 50) perceptions of what they considered to be helpful and unhelpful SS from various sources over the previous six months. Among types of SS, tangible support was most likely to be rated as helpful, whereas emotional support was more likely to be rated as unhelpful. Patients reported only rare instances of dissatisfaction with tangible support across various providers. Among support sources, instances of tangible support from physicians and emotional support from friends, family and spouses were recalled as most helpful. Physical therapists were named as providing the greatest amount of all three types of social support and were rated as rarely providing unhelpful social support. These findings suggest that the desirability of different types of SS varies as a function of the source of support and indicate that physical therapists are perceived by low-back-pain patients as particularly helpful in their provision of social support.

Caregiver burnout is inevitable when dealing with prolonged and chronic illness. Ybema, Kuijer, Hagedoorn, and Buunk (2002) assessed caregiver burnout among intimate partners of 106 cancer and 88 patients with multiple sclerosis. These investigators examined how burnout is related to marital quality and perceptions of inequity in the relationship, finding that higher perceptions of inequity are strongly associated with higher emotional exhaustion and depersonalization and lower feelings of personal accomplishment. Intimate partners of both cancer patients and patients with multiple sclerosis are relatively likely to experience burnout when they feel that they did not invest or benefit enough in the exchange with their ill partner. The relationship between inequity and burnout held when general marital quality, gender, the duration of the illness, the physical and psychological condition of the ill partner, and support from other persons were controlled for. This study shows that the perception of equity or balance in the relationship between patients and their intimate partners are important for preventing caregiver burnout and for enhancing positive caregiver experiences.

HURT FEELINGS IN MENTAL HEALTH

Early identification of disease and intervention when necessary are a cornerstone of contemporary medical practice. The approach has been successful in reducing suffering associated with the progression of unchecked medical problems to full-blown disease. Many health-care systems, in turn, support this approach via routine checkups. The same cannot be said for mental health care. Fox, Halpern, and Forsyth (2008) evaluated a school-based mental health checkup approach in the context of anxiety and depression in children and adolescents. These researchers outlined how checkups can identity children with emotional disorders and with risk factors that, if left unchecked, may contribute to the eventual onset of the disorder.

Although clinical observations suggest that health-related anxiety is present to some extent in a number of anxiety disorders, the relationship has not been examined empirically. Abramowitz, Olatunji, and Deacon (2007), therefore, utilized the Short Health Anxiety Inventory (SHAI) to elucidate the structure of such symptoms among patients with anxiety disorders and to investigate empirically the presence of health anxiety in various anxiety disorders. Confirmatory factor analysis yielded equivalent support for either a two- or three-factor model of the SHAI's latent structure. The measure demonstrated good reliability and convergent and discriminant validities. Comparison of SHAI scores across groups of patients with various anxiety disorders revealed elevated levels of health anxiety among patients with hypochondriasis and panic disorder relative to those with other anxiety disorders. Receiver operating characteristic analyses supported the utility of the SHAI as a diagnostic tool utilizing empirically derived cut scores for screening patients with hypochondriasis.

An example of the principles of equifinality and equipotentiality is found in the research by Hibel, Granger, Blair, and Cox (2009). They examined the relationship of mother and infant adrenocortical levels and reactivity to an emotion-eliciting task. The impact of intimate partner violence (IPV) on these relationships was assessed as a moderator. The samplc (N = 702 mother-infant dyads) was racially diverse and from predominantly lower-class, rural communities. During a home visit, the dyad's saliva was sampled before twenty-minute and forty-minute standardized tasks designed to elicit the infant's emotional arousal and later assayed for cortisol. Mothers completed self-report measures of their partner's violence, and parenting behaviors were assessed via a structural interview and observations of mother-infant interactions. In response to the task, infants had positive and mothers has negative cortisol slopes. Contrary to expectations, there were no IPV-related differences in mean pretask cortisol levels on reactivity in the mothers or infants. Mother-infant dyads from households characterized by either violence or restrictive and punitive parenting behaviors exhibited correlated cortisol reactivity measured in response to the infant challenge task. These findings suggest that social contextual features of the early caregiving environment may influence individual differences in the *coordination* between maternal and infant adrenocortical reactivity.

Hurt Feelings and Alexithymia

Although alexithymia has already been considered as a physical condition, its ubiquitous role in mental health is too important to overlook. Affection has been found to be a fundamental force in any sort of human relationship, influencing such areas as relational closeness, stress, and depression. One psychological condition that may influence the communication of affection is alexithymia, which hinders the ability of an individual both to experience feelings and to express them as emotions. On the basis of affection exchange theory, Hesse and Floyd (2008) hypothesized a mediating effect of affectionate communication on the association between alexithymia and relational and mental health indices. Participants (N = 347) provided self-reports of alexithymia, affectionate communication, depression, stress, relational closeness, nonverbal immediacy, happiness, and relational affection. Findings implicated affectionate communication as a mediator of the relationship between alexithymia and several of the outcome measures. Addictions may be one way to mask hurt feelings that cannot be expressed (Duncan, Duncan, & Hops, 1996).

Hurt Feelings and Expressed Emotions

Expressed Emotions (EE) include any criticism, name calling, and abusive language directed against someone, frequently found in the relapse of patients with schizophrenia. As assessed by a five-minute speech sample, level of EE in parents significantly discriminated between families of seven- to sixteen-year-old children who were referred for mental health treatment and a nonclinical comparison group; however, both groups contained a relatively high proportion of high EE families (Abela, Skitch, Adams, & Hankin, 2006; Cheavens, Rosenthal, Daughters, Nowak, et al., 2005; Hooley & Parker, 2006; Koss-Chioino & Canive, 1996; Nelson, Hammen, Brennan, & Ullman, 2003). Furthermore, EE independently predicted clinical/nonclinical group status when considered in conjunction with overall family functioning and level of psychological distress in mothers. These findings support the relevance of EE, although the measure showed poor specificity and an analysis of the components that comprise the EE Index indicated that only certain components were pertinent. Consequently, it is important to reassess the meaning of the EE construct and strengthen its applicability for the general clinical population of children and their families.

Previous research by Coyne, Rohrbaugh, Shoham, Sonnega, et al., (2001) that suggested that marital functioning predicted mortality among patients with chronic heart failure led to an examination by Benazon, Foster, and Coyne (2006) of whether EE captured negative marital influences on patient survival. These investigators assessed EE using five-minute speech samples obtained from patients (137 men and 47 women) and their spouses. Prevalence of EE was low, and patient and spouse EE were unrelated. Spouse EE was not related to survival, after the authors controlled for severity of illness. Among patient EE variables, high EE status predicted survival, but in the opposite direction of what was anticipated. Overall, relations between EE and self-report measures of adaptation were weak and inconsistent. Despite the strength of findings concerning EE and psychiatric outcomes, EE did not show promise in predicting adaptation to chronic heart failure. Researchers and clinicians should instead seek to identify positive marital factors that may promote patient survival.

These contradictory and relatively weak results raise the question of whether EE should be used specifically with families for which this measure was developed, that is, families of individuals with schizophrenic disorder (Nicholson, 1997), rather than trying to expand its supposed usefulness to families where such feelings are not expected to exist.

Hurt Feelings and Posttraumatic Stress Disorder

Miller, Vogt, Mozicy, Kaloupek, et al. (2006) examined competing hypotheses regarding the role of two personality dimensions, disconstraint and negative affectivity, in mediating the relationship between PTSD and substance-related problems. Data were drawn from a large sample of male Vietnam War veterans. The best fitting structural model included significant indirect paths from PTSD to both alcohol and drug-related outcomes through disconstraint, and a significant indirect path from PTSD to alcohol-related problems through negative emotionality. There were no direct effects of PTSD on either substance-related outcomes. These findings indicate distinct pathways to different forms of substance-related problems in PTSD and underscore the role of personality in mediating these relationships.

Throughout history warriors have been confronted with moral and ethical challenges, and modern unconventional and guerilla wars amplify these challenges (Litz, Stein, Delaney, Lebowitz, Nash, Silva, & Maguen, 2009). Partially morally injurious events, such as perpetrating, failing to prevent or report, and bearing witness to acts that transgress deeply held moral beliefs and expectations may be deleterious in the long term, emotionally, psychologically, behaviorally, spiritually, and socially (what Litz et al., 2009, labeled as "moral injury"). Although there has been some research on the consequences of unnecessary acts of violence in war zones, the lasting impact of morally injurious experience in war has remained largely undressed. To stimulate a critical examination of moral injury, Litz et al. (2009) reviewed the available literature, defined terms, and offered a working conceptual framework and a set of intervention strategies designed to repair moral injury.

More specifically, Monson, Taft, and Fredman (2009) argued that military operations in Iraq and Afghanistan have brought heightened awareness of military-related PTSD, as well as the intimate relationship problems that accompany this disorder and can influence the course of veterans' trauma recovery. Monson et al. (2009) reviewed recent research that documents the association between PTSD and intimate relationship problems in the most recent cohort of returning veterans, and also synthesized research from previous eras to inform future research and treatment efforts with recently returned veterans and their families. These authors highlighted the need for more theoretically driven research that can account for the likely reciprocally causal association between PTSD and intimate relationship problems; such research could advance understanding and inform prevention and treatment efforts for veterans and their families (Ehlers, 2006). To the point of prevention and treatment for PTSD, in addition to what is presented in Chapters 12 and 13 of this volume, the interested reader may want to consult the review of psychological and pharmacological treatments included in Cukor, Spitalnick, Difede, Rizzo, et al. (2009).

Hurt Feelings and Sexual Abuse

Maniglio (2009) reviewed studies and literature reviews from the last twenty years on how childhood sexual abuse effects health: He reviewed the "best available scientific evidence" (p. 647) to include studies and reviews worthy of inclusion in his review. On the basis of fourteen reviews that included 270,000 participants from 587 studies, he concluded that "There is evidence that survivors of childhood sexual abuse are significantly at risk of a wide range of medical, psychological, behavioral, and sexual disorders ... and psychopathology" (p. 647).

Hurt Feelings and Loss of Contact

Grandparents who lose contact with their grandchildren, due to parental separation or divorce, family feud, or sudden event such as relocation, experienced a steeper increase in depressive symptoms for up to three years as compared with other grandparents who did not experience such a loss (Drew & Silverstein, 2007).

Hurt Feelings and Sons of Psychiatric Patients

Wichstrom, Holte, Husby, and Wynne (1994) claimed to be the first researchers to investigate the effects of family communication on changes in offspring competence. Families (N = 46) in which at least one parent had been diagnosed with a functional psychiatric disorder were examined. Male index offspring's (seven to ten years of age at initial testing) competence was assessed by peers, teachers, parents, and the Wechsler Intelligence Scale for Children at the initial testing (Time 1) and at a three-year follow-up (Time 2). Family communication was observed by means of the Consensus Family Rorschach procedure. During this testing, both parents and all of the children more than four years living at home were present. Results showed that the more disqualifying the communication index offspring received from his family at Time 1, the less favorable was the development in social competence during the three years from Time 1 to Time 2. However, changes in cognitive competence from Time 1 to Time 2 were not associated with family communication. This study indicates how crucial is the relationship between pathological parents in their direct effects on their children (Cohler & Musik, 1983).

Hurt Feelings and Memory

Long-term memories are influenced by the emotion experienced during learning as well as by the emotion experienced during memory retrieval. Buchanan (2007) reviewed the literature addressing the effects of emotion on retrieval, focusing on the cognitive and neurological mechanisms that have been revealed. The reviewed research suggested that the amygdala, in combination with the hippocampus and prefrontal cortex, plays an important role in the retrieval of memories for emotional events. The neural regions necessary for online emotional processing also influence emotional memory retrieval, perhaps through the reexperience of emotion during the retrieval process (Kensinger, 2009).

Hurt Feelings: Forgiveness and Intimacy in Physical and Mental Health

> Forgiveness is associated with positive mental health outcomes in numerous studies.
>
> (Branthwaite, Fincham, & Lambert, 2009, p. 390)

The topic of forgiveness had been avoided by the scientific and professional literatures until it was included in a systematic family therapy work leading to an original workbook on intimacy, where three homework assignments, now renamed "interactive practice exercises," were devoted to hurt feelings and forgiveness (L'Abate, 1986). Yet the process of forgiveness is founded on the very original definition of sharing hurt feelings and fears of being hurt. There cannot be forgiveness unless there has been a sharing of whatever error and transgression that produced hurtful feelings (Cann & Baucom, 2004; Gordon, Hughes, Tomcik, Dixon, et al., 2009), and then only if there is a sufficiently high reservoir of "good" feelings to offset the "bad" ones (Hodgson & Wertheim, 2007).

Individuals: What do laypersons think about forgiveness? Younger, Piferi, Jobe, & Lawler, (2004, p. 842) found lay persons perceived the following about forgiveness and nonforgiveness: (1) Definitions of forgiveness were marked by acceptance, dealing with it, getting over it, coming to terms, and moving on. (2) Reasons for forgiving were attributed to importance of relationship, sake of personal health and/or happiness, need to be forgiven for hurts inflicted on others, offender apologized or felt sorry, religious or spiritual beliefs, avoidance of conflict, and striving for peace. (3) Reasons to not forgive included restatement of offense, offender lack of remorse/apology, offender character that does not deserve forgiveness, ongoing event and damage, severity of unforgivable event.

This topic was also explored by Friesen and Fletcher (2007) through four studies employing a prototype approach to test convergent and discriminant validity of a lay forgiveness representation. In study 1, participants nominated a wide range of forgiveness features. In study 2, participants rated the centrality of forgiveness features, which created a reliable graded structure from central to peripheral features. Study 3 tested the convergent validity of the lay forgiveness representation while controlling for various confounding variables. In study 4, the discriminant validity of the lay forgiveness representation was tested through a categorization procedure. The findings replicate and extend prior research on forgiveness (Kearns & Fincham, 2002) and support the psychological reality of a lay forgiveness representation distinct from other victim responses.

How can forgiveness occur unless there is a sharing of hurt feelings from real or perceived transgressions? With whom should such forgiveness occur? Usually it occurs with the very people who have hurt us or whom we have hurt. We do not need, nor might we have occasion, to forgive strangers. Forgiveness, therefore, occurs within the context of intimate relationships (Fincham, 2000; Root & McCullough, 2007). As already noted, it is questionable whether forgiveness and intimacy can occur unless there is a (reciprocal) sharing of joys as well as of hurt feelings and fears of being hurt (Fincham & Beach, 2002a, 2002b; L'Abate, 1986, 1997, 1999a, 2005; Vangelisti & Beck, 2007).

Maltby, Macaskill, and Gillett (2007) investigated forgiveness in a traditional cognitive model of stress appraisal and coping as well as in a more recent model that includes the construct of low-control stressors. One-hundred sixty six men and 168 women completed measures of forgiveness, primary stress appraisals, and coping strategies. For men, forgiveness was found to be positively associated with the use of challenge appraisals and emotion-focused coping. For women, forgiveness was found to be positively associated with emotion-focused coping and acceptance and negatively associated with avoidance. The results for women indicate that when forgiveness situations are conceptualized as low-control stressors, Maltby et al. were able to explain the relationships between forgiveness, appraisal and coping. The results for men are broadly in line with a more traditional model of coping, which does not consider the construct of low control. Crucial differences in the way that men and women appraise and cope with situations involving forgiveness should be related to gender differences discussed in Chapter 9.

Many conceptualizations of forgiveness currently exist in the relevant literature previously reviewed. On the other hand, Hodgson and Wertheim (2007) argued that the ability to forgive is important in the successful maintenance of relationships. These investigators used a multifactorial model predicting two forms of forgiveness in a combined community and university sample (N = 110) who reported on their ability to manage emotions, tendency to empathize (through perspective taking, empathic concern, and personal distress), and disposition to forgive others and self. Findings suggested that the ability to manage and repair emotions predicted a greater disposition to forgive, and that perspective taking mediated the relationship between emotion management and forgiveness of others. Another multifactorial model for other forgiveness was completely replicated in significant others' (N = 104) reports about participants, although significant others' results only partially replicated participant findings for self-forgiveness.

Couples: Given the positive benefits associated with interpersonal forgiveness, Kachadourian, Fincham, and Davila (2004) examined the tendency to forgive in romantic relationships. Two studies tested the hypothesis that the tendency to forgive mediates the association between attachment models of self and other and relationship satisfaction in dating (N = 184) and marital relationships (N = 96). In addition, the extent to which the tendency to forgive predicts forgiveness of an actual transgression was examined among married couples. The tendency to forgive partially mediated the relation between model of other (relationship partner) and satisfaction for those in dating relationships and for husbands. For those in marital relationships, the tendency to forgive partially mediated the relation between model of self and satisfaction. In addition, for wives, endorsing a greater tendency to forgive was related to forgiveness of an actual transgression, regardless of the severity of the transgression, but only for more severe transgressions. It remains unclear who is more likely to forgive by gender, age, and education, as is the role that the tendency to forgive plays in romantic relationships.

To follow-up on the previous research, Fincham, Beach, and Davila (2007), using the same data from that study, attempted to answer the question: "Does forgiveness predict later conflict resolution in married couples?" Their answer was found in gender differences between spouses: For wives, the positive dimension of forgiveness or benevolence predicted husbands' later reports of better conflict resolution after controlling for initial levels of conflict resolution. This finding was independent of wives' marital satisfaction and the degree of hurt engendered by husbands' transgressions. For husbands, the only predictor of wives' reports of later conflict resolution was initial level of conflict resolution. These results tend to show that forgiveness does have a positive outcome in marital relationships.

Friesen, Fletcher, and Overall (2005) investigated forgiveness by examining couples' recollections and perceptions of specific incidents of transgressions in their relationship. Results replicated previous research but also produced new findings, showing that more positive attributions and relationship quality independently predicted higher internal forgiveness, whereas expressed forgiveness was related only to relationship quality. Overall, this sample was negatively biased in their perceptions of their partner's forgiveness, but those participants who tended toward a positive bias reported being happier with their relationships, as were their partners. This issue and related research is found in a model of forgiveness (L'Abate (1986, 1997, 1999a; L'Abate et al., 2010), as shown in Chapter 13 of this volume.

In an Italian sample of seventy-nine husbands and ninety-two wives from long-term marriages that provided data on the role of marital quality, affective reactions, and attributions for hypothetical partner transgressions in promoting forgiveness, Fincham, Paleari, and Regalia (2002) found that positive marital quality was predictive of more benign attributions that, in turn, facilitated forgiveness, both directly and indirectly, via affective reactions and emotional empathy. Unexpectedly, marital quality did not account for unique variance in forgiveness. Compared to husbands, wives' responsibility attributions were more predictive of forgiveness, whereas empathy was a better predictor of forgiveness in husbands than in wives. Too bad that a U.S. sample was not compared to establish a more reliable base for these findings and to furnish further cross-cultural comparisons.

As we have shown, researchers and therapists have argued that forgiveness is essential to the process of relationship reconciliation. Waldron and Kelley (2005) consequently described five types of forgiving communication reported by 187 members of romantic relationships. These investigators labeled these forms of forgiving communication as follows: (1) conditional; (2) minimizing; (3) discussion; (4) nonverbal display; and (5) explicit. As expected, forgivers recalled using more conditional and less minimizing types of communication when relational transgressions were severe. In addition, variations in reported forgiving communication were associated with relational outcomes. Partners who reported using conditional forms of communication also indicated that they experienced relationship deterioration after the forgiveness episode. In contrast, reported explicit and nonverbal forgiveness strategies were positively associated with relationship strengthening. These results were interpreted as further evidence that the role of communication behavior should be expanded in conceptual models of forgiveness and relationship reconciliation.

Families: Gordon, Hughes, Tomcik, Dixon, and Litzinger (2009) examined relations between aspects of family functioning and positive and negative dimensions of forgiveness. Increased understanding of one's partner and decreased anger about betrayal characterize positive forgiveness, whereas experiences such as holding a grudge and desiring revenge indicate negative forgiveness. Their sample included eighty-seven wives and seventy-four husbands who reported experiencing a significant betrayal from their partners and their adolescent children. Analyses of reported forgiveness revealed that more negative forgiveness was associated with lower marital satisfaction for husbands and wives; trust partially mediated their relationship. Greater positive forgiveness reported by husbands and wives predicted their own reports of a stronger parenting alliance, whereas greater negative forgiveness by husbands and wives predicted their spouses' reports of a weaker parenting alliance. For wives, more negative forgiveness also predicted higher levels of children's perceived parental conflict, and parents' reported conflict mediated this association for wives. These findings suggest that forgiveness of a marital betrayal is significantly associated with marital satisfaction, the parental alliance, and children's perceptions of parental marital functioning.

In a hermeneutic-phenomenological study (Ronel & Lebel, 2006), thirteen bereaved parents of fallen soldiers or victims of terrorism described their grief, anger, and forgiveness in relation to their struggle of personal loss. The findings indicate anger aroused by three sources as a major variable among participants: (1) circumstances of the loss; (2) institutionalized response to the loss; and (3) makers of a certain policy. A salient finding is that the "enemy," the target of the most anger, was never the one who actually killed their son, but a political leader who participants perceived to be responsible for the loss. Forgiveness was scarcely relevant to participants. A proposed explanation focused on the meaning of the respective representations of the dead child in the participants' inner and social worlds and their lack of readiness for the necessary transformation of that representation. Recommendations based on these findings include the institutionalized responses that may benefit the parents personally and assist them in reaching forgiveness and reconciliation with their defined enemy.

Forgiveness and SS

More recently, in reviewing the negative health effects of hurt feelings, Braithwaite, Fincham, and Lambert (2009, pp. 385–392) proposed an interesting model of forgiveness as a mediator of hurtful events and psychological well-being that includes: (1) the victim's self-esteem; (2) the nature of a hurtful event, which can be chronic, as in alcoholism, or discrete, as in infidelity; (3) the severity of the hurtful event; (4) the extent of rumination about the event; and (4) attributions made to the self or to the target person to be forgiven. This is an interesting model, but how do we help hurt people learn and cope with forgiveness? The effects of a six-week forgiveness intervention (Harris, Luskin, Norman, Standard, et al., 2006) were evaluated from three perspectives: (1) offense-specific forgiveness; (2) forgiveness likelihood in new situations; and (3) health-related psychosocial variables, such as perceived stress and trait anger. Participants were 259 adults who had experiences a hurtful interpersonal transgression from which they still felt negative consequences. They were randomly assigned to a forgiveness-training program or to a no-treatment control group. The intervention reduced negative thoughts and feelings about the target transgression two or three more times more effectively than the control condition, and it produced significantly greater increases in positive thoughts and feelings toward the transgressor. Significant treatment effects were also found for forgiveness self-efficacy, forgiveness generalized to new situations, perceived stress, and trait anger.

Finally, Romero (2008) applied Pennebaker's expressive writing (EW; Chapters 6 and 12 of this volume) to promote forgiveness that she defined as "forgoing destructive thoughts, feelings, and behaviors, and instead, engaging in constructive responses following an interpersonal offense" (p. 625). According to this definition, Romero (2008) compared two EW tasks with a control task to determine whether EW about an interpersonal offense promotes forgiveness of the offender. She found that participants who empathized with the offender and identified benefits of forgiveness experienced decreases in avoidance and increases in perspective taking. Participants who wrote about their thoughts and feelings or about daily events did not experience such forgiveness outcomes.

CONCLUSION

This chapter attempted to show how hurt feelings emerge into objective, physical events, as well as into negatively perceived behaviors such as mental health. Given the ubiquitous nature of these feelings, it is crucial to help hurt people (that is, most of us) learn how to forgive ourselves and loved ones, when we, sometimes unintentionally, hurt each other.

PART THREE

APPLICATIONS OF HURT FEELINGS
IN MENTAL HEALTH

An issue of major clinical significance is the importance of generating theory and research to help understand to what extent automatic emotion processes can be changed through deliberate conscious cognitive processes of self-control and to what extent they can only be changed through more implicit processes based on new emotional and/or relational experiences.

Greenberg (2007, p. 415)

This section will include many possible interventions available to qualified mental health professionals, ranging all the way from distance writing with workbooks, to Social Support in self-help, health promotion, and prevention of illness, to face-to-face, talk-based support (Chapter 11), and psychotherapy (Chapter 12).

11

Sharing Hurt Feelings in Social-Support: Self-Help, Health Promotion, and Prevention

> It can be therapeutic as well as healing for the bereaved to write their thoughts as they move through their grieving process.
>
> Weiss (2000, p. 5)

Theorists claim that emotional support is one of the most significant provisions of close relationships, and studies suggest that the receipt of sensitive emotional support is associated with diverse indices of well-being (Burleson, 2003). Research highlighting the beneficial outcomes of emotional support raises several important questions. Does emotional support play a similar role in the personal relationship of both men and women and those representing different ethnicities and nationalities? Is what counts as effective, sensitive, emotional support the same for everyone? When seeking to provide emotional support, do members of distinct social groups pursue similar or different goals?

Burleson (2003) attempted to answer these questions by reviewing and synthesizing empirical research assessing gender, ethnic, and cultural differences in emotional support in an effort to ascertain the extent and import of these differences. He particularly noted the attention given to demographic differences in (1) the value placed on the emotional support skills of relationship partners; (2) the intentions or goals viewed as especially relevant in emotional support situations; and (3) evaluation of distinct approaches to providing emotional support. Some of the issues reviewed by Burleson (2003) have been already considered in Chapters 9 and 10 of this volume. Nonetheless, the more specific purpose of this chapter is to review how SS fits into an overall framework of self-help, health promotion, and prevention, as three distinct tiers of change-related approaches.

SHARING OR SELF-DISCLOSURE?

Thus far previous chapters have been devoted to hurt feelings and fears of being hurt, either directly or indirectly. In this chapter, we shall concentrate on the missing term in the original definition of intimacy, that is, *sharing* (Rime', 2009a, 2009b). This simple, everyday term here stands for the more formal and frequently used but by now perhaps outdated term "self-disclosure," originally defined as the verbal transmission of personal information (Chaikin & Derlega, 1974a, 1974b; Derlega & Grzlak, 1979; Derlega, Metts, Petronio, & Margulis, 1993; Tolstedt & Stokes, 1984). Derlega and Chaikin (1977), for instance, argued that adjustment of self-disclosure outputs and inputs involves a process of boundary regulation: The extent of control one maintains over this exchange of information contributes to the amount of privacy one has in a social relationship. Regulation of interpersonal boundaries affects the kinds of relationship we maintain with others, intimates or nonintimates. Note, however, that in this literature, as far as I could discern, there was inclusion of what was being disclosed, such as thoughts, feelings, and experiences. However, this literature furnishes another example of how hurt feelings were specifically avoided, at least at that period in time. Fortunately, things have changed since then. Whether a professional helper should self-disclose depends a great deal on how participants are prepared to receive such disclosure as a reciprocal process (Derlega, Lovell, & Chaikin, 1976).

The process of sharing could occur mutually and reciprocally, as in long-term intimate relationships, or it could be used unilaterally, as in intimate and professional relationships, with one party disclosing hurt feelings and the other party listening, possibly empathizing, being available communally, and providing emotional as well as instrumental support when that support is needed (Bradford, Feeney, & Campbell, 2002). But what is social support (SS)? This question was answered in full by Saitzyk, Floyd, and Kroll's research (1997), which presented two circumplex models of Supporter behaviors consisting of two orthogonal dimensions of Emancipation versus Control and Attack versus Love, with Ignoring, Affirming, Blaming, and Protecting in the respective quadrants. Confider behaviors, on the other hand, consisted of two orthogonal dimensions of Separation versus Submission and Recoil versus Love, with Wall-offing, Disclosing, Sulking, and Trusting in the respective quadrants.

More specifically, Dolgin (1996) found that mothers disclosed more than did fathers, and they were more likely to cite "venting," "asking advice," and "seeking emotional support" as reasons for disclosure. Fathers were more likely to cite "trying to change his/her behavior" as a rationale for disclosure, but sons and daughters were disclosed to for different reasons. Divorced parents disclosed more than did parents from continuously intact families, and they cited somewhat different reasons for disclosure. Bauminger, Finzi-Dottan, Chason, and Har-Even (2008) found that self-disclosure and coherence interacted to influence intimacy, where a tendency toward self-disclosure seemed to contribute to intimacy to a greater extent at low levels of coherence. Self-disclosure, however, can mainly occur when there is trust between two partners; possible gender differences between male partner trust are best explained by his emotional reactivity toward his parents, whereas female partner trust might be best explained by her comfort with self-disclosure (Bartle, 1996).

In two studies, Gore, Cross, and Morris (2006) examined the role of relational self-construal in the development and maintenance of intimacy in roommate relationships. In study 1, ninety-eight roommate pairs completed questionnaires assessing attitudes toward their relationship. Results showed that high relationals disclosed more personal information than lows, which was then associated with their roommates' perceptions of relationship quality. In study 2, 142 roommate pairs followed the study 1 procedure with a three-month follow-up session for the 86 percent of participants who returned. Results replicated the findings of study 1 and showed reciprocated disclosure from the roommates, followed by increased disclosure by participants at Times 2. These findings tend to support Reis and Shaver's (1988) intimacy model and indicate the importance of the self-construal in this interpersonal process.

Hurt Feelings: Social Support and Secrecy

On the other end of a continuum of sharing, there is the process and outcome of keeping family secrets (Selvini, 1997; Vangelisti & Caughlin, 1997). Finkenauer and Hazam (2000), for instance, followed up on Vangelisti and Caughlin's (1997) results by proposing that secrecy, in addition to disclosure, should have a beneficial effect on satisfaction in close relationships. Disclosure and secrecy are determined by dispositional characteristics of relationship partners and by the unique relationship context in which they occur. Dispositional and contextual measures of disclosure and secrecy were included in a correlational study among seventy-three married participants in Belgium who spoke English and answered in response to the following questions: (1) Do dispositional measures of disclosure and secrecy predict marital satisfaction? (2) Do contextual measures of disclosure and secrecy predict marital satisfaction?

In addition, Finkenauer and Hazam examined to what extent dispositional measures of disclosure and secrecy predicted communicative behavior between partners. Results showed that dispositional measures contributed only marginally to marital satisfaction, whereas contextual measures strongly contributed to marital satisfaction. Contextual disclosure and secrecy independently contributed to marital satisfaction. Dispositional measures failed to predict communicative behavior between partners. These findings suggest that both disclosure and secrecy may be powerful mechanisms in marital relationships, and that it is the process that occurs when partners interact with each other, rather than the characteristics of either or both partners, that may effect marital satisfaction.

Furthermore, Foster and Campbell (2005) attempted to answer the question of whether secret romantic relationships are alluring or aversive. Previous research reviewed by these investigators suggests that secrecy (i.e., keeping a romantic relationship secret from others) creates a cognitive preoccupation that enhances romantic attraction. In contrast to that suggestion, Foster and Campbell (2005) predicted that romantic secrecy interferes with relationship interdependence and thereby decreases relationship quality. Three studies of secrecy in ongoing romantic relationships confirmed this prediction. In study 1, romantic secrecy predicted lower levels of initial quality and decreased relationship quality over a two-week period. In study 2, relationship burden mediated partially the negative association between romantic secrecy and relationship quality. In study 3, the negative association between romantic secrecy and relationship quality was primarily explained by decreased relationship satisfaction.

Using the construct and process of sharing will bring us to review selectively whatever approaches are available to decrease the toxic effects of hurt feelings in the population at large through self-help (Harwood & L'Abate, 2010) and in selected at-risk populations (L'Abate, 2007). Approaches not covered elsewhere but related specifically to SS will be included in this chapter.

THE PROXIMAL CONTEXT OF SOCIAL SUPPORT: SELF-HELP, PROMOTION, AND PREVENTION

This section about proximal context consists of a brief historical introduction and a selective review of SS research and applications.

A Brief Historical Introduction

A few years ago, Bradbury (2002a) opened a conceptual can of worms in relationship science by raising serious concerns about the integrity and viability of research on personal relationships without applications. These concerns include a lack of descriptive research and integration in research findings, neglect of ethnically and culturally diverse people and their relationships, inadequacies in sampling, and the absence of interdisciplinary research. Bradbury argued that progress in resolving these problems can be made and the relevance and rigor of relationship science could be enhanced by greater emphasis on *research that aims to improve personal relationships.* Relationship science devoted to the scientific study of interpersonal functioning should be uniquely positioned to address a vast array of problems that arise and impinge upon personal relationships. Failure to pursue the applied potential of relationship science will represent a lost opportunity to develop and demonstrate relationship scholars' expertise in this domain and thus to bring about desirable social change.

Bradbury listed and expanded on five advantages that would derive from an *applied approach* to relationships: (1) better samples; (2) more descriptions; (3) causal analyses; (4) stronger inferences; and (5) clearer criteria. He also supplied three examples of how an applied orientation could improve relationship research.

Among the three relationship scholars who were invited to comment on what seemingly appeared as a controversial position, Reis (2002) took issue with Bradbury's claims of better description, causal analyses, stronger inferences, and clearer criteria. In spite of these arguments, ultimately, however, Reis seemed to agree with Bradbury's position:

> To be sure, translation of basic research into effective interventions should be an important priority, not only to improve our science but also for the more obvious reason: The pressing need of practitioners and policy makers to have access to useful, empirically grounded information and tools. (p. 609)

In a second commentary, Muehlhoff and Wood (2002) agreed with and even admired Bradbury's position on four points: (1) the interpersonal character of many problems; (2) the value of case studies and interviews; (3) the need to move research beyond privileged groups; and (4) valuing research that aims for change. Both authors, however, raised some relevant concerns and questions that relate not only to Bradbury's position, but also to scholarship of relationships; Those questions were: (1) What is the place of theory in the field of relationship science? (2) Is immediate change the best measure of research? (3) Does change-oriented research resolve other problems? Issues of how to relate theory with research and link research with practical applications, however, were still kept open, a topic that will be considered in Chapter 13 of this volume.

In a third commentary, Hendrick (2002) pointed out that Bradbury's position was linked directly to the field of prevention: "[T]he field of close relationships should reorient to focus on *prevention*" (p. 621) as present in psychology and prevention with couples. To support his thesis, Hendrick presented a table (p. 623) with the frequencies of citations for selected terms from the PsycINFO database. These frequencies mounted into the thousands for prevention of couple and marital problems and divorce, among others, as well as for psychotherapy and marital therapy.

Bradbury's (2002b) response to the three commentaries highlighted several factors that may temper enthusiasm for a change-oriented research agenda, including: (1) uncertainty about which research findings ultimately will prove useful in devising interventions; (2) value judgments associated with determining which kinds of changes and outcomes are desirable; and (3) concerns that change-oriented research will undermine theory development. He argued that these factors may limit acceptance and complicate implementation of a change-oriented research agenda, yet they would not diminish the importance of such an agenda or the benefits it is likely to produce.

Instead of relying on an outdated division of primary, secondary, and tertiary prevention (L'Abate, 1990b), in the last generation, the mental health field has differentiated itself according to at least three tiers of self-help (Harwood & L'Abate, 2010): promotion (L'Abate, 2007), prevention proper (L'Abate, 1990b), and tertiary prevention representing the field of psychotherapy. This latter topic will be considered in greater detail in Chapter 12 of this volume. What in the past was called primary prevention has differentiated itself into at least two tiers of its own, represented by the self-help movement (Harwood & L'Abate, 2010) and by promotion of physical and mental health (L'Abate, 2007). The difference between promotion and prevention was highlighted by Higgins & Spiegel (2004), who differentiated between promotion as moving toward health-producing approaches versus prevention as the avoidance of sickness. The third tier of secondary prevention dealing with at-risk populations seems to have proved its mettle in a follow-up report by the National Research Council and Institute of Medicine (Clay, 2009). That report showed that early interventions with children and adolescents significantly improved their long-term welfare and could save billions of dollars in the long run.

A few advances in the last decade, not mentioned in the five articles reviewed previously (Bradbury, 2002a, 2002b; Hendrick, 2002; Muehlhoff &Wood, 2002; Reis, 2002) or in Burleson's (2009) dual-process approach, have changed the landscape of mental health interventions are going to occur in this century, namely: (1) self-help and health promotion; (2) advent of the Internet and online interventions, either self-help, promotional, preventive, or therapeutic; (3) parallel introduction of homework assignments that would justify and support online and offline interventions (Kazantzis & L'Abate, 2007; L'Abate, 2011b); (4) greater reliance on writing and especially distance writing as the inevitable change from face-to-face talk in the field of mental health occurs; and (5) within the field of distance writing, expressive and programmed writing seem the two most relevant and validated approaches to SS.

Developmental Aspects of SS

SS changes in its nature according to various stages of the life cycle (Brock, Pierce, Sarason, & Sarason, 1996). Consequently, SS will be considered within those stages according to available evidence, including the influence of individual personality to the process of SS (Cutrona, Hessling, & Suhr, 1997).

In Preadolescence

Van Aken and Asendorf (1997) had a sample of 138 grade six (twelve-year-olds) complete a social network interview and rated their network members on various dimensions of SS. Low support showed some consistency across members of the nuclear family but was fairly specific for particular network members outside of the family. Children with low support from their mother, father, or classmates reported a low general self-worth, but those with low support from siblings or nonschool peers did not. Low support by one parent could only be compensated for by a supportive relationship with the other parent. Low support by a classmate was not compensated for by supportive siblings or nonschool peers. These findings underscore the relationship specificity of SS and its relation to self-esteem in preadolescence.

In College Students

Korchmaros and Kenny (2006) examined whether relationship factors account for the positive association between genetic relatedness and willingness to help. In college students (thirty-one males and forty-six female), willingness to help family members was measured using hypothetical dilemmas involving life-or-death and everyday-favor situations. Relationship factors were measured using a questionnaire. As expected, emotional close-ness and obligation mediated the association between genetic relatedness and willingness to help. Furthermore, as expected, propinquity, similar-ity, and frequency and amount of interactions mediated the association between genetic relatedness and emotional closeness. Type of situation moderated the association between genetic relatedness and willingness to help, although not entirely as expected. These results suggest that relation-ship factors account for a substantial proportion of the association between genetic relatedness and helping.

SS in Women

Effective SS (SSE; Rini, Schetter, Hobel, Glynn, & Sandman, 2006) takes into account the quantity and quality of support attempts and the extent to which these attempts meet the needs of recipients. SSE was assessed in a sample of 176 pregnant women with regard to their partners' SS behavior. Potential antecedents of SSE were investigated, including individual and relationship variables. In addition, it was hypothesized that women who appraised their partners' support as more effective would have lower pre-natal anxiety, both concurrently (in mid-pregnancy) and prospectively (in late pregnancy).

Factor analyses confirmed that all hypothesized aspects of SSE contrib-uted to a unitary factor of SSE. Structural equation modeling was used to test the proposed antecedents and consequences of SSE. Results revealed that women's ratings of the effectiveness of partner support were predicted by their interpersonal orientation (adult attachment, network orientation, kin individualism-collectivism, and social skills) and by characteristics of their relationships with their partners (relationship quality, emotional closeness and intimacy, and equity). Furthermore, women who perceived themselves to have more effective partner support reported less anxiety in mid-pregnancy and showed a reduction in anxiety from mid- to late-preg-nancy. These findings will be considered below within the proximal and distal contexts of SS.

SS and Personality Characteristics

As indicated in Chapter 8, gender differences in attachment style might be related to many individual differences. For instance, individuals with a more secure attachment style report having larger and more satisfying SS networks (Anders & Tucker, 2000). Individuals with a more anxious or more avoidant attachment style, by contrast, report having smaller and less satisfying support networks. Anders and Tucker (2000) examined the role of interpersonal communication competence (ICC) as a possible mediator of the association between attachment and SS in a sample of undergraduates. Strong support was found for the described model. Mediational analysis revealed that global deficits in ICC could account for the smaller SS network sizes and lower levels of satisfaction among both more anxiously attached and more avoidantly attached participants. Additionally, subsequent analyses examining specific dimensions of ICC revealed that the lower support satisfaction among more anxious individuals could be uniquely accounted for by a lack of assertiveness in social interactions. For more avoidantly attached individuals, smaller network sizes could be uniquely accounted for by lower levels of self-disclosure, and less support satisfaction could be uniquely accounted for by a lack of assertiveness in addition to lower levels of self-disclosure.

Furthermore, perceptual congruency regarding SS interactions does have an impact on key aspects of task relationships between mixed status parties, including relational certainty, trust, talk about new ideas, and performance evaluation. Most support occurs when relationships with the highest perceived reciprocity include performance ratings and most frequent discussions of innovations (Albrecht & Halsey, 1992).

SS in Later Life
Past research has documented a positive association between perceived support availability and well-being in later life (Post, 2007). Other work, reviewed by Reinhardt, Boerner, and Horowitz (2006) shows that actually receiving support can have negative effects. Instrumental support receipt may be negative for persons with chronic impairment because it may emphasize their inability to accomplish daily tasks. Reinhardt et al. contrasted the impact of perceived and received affective and instrumental support on adaptation to chronic vision impairment in 570 elders. After accounting for the significant positive impact of perceived support, receiving instrumental support had a negative effect, whereas receiving affective support had a positive effect on well-being. These findings underscore the importance of distinguishing the association of multiple support components and outcomes to increase understanding of how support affects adaptation in later life.

SS and Emotionality
Bertera (2005) examined positive SS, social negativity, anxiety, and mood disorders in a random sample of 4,688 adults aged twenty-one to fifty-four years from the National Comorbidity Survey (1990–1992). Social

negativity with spouses, relatives, and friends had a strong positive association with the number of anxiety and mood disorder episodes. One surprising finding was that positive support was not strongly associated with the number of anxiety and mood disorder episodes as much as social negativity. Positive support from spouses or friends was not associated with a lower number of episodes of either anxiety or mood disorders. Only positive support from relatives was associated with a lower number of both anxiety and mood disorders. These results, of course, may be due to variations in the link between support and negativity. Given that much previous research has focused on the role of positive support, these findings demonstrate the significant impact that negative social exchanges can have on mental health.

SS and Control

People who have an idiocentric value orientation tend to emphasize their own goals and needs over those of the groups to which they belong, and are often independent and self-reliant. Allocentric individuals tend to be more cooperative, interdependent, and have a stronger need to affiliate with others than idiocentric individuals. Dayan, Doyle, and Markiewicz (2001) investigated how children's social relationships and self-esteem vary as a function of their allocentrism. Participants were 419 children between nine and eighteen years of age from a variety of ethnic backgrounds (French/Canadian/Quebecois, Greek, Arabic, and Caribbean). As expected, allocentric children reported more SS from their peers than did idiocentric children. In addition, idiocentrics and allocentrics differed in their reported sources of intimacy and companionship, for example, from best friends, mothers, and relatives. Also, the self-esteem of idiocentric children, but not of allocentric children, was predicted by SS from their best friend. Implications are that idiocentric and allocentric individuals seek out different members of their social networks to satisfy various needs and to strengthen their self-esteem.

SS, social control, and companionship represent basic elements of many close relationships, yet Rook and Ituarte (1999) argued that relatively little is known about how these distinctive elements separately and jointly influence relationship quality. Control and support may have incompatible effects, with efforts by a family member or friend to influence a focal person's behavior undermining the sense of support in the relationship. These researchers examined the implications of control, support, and companionship for the perceived quality of older adults' family relationships and friendships in a sample of 189 older adults (mean age 70.5 years, ranged from 58 to 90 years), predominantly white (90 percent) women (66 percent), unmarried (64 percent), or widowed (70 percent), and in good to excellent health.

Results from interviews and measures of social network, social control, SS, perceived relationship quality, family versus friend status of network members, and demographic characteristics indicated that the participants' family members and friends were differentially involved in performing control, support, and companionship functions. In addition, perceived relationship quality appeared to be anchored in somewhat different functions for family members versus friends. Perceived quality of family ties was related to emotional support, companionship, and social control, whereas perceived quality of ties with friends was related to emotional support, instrumental support, and companionship. Contrary to expectations, Rook and Ituarte found no evidence that social control detracted from perceived relationship quality or that social control interacted with SS in predicting relationship quality. These results underscore the usefulness of distinguishing social control, SS, and companionship.

SS and Reliance on Others

A component of SS, already mentioned by Burleson (2003), is people's willingness to rely on others for emotional support. Ryan, La Guardia, Solky-Butzel, Chirkof, et al. (2005) proposed that emotional reliance (ER) is typically beneficial to well-being. However, due to different socialization and norms, ER is also expected to differ across gender and cultures. Further, following a self-determination theory perspective, these authors hypothesized that ER is facilitated by social partners who support one's psychological needs for autonomy, competence, and relatedness. Results from studies performed by Ryan et al. (2005) supported the view that ER is generally associated with greater well-being and that it varies significantly across different relationships, cultural groups, and gender. Within-person variation in ER were systematically related to levels of need satisfaction within specific relationships, over and above between-person differences. However, in both Burleson's (2003) and Ryan's (2005) case, among many others, what does ER come down to specifically? The answer by now should be clear: sharing joys, hurts, and fears of being hurt.

SS and Health

It is generally assumed that SS has a favorable impact on the maintenance of health and on coping with illness (Schwarzer & Leppin, 1991). However, results (up to 1990) are inconsistent and even conflicting. This is partly due to conceptual and methodological shortcomings. In order to overcome these problems and to guide better research, Schwarzer and Leppin (1991) presented a taxonomy of social relationships and a causal process model: Social integration, cognitive SS, and behavioral SS were distinguished and related to personality, stress, coping, and the pathogenic process. In the casual model, these authors proposed that SS is depicted both as mediating the effects of stress on illness as well as directly effecting illness. A meta-analysis related SS and social integration to morbidity and mortality based on eighty empirical studies, including more than 60,000 participants. Data subsets revealed disparate patterns of results that give rise to intriguing theoretical questions. Evidently, SS operates in complex ways. Several causal models represented alternative pathways of SS processes. When SS was associated with less illness, a direct effect model was proposed. In cases where more support was seemingly paradoxically associated with illness, it was assumed that a mobilization of support had taken place.

To follow-up the preceding proposal along research that is more relevant to the purposes of this chapter, Schwarzer and Weiner (1991) extended SS through affective reactions toward seven disease-related stigmas using a simulation experiment. The onset of the stigmas was varied as being either controllable or uncontrollable. In addition, a target person was described as either coping with the stigma or not coping. The research question aimed at exploring the effects of controllability and coping efforts on expectations, blame, emotions such as pity, anger and social stress, and on the willingness to support the target person. In a within-group design, each of the eighty-four participants was confronted with all seven stigmas under four different conditions. Both experimental factors elicited affective reactions and judgments to help. However, the coping dimension appeared to be stronger for most dependent variables. In addition, helping behavior was mediated by different affective reactions for disparate stigma groupings.

According to Uchino (2006), SS has been reliably related to lower rates of morbidity and mortality. An important issue concerns the physiological mechanisms by which SS influences such health endpoints. Uchino examined evidence linking SS to changes in cardiovascular, neuroendocrine, and immune functions. Consistent with epidemiological evidence, SS appears related to more positive biological profiles across these disease-relevant systems. Recent research on immune-mediated inflammatory processes is also starting to provide data on more integrative physiological mechanisms potentially linking SS to health.

Related to Vangelisti's (2009a) critical arguments, reviewed elsewhere in this chapter, Uchino (2009) argued that SS has been reliably related to physical health outcomes. However, an examination of mediators of such links have been slowed by the lack of understanding regarding two complex and related questions: What is SS, and what phase of the disease process does it impact? The importance of a lifespan perspective would take into account distinct antecedent processes and mechanisms that are related to measures of support over time. This view makes clear the need to distinguish among measures of perceived and received support and their links to more specific aspects of disease (e.g., acute, chronic, disease incidence).

In the same vein as Uchino, Orth-Gomer (2009) proposed that individuals with few social contacts have an increased risk of dying prematurely from coronary disease. Social ties generally exert general but unspecific health protective effects; however, negative social ties are sometimes harmful for women's cardiac health. In a clinical trial of psychosocial intervention, consecutive female coronary patients received a one-year cognitive-stress-reduction and support-strengthening program. In a nine-year follow up, the program reduced mortality by two-thirds when compared to women in typical care programs. There is additional evidence from population-based clinical observation and controlled intervention studies that SS is health (specifically cardiac) protective and that these effects may generalize to men.

Bass and Stein (1997) administered the SS Questionnaire (SSQ) and the Social Network List (SNL) to 102 undergraduates twice over a four-week interval to find that at both times of measurement, participants delineated significantly larger networks using the SNL than using the SSQ, with a larger average number of friends being elicited by the SNL. However, participants averaged significantly higher global network satisfaction ratings for SSQ networks relative to SNL networks at both times of measurement. These results suggest that both instruments may need to be administered simultaneously to encompass overlapping aspects of social networks.

Ertel, Glymour, and Berkman (2009) stressed the importance of social networks in reducing social isolation, changing network structure, and improving SS. However, these investigators felt that these interventions have had weak or null effects on the health outcomes they were designed to impact. Consequently, Ertel et al. (2009) considered several issues that may help explain why there have been divergent results between observational studies and large-scale randomized clinical trials. These authors relied mostly on the role that social networks and support play in cardiovascular and cerebral-vascular disease by employing life course models of health and development.

SS in Couples

Johnson, Hobfoil, Zalcberg-Linetzy (1993) examined the relationship among SS knowledge, supportive behaviors, intimacy with one's spouse, and satisfaction with support provided by one's spouse among forty-one Israeli kibbutz couples. These investigators tested the hypothesis that support knowledge and support behavior influence the intimacy between couples and increase satisfaction with spouse's SS efforts. Alternative causal mechanisms were also explored with simultaneous equation modeling. Their results indicated that satisfaction with SS behavior by one's spouse is mediated entirely by intimacy with one's spouse. Additionally, partner's knowledge about SS behavior directly affects intimacy and indirectly generated SS satisfaction independent of actual supportive behavior. These findings did not differ by gender. These investigators discussed the consistency of these findings with family behavior exchange theory with their implications for marital therapy.

To compare the extent to which (1) amount versus adequacy of received support and (2) support provision versus solicitation behaviors predict marital satisfaction, married couples from the United States (N = 275) provided perceptions of received support and participated in two support transactions (Lawrence, Bunde, Barry, Brock, et al., 2008). Actor-partner interdependence and structural equation modeling techniques were employed. Husbands' perceptions of support adequacy predicted marital satisfaction more than their perceptions of support amount, whereas the results were generally opposite for wives. Husbands' provision and wives' solicitation behaviors predicted marital satisfaction. These results suggest the need to move beyond simple counts of support received to examining support adequacy – and the various behaviors and roles involved in supportive transactions – in order to enhance theories of support and relationship functioning, as discussed in greater detail in Chapter 13.

Providing SS

To untangle the complexity of SS, Sarason, Sarason, and Pierce (1994) reviewed the development of research on SS that began with the construction of the Quality of Relationships Inventory (QRI) to assess overall support and determination of its correlations with various indicators of adjustment and performance. The administration of this instrument led to inquiries into how people at different support levels behave socially and how they perceive the behavior of others. The results of their studies led, in turn, to focusing attention on the relative contributions to outcomes of both global and relationship-specific perceived support. The authors provided examples of studies that characterize each phase of the research and discussed needs for future research, with special emphasis on the need for closer integration of research on SS and personal relationships.

Brock, Pierce, Sarason, and Sarason (1996) argued that perceived global SS and support from specific relationships are not synonymous, yet existing measures typically assess only one or the other. However, it might be possible to simultaneously assess both using the same instrument. In two studies, the reliability and validity of scores derived for specific relationship categories from the SS Questionnaire were examined. Separate scores were developed for mother and father, and a composite score for friends. Each score exhibited good internal consistency, and correlational analyses revealed both convergent and discriminant validity for each of the scores. Support from friends and mother, but not for father, predicted perceptions of support availability. Parental support was more predictive than support from friends of the self-perceived past and present quality of family relationships. Regression analyses indicated that support from individual relationships predicted relationship quality and adjustment, even after accounting for global support.

Gurung, Sarason, and Sarason (1997) investigated three questions related to SS: (1) Do both personal characteristics and perceived qualities of romantic relationships contribute to partners' perception of support? (2) Do these variables predict supportive behavior in partner interactions that can be observed by others? (3) How do situational characteristics affect the predictors of observed supportive behavior? After signing an informed consent form, eighty-six undergraduates and their romantic partners completed a packet of questionnaires that included the Quality of Relationship Inventory (QRI), a Commitment Scale, the Beck Depression Inventory, the UCLA Loneliness Questionnaire, the State-Trait Anxiety Inventory (Trait Version), and the Rosenberg Self-Esteem Scale; a conflict discussion task was administered twice with and without ratings of several typical relationship issues over which partners might potentially disagree, and they participated in a structured videotaped interaction that included a stress-inducing intervention. Participants' perceived support of the relationship was predicted by participants' own personal characteristics and view of the relationship, as well as by partners' personal characteristics. Observed supportive behavior in a somewhat unfamiliar task was related to personal characteristics of both partners and their views of the relationship. Supportive behavior after an experimenter-administered stressor was predicted only by the couple's personal characteristics. These results might demonstrate how study of SS in close relationships can advance understanding of relations between support perception and support receipt. However, one issue with this study lies in how close these romantic partners were and how adventitious their relationship was to fulfill course credit or recognition. For instance, how long were they involved before participating in the study, and how long did their claimed romantic relationship last?

SS, Help Seeking, and Support Provision

Help seeking in SS is the reverse of help provision. The former addresses the help seeker. The latter addresses the help provider. For instance, Trobst, Collins, and Embree (1994) in two studies examined the association between emotion-related factors and intentions to provide SS to a distressed peer. In both studies, providers' gender and their level of dispositional empathy were related to anticipatory support provision. Women and persons high in trait empathy were more supportive than men and persons low in trait empathy. Consistent with predictions, the gender effect was largely mediated by empathy. Study 2 extended these findings by demonstrating that empathic responses are also subsequently associated with support provision, as well as by exploring the impact of recipients' expression of emotion on empathy and support. As a whole, both studies indicate that emotion plays an important role in support provision in that providers' feelings of concern are a strong determinant of their supportive responses.

Intimate partner violence (IPV), for instance, is one presumed origin of hurt feelings that produces a process of help seeking in victims that unfolds over time rather than occurs once. This presumption, however, has never been explored with longitudinal data. In a study that is relevant to sharing hurt feelings, Cattaneo, Stuewig, Goodman, Kaltman, et al. (2007) described a pattern of formal help-seeking efforts in a sample of 406 IPV victims over the course of one year. Furthermore, these investigators explored the relationship between legal and extralegal help seeking, reflecting current controversy over how these two types of interventions should be coordinated. These investigators found that repeated help seeking was common, with 80 percent seeking additional help during follow-up. Legal and extralegal help seeking decreased together over time, and this similarity in pattern can best described as a connection between behaviors that are similarly influenced by time-specific events like repeated abuse rather than a connection between overarching trajectories. These results suggest that time-varying factors are more important than stable characteristics in predicting help-seeking patterns and support coordination through a one-stop-shopping model rather than primarily through referral systems.

Individuals' perceiving stigma may be unwilling to seek support directly. Instead, they may use indirect strategies due to fear of rejection. Ironically, indirect seeking may lead to unsupportive network responses (i.e., rejection). In study 1, Williams and Mickelson (2008) collected data from structured interviews of a sample of U.S. women in poverty (N = 116); the data showed perceived poverty-related stigma was related to increased fear of rejection, which in turn partially mediated perceived stigma and indirect seeking. In study 2, data gathered from structured interviews of a sample of abused women (N = 177) revealed that perceived abuse-related stigma was linked to increased indirect seeking, which in turn related to increased unsupportive network responses. By contrast, direct support seeking was related to increased supportive and decreased unsupportive responses.

Sometimes reliance on others takes the form of "compensatory support." Milevsky (2005) examined how the compensatory effects of SS received from siblings relate to psychological adjustment in emerging adulthood. Participants completed measures of SS from a variety of sources and several indicators of well-being. Sibling support was associated with lower loneliness and depression and with higher self-esteem and life satisfaction. Also, sibling support compensated for support from low parental and peer support. Sibling support compensated for low support from mothers for depression and self-esteem. Sibling support compensated for low support from fathers for loneliness, self-esteem, and life satisfaction. Finally, sibling support partially compensated for low support from friends for all the well-being measures and completely compensated for self-esteem, depression, and life satisfaction. The potential benefits of sibling support warrant a closer examination of the wide-ranging issues involved in sibling relations.

Perrine (1993) explored supporters' feelings about giving emotional support to a person in distress. In a laboratory setting, participants talked with a confederate enacting a distressed role. The response of the confederate was manipulated either "improvement" or "no improvement." Responses from participants were categorized as either "supportive," that is, primarily listening or providing encouragement, or "active," that is, primarily problem solving. Participants' affect, goal accomplishment, and feelings of responsibility were assessed. Three factors were significantly related to an increase in the participant's anger and sadness (1) when the confederate did not improve, (2) when the participant relied on "supportive" responses, and (3) when participants perceived that they had not accomplished their goal. In addition, the more responsible participants felt for solving the problem, the more negative affect they experienced after talking with a confederate who did not improve. Whether or not the confederate improved, participants who relied on problem solving felt that they had helped more than did participants who relied on listening.

Confidant Support and Marital and Maternal Distress

What happens when a wife or partner cannot confide with her husband or partner because of absence or emotional unavailability? Julien, Markman, Leveille, Chartrand, et al. (1994) attempted to answer this question by coding videotapes of fifteen maritally adjusted and thirteen unadjusted wives' interactions with confidants and interferences with regard to wives' marriages. Adjusted wives' conversations were more supportive of marriage than were unadjusted wives' conversations, but the groups did not differ on sequences involving interference behaviors. The proportion of happily married confidants in wives' networks was associated with the likelihood of confidants reciprocating wives' support of their own marriages, but confidants' characteristics did not predict interference. Regardless of marital adjustment, confidants' interference behaviors predicted wives' levels of distress and distance from husbands after the conversations. These results seem relevant to the social construction of cognitions in marriages.

DeGarmo and Forgatch (1997) investigated confidant support (emotional support, supportive behavior, and likeability of support provider) from friends, family, and intimate partners, along with maternal distress, as predictors of parenting practices for divorced women. Controlling for maternal distress and confidant negativity, observed confidant support predicted higher levels of effective parenting practices. Confidant negativity was associated with maternal distress with a marginal relationship between marital distress and parenting. Confidant negativity had an indirect association with parenting by predicting lower levels of observed support.

What is the difference between "distress" and "acute stress"? If both terms are not operationally defined, it will be practically impossible to distinguish one condition from the other. Nonetheless, emotional support from intimate partners has been shown to have both costs and benefits for daily anxious and depressed moods (Shrout, Herman, & Bolger, 2006). These investigators examined whether similar costs and benefits are found for practical support, and when fatigue, vigor, and anger are outcomes. Results were based on daily diary reports from sixty-eight recent law school graduates and their intimate partners during the month before the New York State Bar examination. Partners' reports of practical support provision to the examinee were beneficial in that they were associated with decreased examinee fatigue and increased examinee vigor. In contrast, examinees' recognition of emotional support receipt was costly in that it was associated with increases in anger as well as anxious and depressed mood. These results highlighted the importance of distinguishing between emotional and practical support and are consistent with findings that suggest that invisible (provided but not recognized) support leads to the best outcome.

Prouix, Helms, Milardo, and Payne (2009) explored the monitoring role of husbands' relational interference in the link between relational support from close friends and wives' marital and family relationship quality. Using data from fifty-two wives rearing school-aged children, results suggested that husbands' interference moderates the association between support from close friends and both wives' marital satisfaction and mother-child relationship quality. At low level of interference from husbands, support from close friends is positively associated with wives' reports of marital satisfaction, and at high levels of spousal interference, support from close friends is positively associated with mother-child relationship quality.

SS and Obesity

Family-based interventions for pediatric obesity are defined by active parent involvement in treatment (Kitzmann & Beech, 2006). In a review, Kitzmann and Beech examined thirty-one family-based interventions with published outcome data and distinguished four categories of family-based interventions: (1) Target a narrow range of parent behaviors related to eating/exercise and assess change only in terms of a child's eating, exercise, or weight; (2) target a similarly narrow range of parent behaviors, but nevertheless assess program-related changes in general parenting skills or family functioning; (3) target a broad range of parent behaviors related to general parenting skills and family functioning, but do not assess program-related changes in this area; and (4) target general parenting or family functioning and also assess program-related changes in these areas. The authors highlighted methodological and conceptual challenges facing researchers in this area and argued that for an even broader family focus in family-based interventions for pediatric obesity.

SS in the Aftermath of Suicide

Survivors of suicide loss include family members, friends, coworkers, and mental health professionals. Survivors may grieve more intensely and for longer periods of time than people mourning other types of losses. Various practical ways to express support can help survivors cope by trying to ease guilt concerning what they could or should have done to prevent the loss, encouraging and suggesting ways in which survivors can express and share their hurt feelings with other loved ones, including writing letters, and even sharing painful details about how the suicide occurred. Additionally, survivors could be aided by making sure they remember anniversaries, birthdays, and special occasions relevant to the decreased. If necessary, they may be encouraged to make connections with existing online resources, and names and addresses of trusted mental health professionals may be furnished (Sakinofsky, 2007).

SS and Marital Violence

To compare the SS behaviors of violent and nonviolent husbands, Holtzworth-Munroe, Stuart, Sandin, Smutzler, et al. (1997) recruited four groups of couples: violent/distressed (VD), violent/nondistressed (VND), nonviolent/distressed (NVD), and nonviolent/nondistressed (NVND). Two systems were used to code couples' discussions of wives' personal problems. Using the SS Interaction Coding System, no violent-nonviolent group differences emerged; however, as listeners NVND husbands were the most positive and tended to be the least negative. Using a coding system designed for this study (i.e., SS Behavior/Affect Rating System), these investigators confirmed the hypothesis that violent husbands would offer less SS than would nonviolent husbands. Relative to nonviolent men, violent husbands were less positive, more belligerent/ domineering, more contemptuous/disgusted, and more upset by the wife's problem. Relative to NVND husbands, violent husbands displayed more anger and tension. VND husbands were more critical of their wives' problems, and VD men were more critical of the possible solutions wives offered. Across both coding systems, few group differences in wife behaviors emerged, suggesting that husband behavior better differentiated violent from nonviolent couples when wives are discussing personal problems.

Recent Contributions to SS

More recently, an entire issue (2009) of the *Journal of Social and Personal Relationships* (ISPR) was devoted to SS, with Mikulincer and Shaver (2009) introducing and updating attachment styles with behavioral systems in SS. Burleson (2009) argued that numerous factors affect the outcome of supportive interactions, including aspects of the supportive message, the helper, the interaction context, and the recipient. He defined supportive communication as "verbal and nonverbal behavior produced with the intention of providing assistance to others perceived as needing that aid" (pp. 21–22). Additionally, Burleson proposed that the direct and interactive effects of these factors can be explained through a dual-process theory of supportive communication outcomes, which provides a comprehensive, integrative treatment of when and why collections of variables in supportive interactions generate the effects they do (p. 29).

Vangelisti's (2009a) critical contribution argued that although research on SS has generated findings that are key to the study of social and personal relationships, scholars have yet to deal with a number of conceptual issues that affect how SS is defined and measured. Research on hurt feelings provides some interesting insights concerning the conceptualization of support. Based on her research (reviewed in Chapter 6 of this volume) as well as a review of the literature on SS, Vangelisti described several issues that scholars ought to consider as they conceptualize, evaluate, and study SS processes.

In line with Uchino's (2009) life span emphasis, Rook (2009) emphasized that gaps in SS resources in later life may arise when older adults lose social network members due to illness, death, or residential relocation. Gaps may also arise when social networks remain intact but are not well suited to meet older adults' intensifying support needs, such as needs for extended or highly personal instrumental support. Significant gaps in support resources are likely to require adaptive responses by older adults. The small literature on these issues suggests that this area of interest is ripe for further development.

In closing this *JSPR* issue, Sarason and Sarason (2009) suggest that SS is a construct with multiple dimensions that can be approached at multiple levels. Findings from a variety of disciplines and recognition of its bidirectional nature can help map the construct. Bidirectionality is a process that requires attention to moderators, such as gender (see Chapter 8 of this volume), cultural change (see Chapter 9 of this volume), and personal development, together with the relationship between the receiver and the provider of support. Both close personal ties and weaker ones that often are part of community involvement need to be taken into account in order to map the construal of SS comprehensively.

THE DISTAL CONTEXT OF SS

Kamholz, Hayes, Carver, Gulliver et al. (2006) argued that the ability to regulate emotions is important to mental health and well-being. However, these investigators felt that relatively little is known about cognitive strategies people used when faced with *negative affect* and the extent to which these strategies reduce such affect. This may be due, in part, to the lack of a comprehensive measure of cognitive-affect-regulation strategies. These investigators conducted three studies to develop a broad-based self-report inventory of fifteen specific strategies, called the Inventory of Cognitive Affect Regulation Strategies (ICARUS). This instrument assesses strategies that are oriented toward avoidance of the feelings (e.g., mental disengagement, thoughts of suicide) or diverting attention (e.g., self-criticism/self-blame, blaming others) as well as strategies that are oriented toward approach or engagement (e.g., reframing and growth, acceptance, mindful observation). Results provided preliminary support for the internal consistency, test-retest reliability, and convergent validity of this measure. This kind of measure would go a long way toward assessing what kind of intervention should be used and could provide a way to intervene directly and specifically as suggested in the following ways.

Telephone-Administered Counseling

Mohr, Vella, Hart, Heckman, et al. (2008) noted that increasingly the telephone is being used to deliver psychotherapy for depression, in part as a means to reduce barriers to treatment. Twelve trials of telephone-administered psychotherapies (TAP) included an assessment of depressive symptoms. There was a significant reduction in depressive symptoms for patients enrolled in TAP as compared to control conditions ($d = .26$, 95% confidence interval [CI] = $.14–.39$, $p < .0001$). There was also a significant reduction in depressive symptoms in analyses of pretreatment to posttreatment change ($d = .81$, 95% CI = $.50–1.13$, $p < .0001$). The mean attrition rate was 7.56% (95% CI = $4.23–10.90$). These findings suggest that TAP can produce significant reduction in depressive symptoms. Attrition rates were considerably lower than rates reported in face-to-face psychotherapy.

Self-Help and Health Promotion

Harwood and L'Abate (2010) reviewed critically the field of self-help and the variety of ways by which hurt feelings can be admitted and processed in a variety of settings, including promotion and prevention (L'Abate, 1990b, 2007). Consequently, all three overlapping approaches (self-help, health promotion, and prevention of illness) will be reviewed here in reference to how hurt feelings can be dealt with helpfully in each of these three overlapping fields.

Self-help: Harwood and L'Abate (2010) distinguished among self-support methods initiated, administered, guided, maintained, and monitored by professionals, such as distance writing, bibliotherapy, online support groups and therapy, and manuals for practitioners. In a separate section, they reviewed self-help and self-change approaches for specific conditions, including anxieties, depressions, eating disorders, addictive behaviors, personality disorders, severe psychopathology, and medical conditions, concluding their critical review with how RCT can help identify who could profit by self-help, health promotion, sickness prevention, or direct professional help.

Advent of Internet Interventions: There is no question that the Internet will inevitably become a major medium of communication and healing in self-help, promotion, prevention, or psychotherapy. This advent will involve mental health professionals working with participants at a distance, without ever seeing them (L'Abate, 2008a, 2008b, 2010). However, Witty (2009) warned about the dark side of the Internet, where flaming, deception, harassment, and even revenge, computer infidelity, and addictions have proliferated. In spite of these potential dangers, the Internet can become an additional way to help people who hurt deal with those hurts successfully.

This conclusion is supported by the research by Fouladi, McCarthy, and Moller (2002), who found that the mode of presentation effects, paper-and-pencil versus online, were statistically significant; the magnitude of the effects was in general very small. The basic similarity of the properties of the measures using paper-and-pencil and online Internet modes of administration suggested the viability of the Internet for assessing these and other psychological phenomena, including, of course, hurt feelings.

Andersson, Carlbring, Holmstrom, Spartham, et al. (2006) assigned sixty-four individuals with social phobia (social anxiety disorder) to a multimodal cognitive-behavioral treatment package or to a waiting-list control group. Treatment consisted of a nine-week, Internet-delivered self-help program combined with two group-exposure sessions in real life and minimal therapist contact via e-mail. From pretest to posttest, treated participants in contrast to controls showed significant improvement on most measured dimensions (social anxiety scales, general anxiety and depression levels, quality of life). The overall within- and between-group effect sizes were Cohen's $d = .87$ and $.70$ respectively. Treatment gains were maintained at a one-year follow-up. The results of this study support the continued use and development of Internet-distributed self-help programs for people diagnosed with social phobia.

Spence, Holmes, March, and Lipp (2006) randomly allocated seventy-two clinically anxious children, aged seven to fourteen years, to (1) clinic-based, cognitive-behavior therapy; (2) the same treatment partially delivered via the Internet; or (3) a wait-list control (WL). Children in the clinic and clinic-plus-Internet conditions showed significantly greater reduction in anxiety from pretreatment to posttreatment and were more likely to be free of their anxiety diagnoses, compared with the WL group. Improvements were maintained at a twelve-month follow-up for both therapy conditions, with minimal difference in outcomes between the two types of interventions. The Internet treatment content was highly acceptable to families, with minimal dropout and a high level of therapy compliance.

The University of Texas Medical Branch, the Robert Wood Johnson Foundation, the Galveston Independent School District, and Galveston's philanthropic community have established and successfully implemented a collaborative Telehealth for School-based Mental Health program to meet the mental health treatment needs of adolescents in the area secondary schools. This program is currently in its third year and has produced promising results in improving access to mental health services for adolescents and their families, and improving outcomes for adolescents living with mental illness www.utmb.edu/hpla.telehealth.asp. Ramirez and Broneck (2009) argued that few studies to date have examined the use of Internet applications in enacting "everyday" routine relational maintenance, and even fewer assess how such tools complement more traditional forms of communication to sustain involvements. These investigators explored the role of one such tool, instant messaging (IM) in relationship maintenance. Participants (N = 402) reported their general use of IM (Stage 1) and subsequently conducted and reported on a specific interaction occurring either through IM or face-to-face (Stage 2). Among IM users, significant gender and the types of relational differences emerged in "every communication." Findings also indicate how IM is being utilized in conjunction with other communication channels. This field is ripe for new research opportunities to examine relational maintenance processes.

Homework Assignments: With the advent of the Internet it will become even more important for mental health practitioners to change from a heretofore relatively passive stance of reactive, face-to-face, talk-based personal contact to a perhaps impersonal but more dynamic and interactive reliance on homework assignments. As Detweiler-Bedell and Whisman (2005) demonstrated, better treatment outcomes are associated with specific therapist behaviors (i.e., setting concrete goals and discussing barriers to completing the homework), characteristics of the homework task (i.e., written reminders of the homework), and client involvement in the discussion. Regardless of theoretical orientation, a more active stance in all kinds of distance programmed writing and interactive practice exercises in self-help, promotion, and prevention can be demonstrated through the routine administration of regular homework assignments requiring continuous pre-post-intervention evaluation and follow-up since termination (Harwood & L'Abate, 2010; Kazantsis & L'Abate, 2007; L'Abate, 2008a, 2008b, 2010).

Gonzales, Schmitz, and DeLaune (2006) found a significant relationship between homework compliance and cocaine use that was moderated by readiness to change. Homework compliance predicted less cocaine use during treatment, but only for participants higher in readiness to change. For those lower in readiness to change homework compliance was not associated with cocaine use during treatment. Homework compliance early in therapy was associated with better retention in treatment. Homework compliance was not predicted by level of education or readiness to change.

Kazantzis, Whittington, and Dattilio (2010) replicated a classical meta-analysis of homework effects by finding a pre-post-treatment estimated size D = .63 for control conditions and a larger d = 1.8 for therapy conditions with homework. These results support effect size estimates found by L'Abate (2004b) and by Smyth and L'Abate (2001).

In toto, this literature points to a view of any self-help, promotional, preventive, therapeutic, or rehabilitative treatment as consisting of tailor-made written interactive practice exercises interspersed with as few as possible face-to-face talk-based sessions. Even more importantly, these findings indicate that change for the better can be obtained at a distance from participants without even talking with them face to face (L'Abate, 2010, 2011b).

Distance Writing: Common to both Internet and homework assignments is the medium of distance writing, a medium that inevitably will supplement and even supplant face-to-face talk (L'Abate, 2011a). There are various forms of distance writing: diaries and journaling, expressive writings as in the work of Pennebaker already reviewed in Chapter 6 of this volume, autobiographies, and guided writing (L'Abate, 2007; L'Abate & Sweeney, 2011). For instance, in an application of Pennebaker's paradigm, Segal, Tucker, and Coolidge (2009) investigated the effects of expressing an upsetting event through writing about either positive feelings, negative feelings, or both in order to assess which mode of expression facilitated greater emotional and cognitive processing. Undergraduate participants with self-reported unresolved upsetting experiences were randomly assigned to the three writing groups. After completing three writing sessions, they were evaluated at baseline, postexperimentally, and at one-month follow-up. All groups demonstrated positive benefits, however, participants in the positive writing group showed greater adaptive cognitive changes than the other groups.

Thus, it appears that the written expression of positive feelings is as therapeutic as the written expression of negative emotions, which may prompt increased cognitive reorganization or benefit finding among a nonclinical sample. There is the possibility that this lack of differences among the groups may be due to limiting the intervention only to three sessions – rather than every day for a month, as in the Cohn et al. (2009) study, reported in Chapter 1 of this volume – too short a time that may not have been sufficient to make much difference in the outcome.

Guided writing may consist of asking participants to keep a journal, and on the basis of Cohn's et al. (2009) findings, to write down five things for which they are grateful; they should phrase them positively rather than negatively; finally, participants should identify people they appreciate for something special they have done for the participant, as well as whatever other experiences that made the participant feel good.

However, within the field of distance writing, programmed writing deserves greater attention, especially in its relevance to intimacy and hurt feelings, as will be discussed. Even though the multimedia program for computer-assisted psychotherapy, proposed and evaluated by Wright, Wright, Salmon, Beck, et al. (2002), was developed to help patients learn cognitive-behavior skills. There is no reason why a similar program could not be developed to teach skills to deal with feelings and emotions, as available in many interactive practice exercises published by L'Abate (2001, 2002, 2011b).

The program developed by Wright et al. was designed to provide psycho-education, teach self-help methods, and give information to clinicians on the patient's progress in using software. Multimedia technology can be utilized to engage users in the learning process and to make the program accessible for persons who do not have computer or keyboard skills. A preliminary study with ninety-six participants (aged eighteen to seventy-five years old) who used the software along with treatment as usual found that seventy-five (78.1 percent) completed the entire program. Users indicated a high rate of acceptance of this form of computer-assisted therapy, and mean scores on a measure of cognitive therapy knowledge were significantly improved.

Programmed Writing and Interactive Practice Exercises: Programmed writing (PW) was developed to provide a structure that participants would understand easily and directly, with a minimum of directions, exhortations, or explanations. Essentially, PW consists of systematically and sequentially presented questions or tasks around a topic that participants can answer in writing as homework assignments (L'Abate, 1986, 1990, 1992, 2001; 2002, 2004a, 2004b; 2011b). Topics may range from time-out for children and sibling rivalry to anxiety, depression, or impulsivity in adults, and lifelong learning for individuals, couples, families, and children with or without their families. The style of these interactive practice exercises or workbooks may vary from linearly worded questions about hurt feelings (L'Abate, 1986) to paradoxically framed ones (L'Abate, 2011b).

What is relevant to applied practice, and especially to hurt feelings and intimacy, consists of a very simple way to produce workbooks or interactive practice exercises. One can take any of the dozens of intimacy-related questionnaires included not only in Prager (1995, pp. 31–42) and in Mashek and Aron (2004), but also in a great deal of research cited in the references of this volume, as in Waring's Intimacy Questionnaire (Waring & Reddon, 1983), Thelen's FIS reviewed in Chapter 6 of this volume, or Schaefer and Olson's (1981) PAIR inventory, and transform them directly and easily into active workbooks or written, interactive practice exercises.

Any list of inert, static items or statements about behaviors, symptoms, or signs composing any questionnaire or rating sheet can be converted directly into a dynamic workbook or interactive practice exercises by asking participants to (1) define the meaning of each term, item, or statement, using even a dictionary if necessary; (2) give two examples of how that item is represented in actual behavior; (3) rank-order items according to how each term or item applies to self; and (4) complete a series of standard practice exercises administered sequentially according to the rank-order given by participants. Such a general practice exercise asks participants to amplify information about the nature, origin, functionality, dysfunctionality, and relation of that item to self and to loved ones. It also includes additional homework between administration of other standard practice exercises for each item that follows the rank-order given in (3). On a more positive side, using the same method, one could develop a series of interactive practice exercises from the list of positive terms describing features of compassionate love developed by Fehr and Sprecher (2009, p. 350).

Through this simple transformation, going from inherently static and inert tests or questionnaires, or factor analyses of items, as well as DSM-IV lists of symptoms to active homework assignments with follow-up feedback from professionals, it is possible to intervene and evaluate very large populations using different questionnaires to evaluate comparatively the outcome of competing questionnaires constructed from different conceptual models or frameworks (L'Abate, 2011a, 2011b). Of course, these applications would involve obtaining a signed informed consent form from participants dealing with such an explosive topic as hurt feelings to protect researchers and participants (Appendixes A and B).

Emotional Skills Training: Brooks and Richardson (1980) investigated the effects of delivering an emotional skills training program to patients with x-ray confirmation of uncomplicated duodenal ulcer. The program, consisting of anxiety management and assertiveness training components, was completed by eleven male veteran patients in eight sixty- to ninety-minute sessions over a two-week period. Eleven similar patients received an attention placebo treatment. Over a sixty-day follow-up period, patients receiving emotional skills training reported less severe ulcer symptomatology, experienced fewer days of symptomatic pain, and consumed less antiacid medication. There were no significant differences between groups in terms of days of unrelieved pain and follow-up x-ray results. Of the patients receiving skills training, those initially reporting high levels of anxiety and unassertiveness constriction were significantly less anxious and constricted at follow-up testing. Comparison of the two groups three and a half years after the program was terminated revealed significantly lower rate of ulcer recurrence in the treatment group.

Exercise: According to Stathopoulou, Powers, Berry, Smiths, Jasper, et al. (2006), associations between exercise and mental well-being have been documented repeatedly over the last two decades. More recently, there has been application of exercise interventions to clinical populations diagnosed with depression, anxiety, and eating disorders with evidence of substantial benefits (Hawood & L'Abate, 2010). Nonetheless, attention to the efficacy of exercise interventions in clinical settings have been notably absent in the psychosocial treatment literature, in spite of calls for the integration of these methods within the clinical practices of mental health professionals.

Those authors provided a quantitative review of efficacy studies in clinical samples and discussed potential mechanisms of action for exercise interventions with attention to both biological and psychosocial processes. A meta-analysis of eleven treatment outcome studies of individuals with depression yielded a very large combined effect size for the advantage of exercise over control conditions: $g = 1.39$ (95%CI: .89 1.88) corresponding to a $d = 1.42$ (95% CI: .92–1. 93). Based on these findings, these researchers encourage clinicians to consider the role of adjunctive exercise interventions in their clinical practice with a discussion of issues concerning this integration.

Commenting on Stathopoulou's et al. results, Seime and Vickers (2006) remarked that the current empirical evidence is convincing that exercise either alone or in combination with other evidence-supported treatment is effective in treating clinically significant depression, where hurt feelings usually remain unexpressed. The challenge produced by this evidence lies in translating it into effective practice. Practicing clinicians encounter many barriers in utilizing exercise in the face of depressive symptoms, including pessimism, low motivation, physical inactivity, and withdrawal. Some practical suggestions are given to increase the likelihood that patients with depression implement and maintain exercise behaviors to improve their mood (Dubbert, 2002).

Smith (2006) picked up on Seime and Vickers's suggestions by suggesting that exercise is also useful in the management of a wide variety of medical disorders that often co-occur with depression and related emotional conditions. Indeed, exercise may be particularly useful in managing emotional-physical comorbidities. Furthermore, the evidence presented by Stathopoulou et al. indicates the importance of using exercise in preventing both emotional and physical disorders, as found in self-help, promotional, and preventive approaches already available (Harwood & L'Abate, 2010; L'Abate, 2007).

Intimacy Workshops: On the basis of the findings from Frey et al. (1979), an intimacy workshop for couples was produced and evaluated (L'Abate & Sloan, 1984, 1985).

Mindful Emotion Regulation: Chambers, Gullone, and Allen (2009) attempted to integrate the constructs of mindfulness and emotion regulation through a review of relatively new research into both areas, considering that to date, no one has directly proposed a conceptual integration that may serve for useful practical applications. After exploring key axioms and assumptions of traditional psychological models of emotion regulation and psychological interventions that are derived from them, such as cognitive behavior therapy, these authors conclude that these interventions differ fundamentally from mindfulness-based approaches in terms of the underlying processes they address, that is, feelings and emotions. Accordingly, mindfulness and emotion regulation can be linked through a conceptual framework, especially the actual reality of both feelings and thoughts "*and the need to move beyond a valence model of emotion*" (Chambers et al., 2009, p. 590; italics mine).

Implications of SS for Preventive and Health Promotional Interventions

No matter what type of direct or indirect treatment is adopted to deal with hurt feelings, the principle remains the same: "Approach what you have avoided" (L'Abate, 1984). This principle is implicit in "exposure therapy" (McNally, 2007) and in the work of Johnson and Greenberg, reviewed in Chapter 12 of this volume. However, how is this approach to hurt feelings to occur? The same way porcupines make love: very carefully. Verbally, in unstructured talk therapy, many symptoms can be traced to past hurts, but this link is not as simple or direct as it seems. One needs to assess the level and type of dysfunctionality before addressing hurt feelings (Kring, 2008; L'Abate, 2009b, 2011b). Are these feelings expressed verbally, psychosomatically, or motorically through acting out, or impulsively, against self, and against others? Or are these feelings directed against the self to protect others? How?

In distance writing, structurally speaking, the options to address hurt feelings are much wider and more specific than in talking (L'Abate, 2009a) One could use autobiographies, diaries, or journals to indirectly infer past hurts (Harwood & L'Abate, 2010; L'Abate, 2007; L'Abate & Sweeney, 2011). More directly, one could use Pennebaker's (Kacewicz et al., 2007) expressive writing about past traumas. However, as noted, even here one needs to assess level and type of functionality before using such an approach, especially when administered to clinical populations.

CONCLUSION

Relationship science has been open to SS for a long time, judging by how many references are found in its two main journals, *Personal Relationships* and the *Journal of Social and Personal Relationships*. Strangely, this field was not considered by Bradbury and by his critics/supporters mentioned earlier in this chapter, even though they published in the very same journals. Nonetheless, there are many ways to deal with the unresolved hurt feelings present in most of us and especially in populations at risk and in need of help.

12

Psychotherapy: Sharing Hurt Feelings and Fears of Being Hurt

The idea that accessing and exploring painful emotions and "bad feelings" in a therapeutic relationship makes one feel better is a widely held belief among several schools of psychotherapy.
                    Greenberg & Pascal-Leone (2006, p. 611)

The purpose of this chapter is to consider how the professional community has dealt with hurt feelings in face-to-face (F2F) talk-based (TB) contacts between psychotherapists and their participants. First, the avoidance of hurt feelings in the professional literature will be reviewed. Second, instead of reviewing and therefore duplicating unstructured, old, tried but not always true, traditionally expensive F2F, TB approaches that continue to dominate the field of psychotherapy, the specific contributions of Susan M. Johnson and Leslie S. Greenberg will be reviewed; their work amounts to a sea change with regard to its inclusion of feelings and emotions in psychotherapy processes and outcomes. This approach is in contrast, if not in opposition to, the behavioral-cognitive school that makes thinking responsible for how we feel. The field of psychotherapy has been dominated heretofore by the behavioral-cognitive school, which does not emphasize the importance of feelings in general and of hurt feelings in particular. Feelings are the product of how we think rather than the other way around. Against such hegemony, for the past twenty years Greenberg and Johnson (1990) have emphasized the importance of feelings and emotions. Hurt feelings are predominant although not addressed specifically by either therapist. Third, research on distance writing (DW) will be reviewed. Fourth, issues of psychotherapy with complex and very likely resistant cases of persistent grief will be reviewed. Fifth, one indirect and one direct prescription relating to hurt feelings will be presented.

AVOIDANCE OF HURT FEELINGS IN THE PROFESSIONAL
LITERATURE

There is plenty of literature showing that the topic of hurt feelings has been avoided consistently in the psychotherapy community, even though these feelings lie at the bottom of a great deal of dysfunctionality and psychopathology, that is, the "unconscious" as discussed in previous chapters of this volume. A few representative examples from relevant professional texts will be included to support the avoidance of or inconsistent reliance on a variety of different feelings, which relies on an explanatory construct to deal with maladaptive behaviors. In an early treatise, Nichols and Zax (1977) included anger, anxiety, depression, and a Discomfort Relief Quotient (p. 177). These authors, like many others to follow, included the term distress throughout the text without defining it. However, the term was not included in the subject index. Pierce, Nichols, and DuBrin (1983) included "recall of repressed material" (p. 4) and "repressed affects" (pp. 5, 30). However, the only affect they included was "embarrassment" (p. 189). Safran and Greenberg (1991) considered at great length affects and emotions including anger, anxiety, depression, embarrassment, fear, and sadness, but neither distress nor hurt feelings were included. Johnson (2002) considered anger, anxiety, depression, and fear, but did not include either distress or hurt feelings, as if these feelings did not exist in trauma survivors.

A classical text on psychotherapy (Bergin & Garfield, 1994) included "affective experiencing" without defining it, as well as anxiety, various types of phobias, and depression. Another treatise (Snyder & Ingram, 2000) covered affect and affect regulation without defining either term; other unexplained terms were anxiety disorders, depression, empathy, and finally "emotional distress in interpersonal psychotherapy" (pp. 269–270). Even though the term distress was repeated three times in as many paragraphs, it was never defined except as being related to psychosomatic symptoms without a physical cause.

Two exceptions to the forgoing review are found in the work by Ogrodniczuk, Piper, and Joyce (2006) and by Marin, Holtzman, and DeLongis (2007). After mentioning "interpersonal distress" nine times and "psychic distress" once in half a page (p. 250), Ogrodniczuk et al. used Horowitz, Rosenberg, Baer, Ureno, & Villasenor's (1988) sixty-four-item, eight-subscales Inventory of Interpersonal Problems as an operational definition of "interpersonal distress." This inventory is a self-report instrument designed to assess problems in interpersonal interactions that either are reflected in difficulties in executing particular behaviors ("It is hard for me to …") or difficulties in exercising restraint ("I do … too much"). Many items at their face value could be considered as being hurtful to the respondent. Another attempt to define distress operationally was conducted by Marin et al., who used the Brief Symptom Inventory as an operational definition of "psychological distress."

From this representative sample one can conclude that at best there is no consistent agreement about what feelings constitute affect in the professional literature. Even when distress is attributed to participants, it is consistently either ignored in the subject index or, when cited in text and in subject index, it is left undefined. When there is an attempt to define distress operationally, at least two completely different measures were applied. Consequently, there is room to question whether the frequently but inconsistently used, generic and undefined terms such as distress, negative emotions, social pain, or emotional disturbances begin to describe the essence and depth of our existence (Bridges, 2006).

Distress as a term does not do justice to, nor is it sufficient to describe, particularly hurtful events that we humans are bound to experience during a lifetime. Can generic terms really begin to capture the loss of a loved one due to accident, disease, murder, or suicide? Can these terms describe the experience of a rape victim? It is doubtful whether the term "distress" or even "upset" would qualify. How can we use either one of these undefined terms without committing a serious conceptual and empirical error, when we do not know whether these feelings refer to anger, anxiety, disgust, fear, or sadness?

Despite increased interest in the role of emotion in the process of psychotherapy, Wiser and Goldfried (1993) argued that we currently lack of a valid gauge of its importance in the change process. Wiser and Goldfried obtained significant sessions from thirteen experienced psychodynamic-interpersonal and seventeen experienced cognitive-behavioral therapists, who were examined to determine the extent of affective exploration and therapists' views of these client states. Results indicated that affective experiencing is present in equivalent amounts in the change sessions of these two orientations. However, therapists' clinical views were dissimilar. Psychodynamic-interpersonal therapists viewed portions containing higher affective experiencing as more critical to the change process, whereas cognitive-behavioral therapists viewed lower levels of experiencing as being therapeutically more significant. These findings suggest that, with regard to emotional experiencing, psychodynamic-interpersonal therapists may share common ground with experiential therapists, whereas cognitive-behavior therapists appear to have a unique perspective (Cukor, Spitalnick, Difede, Rizzo, & Rothbaum, 2007).

More recently, however, results about the negative effects on family functioning from psychosocial treatments (Szapocznik & Prado, 2007) have raised serious questions about their effectiveness with certain populations. These authors argued:

> Whereas medical products are required to be tested for safety with respect to vulnerable organ systems, psychosocial treatments are not required to be tested for safety with respect to vulnerable social systems such as the family.... psychosocial treatments with vulnerable populations have the potential to produce negative side effects on families. (p. 468)

These therapists, therefore, recommended that further research be conducted to determine whether safety studies should be required for psychosocial treatments. I echo this conclusion by recommending making pre-, post-, and follow-up evaluation an ethical, professional, and scientific requirement for licensed mental health professionals involved in psychotherapy (L'Abate, 2011a, b). Nevertheless, not all results of family therapy are as negative as Szapocznik and Prado (2007) made them to be. Hogue, Dauber, Samuolis, and Liddle (2006), for instance, examined the link between treatment techniques and long-term treatment outcomes in an empirically supported treatment for adolescent drug abuse. Observational ratings of therapeutic interventions were used to predict outcomes at six and twelve months post treatment for sixty-three families receiving multidimensional family therapy. Greater use of in-session family-focused techniques predicted reduction in internalizing and externalizing symptoms and family conflict, with an improvement in family cohesion, but only when adolescent focus was also high.

In addition, greater use of adolescent-focused techniques predicted improvement in family cohesion and conflict. These results suggest that both individual and multiperson interventions can exert an influential role in family-based therapy for clinically referred adolescents However, we cannot forget about the high rates of dropouts in mental health treatment (Edlund, Wamg, Berglund, Katz, et al., 2002). Sociodemographic characteristics associated with treatment dropout included low income, young age, and in the United States, a lack of insurance coverage for mental health treatment. Patient attitudes associated with dropout included viewing mental health treatment as relatively ineffective and embarrassment about seeing a mental health provider. Patients who received both medication and talk therapy were less likely to drop out than those who received single-modality treatment. This last finding supports the position that to take care of severe psychopathology, there is a need for a variety of treatment modalities (Drozdek & Wilson, 2007; L'Abate et al., 2010).

THE CONTRIBUTION OF SUSAN M. JOHNSON

The specific contribution of Susan M. Johnson applies to the healing of trauma in couples. For instance, Johnson and Williams-Keeler (1998) discussed the application of emotionally focused marital therapy (EFT) in couples where one or both of the partners have experienced significant trauma. EFT, a marital therapy that particularly focuses on the creation of secure attachment, has proven in empirical studies to be effective for distressed couples. EFT, in this context of trauma, incorporates the nine steps of conventional EFT and also encompasses the three stages of the "constructivist" self-development theory of trauma treatment. A more secure and intimate relationship with a spouse can help the trauma survivor on many levels. This article illustrates how the integration of EFT and trauma treatment can prove effective in treating not only relationship distress, but also the individual symptoms of posttraumatic stress disorder (PTSD).

Johnson (1999) explained how EFT is an effective short-term approach to modifying distressed couples' constricted interaction patterns and emotional responses, and can help foster the development of a secure emotional bond. Such bonds are powerfully associated with physical and emotional health and well-being, resilience in the face of stress and trauma, optimal personality development, and adaptation to the environment. EFT has been used to successfully address marital distress complicated by other problems such as depression, PTSD, and chronic physical illness, and is now one of the best empirically validated approaches to changing distressed relationships. In this chapter, Johnson presented a theoretical model on and goals of EFT and its effect on marital distress and adult intimacy. Key phases in treatment and assessment, as well as the selection of clients, planning the treatment, building an alliance, and core interventions of EFT are discussed. A case description and transcript are also provided.

Saxe and Johnson (1999) examined the effectiveness of a group treatment program on intrapersonal symptomatology and interpersonal difficulties in a clinical population of women with a history of incest. Participants for the study were drawn from a time-limited group-treatment program conducted by a community-based mental health agency: Thirty-two women with a history of childhood incest who participated in the twenty-week program were compared to thirty-one women who were wait-listed for the program for a similar time period on measures of intrapersonal symptomatology and interpersonal difficulties. In addition, the effects of the group treatment program over time were examined by assessment of the treatment group six months following completion of the program. Results indicated that a time-limited group that focuses on the original trauma is effective in reducing intrapersonal symptomatology for women with a history of incest and that this improvement is stable over time. In general, interpersonal difficulties did not show as much improvement as intrapersonal symptomatology.

Johnson and Greenman (2006) argued that EFT for couples combines experiential and systemic techniques to expand emotional responses and cycles of interaction. This approach has also been used to treat depression, chronic illness, and anxiety disorders. EFT appears to translate well across culture and class, focusing on universal key emotions and attachment needs. From the EFT perspective, adult love is a hardwired, adaptive attachment response. The therapist's in-session focus is on the processing of emotions and key interactional patterns as they occur in the present, because emotional experiences are the primary instruments of change in this approach. The therapist is a relationship consultant who offers a safe platform whereby each partner can distill, expand, and transform experience and find new ways to connect with the other. Usually this process occurs in three stages: deescalation, restructuring interactions, and consolidation.

Experiential therapies, such as EFT, share with John Bowlby's attachment theory (Mikulincer & Shaver, 2007) a focus on the way we deal with basic emotions, engage with others on the basis of these emotions, and continually construct a sense of self from the drama of repeated emotionally laden interactions with attachment figures. The relevance of attachment theory to understanding change in adult psychotherapy, whether individual or couple therapy, has become clearer because of the enormous amount of research applying attachment theory to adults in the last two decades. Attachment theory is now used explicitly to inform interventions in individual therapy, and it forms the basis of one of the best-validated and most effective couple interventions – EFT for couples. The attachment perspective may help humanistic experiential therapists address individual problems such as anxiety and depression, as well as the relationship distress that accompanies and maintains these problems. The current humanistic experiential model of individual psychotherapy is perhaps best represented by the systematic and evidence-based interventions of the EFT school. This approach has received considerable empirical validation both for anxiety/trauma-related problems and for depression in individuals (Johnson, 2009).

Complex developmental traumatic stressors that occur in the context of an insecure or chaotic relationship between an infant and a primary caregiver often include recurring episodes of abuse and neglect over the course of childhood, both within and outside of the family. Psychological trauma experienced at the hands of a key attachment figure, on whom a child depends for a basic sense of safety and connection, has a pronounced impact on the developing child's self-identity and self-worth. If opportunities for change or repair via other relationships are not available, resultant negative models of self and others tend to be stable over the lifespan. These identity and relational prototypes and associated strategies for the regulation of emotion come into play in the various aspects of adult relationships, including bonding, emotional intimacy, and sexual interaction. In this chapter, we address the impact of complex traumatic stress disorder on adult intimate partner relationships and describe a form of therapy, EFT for couples, that addresses the needs of couples when one or both partners has such a history (Johnson & Courtois, 2009).

Johnson (2008) outlined the unique contributions of attachment theory to couple and family therapy (C&FT) and explained how these contributions represent significant departures from the field's traditions. She then presented prominent clinical models of C&FT based on attachment theory, along with relevant outcome research. Potential limitations of attachment theory as it relates to C&FT are then outlined, together with future promising directions for attachment-oriented interventions in both the couple therapy and family therapy domains.

PTSD and depression are the two mental health problems that most often accompany significant relationship distress. An anxiety disorder such as PTSD certainly tends to interfere with the formation and maintenance of satisfying close relationships. It is also clear that the lack of such relationships, at the very least, impedes coping mechanisms and prevents healing and growth, and at worst, exacerbates and perpetuates anxiety and depression. Just how crucial the quality of significant relationships is when it comes to dealing with traumatic stress is, however, only now being fully recognized. Emotional attachment to significant others is the "primary protection against feelings of helplessness and meaninglessness." The impact of traumatic experience is most often best predicted, not by trauma history, but by whether survivors can seek comfort in the arms of another – that is, whether they have a bond that offers them a safe haven and a secure base. The promise of couple therapy is just this: that the creation of a more stable, loving relationship can offer such a haven as well as a secure base on which to stand and learn to deal effectively with the echoes of traumatic experience (Johnson & Makinen, 2003).

THE CONTRIBUTION OF LESLIE S. GREENBERG

Leslie S. Greenberg (2007, 2008) for years has been on the forefront of promoting the importance of feelings and emotions in psychotherapy, quite in contrast with the cognitive-behavioral school that focuses mostly on cognitions rather than feelings or emotions, EFT. Greenberg and Pascal-Leone (2006), for instance, emphasized the importance and usefulness of four distinct emotion processes in psychotherapy depending on the client's concerns: (1) emotion arousal and awareness; (2) emotion regulation; (3) active reflection (meaning making); and (4) emotion transformation, that is, changing an emotion with another emotion: "Thus, to overcome emotion avoidance, clients must first be helped to approach emotions by attending to their emotional experience" (Greenberg & Pascal-Leone, 2006, p. 613). This is a principle advocated by this writer years ago (L'Abate, 1984): "Approach what you have avoided." However, Greenberg and Pascal-Leone (2006, p. 624) correctly felt that avoidance, catharsis, and reflection alone (rational thinking) are not sufficient to process adequately painful emotions. Practical implications of these different but possibly sequential processes for other schools of psychotherapy are discussed, such as experiential therapy, among those that include emotions.

More recently, Greenberg (2008, pp. 95–97) detailed how emotional transformation occurs through an eight-step sequence consisting of (1) the therapeutic relationship; (2) shifting attention to background feelings; (3) accessing needs/goals; (4) positive imagery; (5) expressive enactment of the emotion under consideration; (6) remembering another emotion; (7) cognitive change; and (8) using the therapeutic relationship to generate a new (more positive) emotion. Part of this sequence is generated by the overall view of the therapist as an "emotion coach," as a professional expert/specialist in the field of emotion (Greenberg, Elliott, & Pos, 2007).

One method to reach painful feelings is the Empty Chair technique first advocated by Fritz Perls years ago whereby participants are encouraged to speak to another person significant in their lives or even to another self, an alter ego, sitting in that chair. Through this and other methods outlined previously, Greenberg claims with significant evidence that this approach has helped people with depression, couple distress, personality disorders, childhood abuse and trauma, anxiety, and worry.

Greenberg and Goldman (2009) introduced recent developments of an emotion-focused approach to couple therapy. They identified three core motivations that need to be attended to in facilitating conflict resolution in intimate relationships: (1) the need for attachment; (2) the need to have identity validated by the other; and (3) attraction to the other. These motives are governed by the feelings they engender, making couple relationships a key means of emotion regulation. These writers described different categories of feelings, distinguishing between *primary* emotions that are directly related to satisfaction of our core motivations and those emotions that are influenced by other factors in our psychological makeup. A five-stage model of an emotion-focused way of working with couples was outlined. These steps are designed to help partners gain awareness of and constructively express their different emotions. These therapists emphasized that in order to resolve couple conflict, it not only is important to develop the capacity to empathize with and soothe the other in a relationship, but also to be able to soothe one's own anxieties and shame and tolerate disappointments.

Two simple questions can be raised by the foregoing, admittedly too short, review about whether EFT deals specifically with hurt feelings. If these feelings are not specifically mentioned in all the foregoing references and many other references not included here, shall we assume that the feelings generated by this approach are indeed hurt feelings? Shouldn't the nature of these feelings be spelled out more clearly and specifically? Repeated experiences with major depressive disorder (MDD), on the other cognitive hand, may strengthen associations between negative thinking and dysphoria, rendering negative cognition more accessible and pronounced with each episode.

As noted, according to cognitive theory, greater negative cognition should lead to a more protracted episode of depression. To test this prediction, Beevers, Wells, and Miller (2007) found that in 121 adults with MDD, the number of previous episodes was associated with slower change in depression across inpatient and outpatient treatment. Furthermore, although pretreatment negative cognition and pretreatment family impairment both uniquely predicted slower change in depressive symptoms, only negative cognitions mediated the association between depression history and depression change. These findings suggest that repeated MDD episodes are specifically associated with increased negative cognition, which in turn contributes to a more pernicious course of symptom change during treatment for depression.

Leslie S. Greenberg's contribution finds its validation in two whole issues of the *Journal of Clinical Psychology* (Magnavita, 2006) and *Clinical Psychology: Science and Practice*, which are completely dedicated to feelings and emotions: This implies that a possible sea-change may occur in the field of psychotherapy, including its becoming a science rather than an art. Not all the articles included in the *Journal of Clinical Psychology* are relevant to hurt feelings. Selva and Caughlin (2006), for instance, contributed to research that years ago supported a hypothesis clinically suggested decades ago: that those who have functional disorders exhibit deficits in emotional processing. Many studies reviewed by these authors have systematically documented that patients who habitually repress their emotions simultaneously suppress their immune response, rendering them vulnerable to physical illness and early death. Conversely, those who are encouraged to experience and express their feelings demonstrate improvements in immune function, physical condition, and psychological well-being. These authors describe a psychotherapy designed to interrupt defensive processes and facilitate the direct experience of previously disavowed feelings in the treatment of patients who suffer from physical ailments.

Sloan and Kring (2007) provided a selective review of measures that can be used to assess various aspects of emotional responding during the course of psychotherapy. These writers paid particular attention to measures that index emotion regulation, emotional experience, emotional expression, and emotional awareness across self-report, observer-based, and psychophysiological methods. This review concluded with considerations about the need for a clear working definition of emotion, reliability issues that arise when measures reflect a state-dependent construct (e.g., emotional experience), and the potential need to assess more than one component of emotional responding.

Rottenberg and Gross (2007) commented on Sloan and Kring's article by asserting that never before has the pace of research on emotion and emotion regulation been as vigorous as it is today. This news is welcomed by researchers who study psychological therapies and who believe that emotion and emotion-regulation processes are fundamental to normal and abnormal functioning. However, one unwelcome consequence of this otherwise happy state of affairs is that therapy researchers now face an array of bewildering decisions about what to measure and why. What is needed is a map that will help researchers make wise decisions in this domain. In this spirit, Rottenberg and Gross located Sloan and Kring's (2007) important review of available emotion and emotion-regulation measures within the wider field of affective constructs and the broader issue of psychotherapy research. Where appropriate, Rottenberg and Gross illustrated their arguments with examples from their own work that highlight payoffs and challenges of integrating affective and clinical science.

In additional comments on Sloan and Kring's (2007) article, Mennin and Farach (2007) indicated that clinical psychology has historically underplayed the importance of emotions in conceptualizing and treating adult psychopathology. However, these writers assert that there has been a recent convergence among numerous theoretical orientations in drawing from investigations of emotions within basic affective science, which highlight the survival and societal functions of emotions, the involvement of multiple biological systems in emotion generation, and a dynamic model for regulatory aspects of emotions. These characterizations of emotions suggested a number of ways that current treatments may benefit from explicit incorporation of interventions targeting emotions, particularly for resistant forms of adult psychopathology. Specifically, emotion-related skills training and broadening the role of emotions in measuring change may be important areas for expansion within the treatment of adult psychopathology.

Leahy (2007) responded to these articles by arguing that although cognitive-behavioral therapy has been criticized for not addressing the importance of emotion in psychotherapy, recent trends indicate a growing interest in this topic. So-called Third Wave approaches in cognitive-behavioral therapies suggest that "cognitive" processes are often of little importance. Leahy (2007) then proceeded to describe how learning theory, models of emotional processing, exposure treatments, criticisms of "extinction," and even emotion-based approaches rely on cognitive and representational constructs. He attempted to integrate emotion and cognition in emotional schema theory.

Suveg, Southam-Gerow, Goodman, and Kendall (2007) added that a burgeoning of research on emotion has identified the importance of emotionally competent functioning to children's psychosocial adaptation. As a consequence of this basic research, these authors argued that prevention and treatment programs for youth would benefit from direct consideration of the role of emotion when designing developmentally appropriate programs. The rationale for including a greater focus on emotion in youth prevention and treatment programs is drawn from the affective neuroscience and clinical psychology literatures. Preliminary data from prevention and treatment programs that have a strong emotion focus are promising. Future work needs to (1) examine how emotion-related processes are related to psychopathology in youth; (2) develop developmentally sensitive programs that are influenced by basic research on emotions; (3) evaluate the relative effectiveness of prevention and treatment programs; and (4) assess the potential long-term impact of emotion-focused and emotion-informed programs.

In his commentary to Suveg's et al. (2007) spirited argument for the importance of focusing on emotional awareness and emotion processing in prevention and treatment efforts with children, Mark T. Greenberg (2007) noted that their review included substantial empirical evidence for the role of emotions in normal development and psychopathology, as well as recent evidence of our improved understanding of the neuroscience of emotions. Finally, this writer reviewed recent work that focused on emotion-focused models of prevention and treatment with children. More importantly, the developmental understanding of emotions can do much to inform our models of prevention and treatment and improve the healthy development of children. In closing his comments, M. T. Greenberg focused on conceptual and theoretical clarifications that are necessary in this new connection between neuroscience and psychotherapy.

The need for a multimethod approach to the study of emotion in children and adolescents is crucial in a multilevel analysis in which emotional experience is assessed at a variety of levels (Zeman, Klimes-Dougan, Cassano, & Adrian, 2007). These authors highlighted the critical role of emotion theory when constructing and selecting appropriate assessment tools with a focus on functionalist theory that emphasizes the importance of contextual variables. These authors begin with an examination of theoretical and pragmatic issues in emotion measurement followed by discussions of four basic methods of emotion assessment: (1) self-report; (2) other-report; (3) observation; and (4) neurophysiology.

In response to the previous articles, Halberstadt and Parker (2007) considered several conceptual points regarding the measurement of emotion in developing individuals: (1) Questions should guide measurement rather than vice versa; (2) divergent outcomes across multiple measures are informative rather than worrisome; (3) measures can assess across multiple dimensions of emotion (e.g., structure and function); (4) emotions are dynamic functions occurring within changing individuals in changing relationships; (5) emotions and emotional regulation are inextricably interwoven; (6) the effective social competence model allows for the study of dynamic aspects of emotion competence in dynamic ways within relationships and across diverse cultures; and (7) the study of emotional competence is useful for interventions with clinical populations.

Despite ongoing discussions over how best to define and operationalize emotions, therapists increasingly agree on emotions' centrality to psychological health and change (Burum & Goldfried, 2007). Research suggests that accurately recognizing emotions is critical to psychological health, and most major therapeutic approaches aim to address deficits in emotional awareness. Interventions also strive to regulate emotions, with cognitive-behavior therapy typically working to reduce emotions such as anxiety and depression, and experiential and psychodynamic therapists working to augment emotional experiencing. Increasingly, however, these approaches are converging toward using emotional experience within therapy to ultimately reduce *negative emotions*. The application of emotions' role in meaning changes, and human behavior points to the way in which drawing on basic emotion research can enable us to create assessments and treatments grounded in an empirically supported understanding of the mechanisms of change, and in so doing, foster greater psychotherapy integration.

At the end of this series of articles, Leslie S. Greenberg (2007) emphasized viewing emotion regulation as a process that occurs during the generation of emotion with the aim to foster self-maintenance rather than self-control. In a self-maintenance view, the cognitive system is seen as receiving information from the emotion system as well as influencing it, and self-maintenance is seen as occurring (largely below conscious awareness) by means of dynamic processes that involve both self- and other-regulation. Additionally, Greenberg suggested that the field has yet to pay adequate attention to implicit and relational processes of emotion regulation. An issue of major clinical significance is the importance of generating theory and research to help understand to what extent automatic emotion processes can be changed through deliberate conscious cognitive processes of self-control, and to what extent they can only be changed through more implicit processes based on new emotional and/or relational experience.

To conclude, Ehrenreich, Fairholme, Buzzella, Ellard, et al. (2007) reviewed some common themes and challenges to move forward the role of emotion in psychological therapy. These authors emphasized: (1) context in defining emotion concepts and maximizing the relevancy of those concepts to therapy; (2) the importance of imbuing efforts to develop emotion-focused treatments with emphasis on positive as well as negative emotions and flexibility in the expression of those emotions; (3) the relevance of a lifespan developmental approach to the accurate use of emotion and emotion-regulation concepts within treatment; and (4) the importance of a unified approach to the treatment of emotional disorders in youth and adults.

DISTANCE WRITING IN PSYCHOTHERAPY

Distance writing (DW) means writing without the F2F, TB presence of a professional, usually at home using a computer, as already introduced in Chapter 11. DW can be divided into two major approaches as adjuncts or as alternatives to F2F, TB psychotherapy: (1) Pennebaker's Expressive Writing (EW) method, and (2) L'Abate's programmed writing (PW) and interactive practice exercises or workbooks.

Pennebaker's Expressive Writing Method

As already considered in Chapter 6, EW consists of asking participants to write for fifteen to twenty minutes a day for four consecutive days about heretofore undisclosed traumatic experiences (Esterling, L'Abate, Murray, & Pennebaker, 1999; Pennebaker & Chung, 2007). The evidence about this process tends to support administration of this approach either by itself or conjointly with talk-based psychotherapy (Kacewicz, Slatcher, & Pennebaker, 2007). Recent research supporting this paradigm has been reported in De Giacomo et al. (2010).

Interactive Practice Exercises and Psychotherapy

Interactive practice exercises or workbooks are the byproduct of pro-grammed writing (L'Abate, 1986, 1992b, 2003, 2011c), called originally lessons or assignments, eventually workbooks, and finally interactive practice exer-cises (L'Abate, 2004a, 2004b). The reason for finally using the term interac-tive practice exercises lies in trying to come up with a neutral term that does not reflect an academic quality, such as lessons, assignments, or even work-books. As already described in Chapter 11, there are workbooks for nonclini-cal, promotional, life-learning conditions with nondiagnosed populations, targeted populations, and severe psychopathology. Because psychotherapy is an approach that supposedly deals with psychopathology, it is relevant to single out workbooks that deal with various clinical conditions, such as bipolar, severe depression, and schizophrenia (L'Abate, 2011c).

Research by L'Abate, L'Abate, and Maino (2005) is relevant to the rela-tionship between workbooks and psychotherapy. They reviewed all their clinical cases in twenty-five years of part-time private practice with indi-viduals, couples, and families of the first two authors. The first ten years were conducted with regular F2F, TB contacts without any workbooks. The next fifteen years were conducted with workbooks in addition to F2F, TB contacts and signed informed consent forms to administer workbooks. Up to that point (L'Abate, 1986, 1992b, 2003, 2004), including a meta-analysis of workbooks that produced a medium effect size of d = . 44 (Smyth & L'Abate, 2001), this author had proclaimed the cost-effectiveness of using work-books in psychotherapy, citing their likely decreasing the number of F2F, TB sessions. He was completely wrong. Administration of workbooks sig-nificantly increased the number of sessions in individuals, couples, and fam-ilies. On the other hand, Goldstein (L'Abate & Goldstein, 2007) found that a problem-solving workbook administered to decompensating personality disordered women significantly reduced the number of days in the hospital and the number of readmissions to the hospital.

These contradictory results indicate the need to research further what populations (clinical versus nonclinical) – under what conditions (inpatient versus outpatient) and what type and severity of diagnosis – are benefited by workbooks, and what level of education is necessary for the administration of workbooks.

Comparing Expressive and Programmed Writing

A simple comparison of both approaches, that is, expressive and programmed writing, suggests that they are so structurally different that they must be considered complementary in order to help adjunctively and synergistically in the psychotherapeutic process. However, it would be even more tempting to suggest that each approach possesses its pros and cons. EW, for instance, has been validated extensively with a great many populations, whereas PW has thus far only a few experimental studies going back thirty years, recently reanalyzed for their effect sizes (L'Abate, 2004a, 2004b), and a small meta-analysis (Smyth & L'Abate, 2001). Whereas EW may be quite generic, PW is especially targeted in its workbooks. Focusing on intimacy and hurt feelings, for instance, is much more specific in pinpointing not only the nature but also the causes of those feelings (L'Abate, 1997, 2009a, 2011b).

Therefore, EW essentially relies on a one-size-fits-all approach, whereas PW relies on a variety of different and specific workbooks that allow for the consideration of wider contexts for hurt feelings in a more varied manner. Clearly, PW is much more structured and detailed with questions, tasks, and progressions in its homework assignments, whereas EW's only structure lies in its initial instructions and nothing else. This conclusion is in no way meant to detract from the substantial contribution that EW has made in the field of mental health service delivery.

COMPLICATED GRIEF

This condition is very resistant to standard psychotherapeutic approaches and consists of frequent and intense weeping, inability to let go of memories and behaviors of the deceased, and magnifying if not idolizing the memory of the deceased. For instance, Boelen, van den Hout, and van den Bout (2006) introduced a cognitive-behavioral conceptualization of complicated grief (CG) that offers a framework for generating hypotheses about mechanisms underlying CG that can be targeted for treatment. These processes are seen as crucial in the development and maintenance of CG: (1) insufficient integration of the loss into the autobiographical knowledge base; (2) negative global beliefs and misinterpretations of grief reactions; and (3) anxious and depressive avoidance strategies to deal with painful feelings. According to Boelen et al., these three processes should account for the occurrence of CG symptoms, whereas the interaction among these three processes is postulated to be critical to symptoms becoming marked and persistent. This model recognizes that background variables influence CG, but postulates that this influence is mediated by the model's three core processes. The flip side of this condition lies in the inability to grieve, a much less studied reaction to abandonment, abuse, and loss (see Chapter 3 of this volume) that may be responsible for the development of cancer in some cases, specifically of breast cancer in some women who are unable to express and share hurt feelings. This might be the case in individuals who suffer from alexithymia or similar conditions, whose immune system may have been compromised by an inability to feel hurt feelings and to cry (Hesse, & Floyd, 2008).

Bonanno (2006) emphasized that important progress has been made in conceptualizing and demonstrating effective interventions of CG. He argued, however, that the CG construct is still poorly understood and that there remain several unanswered questions about the construct's basic validity. Bonanno reviewed recent research that provides preliminary evidence for the CG's incremental validity over other forms of grief-related psychopathology. However, further evidence of incremental validity is still needed. He also reviewed several perspective studies that tend to support the discriminant validity of CG in relation to more enduring depressive symptoms. However, up to the present most studies of CG have failed to make this distinction and have tended to confound CG with long-term depressive states. Bonanno argued that future research on CG, including intervention studies, needs to allot greater attention to these validity studies.

Ehlers (2006) outlined the possible parallels between the phenomenology and treatment of CG and PTSD. He explored in particular how treatment procedures have usually relied on cognitive therapy for PTSD that could be adapted for the treatment of CG. For instance, "Stimulus Discrimination" may be helpful in breaking the link between everyday triggers and the felt presence of memories about the deceased. "Memory Updating" procedures may help participants accept that the deceased is no longer alive and no longer suffering. "Reclaiming Your Life" procedures may help participants access autobiographical memories that are not linked to the deceased and counteract beliefs about the value of life without the deceased. Ehlers further addressed the necessity of specifying idiosyncratic beliefs that prevent coming to terms with the death as well as understanding the relationship between beliefs and coping strategies and distinguishing between memories and ruminations.

Neimeyer (2006) proposed that a cognitive-behavioral model of CG emphasized the struggle to integrate the loss into autobiographical memory, receiving both conceptual and empirical support from recent constructivist work on the role of "sense-making" as a process in bereavement adaptation. However, globally negative appraisals and anxious and depressive avoidance strategies, factors also posited by the cognitive-behavioral formulation, may play a more circumscribed role, inhibiting adjustment to loss in some, but not all, cases of CG. Converging research programs lend credence to a cognitive-constructivist approach to grief and suggest the relevance of meaning-oriented and narrative strategies for assisting participants whose lives have been devastated by the loss.

Ruscio and Holohan (2006) insisted that among the factors contributing to the underutilization of empirically supported treatments (ESTs), as argued by the four previous authors, are practitioners' concerns about the appropriateness of ESTs for complex clinical problems that are thought to be in significant ways different from populations included in clinical research trials, as seen in CG. Such problems may challenge the best available treatments and may raise important ethical, practical, and empirical questions. Ruscio and Holohan reviewed features that may define complex cases such as CG and considered influences on clinicians' decisions to provide, modify, or abandon an EST approach with such cases. Given a dearth of data to inform this decision, these writers highlighted several questions in need of further investigation faced by clinicians, and suggested avenues for future work that may enhance efforts to disseminate and effectively provide ESTs.

Abramowitz (2006) commented on Ruscio and Holohan's arguments about applying ESTs to complex problems like CG, especially those with comorbid conditions. He argued that many clinicians in some instances abandon ESTs on the assumption that treatment manuals do not apply. Abramowitz also argued that although ESTs may provide the best available guidance for how to treat many psychological disorders, effective treatment does not require rigid adherence to treatment manuals if clinicians are able to develop a case formulation on the basis of functional analysis of behavior and apply empirical treatment procedures accordingly. Development of exposure and response prevention for an obsessive-compulsive disorder case is presented as an example of how knowledge of basic cognitive and behavioral processes transcends ESTs and their manuals. It is important for beginning therapists to learn to apply principles based on these processes rather than rely exclusively on treatment manuals.

Persons (2006) favored a case-formulation-driven approach to psychotherapy by addressing many of the difficulties clinicians experience when using EST protocols to treat complex cases such as CG. A formulation-driven approach provides the flexibility required to work effectively with complex cases by allowing clinicians to make intervention decisions guided by theory and by results of continuous assessment rather than simply by the list of interventions described in the EST protocol. To strengthen the empirical foundations of case-formulation-driven psychotherapy, the therapist can use a hypothesis testing approach to each case, relying on an evidence-based nomothetic formulation and treatment plan and on other empirical findings to guide formulation, intervention, and clinical decision making. Current, recently published EST protocols for complex cases include some of the key elements of case-formulation-driven psychotherapy.

Wolfe (2006) suggested that additional research strategies are necessary to acquire information more useful and relevant to clinical practitioners. These strategies would include (1) integrating information from research on empirically supported relationship factors with findings from EST outcome research; (2) analyzing long-term therapies attempting to address issues beyond the symptoms of the DSM-IV; and (3) investigating the efficacy and effectiveness of integrative forms of psychotherapy. An example of Wolfe's second suggestion about addressing issues beyond symptoms of the DSM-IV is found in the research by L'Abate, van Eigen, Goldstein, And Rigamonti (in press), which evaluates nonviolent, externalizing personality disordered women through a checklist that, once validated cross-culturally, could be transformed into an interactive practice exercise specifically tailored to these women.

SELF-ADMINISTERED TREATMENTS FOR DEPRESSION

Menchola, Arkowitz, and Burke (2007) claimed that self-administered treatments (SATs) are widely used by the general public and mental health professionals. Previous reviews of the efficacy of SATs have included under this category interventions for nonclinical problems, group interventions, and interventions involving significant amounts of therapist contact. The efficacy of SATs for clinical levels of depression and anxiety with minimal therapeutic contact was examined by a meta-analysis of twenty-four studies. Results show large effects for SATs when compared with no-treatment control groups (d = 1.00).

However, unlike previous meta-analyses that found nonsignificant differences between SATs and therapist-administered treatments, in this sample SATs result in significant poorer outcomes (d = −0.31). Some differences in effect size were observed between the clinical targets of depression and anxiety. However, there were high correlations between clinical target, methodological quality of the study, and amount of contact. This makes it impossible to determine whether the observed differences could be explained by the nature of the disorders, methodological quality, or the amount of contact with a member of the research team. These results raise questions about the clinical use of SATs without some degree of contact with a professional. This is why written practice exercises were developed to be "interactive" – that means that a professional must be involved in the process to one extent or another. I do not believe that any form of treatment can be completely self-administered, especially with certain types of participants (L'Abate, 2011 a, b). Of course, I could be completely wrong.

PRESCRIPTIONS IN PSYCHOTHERAPY

The prescriptions presented in Tables 12.1 and 12.2 were originally constructed respectively from Models[7] and [15] of RCT (Cusinato & L'Abate, 2012; L'Abate et al., 2010) to administer to couples and families. However, there is no reason why they could not be applied in groups, at least for the Hugging, Holding, Huddling, and Cuddling (3HC) model in Table 12.1. It is strongly recommended that this prescription not be used in individual psychotherapy unless there are other witnesses present to assure that no untoward results or misunderstandings occur between professionals and participants. Although this prescription admittedly does not deal directly with hurt feelings, it may provide the groundwork for allowing such feelings to come to the fore. If disclosure and sharing of hurtful feelings do not emanate naturally from this prescription, then the next one can be administered.

There is substantive evidence in the literature on depression about the wish to be held, where gender and gender role traits need to be considered. Among many studies on this topic, Sanfilipo (1993), for instance, examined different forms of the wish to be held with measures of femininity, masculinity, and various types of depression in a sample of normal adults whose ethnicity resembled that of national statistics. Women reported greater wish to be held than men. However, the wish to be held, which was uncorrelated with depressive symptomatology, related positively to

TABLE 12.1. *Handout for 3HC with couples and families**

Although at first this task seems very simple, it is not as simple as it may appear. You are being asked to hug and hold each other. You will huddle and cuddle with each other by appointment only at the beginning, and later, if you enjoy doing it for longer than just a few minutes, voluntarily. When you have learned this task well, you may want to do it on your own as often as you like or as is necessary.

. . . .

Step 1

Make an appointment, at least 24 hours before the task is to be performed. Make sure that everybody agrees about how important it is for couples and families to hug and hold each other in ways that are not usually done in our fast-moving culture and with our busy schedules. Unless everybody understands the importance of this task, you may need to hold a couple or family conference to make sure that everybody agrees about how important this task is for the couple's or family's well-being. Determine beforehand how long this task will last (anywhere from 10 to 15 minutes depending how often you perform it, that is, every day, every other day, twice a week, or once a week).

Step 2

Before starting this task, make sure there will not be interruptions. Take the phone off the hook if you do not have an answering machine, put out all the lights including the natural light from windows, and, if necessary put a "Please Do Not Disturb" sign outside your residence door.

Step 3

Find a place in the house that is comfortable for everybody and that will contain all the family members. If a sofa is not roomy enough to hold everybody in the family, if you have a very comfortable thick rug, use that.

Step 4

Before starting this task make sure that you set an alarm or timer for the time agreed upon by everybody.

Step 5

Form a huddle by making sure that everybody is hugging and holding everybody else as much as possible. Allow yourselves to feel whether you are enjoying cuddling and being cuddled.

Step 6

While you are cuddling, it is important that there will be no talk. Everybody needs to be silent; concentrate on being together without any talk or interruptions of any kind. Talking or non-required movements will interfere with the concentration needed to perform and complete this task successfully.

(continued)

TABLE 12.1 *(continued)*

Step 7

Once the alarm or timer goes off, break the huddle and remind each other about the next time you are going to do it again. Partners or caretakers should take down in writing any comments offered freely by any family member. If you do write these comments down and are presently under the care of a mental health professional, bring these notes to your next session.

We hope that you have enjoyed this task and that you will make it an important routine in your marriage and family life.

* Adapted from L'Abate, 2001 and from L'Abate and Cusinato, 2007.

TABLE 12.2. *Instructions for hurt-sharing between partners and among family members**

1. Seat partners or family members facing each other with their eyes closed holding hands.
2. Ask participants to concentrate on how the hands of their partners or family members feel and let them answer.
3. After the answers to the previous question are given, ask participants to concentrate on their hurts. Allow quite a few minutes of silence for this concentration to occur.
4. Suggest that if they have been able to link with and feel their hurts they can now express these feelings by saying repeatedly: "I hurt. I am hurting." Allow sufficient time for all participants to express their feelings if they are able to do so.
5. Ask each partner or participant to express how they feel about the feelings expressed by their partner or loved one(s).
6. If necessary prescribe this exercise as a homework assignment to be performed at specific times and in a particular place, keeping notes of what happened to bring back to the professional.
7. Follow up in the next therapy session by asking participants whether they performed the prescription or not. If Yes, what happened afterward, as shown by notes taken.
   If No, what happened in between sessions.

* Adapted from L'Abate, 1998, 1999, 2000, and L'Abate and Cusinato, 2007.

femininity and feelings of efficacy for men, but positively to anaclitic and introjective depression for women. For women, gender role traits also were important for wishes to be held entailing themes of strategy and deprivation. Because gender differences regarding various depressive experiences did not account for these findings, the wish to be held may have different meanings for men and women: one as an intimate gesture, the other as a sexual request.

The prescription in Table 12.2 was originally developed to deal with hurt feelings in couples (L'Abate, 1999b). This prescription should not be administered at the outset of psychotherapy, because it might be too powerful and could produce possibly negative, unexpected, and unpredictable outcomes. Like the previous prescription, this prescription must be first administered in the professional's office before assigning it as homework. It could be used diagnostically at the beginning of couple therapy after the first three evaluation sessions and an informed consent form has been read and signed. At termination, this prescription could be readministered to evaluate whether partners have learned to share hurt feelings constructively and achieved intimacy as defined here from the outset of this volume.

CONCLUSION

This chapter shows how many choices exist for mental health professionals to help needy participants learn to access heretofore avoided hurt feelings, either in individuals, couples, or families. The more severe a condition, the greater the need to use more than one approach, especially if F2F talk does not produce the desired results. It would not hurt to ask for conjoint medical treatment for severe cases, even though such an approach may make it more difficult to access hurt feelings.

PART FOUR

MODELS OF HURT FEELINGS IN THEORY
AND APPLICATIONS

13

Hurt Feelings: A Construct in Search of a Theory

Although numerous studies have investigated the association between hurt experienced in close relationships and psychopathology, there is little theory pertaining to this association, an omission that begs for attention.... [But] good theory is not enough: The need [is] for greater methodological sophistication.

> Braithwaite, Fisham, & Lambert (2009, p. 392)

Relationship scientists have the responsibility to develop, evaluate, and disseminate theories and protocols that will improve the clinical work of practitioners everywhere.... Application and theory provide reciprocal feedback, so that each is well situated within the other.

> Reis (2007, p. 4)

The role of theory has been discussed at length in previous and recent publications (Cusinato & L'Abate, 2012; L'Abate, 2005, 2009a; L'Abate et al., 2010). However, to my knowledge, there is no theory that can yet encompass hurt feelings in its many ubiquitous manifestations and in its many different models proposed by collaborators in Vangelisti's (2009) recent contribution. Consequently, the purpose of this final chapter is to consider the universality of hurt feelings and to outline sixteen models of RCT that encompass various meanings and manifestations of hurt feelings.

THE UNIVERSALITY OF HURT FEELINGS

One cannot be alive and not be hurt in one way or another and to one degree or another. The universality of hurt feelings, as demonstrated by the literature and evidence gathered in this volume, suggests the importance of developmental aspects and recognition of hurt feelings in all of us. Hurt feelings are related to joys and pleasures. Once hurt feelings overwhelm and offset joys and pleasures, there is the onset of dysfunctionality and psycho-pathology. Joys must offset hurts for us to function adequately.

Any seemingly grandiose claim of universality for hurt feelings should include Pennebaker's research, already reviewed in Chapters 6, 11, and 12 of this volume. In all instances where participants were asked to write about their past, perhaps heretofore undisclosed traumas, there is no recorded instance in which a participant denied not having experienced a trauma (James M. Pennebaker, April 24, 2006, personal communication). Trauma here is another synonymous term for hurt feelings because it means painful experiences and events (Table 1.1). The difference between the two terms lies in the former being used as a technical term, whereas the latter is used in everyday language. Any traumatic event causes physical, emotional, and psychological responses having long-term results. The person experiencing a hurtful event may not know exactly how to respond at that moment; how-ever, with time, memories of the trauma can elicit, among others, feelings of hurt. From Pennebaker's widely cited and replicated research, it is clear that all participants experienced and expressed in writing past traumas that particularly affected them, without exception. No one is immune to being hurt and, if one were, it would be similarly impossible to experience and share joys and pleasures, as in alexithymia or anedonia.

A great deal of evidence is available to connect intensity and frequency of trauma (abuse, adversity, neglect) to physical and mental health, for instance, as in the etiology of criminality (Stoff, Breiling, & Maser, 1997) and psychopathology (Goodyer, 1990; Kring, 2008; Plutchik & Kellerman, 1983, 1990). The pervasiveness of these etiological factors is so extensive that there is no need to document it. Yet what about the consequences and out-comes of hidden abuse that are not reported and therefore undocumented? This question leads to another one: Given such pervasiveness, how many people are hurt by etiologically aversive factors and what will the conse-quences be for whoever has been hurt? Can we indeed conclude that – given the widespread extent of violence, abuse, and neglect – there is still a large proportion of the population whose suffering falls under the umbrella term of hurt feelings?

Given this universality, how can we account for hurt feelings in a way that integrates models that are independent from each other, such as trans-gressions (Vangelisti, 2009b), devaluation of self (Leary & Leder, 2009), cognitive appraisal (Fitness & Warburton, 2009), politeness and face-work (Goldsmith & Donovan-Kicken, 2009), rejection sensitivity (Kang, Downey, Iida, & Rodriquez, 2009), attachment, generation, and regulation of emotions (Shaver, Mikulincer, Lavy, & Cassidy, 2009), rejection (DeWall,

Baumeister, & Masicampo, 2009), conflict (Caughlin, Scott, & Miller, 2009), deception in the name of kindness (DePaulo, Morris, & Sternglanz, 2009), relational and developmental perspectives (Card, Isaacs, & Hodges, 2009; Fehr & Harasymchuk, 2009), couples (Feeney, 2009), families (Mills & Piotrowski, 2009), postdivorce negotiations (Metts, Braithwaite, & Fine, 2009), and settings, as in technology (Whitty, 2009), workplace (Cunningham, Berbee, & Mandal, 2009), and culture (Kowalski, 2009)?

All these models speak to the ubiquitous multicausality and multidimensionality of hurt feelings. How can one make sense of hurt feelings, which comprise so many different models, unless they are integrated into a whole theory? The only theory I am familiar with that could possibly integrate these many disparate models into a whole framework is RCT.

HURT FEELINGS AND RELATIONAL COMPETENCE THEORY

Hierarchical RCT was developed and refined over a span of decades (L'Abate, 1976, 1986, 1990a, 1992a, 1994, 1997, 2003, 2005, 2006; L'Abate & Cusinato, 2007) and validated in some models by L'Abate et al. (2010), and by Cusinato and L'Abate (2012). RCT, akin to the organization table of any human enterprise, be it educational, industrial, military, or religious, is composed of four formal requirements, three meta-theoretical assumptions, three theory-related assumptions, five developmental and normative models, three models dealing with clinical, deviant and dysfunctional populations, and one conclusive and integrative mode of negotiation

Requirements

Models of RCT must fulfill at least four requirements:

Verifiability: Each model from the first to the last must be amenable to empirical verification in the laboratory and in clinical settings.

Applicability: Each model can be applied to functional and dysfunctional relationships with individuals (children, adolescents, adults), couples, and families.

Redundancy: Any construct as represented by a model can be viewed from more than one viewpoint or model of the theory, perhaps a synonymous term for *pluralism*. Consequently, as shown, hurt feelings can be viewed, described, interpreted, and perhaps explained by more than one model of the theory. Complex and multidimensional constructs, such as psychopathology, love, control, and relational creativity, among others, can be viewed by different models of the theory.

Fruitfulness: Each model can generate more than one test or method to be evaluated repeatedly, as done by Cusinato and L'Abate (2005a, 2005b, 2012) and by L'Abate et al. (2010). If the present work on hurt feelings is to be successful, it needs to be cited by more than one scholar or researcher to demonstrate longevity.

Meta-theoretical Assumptions

These assumptions include whatever is known historically about a given topic.

Model[1]: Horizontality

This model views relationships horizontally along a circular recursive communication dimension, already mentioned in Chapter 1 of this volume, starting with the following:

Emotionality: This term describes the whole state of how feelings are experienced from within self and from others, as reviewed in Chapters 1 (Figure 1.1) and 3 of this volume. Emotionality varies along three dimensions: (1) hedonic, whether joyful and pleasant or hurtful and unpleasant; (2) arousal, whether activated or deactivated; and (3) intensity, as powerful or powerless (Frijda et al., 1992).

Rationality: How hurt feelings are appraised and processed cognitively and intellectually (Fitness & Warburton, 2009) as well as how affective states influence everyday judgments in personal relationships (Forgas, Levinger, & Moylan, 1994), including emotional intelligence (Izard, 2001).

Activity: How hurt feelings are expressed, shared, or not shared with self and others through actions rather than just words, roughly equivalent to Frijda's (2007, 2008) action tendencies.

Awareness: There is a feedback loop from how one views what has just occurred, that is, how one is able to evaluate, introspect, reflect, and if necessary change or correct what has already been said or done in relation to hurt feelings (Pennebaker, 1995).

Context: Whatever immediate, proximal or distal, human or material surrounding is perceived subjectively by the individual (Badr, 2004; Brody & Hall, 2008; Mesquita et al., 2010; Rottenberg, 2007; Rottenberg & Vanghan, 2008; Sagarin & Guadagno, 2004; Surra & Perlman, 2003; Thompson & Berenbaum, 2009). A useful conceptualization of context as nested within interactive layers of influence has been proposed by Yang and Rettig (2003). As Goldsmith and Donoval-Kicken (2009, p. 50) commented: "The same action or comment might be more or less hurtful in a different social context." Furthermore, Saarni (2008, p. 333) stressed how context is significant for emotional development according to "affordances" provided in the interaction between organism and environment. Gibson's (1982) original concept of affordances does not seem to be too distant from Rumbaugh and Washburn's (2003) and Kagan's (2007) conceptions of emergence. Saarni (2008, p. 334) emphasized the concept of plasticity as the organism's ability to be sculptured by the immediate environment, that is, context:

> [P]lasticity of emotional development relative to context can be seen in four ways: (1) in a particular style of emotional regulation manifesting itself in different forms in the same individual at different developmental periods, whereby the eliciting situations share some common relational theme for the individual; (2) in the same way that similar emotion-evoking contexts elicit different expressive reactions. This is suggestive of the same hedonic tone with varying manifestations across different individuals (e.g., a "freezing" reaction to a stressful stimulus vs. an agitated reaction); (3) in the "*equipotentiality*" (italics mine) of emotion expressive channels (e.g., facial expression vs. vocal channel or kinesthetic channel; and (4) in judges' ratings of emotion in others that are informed by the context in which the others appear to be responding to relational goals.

This ERAAwC Model has been evaluated with a fifty-item questionnaire originally developed by Cusinato (2001) and validated in many studies reported in Cusinato and L'Abate (2012) and L'Abate et al. (2010). This model also accounts for gender differences in feelings and emotions, as reviewed in Chapter 8 of this volume. Each component of this model has generated major schools of thought and of therapy that claim hegemony over the other schools (L'Abate, 1997, 2005).

Model²: Verticality

This model views hurt feelings within a layered framework consisting of external and internal processes: *description* and *explanation*. Description has two sublevels, the public social façade, impression management, and personal appearance at a *presentational level* in superficial short-term relationships (Leary & Kowalski, 1990; Mor & Winquist, 2002). Here, very likely, hurt feelings are not expressed and shown, as opposed to the *phenotypical* level in the privacy of one' own home. In the home and in prolonged, stressful relationships, hurt feelings may surface appropriately or inappropriately under the stress and pressure of intimate relationships, especially if and when intimacy is inadequate or absent. At this sublevel, hurt feelings are acknowledged and possibly expressed either constructively or destructively within the confines of intimate relationships. Discrepancies between the social façade and the phenotypical level can be accounted for by both politeness and facework theory (Goldsmith & Donovan-Kicken, 2009; Mak et al., 2009) as well as deception in the name of kindness (De Paulo, Morris, & Sternglunz (2009); that is, when we lie to save face for another person or to prevent hurt feelings.

The *explanatory* level consists of two sublevels, the *genotypical* one that includes how an individual feels about oneself, that is, self-identity, which is covered by Model[8], and the historical, generational, and developmental level that relates us to our families of origin and to our families of procreation. Here is where hurt feelings are kept when they are not expressed and shared with intimates. The *historical* sublevel consists of the intergenerational transmission of violence (Ehrensaft, Cohen, Brown, Smailes et al., 2003) and epigenetic inheritance and intergenerational transfer of experience (Harper, 2005).

How hurt feelings are either kept inside or expressed depends a great deal on how they are transmitted from one generation to another. Metts et al. (2009, p. 341) commented on this explanatory level thus: "Although no systematic investigation of the generational transmission of hurt through emotional contagion are available, several studies indicate that a similar emotional complex, sadness and depression, is transferred to children by parents." (Chapters 4 and 5 this volume). This generational transmission occurs also with anger and fears, as in the case of maternal depression and adolescent adjustment among other aversive antecedent conditions, as reviewed in previous chapters of this volume.

Model[3]: Settings

Rather than a poorly defined, generally vague term such as "environment," it is much better to break down this term into specific settings. Settings are a function of the culture in which they are embedded, as discussed in Chapter 9 of this volume. Model[3] divides settings according to a classification as follows: (1) *enduring* settings such as home, school, or work; (2) *temporary* settings, such as (a) *transitory settings*, as in barber shops, beauty salons, movie theaters, and sport venues, and (b) *transit settings*, as in buses, cars, hotels, planes, and roads. (Story & Repetti, 2006; Werner, Altman, & Brown, 1992; Zvonkovic, Pennington, & Schmiege, 1994).

Settings are objective and can be photographed and recorded in contrast to the subjectively perceived contexts considered in Model[1]. Contexts must be elicited in order to assess them. Outside the home, in settings where instrumental competition is present, there are bound to be hurt feelings for those who did not reach the top places. Supposedly, this competition should not occur in communal, intimate relationships. The rub starts when communal relationships are influenced by and mixed with competition. This confusion is visible especially in technological settings (Chapter 11, this volume; Whitty, 2009).

Cunningham, Barbee, and Mandal (2009), for instance, argued: "Hurt feelings can be hurtful in any type of relationship, but hurt feelings may have particular intensity in the workplace" (p. 417). These conclusions are supported by the research of Barnett Marshall, Raudenbush, and Brennan (1993) who found that job role quality was significantly negatively associated with "psychological distress," both for women and men in dual-earner couples. Furthermore, both Krokof's (1991) and Matjasko and Feldman's (2006) findings, indicated how work-home relationships have significant effects on how mothers and fathers feel about how they should manage both settings.

Theoretical Assumptions

The three assumptions specific to RCT consist of the ability to love, ability to control and regulate self, and the ability to integrate both abilities.

Model[4]: Ability to Love

Model[4] defines the ability to love according to a dimension of distance that includes approach toward a loved person, object, or task and avoidance of a disliked, unwanted person, object, or task (Beall & Sternberg, 1995; Ben-Ari & Lavee, 2007; Hess, 2003, Hess et al., 2007; Ickes, Hutchison, & Mashek, 2004; Rempel & Burris, 2005; Repinski & Zook, 2005). We approach pleasurable persons, objects, responsibilities, or tasks and avoid painful, unpleasant, persons, objects, responsibilities, or tasks (Birnie, McClure, Lydon, & Holmgerf, 2009; Feeney, 1999b; Hui & Bond, 2009; Lavee & Ben-Ari, 2007). Unfortunately, sometimes we have to approach people, objects, and tasks we dislike out of necessity, for example, our boss or our job.

Whether closeness and distance are two separate or even orthogonal dimensions remains to be seen. This ability, of course, is just one way to define a multidimensional construct such as love. As other models of RCT show redundantly, the construct of love is too complex (Kovecses, 1991) to be encompassed by one dimension or one model alone. Lack of space does not allow us to include in greater detail Kovecses's original contribution illustrating such complexity. Nonetheless, this approach-avoidance dimension is visible in countless studies concerning the demand-withdraw conflict in many marriages, as well in the avoidance of conflict (Latzer & Gaber, 1998) rather than approaching and welcoming confrontation, as detailed in Model[13]. Thus, avoidance in this context means either denying, repressing, or suppressing hurt feelings and *approaching* mostly pleasurable, joyful experiences (Bureson, 1995).

Model[5]: Ability to Control and Regulate Self

Model[5] defines the ability to control self according to a dimension of time that includes responding through either discharge (quickly) at one end of this dimension and delay (slowly) on the other. This is sometimes called dysinhibition or dysregulation (Baumeister & Vohs, 2004; Eisenberg, 2000; Eisenberg, Hofer, & Vaughn, 2007; Feeney, 1999a; Feldman, Mashala, & Alony, 2006; Fuendeling, 1998; Murray, Holmes, & Collins, 2006; Rook & Ituarte, 1999), that is, how much time it takes to approach or avoid someone or something, including feelings in general and hurt feelings in particular. Prototypes of one extreme are externalizing PDs found in Cluster B, characterized by immediate discharge, whereas internalizing PDs in Cluster C are characterized by relatively greater delay, as in repressive coping style reviewed by Weinberger (1990).

Cappadocia, Desorcher, Pepler, and Schroeder (2009), for instance, found evidence that neurological profiles of individuals with conduct disorders (Model 2.1) compared to peers are characterized by reduced P300 brainwave amplitude, deactivation of the anterior cingulated cortex, reduced activation in the left amygdala in response to negative stimuli, and reduced right temporal lobe volume. These findings, if reliable, may support the view that the left hemisphere, relatively more responsible for logical thought, may be responsible for lower verbal than nonverbal performance in acting-out delinquents. This difference may occur in comparison with the right hemisphere, which is relatively more responsible for feelings, emotions, and actions (L'Abate & Hecker, 2004).

In a related example, Kurdek and Fine (1994) found that both family control and acceptance (that is, approach) are both related to positive adolescent adjustment, but not in an interactive manner. Only control was found to have a curvilinear relation with psychosocial competence and self-regulation. The relation between control and psychosocial competence may become progressively stronger as control increases, suggesting that higher levels of family control are associated with an even greater psychosocial competence, but yet to an unknown limit. The relation between control and self-regulation, on the other hand, might be most pronounced at low levels of control, suggesting that levels of control beyond a moderate level are not associated with any further enhancement of self-regulation. Additionally, parental loss before age sixteen may be associated with diminished feelings of personal control in later life (Krause, 1993). High control may be associated with depressive symptoms in late life (Kraaij & Garnefsky, 2002).

In Luyckx, Soenens, Berzonsky, Vansteenkiste's, et al. (2007) study, longitudinal data were used to evaluate whether parental psychological control would have a negative impact on four identity formation dimensions: commitment making, exploration of breadth, identification with commitment, and exploration of depth. Indeed, psychological control tended to inhibit progress in both commitment dimensions, whereas exploration in depth seemed to lead to increased psychological control. Even though this study is not related to hurt feelings, it is included here for two reasons: (1) because of the relationship between parental control and self-control in their offspring in Model[5], and (2) the importance of an identity construct that is included in Model[8] of RCT.

How does this model relate to hurt feelings? The answer is clear (Figure 2.1): In functional relationships hurt feelings are expressed, accepted, and shared. In Axis II, Cluster B personality disorder, hurt feelings are externalized through angry words and hostile actions against others. In Cluster C personality disorder, hurt feelings are internalized more against self than against others. In Axis I severe disorders, the fear of approaching feelings of any kind, and especially hurt feelings, is so strong that to try to reach those feelings may produce a strong, even psychotic, reaction, as explained in Chapter 2.

A study by Escudero, Rogers, and Gutierrez (1997) analyzed separately and in combination patterns of relational control and nonverbal affect in clinic-distressed and nonclinic-nondistressed couples' interaction. Results indicated that a low to moderate relationship between control and affect may exist. However, each dimension conveyed nonredundant interactional information. Clinic couples displayed more domineeringness, more *affect negativity*, and a stronger association between one-up control and negative affect than nonclinic couples. Lower levels of neutral affect reciprocity and one-down/one-across transitory control interactions were also salient characteristics in differentiating clinic from nonclinic couples' interaction. Furthermore, combined control-affect analysis indicated a higher proportion of escalating competitive symmetry with negative affect for clinic couples. For nonclinic couples, competitive symmetry with negative affect was counterbalanced by competitive symmetry with neutral affect and diverse transitory patterns with neutral or positive affect. Here one would question whether there is such a thing as "neutral affect."

In addition to self-control, control in and of itself can be expanded also to "social control" over others, originally best thought of as the exercise of power and control in close relationships (Guinote & Vescio, 2010; Lewis, Butterfield, Darbes, & Johnston-Brooks, 2004, p. 669). These investigators found that such a definition is not supported by results from a first study. In a second study, Lewis et al. found that many control tactics reported by spouses are not included in the social influence literature, and that the exercise of social control in marriage may best be characterized as a communally oriented process between spouses (p. 669), rather than an agentic-orientation.

Model[6]: Integration of both Abilities

Model[6] integrates both dimensions of distance and self-control into a classification of functional and dysfunctional relationships, as proposed by Bakan's (1988) combination of community and agency or intimacy and autonomy (Dresner & Grolnick, 1996). When both abilities to love and to control self are high and appropriately expressed, there is the highest level of functionality. When either one ability is high and the other is low, there is a borderline level of functionality. When both abilities are low, there is the lowest level of functionality.

This model is supported in part by the review of theory and research of Roemer, Salters, Raffa, and Orsillo (2005) and of Impett, Peplau, and Gable (2005), among others. Roemer et al. (2005), for instance, argued that the tendency to fear and avoid internal (painful) experiences may be an important characteristic of individuals with generalized anxiety disorder (GAD). Individuals with GAD may be experientially avoidant of internal emotional processes, just as repressors are (Weinberger, 1990). Preliminary research seems to support this possibility, indicating that this avoidance and inhibition is prevalent in most psychiatric disorders. Findings from both a clinical and a nonclinical sample suggest that worry and GAD may be associated with a tendency to avoid or control (versus accept and express) internal experiences, as well as a tendency to fear losing control over one's own emotional responses, particularly anxiety.

Furthermore, Hussong's (2000) research supports the orthogonality of the two factors of intimacy and control in adolescents, as predicted by Model[6] and supported by two-factor models of relationships (L'Abate, 2009a; L'Abate et al., 2010), including (Harter, Waters, Pettit, Whitesell, et al., 1997) connectedness and autonomy, individuality and connectedness, (Bengtson and Grotevant, 1999), and Saitzyk, Floyd, and Kroll's (1997) autonomy-interdependence and affiliation-disaffiliation, among many others.

Model ⁷: The Triangle of Living

Although the two previous models deal with processes without contents, Model⁷ deals with the contents of relationships. It is derived from Foa and Foa's (1974) resource exchange theory that includes six classes of behaviors: Love (defined redundantly in different models of RCT), Intimacy (as defined from the outset of this volume), Information, Services, Money, and Possessions. These six classes can be reduced to three modalities. By combining love and intimacy, we obtain being or presence in the communal sense of being available emotionally to self and intimates, as in sharing joys, hurts, and fears of being hurt (Adams & Plaut, 2003; Bakan, 1968; Mills, Clark, Ford, & Johnson, 2004; Reis, 2007; Sturge-Apple at al., 2006).

By combining Information and Services we obtain Doing or Performance. By combining Money with Possessions we obtain Having or Production (Lohman, Arriaga, & Goodfriend, 2003), as in compulsive hoarding (Saxena, 2008). By combining Doing and Having we obtain a supraordinate condition of Power, where joys and hurts are not usually shared (Guinote & Vescio, 2010). The two modalities of Presence and Power find their equivalence in a variety of two-factors models (L'Abate, 2009a; L'Abate et al., 2010) emphasizing distance (Model⁴) and time (Model⁵). An experimental Interview Schedule to evaluate this Model⁷ is available in L'Abate (1986, p. 222).

Hurt feelings are shared by being emotionally available and present in Being, whereas those feelings are usually kept separate in Doing and Having in functional relationships. Dysfunctionality occurs when feelings and especially hurt feelings enter, overlap with, and influence Doing and Having without clear boundaries among the three modalities.

Developmental and Normative Models

Models in this section are developmental and normative in nature, consisting of identity differentiation, styles, interactions, selfhood, and priorities.

Model⁸: Identity Differentiation

Model⁸ expands on a primitive, simple developmental dichotomy of similar-dissimilar into a dialectical curvilinear continuum of Likeness or Resemblance comprised by three degrees of sameness (symbiosis, sameness proper, and similarity) and three degrees of differentiation (differentness, oppositeness, and alienation) (Cusinato & Colesso, 2008; Kay, Banfield, & Laurin, 2010; L'Abate, 1976, p. 79). The process of developmental differentiation can occur at all five levels of Model¹, ERAAwC and according to the independent variables of the theory: gender, age, education, and ethnic background.

Here is where, early in life, feelings (E), cognitions (R), actions (A), awareness (Aw), and context (C) are experienced in a dichotomous, either-or fashion as love-hate, friend-enemy, day-night, black-white; hurt feelings remain at the most unconscious level. The infant grows up to mimic available models according to one, some, or all the five components of Model[1]. From a simple dichotomy of laughing or crying, for instance, the child starts to modulate and differentiate feelings, thinking, actions, awareness, and context according to what is experienced with intimates and nonintimates. Developmentally, from a same/dissimilar dichotomy, feelings, cognitions, actions, awareness, and context become more and more differentiated along this continuum of likeness from the intrapsychic to the cultural and ethnic levels (Umana-Taylor & Yazedjian, 2006). However, if available models are worded in a dichotomous fashion, it will be very difficult for a child to learn otherwise unless or until other, more emotionally sophisticated models are available (Metts, Braithwaite, & Fine, 2009).

More specifically: (1) In *symbiosis*, there is an identity of feelings between partners or in early caretaker-child dyads as in déjà vu; (2) in *sameness*, there is an equality of feelings but not one-on-one identity; (3) in *similarity*, there is less resemblance with the acquisition of some new feelings that are not part of the past repertoire of feelings experienced thus far and in partner selection (Acitelli, Kenny, & Weiner, 2001; Barelds & Barelds-Dijkstra, 2007; Cole & Teboul, 2004; Evans & Brase, 2007; Franiuk, Cohen, & Pomerantz, 2002; Korchmaros & Kenny, 2006; Nezlek, 1995; Urberg, Degirmen-cioglu, & Tolson, 1998); (4) in *differentness*, completely new feelings, cognitions, actions, awareness of self, and awareness of context not experienced heretofore are included experientially; (5) in *oppositeness*, a completely dialectical reversal from sameness occurs, to the point that if anger, sadness, or fears have been experienced in the past or in the present, one may choose to use laughter and humor to offset the influence of those hurtful feelings, a process that may well be present in driven stand-up comics or the like (Baxter, Mazanec, Nicholson, Pittman, et al., 1997); and (6) in *alienation*, it is practically impossible to experience feelings, as in Cluster B personality disorders, alexithymia (Berthoz, Artiges, Van de Moortele, Poline, et al., 2002), or anedonia in schizophrenics (Nicholson, 1997). Creativity in experiencing feelings occurs when similar feelings are integrated with different ones in producing emergent, completely new feelings, especially hurt feelings, as discussed in Chapter 2.

Model⁹: Styles in Intimate Relationships

This model derives from the six degrees of sameness-differentness of Model⁸, which are usually below the level of awareness. By combining Symbiosis with Alienation, we obtain an extremely visible Abusive-Apathetic and Neglectful (AA/N) style. By combining Sameness with Oppositeness, we obtain a borderline Reactive-Repetitive (RR) style. By combining Similarity with Differentness, we obtain a functional Creative-Conductive (CC) style.

Evidence for the existence of either AA or RR styles is available in Chapter 3 of this volume, including also Mikulincer and Shaver's (2005) emotional *reactivity* to relational events and Cunningham, Shamblen, Barber, and Ault's (2005) *repetitiveness* in dating couples, or *"obligatory repetition"* as mentioned by Waring (1984; Chapter 6 of this volume). Competitiveness in intimate relationships would be an example of a reactive-repetitive style (Scinta & Gagle, 2005). These styles interact with psychiatric diagnoses to constitute what are considered "comorbid or coexisting" conditions often present in dual diagnoses (L'Abate, 2005). Stress, of course, increases the likelihood of reactivity emerging in harsh parenting practices (Kim, 2006; Martorell & Bugental, 2006).

Spitzberg (2009, p. 211), in addition to a classification of violence included in Chapter 2, added one more distinction by considering AA/N styles according to their frequency of occurrence as chronic, occasional, or reactive. The reactive nature of abuse merging with the RR style also includes the dimension of repetitiveness, how frequently the same or similar hurtful behavior occurs. This distinction then would mean that infliction of hurt feelings could be chronic, occasional, or reactive-nonreactive, and would include all the possible and assumed origins included in Chapter 2. Furthermore, the best example of an AA style is found in the vast literature on Expressed Emotions (EE), which usually consists of protracted and judgmental criticisms bestowed by relatives on individuals afflicted with schizophrenia, often times producing relapses when extreme (Abela, Skitch, Adams, & Hankin, 2006; Benazon, Foster, & Coyne, 2006; Cheavens, Rosenthal, Daughers, Nowak, et al., 2005; Hooley & Parker, 2006; Nelson, Hammen, Brennan, & Ullman, 2003).

This model is tentatively supported by the research of Negel (2003). She attempted to develop a reliable and valid personality measure of hurt *reactivity* comprising *introjective* hurt, that is, internalizing hurt and engaging in punitive self-blame, as in Cluster C, as well as *retaliatory* hurt, that is, lashing out immediately and aggressively against perpetrators of hurt, as in Cluster B. Those two styles are differentially related to various indices of similar and related personality constructs, as indicated in Figure 2.1 of this volume.

It is important to underscore that reactivity at whatever physiological (Sturge-Apple, Davies, Cicchetti, & Cummings, 2009) or relational levels (Bartle, 1996; Buehler & Welsh, 2009) is a useful, accurate, and necessary construct to describe immediate, oftentimes thoughtless responses to aversive, noxious, or hurtful events. However, in and of itself, as far as I know, reactivity is another orphan construct without a clear connection to a theoretical explanatory framework as offered in Model[9]. By the same token, the basic issue here is to know when to assess overreaction (O'Leary & Vidair, 2005) and when to assess underreaction.

Model[5] would need inclusion here in order to evaluate how fast or how slow one responds to threats, provocation, or any of the presumptive antecedents of hurt feelings. This is another example of the redundancy requirement necessary to describe or even explain a given construct. It takes more then one model to describe complex and ubiquitous constructs such as hurt feelings.

Model[10]: *Types of Interaction*

This model expands arithmetically on the three previous styles by classifying CC styles at (1) two levels of functionality: multiplicative and additive; (2) two levels of borderline functionality: static positive and static negative; and (3) two levels of subtractive and divisive interactions. Intimacy, as defined by the sharing of joys, hurts, and fears of being hurt, is present and active in multiplicative and additive interactions, where relational creativity (L'Abate, 2009c), caregiving, leadership, and volunteering are present (Gillath, Shaver, Mikulincer, Nitzberg, et al., 2005; Post, 2007). Intimacy could be occasional (birthdays, funerals, and marriages) in positive and negative static interactions, and missing in subtractive and divisive interactions (L'Abate et al., 2010),

Consequently, in terms of the joys to hurts ratio discussed in Chapter 5, the ratio of joyful to hurtful events would be approximately: +6 to −1 in multiplicative interactions; + 5 to −2 in additive interactions; + 4 to −3 in positive static interactions; +3 to −4 in negative static interactions; +2 to −5 in subtractive interactions; and maximally +1 to -6 in divisive interactions. Of course, these ratios should be operationalized much more clearly and specifically. However, this approach might be a starting point to relate functionality and dysfunctionality according to ratios of joyful to hurtful feelings.

Model[11]: Selfhood

This model is based on the attribution and bestowal of importance to self and intimates, shown through caring (Blieszner, 2006), commitment, concern (Trobst, Collins, & Embree (1994), and compassion, which produces four relational propensities: *Selfulness*: "I win you win, we both must win" (functional); *Selfishness*: "I win you lose" (borderline); *Selflessness*: "You win I lose" (borderline); and *No-self*: "Neither one wins" (dysfunctional). Dayan, Doyle, and Markiewicz's (2001) differentiation of allocentric and idiocentric children offers a developmental perspective for Selflessness and Selfishness. Piferi, Jobe, and Jones (2006) supported a dimension of altruistic versus egoistic motivations during times of national tragedy on long-term giving. Altruistic motivation should be present in Selfulness, and egoistic motivation in Selfishness. When altruism is performed at the expense of the self, it represents Selflessness. In No-self, neither egotism or altruism are present or available – everybody loses.

Selfulness is where the reciprocal sharing of hurt feelings is more likely to occur, as seen in relational creativity (L'Abate, 2009c). In Selfishness or Selflessness, propensities for sharing hurts might not be reciprocal, with no sharing possible in No-self propensities. In Selfishness (Cluster B personality disorders), one would expect hurt feelings to be produced against others rather than against oneself, as in narcissism (Foster, Shrira, & Campbell, 2006) and murder (Figure 2.1, this volume). In Selflessness (Cluster C personality disorders), one would expect an almost chronic collection and accumulations of hurt feelings against oneself rather than against others to the point that suicide, in whatever direct or indirect form, may occur as the natural outcome of such accumulation. In No-self (Axis I and Cluster A of Axis II in DSM-IV) hurt feelings are so feared that there would not be any awareness of them, nor would expression or sharing be possible. Any attempt to enter into this topic in No-self would be met by strenuous resistance, to the point of provoking a psychotic episode. How Model[11] relates to cultural self-construals (Yum, 2004) is an intriguing question that perhaps future research will be able to answer.

Here is where Leary's devaluation of self fits well, especially in Selfishness and Selflessness, where, respectively, the self of another or of oneself are devaluated. In Selfulness, where hurt feelings are shared reciprocally and helpfully, there is no devaluation of self: There is an enhancement of both self and intimates. In No-self, devaluation is so total that there is little if any possibility of adding more hurt to an already existing mass of hurt feelings.

The construct of importance attribution and bestowal to self and others supersedes the construct "self-esteem." The former is a relational whereas the latter is a ubiquitous, theory-free, intrapsychic, nonrelational construct that has no place in any relational framework, especially RCT (Abe, 2004; Arriaga et al., 2007; Caughlin & Malis, 2004; De Raedt et al., 2006; Finzi-Dottan & Karu, 2006; Ragarajan & Kelly, 2006; Reddy, 2009; Rudy & Rusec, 2006). Self-esteem, nevertheless, should be associated positively with a sense of importance, as measured by the Self-Other Profile Chart, one of the most validated measures of Selfhood in RCT (Cusinato & L'Abate, 2012; L'Abate et al., 2010).

Model[12]: Priorities

This model includes attitudes, goals, intentions, and motivations and consists of horizontal (settings) and vertical intimate relationships (Selfhood) according to how settings and intimates are rank-ordered either consciously or automatically (Costigan, Cox, & Cauce, 2003; Matjasko & Feldman, 2005) – what Meegan and Goedereis, (2006) called "life tasks." This model is also akin to the concept of "competing loyalties" expounded and evaluated by Baxter et al. (1997). Does one spend more time at home than at the office? Is family more important than work? Is self more important than partner? Are children more important than self? What role do leisure-time activities occupy in a hierarchy of priorities? How are horizontal priorities in conflict with vertical intimate priorities? More to the point, what place in these priorities do feelings, especially hurt, feelings occupy? When these priorities are clear and organized appropriately according to one's stage of the life cycle, one would expect the sharing of hurt feelings to be expressed and shared accordingly. If these priorities are confused and unclear, one would expect difficulties in experiencing and expressing hurt feelings (L'Abate, 2005).

Clinical Models

Models in this part of RCT deal with dysfunctional processes where unexpressed hurt feelings are more likely to be found than in previous models.

Model[13]: Distance Regulation

This model is composed of three roles trying to bridge the gulf between wanting and being afraid of intimacy: (1) *Pursuer* or Closeness Seeker: "Come here"; (2) *Distancer* or Closeness Avoider: "Go away"; and (3) *Regulator*, who gives contradictory messages about wanting to be close, but when the message is obeyed, there is then a demand for withdrawal: "Come here ... go away." Parts of this model are seen in the demand-withdraw interaction pattern most common in dysfunctional couple relationships (Bodenmann, Kaiser, Hahlweg, & Fehm-Wolfsdorf, 1998; Weger, 2005), already reviewed in previous chapters of this volume. The Pursuer is the one who feels hurts perhaps more than the Distancer. The Regulator, apparently, is completely impervious to how one feels while provoking hurt feelings in others, including oneself. Loving, Le, and Crockett (2009, pp. 362–368) make the best case for withdrawal (Distancer) as being the most hurtful type of act, as in rejection and ostracism. Outcomes would include definite endocrine outcomes for women who are often the target of withdrawal by men: "The occurrence of withdrawal typically is hurtful because it is easily perceived and reflects a clear attempt at dissociation from the relationship or partner or both" (p. 364). Frequent demand-withdraw may be associated with low self-esteem and alcohol and drug use for both adolescents and parents (Caughlin & Malis, 2004; Papp, Kouros, & Cummings, 2009; Sturge-Apple, Davies, & Cummings, 2006; Vogel & Karney, 2002),

Unfortunately, the demand-withdraw model contains only two roles and does not include the third role of Regulator included in this model, making this dimension of demand-withdraw incomplete (Caughlin & Ramey, 2005; Caughlin & Vangelisti, 2000). This incompleteness may have been filled by Kerig's (1995) study, as replicated by Johnson (2003), which is actually more relevant to Model[14], which contains a measure of distance regulation in families.

Model[14]: The Drama Triangle

This pathogenic triangle, of course, is not found in functional relationships, and is composed of three contemporaneous roles: Victim, Persecutor, and Rescuer. Within this triangle, hurt feelings are produced but not acknowledged or shared. Each party or partner in the transactions plays all three roles simultaneously. Depending on one's viewpoint, all parties feel victimized by the other, although each plays the seemingly perceived role of Persecutor. In this deadly triangle, the roots and the beginning of psychopathology are fermented, hence its pathogenic nature. These three subjectively but unconsciously perceived roles are played contemporaneously and simultaneously by two or more players (L'Abate et al., 2010). Players switch roles continuously on how hurt feelings are inflicted on others, as in scapegoating. The first two roles of Victim and Perpetrator have been considered by Feeney (2009) and Wood (2004). However, one needs to add a third role of Rescuer to complete this model.

As far as hurt feelings are concerned, the one who feels victimized by a Persecutor is the one who feels hurt: The Persecutor is the one who inflicts hurts, whereas the Rescuer is the one who attempts to save the Victim from experiencing hurt feelings (Cattaneo, Stuewig, Goodman, Kaltman, et al., 2007; Feeney & Hill, 2006; Lento, 2006; O'Leary & Williams, 2006; Ray, Cohen, Secrist, & Duncan, 1997; Storch, Ledley, Lewin, Murphy, et al., 2006). The Persecutor, however, feels victimized by the one who is now playing the role of Victim, whereas the Rescuer may have played both roles of Victim or Persecutor under different circumstances. A first example of such a triangle is found in Stockholm Syndrome, where the persons having been held hostage or prisoner by Persecutors – who see themselves as Rescuers – join their Persecutors to assume the role of Rescuers. From having been the Victims of hurt they assume the role of hurt inflictors.

A second example of this triangle not included in previous writings is the Parental Alienation Syndrome (PAS), whereby a parent who wants to rescue the child from an apparently "bad" parent downgrades and criticizes him or her, apparently to rescue the child from the perceived "bad," persecuting parent. Many spouses manipulate their own children solely to inflict revenge and pain on the other partner. Consequently, the Rescuer is also the Persecutor all at the same time, whereas the Victim can be also the Rescuer, as seen in some religions and most wars. For some parents, this seems an enjoyable lifelong game (Bernet, von Boch-Galhau, Baker, & Morrison, 2010; Gardner, Sauber, & Lorandos, 2006).

Baker (2006), for instance, conducted a qualitative retrospective study with forty adults who had experienced parental alienation as a child. Results revealed three distinct patterns of alienation: (1) narcissistic alienating mothers in divorced families; (2) narcissistic alienating mothers in intact families; and (3) abusive/rejecting alienating mothers and fathers. Each of these patterns is described in detail along with five additional notable findings: (1) Alcoholism, maltreatment, and personality disorders co-occurred in most of the alienating families; (2) parental alienation occurred in intact families; (3) parental alienation occurred in nonlitigious divorced families; (4) some of the targeted parents appeared to play a role in their own alienation; and (5) the alienation was not always completely internalized. Additionally, as Lindahl, Clements, and Markman (1997) found, the child becomes triangulated into the marital conflict. Although initially been conceived of (literally and figuratively) by either or both parents as the Savior of their marriage, the newly born child might become the Victim of that very same marriage, with either parent assuming alternatively the roles of

Rescuer (usually and stereotypically more often the mother) and Persecutor (usually and stereotypically more often the father). Another example of triangularization may be present in the research of Mahoney et al., (2003) reported in Chapter 2 of this volume.

A third example of this deadly triangle is visible in schools, where bullies, who oftentimes had been Victims themselves, focus on vulnerable children as their Victims, sometime with bystanders assuming the role of Rescuers of the victims (Salmivalli, 2001). Some bullies, dominated by anger, grow up to be criminals (Wood, 2004).

This triangle is evident also in the process of divorce (Metts et al., 2009). The partner who wants out, that is, to avoid the marriage, hopes to achieve and approach a much better emotional, sexual, or financial arrangement with someone or something else, no matter how much hurt is inflicted on the partner, children, and the extended family. Often the process of dissolution requires demonizing the other partner (Model[9]) while avoiding reflecting on what the dissolver feels except the immediacy of an exiting solution. Although behaving as a Persecutor in the eyes of the remaining partner, the dissolver may view someone or something else (better lifestyle, better sex life, more freedom, less responsibility, etc.) as the Rescuer from victimization of the existing marriage.

Most Cluster B personality disorders more often than not assume the Persecutor role toward Cluster C personality disorders, who willingly assume the role of Victims. Here, in a divorce, children, money, and possessions (Model[7]) may become the ultimate Rescuers.

Evidence of the presence triangulation in families is found in a study by Kerig (1995), who evaluated mothers, fathers, and six- to ten-year-old children with the Family Cohesion Index to type their family system as cohesive (all close), separate (all distant), triangulated (cross-generational coalitions), or detouring (child excluded from the parental system). Family members agreed modestly with one another. Multivariate analyses of variance showed that parents in triangulated families were higher in marital conflict and dissatisfaction than were cohesive and detouring parents. Children in triangulated families reported more interparental conflict and more *negative affect* in the family. Children in detouring families rated themselves higher in self-blame for their parents' conflicts, and their parents rated them highest in internalizing problems. Parents in separate families rated their children highest in externalizing problems. If these results are reliable and valid, they would go a long way in dealing with distance regulation (Model[14]) and triangulation in intimate relationships, that is, Model[15].

Kerig's (1995) study was replicated by Johnson's (2003) followed-up study of fifty-seven two-parent families from kindergarten to the fourth grade. She found that fourth graders in triangulated families were seen (by teachers) as more aggressive at school than were their peers in cohesive or separate families. These studies, apparently, tend to support the generational repetition of this triangle from one family to another.

Model[15]: Intimacy

This entire volume is dedicated to this topic, thus this model does not need to be explained here, except to note that to forgive one's own and intimates' transgressions, one must express, share, and process hurt feelings, a process that cannot occur by completing self-report paper-and-pencil questionnaires. The process of forgiveness is realized only after there has been a full sharing and processing of hurt feelings, that is, self-disclosure as discussed in Chapter 11 and 12 of this volume. This sharing is a *sine qua non conditio* for forgiveness, a step usually not considered by many advocates of forgiveness (Braithwaite et al., 2009). They assume, without mentioning it, that that sharing has indeed occurred. Forgiveness was defined (L'Abate, 1986, p. 285–286) as canceling our expectations of perfection in ourselves and in intimate others. In view of Model[7], one would add also to this definition the canceling of expectations of perfection in problem solving, performance, or production.

To define a multidimensional construct such as love (Beall & Sternberg, 1995; Taraban & Hendrick, 1995; L'Abate et al., 2010), for instance, different models from RCT need inclusion with *redundant* dimensions: (1) Model[4], distance; (2) Model[5], self-control; (3) Model[7], being present and available emotionally and instrumentally; (4) Model[8], relying on a creative-conductive style; (5) Model[10], involvement in multiplicative and additive interactions; (6) Model[11], bestowing importance to self and loved ones; (7) Model[12], including self and loved ones within one's priorities; and ultimately (8) Model[15], forgiving errors and transgressions.

By the same criterion of redundancy, hurt feelings can be defined by many different models of love. To add to the many definitions given by contributors in Vangelisti (2009), I offer another; Where there is the passion of love, there is the fire of hurt (L'Abate, 1999a).

Conclusive Model

This model includes using most models of the RCT and requires a certain degree of functionality in order of be carried out effectively.

Model[16]: Negotiation

The ability to negotiate and problem-solve successfully requires a certain amount of functionality (Alverfer & Navsaria, 2009; Gauven, Fagot, Leve, & Kavanah, 2002; Roloff, Putman, & Anastasiou, 2003). This model involves two major functions: (1) *Authority*, who makes the decisions, and (2) *Responsibility*, who carries out those decisions (Bray & Harvey, 1992). Decisions can be *orchestrational*, involving life-changing events, such as changing jobs or moving to another city, or *instrumentational*, involving making decisions about routine, everyday events such as what toothpaste to use or what kind of food to buy and how to prepare it. Within this framework, one must consider levels of functionality of parties involved in the negotiation process (ILL), their skills in being able to carry out the process of negotiation (SKILL), and motivation to negotiate (WILL).

As far as hurt feelings are concerned, these feelings as subjectively experienced do not require negotiation. Hurt feelings are whatever we experience and are aware of. That process does not need justification or negotiation. However, if hurt feelings are to be expressed and shared positively rather than negatively with loved ones, negotiation is required, especially if such a process has not occurred positively in the past. Hence, the process of negotiation on how hurt feelings are to be expressed and shared requires a direct personal confrontation and a rational discussion of those feelings with intimates and nonintimates alike (Model[1]). Here is where the assumption of self-control or regulation of Model[5] is basic and necessary for a successful completion of the process: the maintenance and outcome of negotiation.

The process of negotiation is especially important in postdivorce proceedings in and out of court (Metts et al., 2009), where a whole gamut of hurtful feelings are experienced while at the same time one has to deal rationally with issues that possess inherently emotional aspects such as alimony, finances, and custody.

CONCLUSION

Hopefully, hurt feelings have found a theoretical home at various levels and models of RCT and can no longer be conceived as conceptual or empirical orphans.

APPENDIX A

An Informed Consent Form to Deal with
Hurt Feelings

I_____(the undersigned) have been informed about the possible use of written practice exercises about hurt feelings as homework assignments, either by themselves written at a distance (by mail, fax, or Internet), or as additions to other verbal, face-to-face professional approaches like promotion, prevention, psychotherapy, or rehabilitation.

I understand that this approach is still experimental and needs to be evaluated before being available to everybody. I am aware of the possible dangerous consequences that may be provoked by answering written practice exercises about hurt feelings at a distance. I agree to participate in this type of intervention with full understanding that it may bring up painful memories of my past and that this approach, at least initially, may produce some upset for me, my partner, or my family. I understand further that all information about me will be considered absolutely confidential because all of my writing will be limited between myself and the professional who is administering these written homework assignments. To maximize this anonymity, I can use the following five-digit number instead of my name in completing practice exercises.

I can drop out of this type of intervention any time I want without any penalty or consequence, and I can only disclose whatever I want at my discretion during the course of these homework assignments. If I were to become upset because of the nature of this homework, it will be up to me to deal with this upset in any way I deem satisfactory to me. I should share this upset with the professional who is administering this intervention if I desire or see fit to do so. Or I can share my upset with whoever I choose. I may continue to keep it to myself or discuss it with my loved ones, friends, clergy, or physician(s).

I can answer and send my completed homework assignments through the Internet, fax, or mail in whatever form will guarantee absolute confidentiality, (i.e., encrypted).

The corresponding professional, after proper evaluation, through either an interview or objective psychological tests, does have the option to inform me whether this approach will or will not be helpful to me. I will be informed of this option verbally or in writing.

I undertake to complete in writing practice exercises about hurt feelings at a distance from a professional of my own free will and choice. I will not hold _____ responsible for any possible upset that may result from this intervention. Doctor (Mr. or Mrs.) _____is offering this intervention in good faith, using as many precautions as humanly and professionally possible. I agree to complete in writing homework assignments given to me until completion of an agreed-on practice exercise and, if necessary, to be evaluated before administration, after completion of these practice exercises, and even at a given period of time after termination, to be agreed on with the professional.

SIGNATURE OF PARTICIPANT SIGNATURE OF PROFESSIONAL

_____ Date_____   _____Date_____

One copy of this signed Informed Consent Form should be kept by the Participant and another copy by the Professional.

Please Note: If presently you use any antidepressant or mood-changing medication, you must inform the mental health professional who is offering these practice exercises about this medication. Ask permission and consent from your attending physician to participate in this type of intervention. Make sure you obtain written consent from your physician that indicates his or her knowledge and consent for you to participate in this type of practice exercises. Give a copy of the physician's signed consent form or letter to the professional. Keep one copy to yourself. If necessary, have the mental health professional talk with your physician. In this case, you will need to give a written permission to this professional to talk with your physician, and vice versa.

APPENDIX B

Experimental Scale of Unexpressed Hurt Feelings

Instructions to a five-point Likert scale of Agreement/Disagreement*

1. My life experiences leave a bitter taste in my mouth.
2. In my life I have suffered many painful experiences.
3. I do not like to go back to whatever I have suffered.
4. It is tiresome for me to approach painful relationships.
5. I am convinced that life holds much more suffering than satisfaction.
6. Relationships with others leave me profoundly wounded.
7. Often I feel completely overwhelmed by others.
8. I experience very few serene moments in my life.
9. Relationships with people close to me are a source of anger that I do not express.
10. I have learned to show indifference to whatever happens around me.
11. I think that it is useless to cry and to complain.
12. Whoever is born with an adverse destiny cannot do anything to change it.
13. What others define as indifference is for me all the pain that I suffered.
14. I am unable to rebel as much as I would like.
15. I experience more sadness than joy.

*Created by Mario Cusinato and published with his permission. This scale has not been validated in English.

REFERENCES

Abe, J. A. (2004). Self-esteem, perception of relationships, and emotional distress: A cross-cultural study. *Personal Relationships*, 11, 231–248.

Abela, J. R. Z., Skitch, S. A., Adams, P., & Hankin, B. L. (2006). Timing of parent and child depression: A hopelessness theory perspective. *Journal of Clinical Child and Adolescent Psychology*, 35, 253–263.

Abelson, J. L., Liberzon, I., Young, E. A., & Khan, S. (2005). Cognitive modulation of the endocrine stress response to a pharmacological challenge in normal and panic disorder subjects. *Archives of General Psychiatry*, 62, 668–675.

Abramowitz, J. (2006). Toward a functional analytic approach to psychologically complex patients: A comment on Ruscio and Holohan (2006). *Clinical Psychology: Science and Practice*, 13, 163–166.

Abramowitz, J., Olatunji, B., & Deacon, B. (2007). Health anxiety, hypochondriasis, and the anxiety disorders. *Behavior Therapy*, 38(1), 86–94.

Acitelli, L. K. Kenny, D. A., & Weiner, D. (2001). The importance of similarity and understanding of partners' marital ideals to relationship satisfaction. *Personal Relationships*, 8, 167–185.

Adams, R. E., & Laursen, B. (2007). The correlates of conflict: Disagreement is not necessarily detrimental. *Journal of Family Psychology*, 21, 445–451.

Adams, G., & Plaut, V. C. (2003). The cultural grounding of personal relationships: Friendship in North American and West African worlds. *Personal Relationships*, 10, 333–348.

Addis, M. E. (2008). Gender and depression in men. *Clinical Psychology: Science and Practice*, 15, 153–168.

Adolphs, R., Tranel, D., & Damasio, A. R. (1998). The human amygdala in social judgment. *Nature*, 393, 470–474.

Adolphs, R., Tranel, D., Damasio, H., & Damasio, A. R. (1995). Fear and the human amygdala. *Journal of Neuroscience*, 15, 5879–5891.

Aggleton, J. P. (1992). The functional effects of amygdala lesions in humans: A comparison with findings from monkeys. In J. P. Aggleton (Ed.), *The amygdala: Neurobiological aspects of emotion, memory, and mental dysfunction* (pp. 485–504). New York: Wiley-Liss.

Ahrens, S., & Deffner, G. (1986). Empirical study of alexithymia: Methodology and results. *American Journal of Psychotherapy*, 40, 430–446.

Akiyama, H., Antonucci, T., Takahashi, K., & Langfahl, E. (2003). Negative interactions in close relationships across the life span. *The Journals of Gerontology: Series B: Psychological Sciences and Social Sciences*, 58B(2), 70–79.

Albrecht, T. A., & Halsey, J. (1992). Mutual support in mixed-status relationships. *Journal of Social and Personal Relationships*, 9, 237–252.

Alexander, P. C., & Schaeffer, C. M. (1994). A typology of incestuous families based on cluster analysis. *Journal of Family Psychology*, 8, 458–470.

Allan, G., & Harrison, K. (2009). Affairs and infidelity. In A. L. Vangelisti (Ed.), *Handbook of hurt feelings in close relationships* (pp. 191–208). New York: Cambridge University Press.

Alverfer, M. A., Navsaria, N., & Kasak, A. E. (2009). Family functioning and post-traumatic stress disorder in adolescent survivors of childhood cancer. *Journal of Family Psychology*, 23, 717–725.

Amaral, D. G. (2002). The primate amygdala and the neurobiology of social behavior: Implications for understanding social anxiety. *Biological Psychiatry*, 51, 11–7.

Anand, A., Li, Y., Wang, Y., Wu, J. W., Gao, S. J., Bukhari, L., Mathews, V. P., Kalnin, A., & Lowe, M. J. (2005). Activity and connectivity of brain mood regulating circuit in depression: A functional magnetic resonance study. *Biological Psychiatry*, 57, 1079–1088.

Anastasi, A. (1985). Reciprocal relations between cognitive and affective development-implications for sex differences. In T. B. Sonderegger (Ed.), *Psychology of gender: Nebraska Symposium on Motivation* 1994 (pp. 1–35). Lincoln: University of Nebraska Press.

Anders, S. L., & Tucker, J. S. (2000). Adult attachment style, interpersonal communication competence, and social support. *Personal Relationships*, 7, 379–391.

Andersson, G., Carlbring, P., Holmström, A., Sparthan, E., et al. (2006). Internet-based self-help with therapist feedback and in vivo group exposure for social phobia: A randomized controlled trial. *Journal of Consulting and Clinical Psychology*, 74, 677–686.

Armey, M., Fresco, D., Moore, M., Mennin, D., Turk, C., Heimberg, R., et al. (2009). Brooding and pondering: Isolating the active ingredients of depressive rumination with exploratory factor analysis and structural equation modeling. *Assessment*, 16, 315–327.

Arriaga, X. B., Slaughterbeck, E. S., Capezza, N. M., & Hmurovic, J. I. (2007). From bad to worse: Relationship commitment and vulnerability to partner imperfections. *Personal Relationships*, 14, 389–410.

Auhagen, A. E., & Hinde, R. A. (1997). Individual characteristics and personal relationships. *Personal Relationships*, 4, 63–84.

Awong, T., Grusec, J., & Sorenson, A. (2008). Respect-based control and anger as determinants of children's socioemotional development. *Social Development*, 17, 941–959.

Aziz, Q., Schnitzler, A., & Enck, P. (2000). Functional neuroimaging of visceral sensation. *Journal of Clinical Neurophysiology*, 17, 604–612.

Bachorowski, J. A., & Owren, M. J. (2008). Vocal expression of emotion. In M. Lewis, J. M. Haviland-Jones, & L. F. Barrett (Eds.), *Handbook of emotions* (3rd ed., pp. 196–210). New York: Guilford.

Badr, H. (2004). Coping in marital dyads: A contextual perspective on the role of gender and health. *Personal Relationships*, 11, 197–212.

Bakan, D. (1968). *Disease, pain, and sacrifice: Toward a psychology of suffering.* Boston, MA: Beacon Press.

Baker, A. (2006). Patterns of Parental Alienation Syndrome: A qualitative a study of adults who were alienated from a parent as a child. *American Journal of Family Therapy*, 34, 63–78.

Banks, N. (2000). The development of sociability and fears. In D. S. Gupta & R. M. Gupta (Eds.), *Psychology for psychiatrists* (pp. 300–317). Philadelphia: Whurr Publishers.

Banks, S. J., Eddy, K. T., Angstadt, M., Nathan, P. J., & Phan, K. L. (2007). Amygdala-frontal connectivity during emotion regulation. *Social Cognitive and Affective Neuroscience*, 2, 303–312.

Barelds, D. P. H., & Barelds-Dijkstra, P. (2007). Love at first sight or friends first? Ties among partner personality trait similarity, relationship onset, relationship quality, and love. *Journal of Social and Personal Relationships*, 24, 479–496.

Bargh, J. A. (2005). Bypassing the will; Toward demystifying the nonconscious control of social behavior. In R. R. Hassin, J. S. Uleman, & J. A. Bargh (Eds.). *The new unconscious* (pp. 37–58). New York: Oxford University Press.

(Ed.). (2007). *Social psychology and the unconscious: The automaticity of higher mental processes.* New York: Psychological Press.

Bargh, J. A., & Williams, L. E. (2007). The nonconscious regulation of emotions. In J. J. Gross (Ed.), *Handbook of emotion regulation* (pp. 429–449). New York: Guilford.

Barnett, R., Marshall, N., Raudenbush, S., & Brennan, R. (1993). Gender and the relationship between job experiences and psychological distress: A study of dual-earner couples. *Journal of Personality and Social Psychology*, 64, 794–806.

Baron, K., Smith, T., Butner, J., Nealey-Moore, J., et al. (2007). Hostility, anger, and marital adjustment: Concurrent and prospective associations with psychosocial vulnerability. *Journal of Behavioral Medicine*, 30, 1–10.

Barrett, L. F. (2006). Solving the emotion paradox: Categorization and the experience of emotion. *Personality and Social Psychology Review*, 10, 20–46.

Barrett, L. F., Mesquita, B., Ochsner, K. N., & Gross, J. J. (2007). The experience of emotion. *Annual Review of Psychology*, 58, 373–403.

Barrett, L. F., Niedenthal, P. M., & Winkielman, P. (Eds.). (2005). *Emotion and consciousness.* New York: Guilford.

Barrett, L. F., Ochsner, K. N., & Gross, J. J. (2007). On the automaticity of emotion. In J. A. Bargh (Ed.), *Social psychology and the unconscious: The automaticity of higher mental processes* (pp. 173–217). New York: Psychology Press.

Barrett, L. F., & Russell, J. A. (1999). Structure of current affect. *Current Directions in Psychological Science*, 8, 10–14.

Barr-Zisowitz, C. (2000). "Sadness" – Is there such a thing? In M. Lewis & J. M. Haviland-Jones (Eds.), *Handbook of emotions* (2nd ed., pp. 607–622). New York: Guilford.

Bartle, S. E. (1996). Family of origin and interpersonal contributions to the interdependence of dating partners' trust. *Personal Relationships*, 3, 197–209.

Bass, L., & Stein, C. (1997). Comparing the structure and stability of network ties using the Social Support Questionnaire and the Social Network List. *Journal of Social and Personal Relationships*, 14(1), 123–132.

Bates, J. E., Goodnight, J. A., & Fite, J. E. (2008). Temperament and emotion. In M. Lewis, J. M. Haviland-Jones, & L. Feldman Barrett (Eds.), *Handbook of emotions* (3rd ed., pp. 485–496). New York: Guilford.

Battaglia, D. F., Richard, F. D., Datteri D. L., & Lord, C. G. (1998). Breaking up is (relatively) easy to do: A script for the dissolution of close relationships. *Journal of Social and Personal Relationships*, 15, 829–845.

Bauman, M. D., Lavenex, P., Mason, W. A., Capitanio, J. P., et al. (2004). The development of mother-infant interactions after neonatal amygdala lesions in rhesus monkeys. *Journal of Neuroscience*, 24, 711–721.

Baumeister, R. F., & Vohs, K. D. (Eds.). (2004). *Handbook of self-regulation: Research, theory, and applications*. New York: Guilford.

Baumeister, R. F., Zell, A. L., & Tice, D. M. (2007). How emotions facilitate and impair self-regulation. In J. J. Gross (Ed.), *Handbook of emotion regulation* (pp. 408–426). New York: Guilford.

Bauminger, N., Finzi-Dottan, R., Chason, S., & Har-Even, D. (2008). Intimacy in adolescent friendship. *Journal of Personal and Social Relationships*, 25, 409–428.

Baxter, L. A., Mazanec M., Nicholson, J., Pittman, et al. (1997). Everyday loyalties and betrayals in personal relationships. *Journal of Social and Personal Relationships*, 14, 655–678.

Beach, S. R. H., & Fincham, F. D. (1994). Toward an integrated model of negative affectivity in marriage. In S. M. Johnson & L. S. Greenberg (Eds.), *The heart of the matter: Perspectives on emotion in marital therapy* (pp. 227–255). New York: Brunner/Mazel.

Beach, S. R. H., Katz, J., Kim, S., & Brody, G. (2003). Prospective effects of marital satisfaction on depressive symptoms in established marriages: A dyadic model. *Journal of Social and Personal Relationships*, 20, 355–371.

Beach, S. R. H., & O'Leary, K. (1993a). Dysphoria and marital discord: Are dysphoric individuals at risk for marital maladjustment? *Journal of Marital and Family Therapy*, 19, 355–368.

(1993b). Marital discord and dysphoria: For whom does the marital relationship predict depressive symptomatology? *Journal of Social and Personal Relationships*, 10, 405–420.

Beach, W. A., & Good, J. S. (2004). Uncertain family trajectories: Interactional consequences of cancer diagnosis, treatment, and prognosis. *Journal of Social and Personal Relationships*, 2, 8–32.

Beall, A. E., & Sternberg, R. J. (1995). The social construction of love. *Journal of Social and Personal Relationships*, 12, 417–438.

Bearison, D. J., & Zimiles, H. (Eds.). (1986). *Thought and emotion: Developmental perspectives*. Hillsdale, NJ: Erlbaum.

Beauregard, M., Levesque, J., & Bourgouin, P. (2001). Neural correlates of conscious self-regulation of emotion. *Journal of Neuroscience*, 21, RC165.

Bechara, A., & Damasio, A. R. (2005). The somatic marker hypothesis: A neural theory of economic decision. *Games and Economic Behavior*, 52, 336–372.

Bechara, A., Damasio, H., & Damasio, A. R. (2003). The role of the amygdala in decision-making. In P. Shinnick-Gallagher, A. Pitkanen, A. Shekhar, & L. Cahill (Eds.), *The amygdala in brain function: Basic and clinical approaches* (pp. 365–369). New York: Annals of the New York Academy of Science.

Bechara, A., Damasio, H., Damasio, A. R., & Lee, G. P. (1999). Different contributions of the human amygdala and ventromedial prefrontal cortex to decision-making. *Journal of Neuroscience*, 19, 5473–5481.

Beck, A. T., Rush, S., Shaw, P., & Emery, N. (1979). *Cognitive therapy of depression*. New York, Guilford.

Becker, D., Sagarin, B., Guadagno, R., Millevoi, A., et al. (2004). When the sexes need not differ: Emotional responses to the sexual and emotional aspects of infidelity. *Personal Relationships*, 11, 529–538.

Beer, J. S., & Lombardo, M. V. (2007). Insights into emotion regulation from neuropsychology. In J. J. Gross (Ed.), *Handbook of emotion regulation* (pp. 69–86). New York: Guilford.

Beevers, C., Wells, T., & Miller, I. (2007). Predicting response to depression treatment: The role of negative cognition. *Journal of Consulting and Clinical Psychology*, 75, 422–431.

Bekker, M. H. J., & Spoor, S. T. P. (2008). Emotional inhibition, health, gender, and eating disorders: The role of (over)sensitivity to others. In A. Vingerhoets, I. Nyklicek, & J. Denollet (Eds.), *Emotional regulation: Conceptual and clinical issues* (pp. 170–183). New York: Springer.

Bell, C., & L'Abate, L. (undated). Crying: A noxious stimulus to be suppressed? Unpublished manuscript. Department of Psychology, Geogia State University, Atlanta, GA.

Belsky, J., Woodworth, S., & Crnic, K. (1996). Trouble in the second year: Three questions about family interaction. *Child Development*, 67, 556–578.

Ben-Ari, A., & Lavee, Y. (2007). Dyadic closeness in marriage: From the inside story to a conceptual model. *Journal of Social and Personal Relationships*, 24, 627–644.

Benazon, N. R., Foster, M. D., & Coyne, J. C. (2006). Expressed emotion, adaptation, and patient survival among couples with chronic heart failure. *Journal of Family Psychology*, 20, 328–334.

Bennett, M. P., Zeller, J. M., Rosenberg, L., & McCann, J. (2003). The effect of mirthful laughter on stress and natural killer cell activity. *Alternative Therapies in Health and Medicine*, 9, 38–45.

Berenbaum, H., Raghanvan, C., Le, H-N, Vernon, L. L., & Gomez, J. J. (2003). A taxonomy of emotional disturbances. *Clinical Psychology: Science and Practice*, 10, 206–226.

Bergin, A. E., & Garfield, S. L. (Eds.). (1994). *Handbook of psychotherapy and behavior change*. New York: Wiley.

Berle, D., & Phillips, E. S. (2006). Disgust and obsessive-compulsive disorder: An update. *Psychiatry: Interpersonal and Biological Processes*, 69, 229–238.

Bernet, W., von Boch-Galhau, W., Baker, A. J., & Morrison, S. L. (2010). Parental alienation, DSM-V, and ICD-11. *American Journal of Family Therapy*, 38, 76–187.

Bersheid, E., & Ammazzalorso, H. (2003). Emotional experience in close relationships. In G. J. O. Fletcher & M. S. Clark (Eds.), *Blackwell handbook of social psychology: Interpersonal processes* (pp. 308–330). Malden, MA: Blackwell.

Bertera, E. M. (2005). Mental health in U.S. adults: The role of positive social support and social negativity in personal relationships. *Journal of Social and Personal Relationships*, 22(1), 33–48.

Berthoz, S., Artiges, E., Van de Moortele, P. F., Jean-Baptiste Poline, J. B., Rouquette, S., Consoli, S. M., & Jean-Luc Martinot, J. L. (2002). Effect of impaired recognition and expression of emotions on frontocingulate cortices: An fMRI study of men with alexithymia. *The American Journal of Psychiatry*, 159, 961–967.

Bielby, D. D. (1999). Gender and family relations. In J. S. Chafetz (Ed.), *Handbook of the sociology of gender* (pp. 391–406). New York: Kluwer Academic.

Birnie, C., McClure, M. J., Lydon, J. E., & Holmberg, D. (2009). Attachment avoidance and commitment aversion: A script for relationship failure. *Personal Relationships*, 16, 79–98.

Bishop, S. J., Duncan, J., & Lawrence, A. D. (2004). State anxiety modulation of the amygdala response to unattended threat-related stimuli. *Journal of Neuroscience*, 24, 10364–10380.

Blanchard, J. J., Cohen, A. S., & Correno, J. T. (2007). Emotion and schizophrenia. In J. Rottenberg & S. L. Johnson (Eds.), *Emotion and psychopathology: Bridging affective and clinical science* (pp. 103–122). Washington, DC: American Psychological Association.

Blaney, P. H. (1999). Paranoid conditions. In T. Millon, P. H. Blaney, & R. D. Davies (Eds.), *Oxford textbook of psychopathology* (pp. 339–364). New York: Oxford University Press.

Blechman, E. A. (Ed.). (1990). *Emotions and the family: For better or for worse.* Hillsdale, NJ: Erlbaum.

Blieszner, R. (2006). A lifetime of caring: Dimensions and dynamics in late-life relationships. *Personal Relationships*, 13, 1–18.

Bodenmann, G., Charviz, L, Bradbury, T. N., Bertoni, A., et al. (2007). The role of stress in divorce: A three-nation retrospective study. *Journal of Social and Personal Relationships*, 24, 707–728.

Bodenmann, G., Kaiser, A., Hahlweg, K., & Fehm-Wolfsdorf, G. (1998). Communication patterns during marital conflict: A cross-cultural replication. *Personal Relationships*, 5, 343–356.

Bodenmann, G., Ledermann, T., & Bradbury, T. N. (2007). Stress, sex, and satisfaction in marriage. *Personal Relationships*, 14, 551–569.

Boelen, P., van den Hout, M., & van den Bout, J. (2006). A cognitive-behavioral conceptualization of complicated grief. *Clinical Psychology: Science and Practice*, 13, 109–128.

Bonanno, G. (2006). Is complicated grief a valid construct? *Clinical Psychology: Science and Practice*, 13, 129–134.

Bonanno, G. A., Goorin, L., & Coifman, K. G. (2008). Sadness and grief. In M. Lewis, J. M. Haviland-Jones, & L. Feldman Barrett (Eds.), *Handbook of emotions* (3rd ed., pp. 797–810). New York: Guilford.

Bonanno, G., Papa, A., Lalande, K., Zhang, N., et al. (2005). Grief processing and deliberate grief avoidance: A prospective comparison of bereaved spouses and parents in the United States and the People's Republic of China. *Journal of Consulting and Clinical Psychology*, 73(1), 86–98.

Boon, S. D., & Holmes, J. G. (1999). Interpersonal risk and the evaluation of transgressions in close relationships. *Personal Relationships*, 6, 151–168.

Borkovic, T., & Hu, S. (1990). The effect of worry on cardiovascular responses to phobic imagery. *Behaviour Research and Therapy*, 28, 69–73.

Bradbury, T. N. (2002a). Invited program overview: Research on relationships as a prelude to action. *Journal of Social and Personal Relationships*, 19, 215–232.

(2002b). Research on relationships as a prelude to action: Response to commentaries. *Journal of Social and Personal Relationships*, 19, 629–638.

Bradbury, T. N., & Fincham, F. D. (1989). Behavior and satisfaction in marriage: Prospective mediating processes. In C. Hendrick (Ed.), *Close relationships: Review of personality and social psychology* (Vol. 10, pp. 119–143). Thousand Oaks, CA: Sage.

Bradford, S. A., Feeney, J. A., & Campbell, L. (2002). Links between attachment orientation and dispositional and diary-based measures of disclosure in dating couples: A study of actor and partner effects. *Personal Relationships*, 9, 491–506.

Braithwaite, S. R., Fincham, F. D., & Lambert, N. M. (2009). Hurt and psychological health in close relationships. In A. L. Vangelisti (Ed.), *Feeling hurt in close relationships* (pp. 376–398). New York: Cambridge University Press.

Branje, S. J. T., Frijns, T., Finkenauer, C., Engels, R., et al. (2007). Are you my best friend: Commitment and stability in adolescents' same-sex friendships. *Personal Relationships*, 14, 587–604.

Brase, G. L., Caprar, D. V., & Voracek, M. (2004). Sex differences in responses to relationship threats in England and Romania. *Journal of Social and Personal Relationships*, 21, 763–778.

Bridges, M. R. (2006). Activating the corrective emotional experience. *Journal of Clinical Psychology*, 62, 551–568.

Briere, J., & Rickards, S. (2007). Self-awareness, affect regulation, and relatedness: Differential sequels of childhood versus adult victimization experience. *Journal of Nervous and Mental Disease*, 195, 497–501.

Brinkman, D. C., & Overholser, J. C. (1994). Emotional distress in adolescent psychiatric inpatients: Direct and indirect measures. *Journal of Personality Assessment*, 62, 472–484.

Brock, D. M., Pierce, G. R., Sarason, I. G., & Sarason, B. R. (1996). Simultaneous assessment of perceived global and relationship-specific support. *Journal of Social and Personal Relationships*, 13, 143–152.

Brody, L. R., & Hall, J. A. (2008). Gender and emotion in context. In M. Lewis, H. M. Haviland-Jones, & L. F. Barrett (Eds.), *Handbook of emotions* (3rd ed., pp. 395–408). New York: Guilford.

Brooks, G. R., & Richardson, F. C. (1980). Emotional skills training: A treatment program for duodenal ulcer. *Behavior Therapy*, 11, 198–207.

Brossshot, W. G., & Thayer, J. (2006). The perseverative cognition hypothesis: A review of worry, prolonged-stress-related physiological activation, and health. *Journal of Psychosomatic Research*, 60, 113–124.

Brown, R. J. (2007). Introduction to the special issue on medically unexplained symptoms: Background and future directions. *Clinical Psychology Review, 27,* 769–780.

Buchanan, T. W. (2007). Retrieval of emotional memories. *Psychological Bulletin, 133,* 761–779.

Buck, R. (1999). The biological affects: A typology. *Psychological Review, 106,* 301–336.

Buckley, K. E., Winkel, R. E., & Leary, M. R. (2004). Reactions to acceptance and rejection: Effects of level and sequence of relational evaluation. *Journal of Experimental Social Psychology, 40,* 14–28.

Buehler, C., & Welsh, D. P. (2009). A process model of adolescents' triagulation into parents' marital conflict: The role of emotional reactivity. *Journal of Family Psychology, 23,* 167–180.

Bugental, D. B. (2010). Paradoxical power manifestations: Power assertion by the subjectively powerless. In A. Guinote & T. K. Vescio (Eds.), *The social psychology of power* (pp. 209–230). New York: Guilford.

Burger, E., & Milardo, R. M. (1995). Marital interdependence and social networks. *Journal of Social and Personal Relationships, 12,* 403–416.

Burleson, B. R. (1995). Personal relationships as a skilled accomplishment. *Journal of Social and Personal Relationships, 12,* 575–582.

(1997). A different voice on different cultures: Illusion and reality in the study of sex differences in personal relationships. *Personal Relationships, 4,* 229–242.

(2003). The experience and the effects of emotional support: What the study of cultural and gender differences can tell us about close relationships, emotions, and interpersonal relationship. *Personal Relationships, 10,* 1–24.

(2009). Understanding the outcomes of supportive communication: A dual-process approach. *Journal of Social and Personal Relationships, 26,* 21–38.

Burum, B. A., & Goldfried, M. R. (2007). The centrality of emotion to psychological change. *Clinical Psychology: Science and Practice, 14,* 407–413.

Buss, D. M., Shackelford, T. K., Kirkpatrick, L. A., Choe, J. C., et al. (1999). Jealousy and the nature of beliefs about infidelity: Tests of competing hypotheses about sex differences in the United States, Korea, and Japan. *Personal Relationships, 6,* 125–150.

Butler, A. B., & Hodos, W. (2005). *Comparative vertebrate neuroanatomy: Evolution and adaptation.* Hoboken, NJ: Wiley.

Butler, E. A., & Gross, J. J. (2009). Emotion and emotion regulation: Integrating individual and social levels of analysis. *Emotion Review, 1,* 86–87.

Butner, J., Diamond, L. M., & Hicks, A. M. (2007). Attachment style and two forms of affect regulation between romantic partners. *Personal Relationships, 14,* 430–456.

Buunk, B. P. (1995). Sex, self-esteem, dependency, and extradyadic sexual experience as related to jealousy responses. *Journal of Social and Personal Relationships, 12,* 147–153.

Buunk, B. P., & Dijkstra, P. (2001). Evidence from a homosexual sample for a sex-specific rival-oriented mechanism: Jealousy as a function of a rival's physical attractiveness and dominance. *Personal Relationships, 8,* 391–406.

Buunk, B. P., & Dijkstra, P. (2004). Gender differences in rival characteristics that evoke jealousy in response to emotional versus sexual infidelity. *Personal Relationships*, 11, 395–408.

Buunk, B., Dijkstra, P., Fetchenhauer, D., & Kenrick, D. (2002). Age and gender differences in mate selection criteria for various involvement levels. *Personal Relationships*, 9, 271–278.

Bylund, C. L., & Duck, S. (2004). The everyday interplay between family relationships and family members' health. *Journal of Social and Personal Relationships*, 21, 5–7.

Campbell, C. M., France, C. R., Robinson, M. E., Logan, H. L., et al. (2008). Ethnic differences in diffuse noxious inhibitory controls. *Journal of Pain*, 9, 759–766.

Campbell, S. B. (2002). *Behavior problems in preschool children: Clinical and developmental issues*. New York: Guilford.

Campbell-Sills, L., & Barlow, D. H. (2007). Incorporating emotion regulation into conceptualizations and treatments of anxiety and mood disorders. In J. J. Gross (Ed.), *Handbook of emotion regulation* (pp. 542–559). New York: Guilford.

Camras, L. A., & Fatani, S. S. (2008). The development of facial expressions: Current perspectives on infant emotions. In M. Lewis, J. M. Haviland-Jones, & L. F. Barrett (Eds.), *Handbook of emotions* (3rd ed., pp. 291–303). New York: Guildford.

Canly, T. (2008). Toward a "molecular psychology" of personality. In O. P. John, R. W. Robins, & L. A. Pervin (Eds.), *Handbook of personality: Theory and research* (pp. 311–327). New York: Guilford.

Cann, A., & Baucom, T. R. (2004). Former partners and new rivals as threats to a relationship: Infidelity type, gender and commitment as factors related to distress and forgiveness. *Personal Relationships*, 11, 305–318.

Capitelli, M., Guerra, C., L'Abate, L., & Rumbaugh, D. M. (2009). Science or mind? Reductionism proper, optimal reductionism, emergent interactionism, and synthetic integration. In L. L'Abate, M. Capitelli, P. De Giacomo, & S. Longo (Eds.), *Science, mind, and creativity: The Bari symposium* (pp. 1–22). New York: Nova Science Publishers.

Cappadocia, M. C., Desorcher, M., Pepler, D., & Schroeder, J. H. (2009). Conceptualizing the neurobiology of conduct disorder in an emotion dysregulation framework. *Clinical Psychology Review*, 29, 506–518.

Caprara, G. V., & Cervone, D. (2000). *Personality: Determinants, dynamics, and potentials*. New York: Cambridge University Press.

Card, N. A., Isaacs, J., & Hodges, E. V. E. (2009). Aggression and victimization in children's peer groups: A relational perspective. In A. L. Vangelisti (Ed.), *Handbook of hurt feelings in close relationships* (pp. 235–259). New York: Cambridge University Press.

Carducci, B. J. (1999). *Shyness: A bold new approach*. New York: HarperCollins.

Carnelley, K. B., Pietromonaco, P. R., & Jaffe, K. (1996). Attachment, caregiving, and relationship functioning in couples: Effects of self and partner. *Personal Relationships*, 3, 257–277.

Carver, C. S. (1997). You want to measure coping but your protocol's too long: Consider the Brief COPE. *International Journal of Behavioral Medicine*, 4, 92–100.

Cattaneo, L. B., Stuewig, J., Goodman, L. A., Kaltman, S., et al. (2007). Longitudinal helpseeking patterns among victims of intimate partner violence: The relationship between legal and extralegal services. *American Journal of Orthopsychiatry, 77,* 467–477.

Caughlin, J. P., & Malis, R. S. (2004). Demand/withdraw communication between parents and adolescents: Connections with self-esteem and substance abuse. *Journal of Social and Personal Relationships, 21,* 125–148.

Caughlin, J. P., & Ramey, M. A. (2005). The demand/withdraw pattern of communication in parent-adolescent dyads. *Personal Relationships, 12,* 337–356.

Caughlin, J. P., Scott, A. M., & Miller, L. E. (2009). Conflict and hurt in close relationships. In A. L. Vangelisti (Ed.), *Handbook of hurt feelings in close relationships* (pp. 143–166). New York: Cambridge University Press.

Caughlin, J. P., & Vangelisti, A. L. (2000). An individual difference explanation of why married couples engage in the demand/withdrawal pattern of conflict. *Journal of Social and Personal Relationships, 17,* 523–551.

Cechetto, D. F., & Saper, C. B. (1987). Evidence for a viscerotopic sensory representation in the cortex and thalamus in the rat. *The Journal of Comparative Neurology, 262,* 27–45.

Chaikin, A. L., & Derlega, V. J. (1974a). Liking for the norm-breaker in self-discosure. *Journal of Psychology, 42,* 117–129.

(1974b). Variables affecting the appropriateness of self-disclosure. *Journal of Consulting and Clinical Psychology, 42,* 585–593.

Chambers, R., Guilone, E., & Allen, N. B. (2009). Mindful emotion regulation: An integrative review. *Clinical Psychology Review, 29,* 560–572.

Chang, L., Schwartz, D., Dodge, K. A., & McBride-Chang, C. (2003). Harsh parenting in relation to child emotion regulation and aggression. *Journal of Family Psychology, 17,* 598–606.

Chapman, T., & Foot, H. (Eds.). (1976). *Humor and laughter: Theory, research and applications.* New York: Wiley.

Cheavens, J. S., Rosenthal, M. Z., Daughers, S. B., Nowak, J., et al. (2005). An analogue investigation of the relationship among perceived parental criticism, negative affect, and borderline personality disorder features: The role of thought suppression. *Behaviour Research & Therapy, 43,* 257–268.

Chikama, M., McFarland, N. R., Amaral, D. G., & Haber, S. N. (1997). Insular cortical projections to functional regions of the striatum correlate with cortical cytoarchitectonic organization in the primate. *Journal of Neuroscience, 17,* 9686–9705.

Christian, J. L., O'Leary, K. D., & Vivian, D. (1994). Depressive symptomatology in maritally discordant women and men: The role of individual and relationship variables. *Journal of Family Psychology, 8,* 32–42.

Ciompi, L. (1998). Is schizophrenia an affective disease? The hypothesis of affect-logic and its implications for psychopathology. In W. F. Flack, Jr., & J. D. Laird (Eds.), *Emotions in psychopathology: Theory and research* (pp. 283–297). New York: Oxford University Press.

Clark, J. C. (2009). Inequality in prison. *Monitor on Psychology, 40,* 55.

Clark, L. A., & Watson, D. (2008). Temperament: An organizing paradigm for trait psychology. In O. P. John, R. W. Robins, & L. A. Pervin (Eds.), *Handbook of personality: Theory and research* (pp. 265–286). New York: Guilford.

Clark, M. S., & Fiske, S. T. (Eds.). (1982). *Affect and cognition*. Hillsdale, NJ: Erlbaum.

Clark, M. S., Fitness, J., & Brissette, I. (2003). Understanding people's perceptions of relationships is crucial to understanding their emotional lives. In G. J. O. Fletcher & M. S. Clark (Eds.), *Blackwell handbook of social psychology: Interpersonal processes* (pp. 253–278). Malden, MA: Blackwell.

Clark, R. A. (1994). Children's and adolescents' gender preferences for conversational partners for specific communicative objectives. *Journal of Social and Personal Relationships*, 11, 313–319.

Clark, S. L., & Stephens, M. A. (1996). Stroke patients' well-being as a function of caregiving spouses' helpful and unhelpful actions. *Personal Relationships*, 3, 171–184.

Clarkin, J. F., Haas, G. L., & Glick, I. D. (Eds.). (1988). *Affective disorders and the family: Assessment and treatment*. New York: Guilford.

Clay, R. A. (2009). Prevention works. *Monitor on Psychology, September*, 42–44.

Cleary, R. P., & Katz, L. F. (2008). Family-level emotion socialization and children's comfort with emotional expressivity. *The Family Psychologist*, 24, 7–13.

Clements, K., Holtzworth-Munroe, A., Schweinle, W., & Ickes, W. (2007). Empathy accuracy of intimate partners in violent versus nonviolent relationships. *Personal Relationships*, 14, 369–388.

Clore, G. L., & Huntsinger, J. R. (2009). How the object of affect guides its impact. *Emotion Review*, 1, 39–54.

Clore, G. L., & Ortony, A. (2008). Appraisal theories: How cognition shapes affect into emotion. In M. Lewis, J. M. Haviland-Jones, & L. Feldman Barrett (Eds.), *Handbook of emotions* (3rd ed., pp. 628–643). New York: Guilford.

Coan, J. A., & Allen, J. J. B. (Eds.). (2007). *Handbook of emotion elicitation and assessment*. New York: Oxford University Press.

Cocking, R. R., & Renninger, K. A. (Eds.). (1993). *The development and meaning of psychological distance*. Mahwah, NJ: Erlbaum.

Cohan, C. L., Booth, A., & Granger, D. A. (2003). Gender moderates the relationship between testosterone and marital interaction. *Journal of Family Psychology*, 17, 29–40.

Cohen, S., Klein, D. N., & O'Leary, K. D. (2007). The role of separation/divorce in relapse and recovery from major depression. *Journal of Social and Personal Relationships*, 24, 855–874.

Cohler, B. J., & Musik, J. S. (1983). Psychopathology of parenthood: Implications for mental health of children. *Infant Mental Health Journal*, 4, 140–164.

Cohn, M., Fredrickson, B., Brown, S., Mikels, J., et al. (2009). Happiness unpacked: Positive emotions increase life satisfaction by building resilience. *Emotion*, 9, 361–368.

Cole, T. (2001). Lying to the one you love: The use of deception in romantic relationships. *Journal of Social and Personal Relationships*, 18, 107–129.

Cole, T., & Teboul, J. C. B. (2004). Non-zero-sum collaboration, reciprocity, and the preference for similarity: Developing an adaptive model of close relational functioning. *Personal Relationships*, 11, 135–160.

Collins, N. L., & Feeney, B. C. (2004). An attachment theory perspective on closeness and intimacy. In D. J. Mashek & A. Aron (Eds.), *Handbook of closeness and intimacy* (pp. 163–187). Mahwah, NJ: Erlbaum.

Combs, D. R., Michael, C. O., & Penn, D. L. (2006). Paranoia and emotion perception across the continuum. *British Journal of Clinical Psychology*, 45, 19–41.

Conger, J. C., Conger, A. J., Edmondson, C., Tescher, B., et al. (2003). The relationship of anger and social skills to psychological symptoms. *Assessment*, 10, 248–258.

Consedine, N. S. (2008). Health-promoting and health-damaging effects of emotion: The view from developmental functionalism. In M. Lewis, J. M. Haviland-Jones, & L. Feldman Barrett (Eds.), *Handbook of emotions* (3rd ed., pp. 676–690). New York: Guilford.

Conway, A. M. (2005). Girls, aggression, and emotion regulation. *American Journal of Orthopsychiatry*, 75, 334–339.

Corr, P. J. (2005). Social exclusion and the hierarchical defense system: Comment on MacDonald and Leary (2005). *Psychological Bulletin*, 131, 231–236.

Corrigan, P. W., Watson, A. C., & Miller, F. E. (2006). Blame, shame, and contamination: The impact of mental illness and drug dependence stigma on family members. *Journal of Family Psychology*, 20, 239–246.

Costigan, C. L., Cox, M. J., & Cauce, A. M. (2003). Work-parenting linkages among dual-earner couples as the transition to parenthood. *Journal of Family Psychology*, 17, 397–408.

Coyne, J. C. (1976). Toward an interactional description of depression. *Psychiatry*, 39, 28–40.

Coyne, J. C., Kahn, J., & Gotlib, I. H. (1987). Depression. In T. Jacob (Ed.), *Family interaction and psychopathology: Theories, methods, and findings* (pp. 509–534). New York: Plenum.

Coyne, J. C., Rohrbaugh, M. J., Shoham, V., Sonnega, J. S., et al. (2001). Prognostic importance of marital quality for survival of congestive heart failure. *The American Journal of Cardiology*, 88, 526–529.

Coyne, J. C., & Smith, D. A. F. (1991). Couples coping with a myocardial infarction: A contextual perspective on wives' distress. *Journal of Personality and Social Psychology*, 61, 404–412.

(1994). Couples coping with a myocardial infarction: Contextual perspective on patient self-efficacy. *Journal of Family Psychology*, 8, 43–54.

Coyne, J. C., Thompson, R., & Palmer, S. C. (2002). Marital quality, coping with conflict, marital complaints, and affection in couples with a depressed wife. *Journal of Family Psychology*, 16, 26–37.

Craig, A. D. (2002). How do you feel? Interoception: The sense of the physiological condition of the body. *Nature Reviews Neuroscience*, 3, 655–666.

(2008). Interoception and emotion: A neuroanatomical perspective. In M. Lewis, J. M. Haviland-Jones, & L. F. Barrett (Eds.), *Handbook of emotions* (3rd ed., pp. 272–288). New York: Guilford.

Craig, J-J., Koestner, R., & Zuroff, D. C. (1994). Implicit and self-attributed intimacy motivation. *Journal of Social and Personal Relationships*, 11, 491–508.

Critchley, H. D. (2005). Neural mechanisms of autonomic, affective, and cognitive integration. *The Journal of Comparative Neurology*, 493, 154–166.

Critchley, H. D., Wiens, S., Rotshrein, P., Ohman, A., et al. (2004). Neural systems supporting interoceptive awareness. *Nature Neuroscience*, 7, 189–195.

Crockenberg, S., & Langrock, A. (2001). The role of specific emotions in children's responses to interparental conflict: A test of the model. *Journal of Family Psychology*, 15, 163–182.

Cross, N. E., & Gore, J. S. (2004). The relational self-construal and closeness. In D. J. Mashek & A. Aron (Eds.), *Handbook of closeness and intimacy* (pp. 229–245). Mahwah, NJ: Erlbaum.

Croyle, R. T. (1992). Appraisals of health threats: Cognition, motivation, and social comparison. *Cognitive Therapy and Research*, 16, 165–182.

Cukor, J., Spitalnick, J., Difede, J-A, Rizzo, A., et al. & Rothbaum, B. O. (2007). Emerging treatments for PTSD. *Clinical Psychology Review*, 29, 715–726.

Cummings, E. M., Davies, P. T., & Campbell, S. B. (2000). *Developmental psychopathology and family process*. New York: Guilford.

Cummings, E. M., Davies, P. T., & Simpson, K. S. (1994). Marital conflict, gender, and children's appraisal and coping efficacy as mediators of child adjustment. *Journal of Family Psychology*, 8, 141–149.

Cummings, E. M., Goeke-Morey, M., Papp, L. M., & Dukewich, T. L. (2002). Children's responses to mothers, and fathers' emotionality and tactics in marital conflict in the home. *Journal of Family Psychology*, 16, 478–492.

Cunningham, M. R., Barbee, A. P., & Mandal, E. (2009). Hurt feelings and the work place. In A. L. Vangelisti (Ed.), *Handbook of hurt feelings in close relationships* (pp. 417–456). New York: Cambridge University Press.

Cunningham, M. R., Samblen, S. R., Barber, A. P., & Ault, L. K. (2005). Social allergies in romantic relationships: Behavioral repetition, emotional sensitization, and dissatisfaction in dating couples. *Personal Relationships*, 12, 273–296.

Cunningham, W. A., Johnson, M. K., Gatenby, J. C., Gore, J. C., et al. (2003). Neural components of social evaluation. *Journal of Personality and Social Psychology*, 85, 639–649.

Curran, M., Hazen, N., Jacobvitz, D., & Sasaki, T. (2006). How representations of the parental marriage predict marital emotional attunement during the transition to parenthood. *Journal of Family Psychology*, 20, 477–484.

Cusinato, M., & Colesso, W. (2008). Validation of a continuum of likeness in intimate relationships. In L. L'Abate (Ed.), *Toward a science of clinical psychology: Laboratory evaluations and interventions* (pp. 337–352). New York: Nova Science Publishers.

Cusinato, M., & L'Abate, L. (Eds.). (2012). *Advances in relational competence theory: With special attention to alexithymia*. New Work: Nova Science Publishers.

Cutrona, C. E., Hessling, R. M., & Suhr, J. A. (1997). The influence of husband and wife personality on marital social support interactions. *Personal Relationships*, 4, 379–394.

Dallaire, D. H., Pineda, A. O., Colem D. A., Ciesla, J. A., et al. (2006). Relation of positive and negative parenting to children's depressive symptoms. *Journal of Clinical Child and Adolescent Psychology*, 35, 313–322.

Damasio, A. R. (1994). *Descartes' error: Emotion, reason, and the human brain*. New York: Grosset/Putnam.

(1999). *The feeling of what happens: Body and emotion in the making of consciousness*. New York: Harcourt Brace & Company.

Damasio, A. R. (2003). *Looking for Spinoza: Joy, sorrow, and the feeling brain.* New York: Harcourt.

Davidson, R. J., Fox, A., & Kalin, N. H. (2007). Neural bases of emotion regulation in nonhuman primates and humans. In J. J. Gross (Ed.), *Handbook of emotion regulation* (pp. 47–68). New York: Guilford.

Davila, J., Bradbury, T. N., & Fincham, F. (1998). Negative affectivity as a mediator of the association between adult attachment and marital satisfaction. *Personal Relationships,* 5, 467–484.

Davila, J., Karney, B. R., Hall, T. W., & Bradbury, T. N. (2003). Depressive symptoms and marital satisfaction: Within-subject associations and the moderating effects of gender and neuroticism. *Journal of Family Psychology,* 17, 557–570.

Davitz, J. R. (1969). *The language of emotion.* New York: Academic Press.

Dayan, J., Doyle, A-B., & Markiewicz, D. (2001). Social support networks and self-esteem of idiocentric and allocentric children and adolescents. *Journal of Social and Personal Relationships,* 18, 767–784.

Deary, V., Chalder, T., & Sharpe, M. (2007). The cognitive-behavioral model of medically unexplained symptoms: A theoretical and empirical review. *Clinical Psychology Review,* 27, 781–797.

Deater-Deckard, K., Lansford, J. E., Dodge, K. A., Pettit, G. S., et al. (2003). The development of attitudes about physical punishment: An 8-year longitudinal study. *Journal of Family Psychology,* 17, 351–360,

Deater-Deckard, K., & Scarr, S. (1996). Parental stress among dual-earner mothers and fathers: Are there gender differences? *Journal of Family Psychology,* 10, 45–59.

DeGarmo D. S., & Forgatch, M. S. (1997). Confident support and maternal distress: Predictors of parenting practices for divorced mothers. *Personal Relationships,* 4, 305–318.

De Giacomo, P., L'Abate, L., Pennebaker, J. M., & Rumbaugh, D. M. (2010). Amplifications and applications of Pennebaker's analogic to digital model in psychotherapy and mental health interventions. *Clinical Psychology and Psychotherapy,* 17, 355–362.

Dekel, R., & Solomon, Z. (2006). Marital relations among former prisoners of war: Contribution of posttraumatic stress disorder, aggression, and sexual satisfaction. *Journal of Family Psychology,* 20, 709–712.

Del Vecchio, T., & O'Leary, S. G. (2006). Antecedent of toddler aggression: Dysfunctional parenting in mother-toddler dyads. *Journal of Clinical Child and Adolescent Psychology,* 35, 194–202.

Denollet, J., Nyklicek, I., & Vingerhoets, A. J. J. M. (2008). Introduction: Emotions, emotion regulation, and health. In A. J. J. M. Vingerhoets, I. Nyklicek, & J. Denollet (Eds), *Emotion regulation: Conceptual and clinical issues* (pp. 3–11). New York: Springer.

Denton, W. H. (1996). Problems encountered in reconciling individual and relational diagnosis. In F. W. Kaslow (Ed.), *Handbook of relational diagnosis and dysfunctional family patterns* (pp. 35–45). New York: Wiley.

DePaulo, B. M., Morris, W. L., & Sternglanz, R. W. (2009). When the truth hurts: Deception in the name of kindness. In A. L. Vangelisti (Ed.), *Handbook of hurt feelings in close relationships* (pp. 167–190). New York: Cambridge University Press.

De Raedt, R., Schacht, R., Franck, E., De Houwer, J. (2006). Self-esteem and depression revisited: Implicit self-esteem in depressed patients? *Behavior research and therapy*, 44, 1017–1028.

Derlega, V. J., & Chaikin, A. L. (1977). Privacy and self-disclosure in social relationships. *Journal of Social Issues*, 33, 102–115.

Derlega, V. J., & Grzlak, J. (1979). Appropriateness of self-disclosure. In C. Chelune (Ed.), *Self-disclosure: Origins, patterns, and implications of openness in interpersonal relationships* (pp. 151–178). San Francisco: Jossey-Bass.

Derlega, V. J., Lovell, R., & Chaikin, A. L. (1976). Effects of therapist disclosure and its perceived appropriateness on client self-disclosure. *Journal of Consulting and Clinical Psychology*, 44, 866.

Derlega, V. J., Metts, S., Petronio, S., & Margulis, S. T. (1993). *Self-disclosure*. Newbury Park, CA: Sage.

Derlega, V., & Stepien, E. (1977). Norms regulating self-disclosure among Polish university students. *Journal of Cross-Cultural Psychology*, 8, 369–376.

Descountner, C. J., & Thelen, M. H. (1991). Development and validation of a Fear-of-Intimacy scale. *Psychological Assessment: A Journal of Consulting and Clinical Psychology*, 3, 218–225.

Detweiler-Bedell, J. B., & Whisman, M. A. (2005). A lesson in assigning homework: Therapist, client, and task characteristics in cognitive therapy for depression. *Professional Psychology: Research and Practice*, 36, 219–223.

DeWall, C. N., Baumeister, R. E., & Masicampo, E. J. (2009). Rejection: Resolving the paradox of emotional numbness after exclusion. In A. L. Vangelisti (Ed.), *Handbook of hurt feelings in close relationships* (pp. 123–141). New York: Cambridge University Press.

Diamond, L. M., Hicks, A. M., & Otter-Henderson, K. (2006). Physiological evidence for repressive coping among avoidantly attached adults. *Journal of Social and Personal Relationships*, 23, 230–242.

Diatchenko, L., Nackley, A. B., Slade, G. D., Fllingim, R. B., & Maixner, W. (2006). Ideopathic pain disorders – Pathways to vulnerability. *Pain*, 123, 226–230.

Diatchenko, L., Nackley, A. G., Tchivileva, I. E., Shabalina, S. A., & Maixner, W. (2007). Genetic architecture of human pain perception. *Trends in Genetics*, 23, 605–613.

Diefenbach, M. A., Miller, S. M., Porter, M., Peters, E., et al. (2008). Emotions and health behaviors: A self-regulation perspective. In M. Lewis, J. M. Haviland-Jones, & L. Feldman Barrett (Eds.), *Handbook of emotions* (3rd ed., pp. 645–690). New York: Guilford.

Diener, E., Emmons, R. A., Larsen, R. J., & Griffin, S. (1985). The Satisfaction with Life Scale. *Journal of Personality Assessment*, 49, 71–75.

Dindia, K., & Allen, M. (1992). Sex differences in self-disclosure: A meta-analysis. *Psychological Bulletin*, 112, 106–124.

Doi, S. C., & Thelen, M. H. (1993). The Fear-of-Intimacy Scale: Replication and extension. *Psychological Assessment*, 5, 377–383.

Dolan, R. J., Morris, J. S., & de Gelder, B. (2001). Crossmodal binding of fear in voice and face. *Proceedings of the National Academy of Sciences USA*, 98, 10006–10010.

Dolgin, K. G. (1996). Parents' disclosure of their own concerns to their adolescent children. *Personal Relationships*, 3, 159–170.

Domes, G., Heinrichs, M., Glascher, J., Buchel, C., et al. (2007). Oxytocin attenuates amygdala responses to emotional faces regardless of valence. *Biological Psychiatry*, 62, 1187–1190.

Donnellan, M. B., Assad, K. K., Robins, R. W., & Conger, R. D. (2007). Do negative interactions mediate the effects of negative emotionality, communal positive emotionality, and constraint on relationship satisfaction? *Journal of Social and Personal Relationships*, 24, 557–574.

Drabant, E. M., McRae, K., Manucj, S. B., Hariri, A. R., et al. (2009). Individual differences in typical reappraisal use predict amygdala and prefrontal responses. *Biological Psychiatry*, 65, 367–373.

Dresner, R., & Grolnick, W. S. (1996). Construction of early parenting, intimacy, and autonomy in young women. *Journal of Social and Personal Relationships*, 13, 25–40.

Drevets, W. C., Price, J. L., Simpson, Jr., J. R., Todd, R. D., Reich, T., Vannier, M., & Raichle, M. E. (1997). Subgenual prefrontal cortex abnormalities in mood disorders. *Nature*, 386, 824–827.

Drew, L. M., & Silverstein, M. (2007). Grandparents' psychological well-being after loss of contact with their grandchildren. *Journal of Family Psychology*, 21, 371–380.

Drew, S. S., Heesacker, M., Frost, H. M., & Oelke, L. E. (2004). The role of relationship loss and self-loss in women's and men's dysphoria. *Journal of Social and Personal Relationships*, 21, 381–398.

Drozdek, B., & Wilson, J. P. (Eds.). (2007). *Voices of trauma: Treating survivors across cultures.* New York: Springer-Science.

Dubbert, P. M. (2002). Physical activity and exercise: Recent advances and current challenges. *Journal of Consulting and Clinical Psychology*, 70, 526–536.

Duck, S., Pond, K., & Leathem, G. (1994). Loneliness and the evaluation of relational events. *Journal of Social and Personal Relationships*, 11, 253–276.

Duncan, T. E., Duncan, S. C., & Hops, H. (1996). The role of parents and older siblings in predicting adolescent substance abuse use: Modeling development via structural equation latent growth. *Journal of Family Psychology*, 10, 158–172.

Dunn, J. (1994). Lessons from the study of bidirectional effects. *Journal of Social and Personal Relationships*, 14, 465–573.

Eagly, A. M. (2009). The his and hers of prosocial behavior: An examination of the social psychology of gender. *American Psychologist*, 64, 644–658.

Easterbrooks, M. A., Cummings, E. A., & Emde, R. N. (1994). Young children's responses to constructive marital disputes. *Journal of Family Psychology*, 8, 161–169.

Eaton, L. G., & Funder, D. C. (2001). Emotional experience in daily life: Valence, variability, and rate of change. *Emotion*, 1, 413–421.

Eberhart, N. K., & Hammen, C. (2006). Interpersonal predictors of onset of depression during the transition to adulthood. *Personal Relationships*, 13, 195–206.

Eccles, J. (1985). Sex differences in achievement patterns. In T. B. Sonderegger (Ed.), *Nebraska symposium on motivation 1984* (pp. 97–131). Lincoln: University of Nebraska Press.

Edelstein, R. S., & Shaver, P. R. (2004). Avoidant attachment: Exploration of an oxymoron. In D. J. Masheck & A. Aron (Eds.), *Handbook of closeness and intimacy* (pp. 397–412). Mahwah, NJ: Erlbaum.

Edlund, J. E., & Sagarin, B. J. (2009). Sex differences in jealousy: Misinterpretation of nonsignificant results as refuting the theory. *Personal Relationships*, 16, 67–78.

Edlund, M. J., Wamg, P. S., Berglund, P. A., Katz, S. J., et al. (2002). Dropping out of mental health treatment: Pattern and predictors among epidemiological survey respondents in the United States and Ontario. *American Journal of Psychiatry*, 159, 845–851.

Ehlers, A. (2006). Understanding and treating complicated grief: What can we learn from Posttraumatic Stress Disorder? *Clinical Psychology: Science and Practice*, 13, 135–140.

Ehrenreich, J. T., Fairholme, C. P., Buzzella, B. A., Ellard, K. K., et al. (2007). The role of emotion in psychological theory. *Clinical Psychology: Science and Practice*, 14, 422–428.

Ehrensaft, M. K., Cohen, P., Brown, J., Smailes, E., et al. (2003). Intergenerational transmission of partner violence: A 20-year perspective study. *Journal of Consulting & Clinical Psychology*, 71, 741–753.

Ehrhardt, A. A. (1985). Gender differences: A biosocial perspective. In T. B. Sonderegger (Ed.), *Nebraska symposium on motivation 1984* (pp. 37–57). Lincoln: University of Nebraska Press.

Eippert, F., Veit, R., Weiskopf, N., Erb, M., Birbaumer, N., et al. (2007). Regulation of emotional responses elicited by threat-related stimuli. *Human Brain Mapping*, 28, 409–423.

Eisenberg, N. I. (1986). *Altruistic emotion, cognition, and behavior*. Hillsdale, NJ: Erlbaum.

(2000). Emotion, regulation, and moral development. *Annual Review of Psychology*, 51, 665–697.

(2006). Identifying the neural correlates underlying social pain: Implications for developmental processes. *Human Development*, 49, 273–293.

Eisenberg, N. I., Hofer, C., & Vaughn, J. (2007). Effortful control and its socioemotional consequences. In J. J. Gross (Ed.), *Handbook of emotion regulation* (pp. 287–660). New York: Guilford.

Eisenberg, N. I., Losoya, S., Fabes, R. A., Guthrie, I. K., et al. (2001). Parental socialization of children's disregulated expression of emotion and externalizing behavior. *Journal of Family Psychology*, 15, 183–205.

Eisenberg, N. I., Smith, C. L., Sadovsky, A., & Spinrad, T. L. (2004). Effortful control: Relations with emotion regulation, adjustment, and socialization in childhood. In R. F. Baumeister & K. D. Vohs (Eds.), *Handbook of self-regulation: Research, theory, and applications* (pp. 259–282). New York: Guilford.

Eisenberg, S. D. (2009). Coming home. *Opera News*, 74, 35–36.

Eisenberger, N. I., Lieberman, M. D., & Williams, K. D. (2003). Does rejection hurt? An fMRI study of social exclusion. *Science*, 302, 290–292.

Eisler, R. (2009). Roadmap to a new economics: Beyond capitalism and socialism. *Tikkun,17–20*, 69–72.

Ekman, P. (1993). Facial expression and emotion. *American Psychologist*, 48, 384–392.

Ekman, P., & Davidson, R. J. (Eds.). (1994). *The nature of emotion: Fundamental questions*. New York: Oxford University Press.

Ellgring, H., & Smith, M. (1998). Affect regulation during psychosis. In W. F. Flack, Jr., & J. D. Laird (Eds.), *Emotions in psychopathology: Theory and research* (pp. 323–335). New York: Oxford University Press.

El-Sheikh, M., & Whitson, S. A. (2006). Longitudinal relations between marital conflict and child adjustment: Vagal regulation as a protective factor. *Journal of Family Psychology*, 20, 30–41.

Elwood, W. N. (2002). The head that doesn't speak one calls a cabbage: HIV, AIDS, risk, and social support in the 21st century. *Journal of Social and Personal Relationships*, 19, 143–150.

Eminson, D. M. (2007). Medically unexplained symptoms in children and adolescents. *Clinical Psychology Review*, 27, 855–871.

Emmons, R., & McCullough, M. (2003). Counting blessings versus burdens: Experimental studies of gratitude and subjective well-being. *Journal of Personality and Social Psychology*, 84, 377–389.

Ennis, E., Vrij. A., & Chance, C. (2008). Individual differences and lying in everyday life. *Journal of Social and Personal Relationships*, 25, 105–118.

Erath, S. A., Bierman, K. L., & the Conduct Problems Prevention Research Group (2006). Aggressive marital conflict, maternal harsh punishment, and child aggressive-disruptive behavior: Evidence for direct and mediated relations. *Journal of Family Psychology*, 20, 217–226.

Ertel, K. A., Glymour, M.M., & Berkman, L. F. (2009). Social networks and health: A life course perspective integrating observational and experimental evidence. *Journal of Social and Personal Relationships*, 26, 73–92.

Escudero, V., Rogers, L. E., & Gutierrez, E. (1997). Patterns of relational control and nonverbal affect in clinic and nonclinic couples. *Journal of Social and Personal Relationships*, 14, 5–30.

Esposito, C. L., & Clum, G. A. (2003). The relative contribution of diagnostic and psychosocial factors in the prediction of adolescent suicidal ideation. *Journal of Clinical Child & Adolescent Psychology*, 32, 386–395.

Esterling, B. A., L'Abate, L., Murray, E., & Pennebaker, J. M. (1999). Empirical foundations for writing in prevention and psychotherapy: Mental and physical outcomes. *Clinical Psychology Review*, 19, 79–96.

Etcheverry, P. E., & Le, B. (2005). Thinking about commitment: Accessibility of commitment and prediction of relationship persistence, accommodation, and willingness to sacrifice. *Personal Relationships*, 12, 103–124.

Etcheverry, P. E., Le, B., & Charania, M. R. (2008). Perceived versus reported social referent: Approval and romantic relationship commitment and persistence. *Personal Relationships*, 15, 281–296.

Evans, K., & Brase, G. L. (2007). Assessing sex differences and similarities in mate preferences: Above and beyond domain characteristics. *Personal Relationships*, 24, 781–792.

Feder, J., Levant, R. F., & Dean, J. (2007). Boys and violence: A gender-informed analysis. *Professional Psychology, Research and Practice*, 38, 385–391.

Feeney, J. A. (1996). Attachment, caregiving, and marital satisfaction. *Personal Relationships*, 3, 401–416.

(1999a). Adult attachment, emotional control, and marital satisfaction. *Personal Relationships*, 6, 169–186.

(1999b). Issues of closeness and distance in dating relationships: Effects of sex and attachment style. *Journal of Social and Personal Relationships*, 16, 571–590.

(2004). Hurt feelings and couple relationships: Towards integrative models of the negative effects of hurtful events. *Journal of Social and Personal Relationships*, 21, 487–508.

(2005). Hurt feelings in couple relationships: Exploring the romantic attachment and perceptions of personal injury. *Personal Relationships*, 12, 253–271.

(2006). Parental attachment and conflict behavior: Implications for offspring's attachment, loneliness, and relationship satisfaction. *Personal Relationships*, 13, 19–36.

(2009). When love hurts: Understanding hurtful events in couple relationships. In A. L. Vangelisti (Ed.), *Feeling hurt in close relationships* (pp. 313–335). New York: Cambridge University Press.

Feeney, J. A., & Hill, A. (2006). Victim-perpetrator differences in reports of hurtful events. *Journal of Social and Personal Relationships*, 23, 507–522.

Feeney, J. A., & Hohaus, L. (2001). Attachment and spousal caregiving. *Personal Relationships*, 8, 21–40.

Fehr, B. (2003). The status of theory and research on love and commitment. In G. J. O. Fletcher & M. S. Clark (Eds.), *Blackwell handbook of social psychology: Interpersonal processes* (pp. 331–356). Malden, MA: Blackwell.

(2004). A prototype model of intimacy interactions in same-sex friendships. In D. J. Mashek & A. Aron (Eds.), *Handbook of closeness and intimacy* (pp. 9–26). Mahwah, NJ: Erlbaum.

Fehr, B., & Broughton, R. (2001). Gender and personality differences in conceptions of love: An interpersonal theory analysis. *Personal Relationships*, 8, 115–136.

Fehr, B., & Harasymchuk, C. (2005). The experience of emotion in close relationships: Toward an integration of the emotion-in-relationships and interpersonal script models. *Personal Relationships*, 12, 181–196.

(2009). Hurt feelings in adult relationships. In A. L. Vangelisti (Ed.), *Feeling hurt in close relationships* (pp. 288–311). New York: Cambridge University Press.

Fehr, B., & Sprecher, S. (2009). Prototype analysis of the concept of compassionate love. *Personal Relationships*, 16, 343–364.

Fekete, E. M., Stephens, M. A. P., Druley, J. A., & Greene, K. A. (2006). Effects of spousal control and support in older adults recovering from knee surgery. *Journal of Family Psychology*, 20, 302–310.

Feldman, R., Mashala S., & Alony, D. (2006). Microregulatory patterns of family interactions: Cultural pathways to toddlers' self-regulation. *Journal of Family Psychology*, 20, 614–623.

Felitti, V. J., Anda, R. F., Nordenberg, D., Williamson, D. F., Spitz, A. M., Edwards, V., Koss, M. P., & Marks, J. S. (1998). Relationship of childhood abuse and household dysfunction to many of the leading causes of death in adults: The Adverse Childhood Experiences (ACE) study. *American Journal of Preventive Medicine*, 14, 245–258.

Festa, J. R., & Lazar, R. (Eds.). (2009). *Neurovascular neuropsychology*. New York: Springer-Science.

Field, N., Hart, D., & Horowitz, M. D. (1999). Representations of self and other in conjugal bereavement. *Journal of Social and Personal Relationships*, 16, 407–414.

Field, N., & Sundin, E. C. (2001). Attachment style in adjustment to conjugal bereavement. *Journal of Social and Personal Relationships*, 18, 347–361.

Fields, R. D. (2009). *The other brain: From dementia to schizophrenia, how new discoveries about the brain are revolutionizing medicine and science*. New York: Simon and Schuster.

Fincham, F. D. (1994). Understanding the association between marital conflict and child adjustment: Overview. *Journal of Family Psychology*, 8, 123–127.

   (2000). The kiss of the porcupine: From attributing responsibility to forgiving. *Personal Relationships*, 7, 1–23.

Fincham, F. D., & Beach, S. R. H. (2002a). Forgiveness in marriage: Implications for psychological aggression and constructive communication. *Personal Relationships*, 9, 239–251.

   (2002b). Forgiveness: Toward a public health approach to intervention. In J. H. Harvey & A. E. Wenzel (Eds.), *A clinician's guide to maintaining and enhancing close relationships* (pp. 277–300). Mahwah, NJ: Erlbaum.

Fincham, F. D., Beach, S. R. H., & Davila, J. (2007). Longitudinal relations between forgiveness and conflict resolution in marriage. *Journal of Family Psychology*, 21, 542–545.

Fincham, F. D., Crych, J. H., & Osborne, L.N. (1994). Does marital conflict cause child maladjustment? Directions and challenges for longitudinal research. *Journal of Family Psychology*, 8, 128–140.

Fincham, F. D., Paleari, F. G., & Regalia, C. (2002). Forgiveness in marriage: The role of relationship quality, attributions, and empathy. *Personal Relationships*, 9, 27–38.

Finkenauer, C., & Hazam, H. (2000). Disclosure and secrecy in marriage: Do both contribute to marital satisfaction? *Journal of Social and Personal Relationships*, 17, 245–264.

Finzi-Dottan, R., & Karu, T. (2006). From emotional abuse in childhood to psychopathology in adulthood: A path mediated by immature defense mechanisms and self-esteem. *Journal of Nervous and Mental Disease*, 194, 616–621.

Firestone, R. W., & Catlett, J. (1999). *Fear of intimacy*. Washington, DC: American Psychological Association.

Firestone, R. W., & Firestone, L. (2004). Methods for overcoming the fear of intimacy. In D. J. Masheck & A. Aron (Eds.), *Handbook of closeness and intimacy* (pp. 375–395). Mahwah, NJ: Erlbaum.

Fischer, J. L., Fitzpatrick, J., & Cleveland, H. H. (2007). Linking family functioning to dating relationship quality via novelty-seeking and harm-avoidance personality pathways. *Journal of Social and Personal Relationships*, 24, 575–590.

Fitness, J., & Warburton, W. (2009). Thinking the unthinkable: Cognitive appraisal and hurt feelings. In A. L. Vangelisti (Ed.), *Handbook of hurt feelings in close relationships* (pp. 34–48). New York: Cambridge University Press.

Fitzsimons, G. M., & Bargh, J. A. (2004). Automatic self-regulation. In R. F. Baumeister & K. D. Vohs (Eds.), *Handbook of self-regulation: Research, theory, and applications* (pp. 151–171). New York: Guilford.

Fivush, R., & Buckner, J. (2000). Gender, sadness, and depression: The development of emotional focus through gendered discourse. In A. Fischer (Ed.), *Gender and emotion: Social psychological perspectives* (pp. 232–253). New York: Cambridge University Press.

Flack, W. F. Jr., Laird, J. D., Cavallaro, L. A., & Miller, D. R. (1998). Emotional expression and experience: A psychosocial perspective in schizophrenia. In W. F. Flack, Jr., & J. D. Laird (Eds.), *Emotions in psychopathology: Theory and research* (pp. 315–322). New York: Oxford University Press.

Flannery, D. J., Montemayor, R., & Eberly, M. B. (1994). The influence of parent negative-emotional expression on adolescents' perceptions of their relationships with their parents. *Personal Relationships*, 1, 259–274.

Fleischman, A. A., Spitzberg, B. H., Andersen, P. A., & Roesch, S. C. (2006). Tickling the monster: Jealousy induction in relationships. *Journal of Social and Personal Relationships*, 22, 49–74.

Flora, J., & Segrin, C. (2000). Relationship development in dating couples: Implications for relational satisfaction and loneliness. *Journal of Social and Personal Relationships*, 17, 811–826.

Foa', U. G., & Foa', E. B. (1974). *Societal structures of the mind*. Springfield, IL: C. C. Thomas.

Forabosco, G., Ruch, W., & Nucera, P. (2009). The fear of being laughed at among psychiatric patients. *Humor: International Journal of Humor Research*, 22, 233–251.

Forouzan, E., & Cooke, D. J. (2005). Figuring out *la femme fatale*: Conceptual and assessment issues concerning psychopathy in females. *Behavioral Sciences and the Law*, 23, 765–778.

Foster, C. A., & Campbell, W. K. (2005). The adversity of secret relationships. *Personal Relationships*, 12, 125–144.

Foster, J. D., Shrira, I., & Campbell, W. K. (2006). Theoretical models of narcissism, sexuality, and relationship commitment. *Journal of Social and Personal Relationships*, 23, 367–386.

Fouladi, R. T., McCarthy, C. J., & Moller, N. P. (2002). Paper-and-pencil or online? Evaluating mode effects on measures of emotional functioning and attachment. *Assessment*, 9, 204–215.

Fox, J. K., Halpern, L. F., & Forsyth, J. P. (2008). Mental health checkups for children and adolescents: A means to identify, prevent, and minimize suffering associated with anxiety and mood disorders. *Clinical Psychology: Science and Practice*, 15, 182–211.

Fox, N. A., & Calkins, S. D. (2000). Multiple-measure approaches to the study of infant emotion. In M. Lewis & J. M. Haviland-Jones (Eds.), *Handbook of emotions* (2nd ed., pp. 203–219). New York: Guilford.

Franiuk, R., Cohen, D., & Pomerantz, E. M. (2002). Implicit theories of relationships: Implications for relationship satisfactions and longevity. *Personal Relationships*, 9, 345–368.

Franko, D. L., Powers, T. A., Zuroff, D. C., & Moskowitz, D. S. (1985). Children and affect: Strategies of self-regulation and sex differences in sadness. *American Journal of Orthopsychiatry*, 55, 210–218.

Franks, D. D., & Hefferman, S. M. (1998). The pursuit of happiness. In W. F. Flack, Jr., & J. D. Laird (Eds.), *Emotions in psychopathology: Theory and research* (pp. 145–157). New York: Oxford University Press.

Franks, M. M., Stephens, M. A. P., Rook, K. S., Franklin, B. A., et al. (2006). Spouses' provision of health-related support and control to patients participating in cardiac rehabilitation. *Journal of Family Psychology*, 20, 311–318.

Fredrickson, B. L., & Cohn, M. A. (2008). Positive emotions. In M. Lewis, J. M. Haviland-Jones, & L. Feldman Barrett (Eds.), *Handbook of emotions* (3rd ed., pp. 777–796). New York: Guilford.

Fredrickson, B. L., & Losada, M. F. (2005). Positive affect and the complex dynamics of human flourishing. *American Psychologist*, 60, 678–686.

Freed, P. J., Yanagihara, T. K., Hirsch, J., & Mann, J. J. (2009). Neural mechanisms of grief regulation. *Biological Psychiatry*, 66, 33–40.

Frey, J., Holley, J., & L'Abate, L. (1979). Intimacy is the sharing of hurt feelings: A comparison of three conflict resolution models. *Journal of Marital & Family Therapy*, 5, 35–41.

Friesen, M. D., & Fletcher, G. J. O. (2007). Exploring the lay representation of forgiveness: Convergent and discriminant validity. *Personal Relationships*, 14, 209–224.

Friesen, M. D., Fletcher, G. J. O., & Overall, N. C. (2005). A dyadic assessment of forgiveness in intimate relationships. *Personal Relationships*, 12, 61–78.

Frijda, N. H. (2007). *The laws of emotion*. Mahwah, NJ: Erlbaum.
    (2008). The psychologist's point of view. In M. Lewis, J. M. Haviland Jones, & L. F. Barrett (Eds.), *Handbook of emotions* (3rd ed., pp. 68–87). New York: Guildford.

Frijda, N. H. (2009). Emotion experience and its varieties. *Emotion Review*, 1, 264–271.

Frijda, N. H., Ortony, A., Sonnemans, J., & Clore, G. L. (1992). The complexity of intensity: Issues concerning the structure of emotion intensity. In M. S. Clark (Ed.), *Emotion* (pp. 60–89). Newbury Park, CA: Sage.

Fuendeling, J. M. (1998). Affect regulation as a stylistic process within adult attachment. *Journal of Social and Personal Relationships*, 15, 291–322.

Fuller, J. L. (1967). Experimental deprivation and later behavior. *Science*, 158, 1645–1652.

Gaertner, L., & Foshee, V. (1999). Commitment and the perpetration of relationship violence. *Personal Relationships*, 6, 227–240.

Gaines, Jr., S. O. (2007). Personality and personal relationship processes: Concluding thoughts. *Journal of Social and Personal Relationships*, 24, 613–617.

Gaines, Jr., S. O., Rugg, M. A., Zemore, S. E., Armm, J. L., et al. (1999). Gender-related personality traits and interpersonal resource exchange among brother-sisters relationships. *Personal Relationships*, 6, 187–198.

Gamble, S. A., Talbot, N. L., Duberstain, P. R., Conner, K. R., et al. (2006). Childhood sexual abuse and depressive symptom severity: The role of neuroticism. *Journal of Nervous and Mental Disease*, 194, 382–385.

Ganiban, J. M., Ulbricht, J. A., Spotts, E. L., Lichtenstein, P., et al. (2009). Understanding the role of personality in explaining association between marital quality and parenting. *Journal of Family Psychology*, 23, 646–660.

Gardner, R. A., Sauber, S. R., & Lorandos, D. (Eds.). (2006). *The international handbook of parental alienation syndrome: Conceptual, clinical, and legal considerations*. Springfield, IL: C. C. Thomas.

Gauven, M., Fagot, B. I., Leve, C., & Kavanah, K. (2002). Instructions by mothers and fathers during problem-solving with their children. *Journal of Family Psychology*, 16, 81–90.

Geronimus, A., Colen, C., Shochet, T., Ingber, L., et al. (2006). Urban-rural Differences in excess mortality among high-poverty populations: Evidence from the Harlem Household Survey and the Pitt County, North Carolina Study of African American Health. *Journal of Health Care for the Poor and Underserved*, 96, 532–558.

Geronimus, A., Hicken, M., Keene, D., & Bound, J. (2006). "What's Missing from the Weathering Hypothesis?": Geronimus et al. Respond. *American Journal of Public Health*, 96, 955–956.

Gibson, E. J. (1982). The concept of affordance in development: The renascence of functionalism. In A. W. Collins (Ed.), *Minnesota symposium on child psychology: Vol. 13. Theoretical perspectives on development* (pp. 55–81). Hillsdale, NJ: Erlbaum.

Gilbert, P. (1992). *Human nature and suffering*. New York: Guilford.
    (2005). Compassion: Conceptualizations, research and use in psycho-therapy. New York: Rutledge.

Gilbert, P., & Andrews, B. (1998). *Shame: Interpersonal behavior, psychopathology, and culture*. New York: Oxford University Press.

Gillath, O., Shaver, P. R., Mikulincer, M., Nitzberg, R. E., et al. (2005). Attachment, caregiving, and volunteering: Placing volunteerism in an attachment-theoretical framework: *Personal Relationships*, 12, 425–446.

Glascher, J., Tuscher, O., Weiller, C., & Buchel, C. (2004). Elevated responses to constant facial emotions in different faces in the human amygdala: An fMRI study of facial identity and expression. *BMC Neurosciences*, 5, 45.

Glenberg, A. M., Webster, B. J., Mouilso, E., Havas, D., et al. (2009). Gender, emotion, and the embodiment of language comprehension. *Emotion Review*, 1, 151–161.

Goff, B., Crow, J., Reisbig, A., & Hamilton, S. (2007). The impact of individual trauma symptoms of deployed soldiers on relationship satisfaction. *Journal of Family Psychology*, 21(3), 344–353.

Goldie, P. (2009). Getting feelings into emotional experience in the right way. *Emotion Review*, 1, 232–239.

Goldin, P. R., Mcrae, K., Ramel, W., & Gross, J. J. (2008). The neural bases of emotion regulation: Reappraisal and suppression of negative emotion. *Biological Psychiatry*, 63, 577–586.

Goldsmith, D. J., & Donovan-Kicken, E. (2009). Adding insult to injury: The contribution of politeness theory to understanding hurt feelings in close relationships. In A. L. Vangelisti (Ed.), *Handbook of hurt feelings in close relationships* (pp. 50–72). New York: Cambridge University Press.

Golish, T. D., & Powell, K. A. (2003). "Ambiguous loss": Managing the dialectics of grief associated with premature birth. *Journal of Social and Personal Relationships*, 20, 309–334.

Gonzales, V. M., Schmitz, J. M., & DeLaune, K. A. (2006). The role of homework in cognitive-behavioral therapy for cocaine dependence. *Journal of Consulting and Clinical Psychology*, 74, 633–637.

Goodwin, R., Cook, O., & Yung, Y. (2001). Loneliness and life satisfaction among three cultural groups. *Personal Relationships*, 8, 225–230.

Goodwin, R., & Gaines, Jr., S. O. (2004). Relationship beliefs and relationship quality across cultures: Country as a moderator of dysfunctional beliefs and relational quality in three former Communist societies. *Personal Relationships*, 11, 267–280.

Goodwin, R. D., Cox, B. J., & Clara, I. (2006). Neuroticism and physical disorders among adults in the community: Results from the National Comorbidity Survey. *Journal of Behavioral Medicine*, 29, 229–238.

Goodyer, J. M. (1990). *Life experiences, development, and childhood psychopathology*. New York: Wiley.

Gordon, C. L., & Baucom, D. H. (2009). Examining the individual within marriage: Personal strengths and relationship satisfaction. *Personal Relationships*, 16, 421–436.

Gordon, K. C., Hughes, F. M., Tomcik, N. D., Dixon, L. J., et al. (2009). Widening the sphere of impact: The role of forgiveness in marital and family functioning. *Journal of Family Psychology*, 23, 1–13.

Gore, J. S., Cross, S. E., & Morris, M. L. (2006). Let's be friends: Relational self-construal and the development of intimacy. *Personal Relationships*, 13, 83–102.

Gottman, J. M. (1999). *The marriage clinic*. New York: W. W. Norton.

Gottman, J. M., Fainsilber-Katz, L., & Hooven, C. (1997). *Meta-emotion: How families communicate emotionally*. Mahwah, NJ: Erlbaum.

Gottman, J. M., Katz, L. F., & Hooven, C. (1996). Parental meta-emotion philosophy and the emotional life of families: Theoretical model and preliminary data. *Journal of Family Psychology*, 10, 243–268.

Graham, J. E., Christian, L. M., & Kiecolt-Glaser, J. K. (2006). Stress, age, and immune function: Toward a lifespan approach. *Journal of Behavioral Medicine*, 29, 389–400.

Graham, K., Tremblay, P. F., Wells, S., Pernanen, K., et al. (2006). Harm, intent, and the nature of aggressive behavior: Measuring naturally occurring aggression in barroom settings. *Assessment*, 13, 280–296.

Graham-Bermann, S. A., Cutler, S. E., Litzenberger, B. W., & Schwartz, W. E. (1994). Perceived conflict and violence in childhood sibling relationships and later emotional adjustment. *Journal of Family Psychology*, 8, 85–97.

Gray, E. K., & Watson, D. (2007). Assessing positive and negative affect via self-report. In J. A. Coan & J. J. B. Allen (Eds.), *Handbook of emotion elicitation and assessment* (pp. 171–183). New York: Oxford University Press.

Gray, J. A., & McNaughton, N. (2000). *The neuropsychology of anxiety*. New York: Oxford University Press.

Greenberg, L. S. (2007). Emotion coming of age. *Clinical Psychology: Science and Practice*, 14, 414–421.

(2008). The clinical applications of emotion in psychotherapy. In M. Lewis, J. M. Haviland-Jones, & L. Feldman Barrett (Eds.), *Handbook of emotions* (3rd ed., pp. 88–100). New York: Guilford.

Greenberg, L. S., Elliott, R., & Pos, A. (2007). Emotion-focused therapy: An overview. *European Psychotherapy*, 7, 19–39.

Greenberg, L. S., & Goldman, R. N, (2009). The dynamics of emotion love, & power in emotion-focused approach to couples therapy. *Person Centered & Experiential Psychotherapies*, 7, 71–86.

Greenberg, L. S., & Johnson, S. M. (1990). Emotional change processes in couple therapy. In E. A. Blechman (Ed.), *Emotions and the family: For better or for worse* (pp. 137–154).Hillsdale, NJ: Erlbaum.

Greenberg, L. S., & Pascual-Leone, A. (2006). Emotion in psychotherapy: A practice-friendly research review. *Journal of Clinical Psychology: In Session*, 62, 611–630.

Greenberg, M. T. (2007). Commentary on "The role of emotion theory and research in child therapy development." *Clinical Psychology: Science and Practice*, 14, 372–376.

Greene, K., Frey L. R., & Derlega, V. J. (2002). Interpersonalizing AIDS: Attending to the personal and social relationships of individuals living with HIV and/or AIDS. *Journal of Social and Personal Relationships*, 19, 5–18.

Greenfield, S. (2000). *The private life of the brain*. New York: Wiley.

Greenfield, S., & Thelen, M. (1997). Validation of the Fear of Intimacy Scale with a lesbian and gay male population. *Journal of Social and Personal Relationships*, 14, 707–716.

Griffin, W. A. (1993). Transition from negative affect during marital interaction: Husband and wife differences. *Journal of Family Psychology*, 6, 211–229.

Gross, J. J. (1998). Antecedent- and response-focused emotion regulation: Divergent consequences for experience, expression, and physiology. *Journal of Personality and Social Psychology*, 74(1), 224–237.

(2002). Emotion regulation: Affective, cognitive, and social consequences. *Psychophysiology*, 39, 281–291.

(Ed.). (2007). *Handbook of emotion regulation*. New York: York: Guilford.

Gross, J. J., & Levenson, R. W. (1997). Hiding feelings: The acute effects of inhibiting negative and positive emotion. *Journal of Abnormal Psychology*, 106, 95–103.

Guerrero, L. K., La Valley, A. G., & Farinelli, L. (2008). The experience and expression of anger, guilt, and sadness in marriage: An equity theory explanations. *Journal of Social and Personal Relationships*, 25, 699–724.

Guerrero, L. K., Trost, M. R., & Yoshimura, S. M. (2005). Romantic jealousy: Emotions and communicative responses. *Personal Relationships*, 12, 233–252.

Guinote, A., & Vescio, T. K. (Eds.). (2010). *The social psychology of power*. New York: Guilford.

Gulaux, M., van Tilburg, T., & van Graenou. M. B. (2007). Changes in contact and support exchange in personal network in widowhood. *Personal Relationships*, 14, 457–474.

Gurung, R. A. R., Sarason, B. R., & Sarason, I. G. (1997). Personal characteristics, relationship quality, and social support perceptions and behavior in young adult romantic relationships. *Personal Relationships*, 4, 319–340.

Haas, S. M. (2002). Social support as relationship maintenance in gay male couples coping with HIV or AIDS. *Journal of Social and Personal Relationships*, 19, 87–112.

Haden, S. C., & Hojjat, M. (2006). Aggressive responses to betrayal: Type of relationship, victim's sex, and nature of aggression. *Journal of Social and Personal Relationships*, 23, 101–116.

Hafen, B. Q., Karren, K. J., Frandsen, K. J., & Smith, N. L. (1996). *Mind, body, health: The effects of attitudes, emotions, and relationships*. Boston, MA: Allyn & Bacon.

Hakansson, J., & Montgomery, H. (2003). Empathy as an interpersonal phenomenon. *Journal of Social and Personal Relationships*, 20, 267–285.

Halberstadt, A. G., & Parker, A. E. (2007). Function, structure, and process as independent dimensions in research on emotion. *Clinical Psychology: Science and Practice*, 14, 402–406.

Hall, J., Whalley, H., McKirdy, J., Romaniuk, L., McGonigle, D., McIntosh, A., et al. (2008). Overactivation of fear systems to neutral faces in schizophrenia. *Biological Psychiatry*, 64, 70–73.

Hall, J. H., & Fincham, F. D. (2009). Psychological distress: Precursor or consequence of dating infidelity? *Personality and Social Psychology Bulletin*, 35, 143–159.

Hammen, C. (1991). *Depression runs in families*. New York: Springer-Verlag

Handel, G., & Whitchurch, G. G. (Eds.). (1994). *The psychosocial interior of the family*. New York: Aldine De Gruyter.

Hardcastle, V. G. (1999). It's OK to be complicated: The case of emotion. *Journal of Consciousness Studies*, 6, 237–250.

Hare, R. D., Cooke, D. J., & Hart, S. D. (1999). Psychopathy and sadistic personality disorder. T. Millon, P. H. Blaney, & R. D. Davis (Eds.), *Oxford textbook of psychopathology* (pp. 555–584). New York: Oxford University Press.

Hareli, S., Karnieli-Miller, O., Hermoni, D., & Eidelman, S. (2007). Factors in the doctor-patient relationship that accentuate physicians' hurt feelings when patients terminate the relationship with them. *Patient Education and Counseling*, 67, 169–175.

Hariri, A. R., Bookheimer, S. Y., & Mazziotta, J. C. (2000). Modulating emotional responses: effects of a neocortical network on the limbic system. *NeuroReport*, 11, 43–48.

Hariri, A. R., & Forbes, E. E. (2007). Genetics of emotion regulation. In J. J. Gross (Ed.), *Handbook of emotion regulation* (pp. 110–133). New York: Guilford.

Harris, A. H. S., Luskin, F., Norman, S. B., Standard, S., et al. (2006). Effects of group forgiveness intervention on forgiveness, perceived stress, and trait-anger. *Journal of Clinical Psychology*, 62, 715–733.

Harris, P. L. (1989). *Children and emotion*. Malden, MA: Blackwell.

Harrison, K. (2009). The Multidimensional Media Influence Scale: Confirmatory factor structure and relationship with body dissatisfaction among African American and Anglo American children. *Body Image*, 6, 207–215.

Harter, S., Waters, P.L., Pettitt, L. M., Whitesell, N., et al. (1997). Autonomy and connectedness as dimensions of relationship styles in men and women. *Journal of Social and Personal Relationships*, 14, 147–164.

Harvey, J. H., & Wenzel, A. (2002). HIV, AIDS, and close relationships. *Journal of Social and Personal Relationships*, 19, 135–142.

Harwood, T. M., & L'Abate, L. (2010). *Self-help in mental health: A critical review*. New York: Springer-Science.

Hass, A. (1979). The acquisition of gender. *Annals of the New York Academy of Sciences*, 327, 101–113.

Hassin, R. R., Uleman, J. S., & Bargh, J. A. (Eds.). (2005). *The new unconscious*. New York: Oxford University Press.

Hastrup, J. L., Baker, J. G., Kraemer, D. L., & Bornstein, R. F. (1986). Crying and depression among older adults. *The Gerontologist*, 26, 91–96.

Haviland-Jones, J. M., & Wilson, P. J. (2008). A "nose" for emotion: Emotional information and challenges of odors and semiochemicals. In M. Lewis, J. M. Haviland-Jones, & L. F. Barrett (Eds.), *Handbook of emotions* (3rd ed., pp. 235–248). New York: Guilford.

Hay, E. L., Fingerman, K. I., & Lefkowitz, E. S. (2007). The experience of worry in parent-adult child relationships. *Personal Relationships*, 14, 605–622.

Helgeson, V. S., Novak, S. A., Lepore, S. J., & Eton, D. T. (2004). Spouse social control efforts: Relation to health behavior and well-being among men with prostate cancer. *Journal of Social and Personal Relationships*, 21, 53–68.

Helm, B. W. (2009). Emotions as evaluative feelings. *Emotion Review*, 1, 248–255.

Hendrik, C. (2002). A new age of prevention? *Journal of Social and Personal Relationships*, 12, 621–628.

Hendriks, M. C. P., Nelson, J. K., Cornelius, R. R., & Vingerhoets, A. J. J. M. (2008). Why crying improves our well-being: An attachment-theory perspective on the functions of adult crying. In A. Vingerhoets, Nyklicek, & Denollet (Eds.), *Emotion regulation: Conceptual and clinical issues* (pp. 87–96). New York: Springer.

Henline, B. H., Lamke, L. K., & Howard, M. D. (2007). Exploring perceptions of online infidelity. *Personal Relationships*, 14, 113–128.

Hemenover, S. H. (2003). The good, the bad, and the healthy: Impacts of emotional disclosure of trauma on resilient self-concept and psychological distress. *Personality and Social Psychology Bulletin*, 29, 1236–1244.

Herbert, T. B., & Cohen, S. (1993). Depression and immunity: A meta-analytic review. *Psychological Bulletin*, 113, 472–486.

Herrenkohl, E. C., Herrenkohl, R. C., & Egolf, B. (1994). Resilient early school-age children from maltreating homes: Outcomes in late adolescence. *American Journal of Orthopsychiatry*, 64, 301–309.

Herpertz, S. C., Dietrich, T. M., Wenning, B., Krings, T., et al. (2001). Evidence of abnormal amygdala functioning in borderline personality disorder: A functional MRI study. *Biological Psychiatry*, 50, 292–298.

Hess, J. A. (2003). Measuring distance in personal relationships: The Relational Distance Index. *Personal Relationships*, 10, 197–216.

Hess, J. A., Fannin, A. D., & Pollom, L. H. (2007). Creating closeness: Discerning and measuring strategies for fostering closer relationships. *Personal Relationships*, 14, 25–44.

Hesse, C., & Floyd, K. (2008). Affectionate experience mediates the effects of alexithymia on mental health and interpersonal relationships. *Journal of Social and Personal Relationships, 25*, 793–810.

Hettema, J. M., Neale, M. C., Myers, J. M., Prescott, C. A., et al., (2006). A population-based twin study of the relationship between neuroticism and internalizing disorders. *American Journal of Psychiatry, 163*, 857–864.

Heyman, R. E., Feldbau-Kohn. S. R., Ehrensaft, M. K., Langhinrichsen-Rohling, J., et al. (2001). Can questionnaire reports correctly classify distress and partner physical abuse? *Journal of Family Psychology, 15*, 134–346.

Hibel, L. C., Granger, D. A., Blair, C., Cox, M. J., & the Family Life Project Key Investigators (2009). Intimate partner violence moderates the association between mother-infant adrenocortical activity across an emotional challenge. *Journal of Family Psychology, 23*, 615–625.

Hicks, B., Blonigen, D., Kramer, M., Krueger, R., et al. (2007). Gender differences and developmental change in externalizing disorders from late adolescence to early adulthood: A longitudinal twin study. *Journal of Abnormal Psychology, 116*, 433–447.

Higgins, E. T., & Spiegel, S. (2004). Promotion and prevention strategies for self-regulation. In R. F. Baumeister & K. D. Vohs (Eds.), *Handbook of self-regulation: Research, theory, and applications* (pp. 173–187). New York: Guilford.

Hill, C., Stein J., Keenan, K., & Wakschlag, L. S. (2006). Mother's childrearing history and current parenting: Patterns of association and the moderating role of current life stress. *Journal of Clinical Child and Adolescent Psychology, 35*, 412–419.

Hodgson, J., & Fischer, J. (1979). Sex differences in identity and intimacy development in college youth. *Journal of Youth and Adolescence, 8*, 37–50.

Hodgson, L. K., & Wertheim, E. H. (2007). Does good emotion management aid forgiving? Multiple dimensions of empathy, emotion management and forgiveness of self and others. *Journal of Social and Personal Relationships, 24*, 931–949.

Hofferth, S. L., & Casper, L. M. (Eds.). (2007). *Handbook of measurement issues in family research.* Mahwah, NJ: Erlbaum.

Hoffman, M. L. (2008). Empathy and prosocial behavior. In M. Lewis, J. M. Haviland-Jones, & L. F. Barrett (Eds.), *Handbook of emotions* (3rd ed., pp. 440–455). New York: Guildford.

Hogue, A., Dauber, S., Samuolis, J., & Liddle, H. A. (2006). Treatment techniques and outcomes in multidimentional family therapy for adolescent behavior problems. *Journal of Family Psychology, 20*, 535–543.

Hojjat, M. (2000). Sex differences and perceptions of conflict in romantic relationships. *Journal of Social and Personal Relationships, 17*, 598–617.

Holman, T. B., & Jarvis, M. O. (2003). Hostile, volatile, avoiding, and validating couple-conflict types: An investigation of Gottman's couple-conflict types. *Personal Relationships, 10*, 267–282.

Holmes, J. G. (2002). Interpersonal expectations as the building blocks of social cognition: An interdependence theory perspective. *Personal Relationships, 9*, 1–26.

Holtzworth-Munroe, A., Stuart, G. L., Sandin, E., Smurzler, N., & McLaughlin, W. (1997). Comparing social support behaviors of violent and nonviolent husbands during discussions of wife personal problems. *Personal Relationships*, 4, 395–412.

Hooley, J. M., & Parker, H. A. (2006). Measuring expressed emotion: An evaluation of the shortcuts. *Journal of Family Psychology*, 20, 386–396.

Hopkins, W., Russell, J., Cantalupo, C., Freeman, H., et al. (2005). Factors Influencing the prevalence and handedness for throwing in captive chimpanzees (Pan troglodytes). *Journal of Comparative Psychology*, 119, 363–370.

Horowitz, L., Rosenberg, S. E., Baer, B. A., Ureno, G., et al. (1988). Inventory of interpersonal problems: Psychometric properties and clinical application. *Journal of Consulting and Clinical Psychology*, 56, 885–892.

Howell, A. J., & Watson, D. C. (2005). Impairment and distress associated with symptoms of male-typed and female-typed DSM-IV Axis I disorders. *Journal of Clinical Psychology*, 61, 389–400.

Howland, R. H., & Thare, M. W. Affective disorders: Biological aspects. In T. Millon, P. H. Blaney, & R. D. Davis (Eds.), *Oxford textbook of psychopathology* (pp. 166–202). New York: Oxford University Press.

Hughes, C. F., Uhlmann, C., & Pennebaker, J. W. (1994). The body's response to processing emotional trauma: Linking verbal text with autonomic activity. *Journal of Personality*, 62, 565–585.

Hui, V. K-Y, & Bond, M. H. (2009). Target's face loss, motivations, and forgiveness following relational transgression: Comparing Chinese and US cultures. *Journal of Social and Personal Relationships*, 26, 123–140.

Hussong, A. M. (2000). Distinguishing mean and structural sex differences in adolescent friendship quality. *Journal of Social and Personal Relationships*, 17, 223–244.

Hussong, A. M., Wirth, R. J., Edwards, M. C., Curran, P. J., et al. (2007). Externalizing symptoms among children of alcoholic parents: Entry points for an antisocial pathway to alcoholism. *Journal of Abnormal Psychology*, 116, 529–542.

Huston T. L. (2009). What's love got to do with it? Why some marriages and others fail. *Personal Relationships*, 16, 301–328.

Huston, T. L., & Chorost, A. F. (1994). Behavioral buffers on the effect of negativity on marital satisfaction: A longitudinal study. *Personal Relationships*, 1, 223–240.

Iaccino, J. F. (1993). *Left brain–right brain differences: Inquiries, evidence, and new applications.* Hillsdale, NJ: Erlbaum

Ickes, W. (1997). *Empathic accuracy.* New York: Guilford.
   (2007). Empathic accuracy of intimate partners in violent versus nonviolent relationships. *Personal Relationships*, 14, 369–387.

Ickes, W., Dugosh, J. W., Simpson, J. A., & Wilson, C. L. (2003). Suspicious minds: The motive to acquire relationship-threatening information. *Personal Relationships*, 10, 131–148.

Ickes, W., Gesn, P. R., & Graham, T. (2000). Gender differences in empathic accuracy: Differential ability or differential motivation? *Personal Relationships*, 7, 95–109.

Ickes, W., Hutchison, J., & Mashek, D. (2004). Closeness as intersubjectivity: Social absorption and social individuation. In D. J. Masheck & A. Aron (Eds.), *Handbook of closeness and intimacy* (pp. 357–373). Mahwah, NJ: Erlbaum.

Impett, E. A., Peplau, L.A., & Gable, S. L. (2005). Approach and avoidance sexual motives: Implications for personal and interpersonal well-being. *Personal Relationships, 12,* 465–482.

Ingram, R. E., Scott, W., & Siegle, G. (1999). Depression: Social and cognitive aspects. In T. Millon, P. H. Blaney, & R. D. Davis (Eds.), *Oxford textbook of psycho-pathology* (pp. 203–226). New York: Oxford University Press.

Isen, A. M. (2008). Some ways in which positive affect influences decision making. In M. Lewis, J. M. Haviland-Jones, & L. Feldman Barrett (Eds.), *Handbook of emotions* (3rd ed., pp. 548–543). New York: Guilford.

Iversen, A., Chalder, T., & Wessely, S. (2007). Gulf war illness: Lessons from medically unexplained symptoms. *Clinical Psychology Review, 27,* 842–854.

Izard, C. E. (1979). Emotions and motivations: An evolutionary-developmental perspective. In R. A. Dienstbier (Ed.), *Nebraska symposium on motivation: Human emotion* (pp. 163–200). Lincoln: University of Nebraska Press.

(2001). Emotional intelligence or adaptive emotions? *Emotion, 1,* 249–257.

Izard, C. E., Libero, D. Z., Putman, P., & Haynes, O. M. (1993). Stability of emotion experience and their relations to traits of personality. *Journal of Personality and Social Psychology, 64,* 847–860.

Jabbi, M., Swart, M., & Keysers, C. (2007). Empathy for positive and negative emotions in the gustatory cortex. *NeuroImage, 34,* 1744–1753.

Jack, D. (1987). Silencing the self: The power of social imperatives in female depression. *Women and depression: A lifespan perspective* (pp. 161–181). New York: Springer Publishing Co.

(1991). *Silencing the self: Women and depression.* Cambridge, MA US: Harvard University Press.

(2001). Understanding women's anger: A description of relational patterns. *Health Care for Women International, 22,* 385–400.

Jack, D., & Dill, D. (1992). The Silencing the Self Scale: Schemas of intimacy associated with depression in women. *Psychology of Women Quarterly, 16,* 97–106.

Jacob, T. (Ed.). (1987). *Family interaction and psychopathology: Theories, methods, and findings.* New York: Plenum.

Jacob, T., & Seilhamer, R. A. (1987). Alcoholim and family interaction. In T. Jacob (Ed.), *Family interaction and psychopathology: Theories, methods, and findings* (pp. 535–580). New York: Plenum.

Jandasek, B., Holmbeck, G. N., DeLucia, C., Zabracki, K., & Friedman, D. (2009). Trajectories of family processes across the adolescent transition to youth with spina bifida. *Journal of Family Psychology, 23,* 726–738.

John, O. P., & Gross, J. J. (2007). Individual differences in emotion regulation. In J. J. Gross (Ed.), *Handbook of emotion regulation* (pp. 351–372). New York: Guilford.

Johnson, R., Hobfoll, S. W., & Zalchberg-Linetzy, A. (1993). Social support knowledge and behavior and relational intimacy: A dyadic study. *Journal of Family Psychology, 6,* 266–277.

Johnson, S. L., Gruber, J., & Eisner, L. R. (2007). Emotion and bipolar disorder. In J. Rottenberg & S. L. Johnson (Eds.), *Emotion and psychopathology: Bridging affective and clinical science* (pp. 123–150). Washington, DC: American Psychological Association.

Johnson, S. M. (1999). Emotionally focused couple therapy: Straight to the heart. In J. M. Donovan (Ed.), *Short-term couple therapy* (pp. 13–42). New York: Guilford Press.

(2002). *Emotionally focused couple therapy with trauma survivors: Strengthening attachment bonds.* New York: Guilford.

(2008). Couple and family therapy: An attachment perspective. In J. Cassidy & P. R. Shaver (Eds.), *Handbook of attachment: Theory, research, and clinical application* (pp. 811–829). New York: Guilford Press.

(2009). Attachment theory and emotionally focused therapy for individuals and couples: Perfect partners. In J. H. Obegi & E. Berant (Eds.), *Attachment theory and research in clinical work with adults* (pp. 410–433). New York: Guilford Press.

Johnson, S. M. & Courtois, C. A. (2009). Couple therapy. In C. A. Courtois & J. D. Ford (Eds.), *Treating complex traumatic stress disorders: An evidence-based guide* (pp. 371–390). New York: Guilford Press.

Johnson, S. M., & Greenman P. S. (2006). The path to a secure bond: Emotionally focused couple therapy. *Journal of Clinical Psychology, 62,* 597–609.

Johnson, S. M., & Makinen, J. (2003). Posttraumatic stress. In D. K. Snyder & M. A. Whisman (Eds.), *Treating difficult couples: Helping clients with coexisting mental and relationship disorders* (pp. 308–329). New York: Guilford Press.

Johnson, S. M., & Williams-Keeler, L. (1998). Creating healing relationships for couples dealing with trauma: The use of emotionally focused marital therapy. *Journal of Marital and Family Therapy, 24,* 25–40.

Johnson, V. K. (2003). Linking changes in whole family functioning and children's externalizing behavior across the elementary school years. *Journal of Family Psychology, 17,* 499–509.

Jolly, J. B., Dyck, M. J., Kramer, T.A., & Wherry, J. N. (1994). Discriminating anxiety and depression in adults. *Journal of Abnormal Psychology, 103,* 544–552.

Jones, W. H., Kugler, K., & Adams, P. (1995). You always hurt the one you love: Guilt and transgressions against relationship partners. In J. P. Tangney & K. W. Fischer (Eds.), *Self-conscious emotions: The psychology of shame, guilt, embarrassment and pride* (pp. 301–321). New York: Guilford.

Julien, D., Markman, H. J., Leveille, S., Chartrand, E., et al. (1994). Networks' support and interference with regard to marriage disclosures of marital problems with confidants. *Journal of Family Psychology, 8,* 16–31.

Kacewicz, E., Slatcher, R. B., & Pennebaker, J. W. (2007). Expressive writing: An alternative to traditional methods. In L. L'Abate (Ed.), *Low-cost approaches to promote physical and mental health* (pp. 271–284). New York: Springer Science.

Kachadourian, L. K., Fincham. F., & Davila, J. (2004). The tendency to forgive in dating and married couples: The role of attachment and relationship satisfaction. *Personal Relationships, 11,* 373–393.

Kaczynski, K. J., Lindahl, K. M., Malik, N. M., & Laureceau, J-P. (2006). Marital conflict, maternal and paternal parenting, and child adjustment: A test of mediation and moderation. *Journal of Family Psychology*, 20, 199–208.

Kagan, J. (2007). *What is emotion?* New Haven, CT: Yale University Press.

Kamholz, B. W., Hayes, A. M., Carver, C. S., Gulliver, S. B., et al. (2006). Identification and evaluation of cognitive affect-regulation strategies: Development of a self-report measure. *Cognitive Therapy and Research*, 30, 227–262.

Kang, N. J., Downey, G., Iida, M., & Rodriquez, S. (2009). Rejection sensitivity: A model of how individual difference factors affect the experience of hurt feelings in conflict and support. In A. L. Vangelisti (Ed.), *Handbook of hurt feelings in close relationships* (pp. 73–91). New York: Cambridge University Press.

Kanoy, K., Ulku-Steiner, B., Cox, M., & Burchinal, M. (2003). Marital relationship and individual psychological characteristics that predict physical punishment in children. *Journal of Family Psychology*, 17, 20–28.

Kaplar, M. E., & Gordon, A. K. (2004). The enigma of altruistic lying: Perspective differences in what motivates and justifies lie telling within romantic relationships. *Personal Relationships*, 11, 489–508.

Karasek, R., & Theorell, T. (1990). *Healthy work: Stress, productivity, and the reconstruction of working life*. New York: Basic Books.

Kasak, A. E., Christakis, D., Alderfer, M., & Coiro, M-J. (1994). Young adolescent cancer survivors and their parents: Adjustment, learning problems, and gender. *Journal of Family Psychology*, 8, 74–84.

Kaslow, F. W. (Ed.). (1996). *Handbook of relational diagnosis and dysfunctional families*. New York: Wiley.

Katz, J., Beach, S. R. H., & Joiner, T. E., Jr. (1998). When does partner devaluation predict emotional distress? Prospective moderating effects of reassurance-seeking and self-esteem. *Personal Relationships*, 5, 409–422.

Katz, L. D. (2009). Love, loss, and hope go deeper than language: Linguistic semantics has only a limited role in the interdisciplinary study of affect. *Emotion Review*, 1, 19–20.

Katz, L. F., & Windecker-Nelson, B. (2006). Domestic violence, emotion couching, and child adjustment. *Journal of Family Psychology*, 20, 56–67.

Kay, A. C., Banfield, J. C., & Laurin, K. (2010). The system justification motive and the maintenance of social power. In A. Guinote, & T. K. Vescio (Eds.), *The social psychology of power* (pp. 313–340). New York: Guilford.

Kazantzis, N., & L'Abate, L. (Eds.). (2007). *The handbook of homework assignments in psychotherapy: Practice, research, and prevention*. New York: Springer-Science

Kazantzis, N., Whittington, C., & Dattilio, F. (2010). Meta-analysis of homework effects in cognitive and behavioral therapy: A replication and extension. *Clinical Psychology: Science and Practice*, 17, 144–156.

Kearns, J. N., & Fincham, F. D. (2004). A prototype analysis of forgiveness. *Personality and Social Psychology Bulletin*, 30, 838–885.

Keenan-Miller, D., Hammen, C., & Brennan, P. A. (2007a). Adolescent psychosocial risk factors for severe intimate partner violence in young adulthood. *Journal of Consulting and Clinical Psychology*, 75, 456–463.

(2007b). Health outcomes related to early adolescent depression. *Journal of Adolescent Health*, 41, 256–262.

Kelley, H. H., & Thibaut, J. W. (1978). *Interpersonal relations: A theory of interdependence*. New York: Wiley.

Kemeny, M. E., & Shestyuk, A. (2008). Emotions, the neuroendocrine and immune systems, and health. In M. Lewis, J. M. Haviland-Jones, & L. F. Barrett (Eds.), *Handbook of emotions* (3rd ed., pp. 661–675). New York: Guildford.

Kendler, K., Gardner, C., Annas, P., & Lichtenstein, P. (2008). The development of fears from early adolescence to young adulthood: A multivariate study. *Psychological Medicine*, 38, 1759–1769.

Kennedy, H., Kemp, L., & Dyer, D. (1992). Fear and anger in delusional paranoid disorder: The association with violence. *British Journal of Psychiatry*, 160, 488–492.

Kensinger, E. A. (2009). Remembering the details: Effects of emotion. *Emotion Review*, 1, 99–112.

Kensiger, E. A., & Schachter, D. L., (2008). Memory and emotion. In M. Lewis, J. M. Haviland-Jones, & L. F. Barrett (Eds.), *Handbook of emotions* (3rd ed., pp. 601–617). New York: Guildford.

Kerig, P. K. (1995). Triangles in the family circle: Effects of family structure on marriage. *Journal of Family Psychology*, 9, 28–43.

Kerig, P. K., Cowan, P. A., & Cowan, C. P. (1993). Marital quality and gender differences in parent-child interaction. *Developmental Psychology*, 29, 931–939.

Kersting, A., Ohrmann, P., Pedersen, A., Kroker, K., Samberg, D., Bauer, J., Kugel, H., Koelkebeck, K., Steinhard, J., Heindel, W., Arolt, V., & Suslow, T. (2009). Neural activation underlying acute grief in women after the loss of an unborn child. *American Journal of Psychiatry*, 166, 1402–1410.

Kiecolt-Glaser, J. K., McGuire, L., Robles, T. F., & Glaser, R. (2002). Psychoneuroimmunology: Psychological influences on immune function and health. *Journal of Consulting and Clinical Psychology*, 70, 537–547.

Kiefer, A. K., & Sanchez, D. T. (2007). Scripting sexual passivity: A gender role perspective. *Personal Relationships*, 14, 269–290.

Kilpatrick, S. D., Bissonnnette, V. L., & Rusbult, C. E. (2002). Empathic accuracy and accommodative behavior among newly married couples. *Personal Relationships*, 9, 369–394.

Kim, Y. (2006). Gender, attachment, and relationship duration on cardiovascular reactivity to stress in a laboratory study of dating couples. *Personal Relationships*, 23, 103–114.

Kim-Cohen, J., Caspi, A., Rutter, M., Tomas, M. P., et al. (2006). The caregiving environment provided children by depressed mothers with or without an antisocial history. *American Journal of Psychiatry*, 163, 1009–1018.

King, A. R., & Terrance, C. (2006). Relationship between personality disorder attributes and friendship qualities among college students. *Journal of Social and Personal Relationships*, 23, 5–20.

Kirsch, P., Esslinger, C., Chen, Q., Mier, D., et al. (2005). Oxytocin modulates neural vircuitry for social cognition and fear in humans. *Journal of Neuroscience*, 25, 11489–11493.

Kitzmann, K. M., & Beech, B. M. (2006). Family-based interventions for pediatric obesity: Methodological and conceptual challenges for family psychology. *Journal of Family Psychology, 20,* 175–189.

Kitzmann, K. M., & Emery, R. E. (1994). Child and family coping one year after mediated and litigated child custody disputes. *Journal of Family Psychology, 8,* 150–161.

Kluver, H., & Bucy, P. C. (1939). Preliminary analysis of functions of the temporal lobes in monkeys. *Archives of Neurology and Psychiatry, 42,* 979–1000.

Knobloch, L. K., Solomon, D. H., & Cruz, M. G. (2001). The role of relationship development and attachment in the experience of romantic jealousy. *Personal Relationships, 8,* 205–224.

Kolb, B., & Whishaw, I. Q. (1986). *Fundamentals of human neuropsychology.* New York: W. H. Freeman and Company.

Komproe, I. H., Rijken, M., Ros, W. J. G., Winnubst, J. A. M., et al. (1997). Available support and receive support: Different effects under stressful circumstances. *Journal of Social and Personal Relationships, 14,* 59–78.

Korchmaros, J. D., & Kenny, D. A. (2006). An evolutionary and close-relationship model of helping. *Journal of Social and Personal Relationships, 23,* 21–44.

Koss-Chioino, J. D., & Canive, J. M. (1996). Cultural issues in relational diagnosis: Hispanics in the United States. In F. W. Kaslow (Ed.), *Handbook of relational diagnosis and dysfunctional family patterns* (pp. 137–151). New York: Wiley.

Kovecses, A. (1991). A linguist's quest for love. *Journal of Social and Personal Relationships, 8,* 77–97.

Kowalski, R. M. (2009). Cultural influences on the causes and experiences of hurt feelings. In A. L. Vangelisti (Ed.), *Feeling hurt in close relationships* (pp. 457–478). New York: Cambridge University Press.

Kraaij, V., & Garnefski, N. (2002). Negative life events and depressive symptoms in late life: Buffering effects of parental and partner bonding? *Personal Relationships, 9,* 205–214.

Kraemer, D. L., & Hastrup, J. L. (1983a). Crying in adults: Self-control and autonomic correlates. Paper presented at the Meetings of the Society for Psychophysiological Research, Pacific Grove, CA, September 25–28.

(1983b). Crying in natural settings: Global estimates, self-monitoring functions, causes, and sex differences in an undergraduate population. Paper presented at the 44th Meeting of the Eastern Psychological Association, Philadelphia, PA, April 6–9.

Krause, N. (1993). Early parental loss and personal control in later life. *Journal of Gerontology-Psychological Sciences, 48,* P117–P126.

Kring, A. M. (2008). Emotion disturbances as transdiagnostic processes in psychopathology. In M. Lewis, J. M. Haviland-Jones, & L. F. Barrett (Eds.), *Handbook of emotions* (3rd ed., pp. 691–705). New York: Guildford.

Kringelbach, M. L., & Rolls, E. T. (2004). The functional neuroanatomy of the human orbitofrontal cortex: Evidence from neuroimaging and neuropsychology. *Progress in Neurobiology, 72,* 341–372.

Krokoff, L. J. (1991). Job distress is no laughing matter in marriage, or is it? *Journal of Social and Personal Relationships, 8,* 5–26.

Krueger, R. F., & Johnson, W. (2008). Behavioral genetics and personality: A new look at the integration of nature and nurture. O. P. John, R. W. Robins, & L. A. Pervin (Eds.), *Handbook of personality: Theory and research* (pp. 287–310). New York: Guilford.

Kuijer, R. G., Buunk, B. P., & Ybema, J. F. (2001). Justice of give-and-take in the intimate relationship: When one partner of a couple is diagnosed with cancer. *Personal Relationships*, 8, 75–92.

Kurdek, L. A. (2007). Avoidance motivation and relationship commitment in heterosexual, gay male, and lesbian partners. *Personal Relationships*, 14, 291–306.

(2008). A general model of relationship commitment: Evidence from same-sex partners. *Personal Relationships*, 15, 391–405.

Kurdek, L. A., & Fine, M. A. (1994). Relation among control, acceptance, and adolescent adjustment. *Child Development*, 65, 1137–1146.

L'Abate, L. (1977). Intimacy is sharing hurt feelings: A reply to David Mace. *Journal of Marriage and Family Counseling*, 3, 13–16.

(1984). Beyond paradox: Issues of control. *American Journal of Family Therapy*, 12, 12–20.

(1986). *Systematic family therapy*. New York: Brunner/Mazel.

(1990a). A theory of competencies x settings interactions. *Marriage and Family Review*, 15, 253–269.

(1990b). *Building family competence: Primary and secondary prevention strategies*. Newbury Park, CA: Sage.

(1992a). A theory of family competence and coping. In B. N. Carpenter (Ed.), *Personal coping: Theory, research, and application* (pp. 198–217). Westport, CT: Praeger.

(1992b). *Programmed writing: A self-administered approach for interventions with individuals, couples, and families*. Pacific Grove, CA: Brooks/Cole.

(1994). *A theory of personality development*. New York: Wiley.

(1997). *The self in the family: Toward a classification of personality, criminality, and psychopathology*. New York: Wiley.

(1999a). Being human: Loving and hurting. In A. C. Richards & T. Schumrum (Eds.), *Invitations to dialogue: The legacy of Sidney Jourard* (pp. 81–90). Dubuque, IO: Kent/Krandall.

(1999b). Increasing intimacy in couples through distance writing and face-to-face approaches. In J. Carlson & L. Sperry (Eds.), *The intimate couple* (pp. 328–340). Philadelphia: Brunner/Mazel.

(2001). Hugging, holding, huddling, and cuddling (3HC): A task prescription in couple and family therapy. *The Journal of Clinical Activities, Assignments, & Handouts in Psychotherapy Practice*, 1, 5–18.

(2003). *Beyond psychotherapy: Programmed writing and structured computer-assisted interventions*. Westport, CT: Ablex.

(2004). Systematically written homework assignments: The case for homework-based treatment. In L. L'Abate (Ed.), *Using workbooks in mental health: Resources in prevention, psychotherapy, and rehabilitation for clinicians and researchers* (pp. 65–102). Binghamton, NY: Haworth.

(2005). *Personality in intimate relationships: Socialization and psychopathology*. New York: Springer.

(2006). Toward a relational theory for psychiatric classification. *American Journal of Family Therapy*, ap34, 1–15.

(Ed.). (2007). *Low-cost approaches to promote physical and mental health*. New York: Springer-Science.

(2008a). A proposal for including distance writing in couple therapy. *Journal of Couple & Relationship Therapy*, 7, 337–362.

(2008b). Working at a distance from participants: Writing and non-verbal media. In L. L'Abate (Ed.), *Toward a science of clinical psychology: Laboratory evaluations and interventions* (pp. 355–383). New York: Nova Science Publishers.

(2009a). An historical and systematic perspective about distance writing and wellness. In J. F. Evans (Ed.), *Wellness & writing connections: Writing for better physical, mental, and spiritual health* (pp. 53–74). Enumclaw, WA: Idyll Arbor.

(2009b). Hurt Feelings: The last taboo for researchers and clinicians? In A. L. Vangelisti (Ed.), *Feeling hurt in close relationships* (pp. 479–497). New York: Cambridge University Press.

(2009c). Paradigms, theories, and models: Two hierarchical frameworks. In L. L'Abate, P. De Giacomo, M. Capitelli, & S. Longo (Eds.), *Science, mind, and creativity: The Bari symposium* (pp. 107–153). New York: Nova Science Publishers.

(2009d). *The Praeger handbook of play across the life cycle: Fun from infancy to old age*. Westpost, CT: Praeger.

(2011a). Psychotherapy consists of homework assignments with less talk and more interaction: An iconoclastic conviction. In H. Rosenthal (Ed.), *Favorite counseling and therapy homework assignments: Classic anniversary edition* (pp. 219–229). New York: Routledge.

(2011b). *Sourcebook of interactive exercises in mental health*. New York: Springer-Science.

(2011c). *The seven sources of pleasure in life: Making way for the upside in the midst of modern demands*. Westport, CT: Praeger.

(2012). *Clinical psychology and psychotherapy as a science*. New York: Springer-Science.

L'Abate, L., & Cusinato, M. (1994). A spiral model of intimacy. In S. M. Johnson & L. S. Greenberg (Eds.), *The heart of the matter: Perspectives on emotion in marital therapy*, (pp. 122–138). New York: Brunner/Mazel.

L'Abate, L., Cusinato, M., Maino, E., Colesso, W., & Scilletta, C. (2010). *A theory of relational competence: Research and mental health applications*. New York: Springer-Science.

L'Abate, L., & Goldstein. J. (2007). Workbooks to promote mental health and life-long learning. In L. L'Abate (Ed.), *Low-cost approaches to promote physical and mental health: Theory, research, and practice* (pp. 285–303). New York: Springer-Science.

L'Abate, L., & Hecker, L. L. (2004). The status and future of workbooks in mental health: Concluding commentary. In L. L'Abate (Ed.), *Using workbooks in mental health: Resources in prevention, psychotherapy, and rehabilitation for clinicians and researchers* (pp. 351–373). Binghamton, NY: Haworth.

L'Abate, L., L'Abate, B. L., & Maino, E. (2005). A review of 25 years of part-time professional practice: Workbooks and length of psychotherapy. *American Journal of Family Therapy, 33,* 19–31.

L'Abate, L., & Sloan, S. Z. (1984). A workshop format to facilitate intimacy in married couples. *Family Relations, 3,* 245–250.

(1985). Intimacy. In L. L'Abate (Ed.), *Handbook of family psychology and therapy* (pp. 305–329), Pacific Grove, CA: Brooks/Cole.

L'Abate, L., & Sweeney, L. G. (Eds.). (2011). *Research on writing approaches in mental health.* Bingley, UK: Emerald Publishing Group.

L'Abate, L., van Eiden, A., & Rigamonti, S. (2011). Cross-cultural and relational perspectives on non-aggressive, personality disordered women. *American Journal of Family Therapy.*

Labor, K. S., Leduc, J. E., Spencer, D. D., & Phelps, E. A. (1995). Impaired fear conditioning following unilateral temporal lobotomy in humans. *Journal of Neuroscience, 15,* 6846–6855.

Laird, J. D., & Stout, S. (2007). Emotional behavior as emotional stimuli. In J. A. Coan & J. J. B. Allen (Eds.), *Handbook of emotion elicitation and assessment* (pp. 54–64). New York: Oxford University Press.

Lambert, N. M., Graham, S. M., & Fincham, F. D. (2009). A prototype analysis of gratitude: Varieties of gratitude experiences. *Personality and Social Psychology Bulletin, 35,* 195–207.

Lambie, J. A. (2009). Emotion experience, rational action, and self-knowledge. *Emotion Review, 1,* 272–280.

Lane, R. D., Reiman, E. M., Ahern, G. L., Schwartz, G. E., et al. (1997). Neuroanatomical correlates of happiness, sadness, and disgust. *American Journal of Psychiatry, 154,* 926–933.

Lang, F. R. (2000). Ending and continuity of social relationships: Maximizing intrinsic benefits within personal networks when feeling near death. *Journal of Social and Personal Relationships, 17,* 155–182.

Langhinrichsen-Rohling, J., Heyman, R. E., Schlee, K., & O'Leary, K. D. (1997). Before children: Preparenthood cognitions of distressed and husband-to-wife aggressive couples. *Journal of Family Psychology, 11,* 176–187.

Lansford, J. E., Malone, P. S., Castellino, D. R., Dodge, K. A., et al. (2006). Trajectories of internalizing, externalizing, and grades for children who have and have not experienced their parents' divorce or separation. *Journal of Family Psychology, 20,* 292–301.

Lara, D., Pinto, O., Akiskal, K., & Akiskal, H. (2006). Toward an integrative model of the spectrum of mood, behavioral and personality disorders based on fear and anger traits: I. Clinical implications. *Journal of Affective Disorders, 94,* 67–87.

Larsen, J. T., Berntson, G. G., Poehlmann, K. M., Ito, T. A., et al. (2008). The psychophysiology of emotion. In M. Lewis, J. M. Haviland-Jones, & L. F. Barrett (Eds.), *Handbook of emotions* (3rd ed., pp. 180–195). New York: Guilford.

Larsson, J. O. (2004). Behavioural outcomes of regulatory problems in infancy. *Acta Poediatrica, 93,* 1421–1423.

Latzer, Y., & Gaber, L. B. (1998). Pathological conflict avoidance in anorexia nervosa: Family perspectives. *Contemporary Family Therapy: An International Journal, 20,* 539–551.

Laurenceau, J-P., Barrett, L. F., & Rovine, M. J. (2005). The Interpersonal Process Model of intimacy in marriage: A daily-diary and multi-level modeling approach. *Journal of Family Psychology*, 19, 314–323.

Laurenceau, J-P., Rivera, L. M., Schaffer, A. R., & Pietromonaco, P. R. (2004). Intimacy as an interpersonal process: Current status and future directions. In D. J. Mashek & A. Aron (Eds.), *Handbook of closeness and intimacy* (pp. 61–78). Mahwah, NJ: Erlbaum.

Lavee, Y., & Ben-Ari, A. (2007). Dyadic distance: From the inside story to a conceptual model. *Journal of Social and Personal Relationships*, 24, 645–656.

Lawrence, E., Bunde, M., Barry, R. A., Brock, R. L., et al. (2008). Partner support and marital satisfaction: Support amount, adequacy, provision, and solicitation. *Personal Relationships*, 15, 445–464.

Lawrance, K-A., & Byers, E. S. (1995). Sexual satisfaction in long-term heterosexual relationships: The interpersonal exchange model of sexual satisfaction. *Personal Relationships*, 2, 267–278.

Lawrence, J. A., Goodnow, J. J., Woods, K., & Karantzas, G. (2002). Distributions of caregiving tasks among family members: The place of gender and availability. *Journal of Family Psychology*, 16, 493–509.

Lazarus, R. S., & Folkman, S. (1984). *Stress, appraisal, and coping*. New York: Springer.

Lazarus, R. S., & Lazarus, B. N. (1994). *Passion & reason: Making sense of our emotions*. New York: Oxford University Press.

Le, B., & Agnew, C. R. (2003). Commitment and its theorizing determinants: A meta-analysis of the Investment Model. *Personal Relationships*, 10, 37–58.

Leahy, R. L. (2007). Emotion and psychotherapy. *Clinical Psychology: Science and Practice*, 14, 353–357.

Leary, M. R., Koch, E. J., & Hechenbleikner, N. R. (2001). Emotional responses to interpersonal rejection. In M. R. Leary (Ed.), *Interpersonal rejection* (pp. 145–166). New York: Oxford University Press.

Leary, M. R., & Kowalski, R. M. (1990). Impression management: A literature review and two component model. *Psychological Bulletin*, 107, 34–47.

Leary, M. R., & Leder, S. (2009). The nature of hurt feelings: Emotional experience and cognitive appraisals. In A. L. Vangelisti (Ed.), *Feeling hurt in close relationships* (pp. 15–33). New York: Cambridge University Press.

Leary, M. R., & Springer, C. S. (2001). Hurt feelings: The neglected emotion. In R. M. Kowalski (Ed.), *Aversive behaviors and interpersonal transgressions: The underbelly of social interaction* (pp. 151–175). Washington, DC: American Psychological Association.

Leary, M. R., Springer, C., Negel, L., Ansell, E., & Evans, K. (1998). The causes, phenomenology, and consequences of hurt feelings. *Journal of Personality and Social Psychology*, 74, 1225–1237.

LeDoux, J. E. (1996). *The emotional brain*. New York: Simon & Schuster.

LeDoux, J. E., & Phelps, E. A. (2008). Emotional networks in the brain. In M. Lewis, J. M. Haviland-Jones, & L. F. Barrett (Eds.), *Handbook of emotions* (3rd ed., pp. 159–179). New York: Guilford.

Lee, G. P., Arena, J. G., Meador, K. J., Smith, J. R., et al. (1988). Changes in autonomic responsiveness following bilateral amydalotomy in humans. *Neuropsychiatry, Neuropsychology and Behavioral Neurology*, 1, 119–129.

Lee, G. P., Bechara, A., Adolphs, R., Arena, J., et al. (1998). Clinical and physiological effects of stereotaxic bilateral amygdalotomy for intractable aggression. *The Journal of Neuropsychiatry and Clinical Neurosciences*, 10, 413–420.

Lefkowitz, M. M., & Tesiny, E. P. (1984). Rejection and depression: Prospective and contemporaneous analyses. *Developmental Psychology*, 20, 776–785.

Leitman, D., Loughead, J., Wolf, D., Ruparel, K., et al. (2008). Abnormal superior temporal connectivity during fear perception in schizophrenia. *Schizophrenia Bulletin*, 34, 673–678.

Lejoyeux, M., Arbaretaz, M., McLoughlin, M., & Ades, J. (2002). Impulse control disorders and depression. *Journal of Nervous & Mental Disease*, 190, 310–314.

Lemerise, E. A., & Dodge, K A. (2008). The development of anger and hostile interactions. In M. Lewis, J. M. Haviland-Jones, & L. F. Barrett (Eds.), *Handbook of emotions* (3rd ed., pp. 730–741). New York: Guilford.

Lento, J. (2006). Relational and physical victimization by peers and romantic partners in college students. *Journal of Social and Personal Relationships*, 23, 331–348.

Lenton, A. P., & Bryan, A. (2005). An affair to remember: The role of sexual scripts in perceptions of sexual intent. *Personal Relationships*, 12, 483–498.

Lepore, S. J., & Smyth, J. M. (Eds.). (2002). *The writing cure: How expressive writing promotes health and emotional well-being*. Washington, DC: American Psychological Association.

Leung, D. W., & Slep, A. M. S. (2006). Predicting inept discipline: The role of parental depressive symptoms, anger, and attributions. *Journal of Consulting and Clinical Psychology*, 74, 524–534.

Levendosky, A. A., Hugh-Bocks, A. C., Shapiro, D. L., & Semel, M. A. (2003). The impact of domestic violence on the maternal-child relationship and preschool-age children's functioning. *Journal of Family Psychology*, 17, 275–287.

Levendosky, A. A., Leahy, K. L., Bogat, G. A., Davidson, W. S., et al. (2006). Domestic violence, maternal parenting, maternal mental health, and infant externalizing behavior. *Journal of Family Psychology*, 20, 544–552.

Leventhal, H., Nerenz, D. R., & Steele, D. J. (1984). Illness representation and coping with health threats. In A. Baum, S. E. Taylor, & J. E. Singer (Eds.), *Handbook of psychology and health* (pp. 219–252). Hillsdale, NJ: Erlbaum.

Levesque, J., Joanette, Y., Mensour, B., Beaudoin, G., et al. (2004). Neural basis of emotional self-regulation in childhood. *Neuroscience*, 129, 361–369.

Levine, S. B. (1991). Psychological intimacy. *Journal of Sex & Marital Therapy*, 17, 259–268.

Levitt, S. D., & Dubner, S. J. (2009). *Super-freakonomics: Global cooling, patriotic prostitutes, and why suicide bombers should buy life insurance*. New York: William Morrow.

Lewis, M. (2008). The emergence of human emotions. In M. Lewis, J. M. Haviland-Jones, & L. F. Barrett (Eds.), *Handbook of emotions* (3rd ed., pp. 304–319). New York: Guildford.

Lewis, M., & Haviland-Jones, J. M. (Eds.). (1993). *Handbook of emotions* (1st ed.). New York: Guilford.

(Eds.). (2000). *Handbook of emotions* (2nd ed.). New York: Guilford.

Lewis, M., Haviland-Jones, J. M., & Barrett, L. F. (Eds.). (2008). *Handbook of emotions* (3rd ed.). New York: Guilford.

Lewis, M. A., Butterfield, R. M., Darbes, L. A., & Johnston-Brooks, C. (2004). The conceptualization of assessment of health-related social control. *Journal of Social and Personal Relationships*, 21, 669–687.

Lewis, N. (2008b). Self-conscious emotions: Embarrassment, pride, shame, and guilt. In M. Lewis, J. M. Haviland -Jones, & L. F. Barrett (Eds.), *Handbook of emotions* (3rd ed., pp. 742–755). New York: Guildford.

Lieberman, M. D., Eisenberger, N. I., Crockett, M. J., Tom, S. M., et al. (2007). Putting feelings into words: Affect labeling disrupts amygdala activity in response to affective stimuli. *Psychological Science*, 18, 421–428.

Lieberman, M. D., Jarcho, J. M., Berman, S., Naliboff, B. D., et al. (2004). The neural correlates of placebo effects: A disruption account. *NeuroImage*, 22, 447–455.

Lindahl, K. M., Clements, M., & Markman, H. (1997). Predicting marital and parent functioning in dyads and tryads: A longitudinal investigation of marital process. *Journal of Family Psychology*, 11, 139–151.

Lindquist, K.A., & Feldman Barrett, L. (2008). Emotional complexity. In M. Lewis, J. M. Haviland-Jones, & L. Feldman Barrett (Eds.), *Handbook of emotions* (3rd ed., pp. 17–31). New York: Guilford.

Lindsey, E. W., Colwell, M. J., Frabutt, J. M., & McKinnon-Lewis, C. (2006). Family conflict in divorced and non-divorced families: Potential consequences for boys' friendship status and friendship quality. *Journal of Social and Personal Relationships*, 23, 45–64.

Lindsey, E. W., MacKinnon-Lewis, C., Campbell, J., Frabutt, J. M., et al. (2002). Maternal conflict and boys' peer relationships: The mediating role of mother-son emotional reciprocity. *Journal of Family Psychology*, 16, 466–477.

Litz, B. T. (2003). A taxonomy of emotional functioning problems: A good idea in need of more research. *Clinical Psychology: Science and Practice*, 10, 239–244.

Litz, B. T., Stein, N., Delaney, E., Lebowitz, L., et al. (2009). Moral injury and moral repair in war veterans: A preliminary model and intervention strategy. *Clinical Psychology Review*, 29, 695–706.

Loewenstein, G. (2007). Affect regulation and affective forecasting. In J. J. Gross (Ed.), *Handbook of emotion regulation* (pp. 180–203). New York: Guilford.

Lohman, A., Arriaga, X. B., & Goodfriend, W. (2003). Close relationships and placemaking: Do objects in a couple's home reflect couplehood? *Personal Relationships*, 11, 437–450.

Lollis, S., & Kucxynski, L. (1997). Beyond one hand clapping: Seeing bidirectionality in parent-child relations. *Journal of Social and Personal Relationships*, 14, 441–462.

Loving, T. J., Le, B., & Crockett, E. E. (2009). The physiology of feeling hurt. In A. L. Vangelisti (Ed.), *Feeling hurt in close relationships* (pp. 359–375). New York: Cambridge University Press.

Lucas, R. E., & Diener, E. (2008). Subjective well-being. In M. Lewis, J. M. Haviland-Jones, & L. Feldman Barrett (Eds.), *Handbook of emotions* (3rd ed., pp. 471–484). New York: Guilford.

Lundy, D.E., Tan, J., & Cunningham, M.R. (1998). Heterosexual romantic preferences: The importance of humor and physical attractiveness for different types of relationships. *Personal Relationships*, 5, 311–325.

Luria, A. R., Pribram, K. H., & Homskaya, E. D. (1964). An experimental-analysis of the behavioral disturbance produced by a left frontal arachnoidal endothelioma (Meningioma). *Neuropsychologia*, 2, 257–280.

Lutz, T. (1999). *Crying: The natural & cultural history of tears*. New York: W. W. Norton.

Luyckx, K., Soenens, B., Berzonsky, M. D., Vansteenkiste, M., et al. (2007). Parental psychological control and dimensions of identity formation in emerging adulthood. *Journal of Family Psychology*, 21, 546–550.

Lynch, S. K., Turkheimer, E., D'Onofrio, B. M., Mendle, J., et al. (2006). A genetically informed study of the association between harsh punishment and offspring behavioral problems. *Journal of Family Psychology*, 20, 190–198.

Lyons, R. F., Mickelson, K., Sullivan, M. J. L., & Coyne, J. C. (1998). Coping as a communal process. *Journal of Social and Personal Relationships*, 15, 579–606.

Maccoby, E. E., & Jacklin, C. N. (1974). *The psychology of sex differences*. Stanford, CA: Standord University Press.

MacDonald, G., & Jensen-Campbell, L. D. (Eds.).(2011). *Social pain: Neuropsychological and health implications of loss and exclusion*. Washington, DC: American Psychological Association.

MacDonald, G., & Leary, M. R. (2005). Why does social exclusion hurt? The relationship between social and physical pain. *Psychological Bulletin,* 131, 202–223.

Mace, D. R. (1976). Marital intimacy and the deadly love-anger cycle. *Journal of Marriage and Family Counseling*, 2, 131–137.

Magai, C. (2008). Long-lived emotions: A life course perspective on emotional development. In M. Lewis, H. M. Haviland-Jones, & L. F. Barrett (Eds.), *Handbook of emotions* (3rd ed., pp. 376–394). New York: Guilford.

Magnavita, J. J. (2006). The centrality of emotion in unifying and accelerating psychotherapy. *Journal of Clinical Psychology*, 62, 585–596.

Mahalik, J. R. (2008). A biopsychosocial perspective on men's depression. *Clinical Psychology: Science and Practice*, 15, 174–177.

Mahoney, A., O'Donnelly, W. O., Boxer, P., & Lewis, T. (2003). Marital and severe parent-to-adolescent physical aggression in child-referred families: Mother and adolescent reports on co-occurence and links to child behavior problems. *Journal of Family Psychology*, 17, 3–19.

Maino, E. (2012). The validity of an information processing model with alexithymic participants. In M. Cusinato & L. L'Abate (Eds.) *Advances in relational competence theory: With special attention to alexithymia*. New Work : Nova Science Publishers .

Mak, W. W. S., Chen, S. X., Lam, A. G., & Yiu, V. F. L. (2009). Understanding distress. *The Counseling Psychologist*, 37, 239–248.

Malatesta-Magai, C. (1991). Emotional socialization: Its role in personality and developmental psychopathology. In D. Cicchetti & S. L. Toth (Eds.), *Internalizing and externalizing expressions of dysfunction* (pp. 203–224). Hillsdale, NJ: Erlbaum.

Maltby, J., Macaskill, A., & Gillet, R. (2007). The cognitive nature of forgiveness: Using cognitive strategies of primary appraisal and coping to describe the process of forgiving. *Journal of Clinical Psychology*, 63, 555–566.

Maniglio, R. (2009). The impact of child sexual abuse on health: A systematic review of reviews. *Clinical Psychology Review*, 29(7), 647–657.

Manne, S. L., Norton, T. R., Ostroff, J. S., Winker, G., et al. (2007). Protecting buffering and psychological distress among couples coping with breast cancer: The moderating role of relationship satisfaction. *Journal of Family Psychology*, 21, 380–388.

Margolin G., Christensen, A., & John, R. S. (1996). The continuance and spillover of everyday tensions in distressed and nondistressed families. *Journal of Family Psychology*, 10, 304–321.

Marin, T., Holtzman, S., DeLongis, A., & Robinson, L. (2007). Coping and the response of others. *Journal of Social and Personal Relationships*, 24, 951–969.

Markus, H., & Kitayama, S. (1991). Culture and self: Implications for cognition, emotion, and motivation. *Psychological Review*, 98, 224–253.

Marshall, T. C. (2008). Cultural differences in intimacy: The influence of gender-role ideology and individualism-collectivism. *Journal of Social and Personal Relationships*, 25, 143–168.

Marston, P. J., Hecht, M. L., Manke, M. L., McDaniel, S., et al. (1998). The subjective experience of intimacy, passion, and commitment in heterosexual loving relationships. *Personal Relationships*, 5, 15–30.

Martorell, G. A., & Bugental, D. B. (2006). Maternal variations in stress reactivity: Implications for harsh parenting practices with very young children. *Journal of Family Psychology*, 20, 641–647.

Mascolo, M. F., & Griffin, S. (Eds.). (1998). *What develops in emotional development?* New York: Plenum.

Mashek. D. J., & Aron, A. (Eds.). (2004). *Handbook of closeness and intimacy.* Mahwah, NJ: Erlbaum.

Masten, C. L., Eisenberger, N. I., Borofsky, L.A., Pfiefer, J. H., et al. (2009). Neural correlates of social exclusion during adolescence: Understanding the distress of peer rejection. *Social Cognitive and Affective Neuroscience*, 4, 143–157.

Masters, K. S., Stillman, A. M., & Spielman, G. (2007). Specificity of social support for back pain patients: Do patients care who provides what? *Journal of Behavioral Medicine*, 30, 11–20.

Matjasko, J. L., & Feldman, A. F. (2006). Bringing work home: The emotional experiences of mothers and fathers. *Journal of Family Psychology*, 20, 47–55.

Matsumoto, D., Keltner, D., Shiota, M. N., O'Sullivan, M., et al. (2008). Facial expression of emotion. In M. Lewis, J. M. Haviland-Jones, & L. F. Barrett (Eds.), *Handbook of emotions* (3rd ed., pp. 211–234). New York: Guilford.

May, L. N., & Jones, W. H. (2007). Does hurt linger? Exploring the nature of hurt feelings over time. *Current Psychology: Developmental, Learning, Personality, Social*, 25, 245–256.

Mayerfeld, J. (1999). *Suffering and moral responsibility.* New York: Oxford University Press.

Mayne, T. (2001). Emotions and health. In T. Mayne & G. Bonanno (Eds.), *Emotions: Currrent issues and future directions* (pp. 361–397). New York: Guilford Press.

McCabe, S. B., & Gotlib, I. H. (1993). Interaction of couples with and without a depressed spouse: Self-report and observations of problem-solving situations. *Journal of Social and Personal Relationships*, 10, 589–600.

McDonald, E., & Grych, J. H. (2006). Young children's appraisals of interparental conflict: Measurement and links with adjustment problems. *Journal of Family Psychology*, 20, 88–99.

McLean, C. P., & Anderson, E. R. (2009). Brave men and timid women? A review of gender differences in fear and anxiety. *Clinical Psychology Review*, 29, 496–505.

McNally, R. J. (2007). Mechanisms of exposure therapy: How neuroscience can improve psychological treatments for anxiety disorders. *Clinical Psychology Review*, 27, 750–759.

McRae, K., Hughes, B., Chopra, S., Gabrieli, J. D., et al. (2009). The neural bases of distraction and reappraisal. *Journal of Cognitive Neuroscience*, 22, 248–262.

Meegan, S. P., & Goedereis, E. R. (2006). Life task appraisals, spouse involvement in strategies, and daily affect among short- and long-term married couple. *Journal of Family Psychology*, 20, 319–327.

Menchola, M., Arkowitz, H., & Burke, B. L. (2007). Efficacy of self-administered treatments for depression and anxiety. *Professional Psychology: Research and Practice*, 38, 421–429.

Mendoza, J. E., & Foundas, A. L. (2008). *Clinical neuroanatomy: A neurobehavioral approach*. New York: Springer-Science.

Mennin, D., & Farach, F. (2007). Emotion and evolving treatments for adult psycho-pathology. *Clinical Psychology: Science and Practice*, 14, 329–352.

Menuck, M. (1992). Differentiating paranoia and legitimate fears. *The American Journal of Psychiatry*, 149, 140–141.

Menzies-Toman, D. A. & Lydon, J. E. (2005). Commitment-motivated benign appraisal of partner transgressions: Do they facilitate accommodation? *Journal of Social and Personal Relationships*, 22, 111–128.

Mesquita, B., & Albert, D. (2007). The cultural regulation of emotions. In J. J. Gross (Ed.), *Handbook of emotion regulation* (pp. 486–502). New York: Guildford.

Mesquita, B., Barrett, L. F., & Smith, E. R. (Eds.). (2010). *The mind in context*. New York: Guildford.

Mesulam, M. M., & Mufson, E. J. (1982a). Insula of the old world monkey. I. Architectonics in the insulo-orbito-temporal component of the paralimbic brain. *The Journal of Comparitive Neurology*, 212, 1–22.

(1982b). Insula of the old world monkey. III: Efferent cortical output and comments on function. *The Journal of Comparative Neurology*, 212, 38–52.

Metts, S., Braithwaite, D. O., & Fine, M. A. (2009). Hurt in post-divorce relationships. In A. L. Vangelisti (Ed.), *Feeling hurt in close relationships* (pp. 336–358). New York: Cambridge University Press.

Mikulincer, M., & Shaver, P. S. (2005). Attachment theory and emotions in close relationships: Exploring the attachment-related dynamics of emotional reactions to relational events. *Personal Relationships*, 12, 149–168.

(2007). *Attachment in adulthood: Structure, dynamics, and change*. New York: Guilford.

Mikulincer, M., & Shaver, P. S. (2009). An attachment and behavioral systems perspective on social support. *Journal of Social and Personal Relationships*, 26, 7–19.

Milardo, R. M. (1998). Gender asymmetry in common couple violence. *Personal Relationships*, 5, 423–438.

Milevsky, A. (2005). Compensatory patterns of sibling support in emerging adulthood: Variations in loneliness, self-esteem, depression and life satisfaction. *Journal of Social and Personal Relationships*, 22, 743–756.

Miller, J. D., & Pilkonis, P. A. (2006). Neuroticism and affective instability: The same or different? *American Journal of Psychiatry*, 163, 839–845.

Miller, M. W., Vogt, D. S., Mozicy, S. L., Kaloupek, D. G., et al. (2006). PTSD and substance-related problems: The mediating roles of disconstraint and negative emotionality. *Journal of Abnormal Psychology*, 115, 369–379.

Mills, J., Clark, M. S., Ford, T. E., & Johnson, M. (2004). Measurement of communal strength. *Personal Relationships*, 11, 213–230.

Mills, R. S. L., Nazar, J., & Farrell, H. M. (2002). Child and parent perceptions of hurtful messages. *Journal of Social and Personal Relationships*, 19, 731–754.

Mills, R. S. L., & Piotrowski, C. C. (2009). Heaven in a heartless world? Hurt feelings in the family. In A. L. Vangelisti (Ed.), *Handbook of hurt feelings in close relationships* (pp. 260–286). New York: Cambridge University Press.

Minsky, M. (2008). A framework for representing emotional states. In M. Lewis, J. M. Haviland-Jones, & L. F. Barrett (Eds.), *Handbook of emotions* (3rd ed., pp. 618–627). New York: Guildford.

Mohr, D. C., Vella, L., Hart, S., Heckman, J., & Simon, G. (2008). The effect of telephone-administered psychotherapy on symptoms of depression and attrition: A meta-analysis. *Clinical Psychology: Science and Practice*, 15, 243–253.

Mongrain, M., & Leather, F. (2006). Immature dependence and self-criticism predict recurrence of major depression. *Journal of Clinical Psychology*, 62, 705–713.

Monson, C. M., Taft, C. T., & Fredman, S. J. (2009). Military-related PTSD and intimate relationships: From description to theory-driven research and development. *Clinical Psychology Review*, 29, 707–714.

Monsour, M. (1992). Meanings of intimacy in cross- and same-sex friendships. *Journal of Social and Personal Relationships*, 9, 277–296.

Mor, N., & Winquist, J. (2002). Self-focused attention and negative affect: A meta-analysis. *Psychological Bulletin*, 128, 638–662.

Morino, J. L. (1953). *Who shall survive? Foundations of group psychotherapy and sociodrama*. New York: Beacon House.

Morris, J. S., Friston, K. J., Buchel, C., Frith, C. D., et al. (1998). A neuromodulatory role for the human amygdala in processing emotional facial expressions. *Brain*, 121, 47–57.

Morris, J. S., Frith, C. D., Perrett, D. I., Rowland, D., et al. (1996). A differential neural response in the human amygdala to fearful and happy facial expressions. *Nature*, 383, 812–815.

Morrison, A. P., & Wells, A. (2007). Relationships between worry, psychotic experiences and emotional distress in patients with schizophrenia spectrum diagnoses and comparison with anxious and non-patient groups. *Behavior Research and Therapy*, 45, 1593–1600.

Moss, B. F., & Schwebel, A. L. (1993). Defining intimacy in romantic relationships. *Family Relations*, 42, 31–37.

Muehlhoff, T. M., & Wood, J. T. (2002). Speaking of marriage communication: The marriage between theory and practice. *Journal of Social and Personal Relationships*, 19, 613–620.

Mueser, K. T., Bellack, A. S., Wade, J. H., Sayers, S. L., et al. (1991). Expressed emotion, social skill, and response to negative affect in schizophrenia. *Journal of Abnormal Psychology*, 102, 339–351.

Mufson, E. J., Mesulam, M. M. (1982). Insula of the old world monkey. II: Afferent cortical input and comments on the claustrum. *The Journal of Comparative Neurology*, 212, 23–37.

Mullin, B. C., & Hinshaw, S. P. (2007). Emotion regulation and externalizing disorders and children and adolescents. In J. J. Gross (Ed.), *Handbook of emotion regulation* (pp. 523–541). New York: Guilford.

Mulvaney, M. K., & Mebert, C. J. (2007). Parental corporal punishment predicts behavior problems in early childhood. *Journal of Family Psychology*, 21, 389–391.

Murray, S. L., & Holmes, J. G. (2009). The architecture of interdependent minds: A motivation management theory of mutual responsiveness. *Psychological Review*, 116, 908–928.

Murray, S. L., Holmes, J. G., & Collins, N. L. (2006). Optimizing assurance: The risk regulation system in relationships. *Psychological Bulletin*, 132, 641–666.

Myers, L. B., Burns, J. W., Derakshan, N., Elfant, E., et al. (2008). Current issues in repressive coping and health. In A. J. J. M. Vingerhoets, I. Nyklicek, & J. Denollet (2008). *Emotion regulation: Conceptual and clinical issues* (pp. 69–86). New York: Springer.

Naqvi, N. H., Rudrauf, D., Damasio, H., & Bechara, A. (2007). Damage to the insula disrupts addiction to cigarette smoking. *Science*, 315, 531–534.

Nathanson, D. L. (1992). *Shame and pride: Affect, sex, and the birth of self*. New York: Norton.

National Institute of Drug Abuse (2009). NIDA NOTES, volume 15, p. 15.

Nauta, W. J. H. (1971). The problem of the frontal lobe: A reinterpretation. *Journal of Psychiatric Research*, 8, 167–187.

Neafsey, E. J. (1990). Prefrontal cortical control of the autonomic nervous system: Anatomical and physiological observations. In H. B. M. Uylings, C. G. Van Eden, J. P. C. De Bruin, M. A. Corner, & M. G. P. Feenstra (Eds.), *Progress in brain research* (pp. 147–166). New York, Elsevier.

Negel, L. A. (2003). Exploring the nature of hurt feelings. Dissertation Abstracts International: Section B. The Sciences and Engineering, 63, 6133.

Neimeyer, R. A. (2006). Complicated grief and the reconstruction of meaning: Conceptual and empirical contribution to a cognitive-constructivist model. *Clinical Psychology: Science and Practice*, 13, 141–145.

Nelson, D. R., Hammen, C., Brennan, P. A., & Ullman, J. B. (2003). The impact of maternal depression on adolescent adjustment: The role of expressed emotions. *Journal of Consulting & Clinical Psychology*, 7, 935–944.

Nelson, J. A., O'Brien, M., Blankson, A. N., Calkins, S. D., et al. (2009). Family stress and parental responses to children's negative emotions: Tests of the Spillover, crossover, and compensatory hypotheses. *Journal of Family Psychology*, 23, 671–679.

Nelson, J. K. (2008). Crying in psychotherapy: Its meaning, assessment, and management based on attachment theory. In A. Vingerhoets, I. Nyklicek, & J. Denollet (Eds.), *Emotion regulation: Conceptual and clinical issues* (pp. 202–214). New York: Springer.

Newall, N. E., Chipperfield, J. G., Clifton, R. A., Perry, R. P., et al. (2009). Casual beliefs, social participation, and loneliness among older adults: A longitudinal study. *Journal of Social and Personal Relationships*, 26, 273–290.

Nezlek, J. B. (1995). Social construction, gender/sex similarity, and social interaction in close personal relationships. *Journal of Social and Personal Relationships*, 12, 503–520.

Nichols, M. P., & Zax, M. (1977). *Catharsis in psychotherapy*. New York: Gardner Press.

Nicholson, I. R. (1997). Schizophrenia and the family. In L. L'Abate (Ed.), *Family psychopathogy: The relational roots of dysfunctional behavior* (pp. 281–310). New York: Guilford.

Niedenthal, P. M., Krauth-Gruber, S., & Ric, F. (2006). *Psychology of emotion: Interpersonal, experiential, and cognitive approaches*. New York: Psychology Press.

Nielsen, C. S., Staud, R., & Price, D. D. (2009). Individual differences in pain sensitivity: Measurement, causation, and consequences. *Journal of Pain*, 10, 231–237.

Nielsen, L., & Kaszniak, A. W. (2007). Conceptual, theoretical, and methodological issues in inferring subjective emotion experience: Recommendations for researchers. In J. A. Coan & J. J. B. Allen (Eds.), *Handbook of emotion elicitation and assessment* (pp. 361–375). New York: Oxford University Press.

Nolen-Hoeksema, S. (1987). Sex differences in unipolar depression: Evidence and theory. *Psychological Bulletin*, 101, 259–282.

(1995). Epidemiology and theories of gender differences in unipolar depression. In M. V. Seeman (Ed.), *Gender and psychopathology* (pp. 63–87). Washington, DC: American Psychiatric Press.

(2008). It is not what you have, it is what you do with it: Support for Addis's gendered responding framework. *Clinical Psychology: Science and Practice*, 15, 178–191.

Nomura, M., Iidaka, T., Kakehi, K., Tsukiura, T., et al. (2003). Frontal lobe networks for effective processing of ambiguously expressed emotions in humans. *Neuroscience Letters*, 348, 113–116.

Novy, D. M. (1993). An investigation of the progressive sequence of ego development levels. *Journal of Clinical Psychology*, 49, 332–338.

Oatley, K. (2009a). An emotion's emergence, unfolding, and potential for empathy: A study of resentment by the "Psychologist of Avon." *Emotion Review*, 1, 24–30.

Oatley, K., & Jenkins, J. M. (1996). *Understanding emotions*. Cambridge, MA: Blackwell.

Ochsner, K. N., Bunge, S.A., Gross, J. J., & Gabrieli, J. D. (2002). Rethinking feelings: An fMRI study of the cognitive regulation of emotion. *Journal of Cognitive Neuroscience*, 14, 1215–1229.

Ochsner, K. N., & Gross, J. J. (2007). The neural architecture of emotion regulation. In J. J. Gross (Ed.), *Handbook of emotion regulation* (pp. 87–109). New York: Guilford.

Ochsner, K. N., Ray, R. D., Cooper, J. C., Robertson, E. R., et al. (2004). For better or for worse: Neural systems supporting the cognitive down- and up-regulation of negative emotion. *NeuroImage*, 23, 483–499.

O'Connor, T. G., Hetherington, E. M., & Clingempeel, W. G. (1997). Systems of bidirectional influences in families. *Journal of Social and Personal Relationships*, 14, 491–504.

Ogolsky, B. G. (2009). Deconstructing the association between relationship maintenance and commitment: Testing two competing models. *Personal Relationships*, 16, 99–116.

Ogrodniczuk, J. S., Piper, W. E., & Joyce, A. S. (2006). Treatment compliance among patients with personality disorders receiving group psychotherapy: What are the roles of interpersonal distress and cohesion? *Psychiatry: Interpersonal and Biological Processes*, 69, 249–261.

Ohira, H., Nomura, M., Ichikawa, N., Isowa, T., et al. (2006). Association of neural and physiological responses during voluntary emotion suppression. *NeuroImage*, 29, 721–733.

Ohman, A. (1993). Fear and anxiety as emotional phenomena: Clinical phenomenology, evolutionary perspectives, and information-processing mechanisms. In M. Lewis & J. M. Haviland (Eds.), *Handbook of emotions* (1st ed., pp. 511–536). New York: Guilford.

(2000). Fear and anxiety: Evolutionary, cognitive, and clinical perspectives. In M. Lewis & J. M. Haviland-Jones (Eds.), *Handbook of emotions* (2nd ed., pp. 573–593). New York: Guilford.

(2008). Fear and anxiety: Overlap and dissociation. In M. Lewis, J. M. Haviland-Jones, & L. Feldman Barrett (Eds.), *Handbook of emotions* (3rd ed., pp. 709–729). New York: Guilford.

Ohman, A., & Ruck, C. (2007). Four principles of fear and their implications for phobias. In J. Rottenberg & S. L. Johnson (Eds.), *Emotion and psychopathology: Bridging affective and clinical science* (pp. 167–189). Washington, DC: American Psychological Association.

O'Leary, K. D., & Williams, M. C. (2006). Agreement about acts of aggression in marriage. *Journal of Family Psychology*, 20, 656–662.

O'Leary, S. G., & Slep, A. M. S. (2006). Precipitants of partner aggression. *Journal of Family Psychology*, 20, 344–347.

O'Leary, S. G., & Vidair, H. B. (2005). Marital adjustment, childrearing disagreements, and overreactive parenting: Predicting child behavior problems. *Journal of Family Psychology*, 19, 208–216.

Ongur, D., & Price, J. L. (2000). The organization of networks within the orbital and medial prefrontal cortex of rats, monkeys and humans. *Cerebral Cortex*, 10, 206–219.

Onoda, K., Okamoto, Y., Nakashima, K., Nittono, H., et al. (2009). Decreased ventral anterior cingulate cortex activity is associated with reduced social pain during emotional support. *Society for Neuroscience*, 4, 443–454.

Orth-Gomer, K. (2009). Are social relations less health protective in women than in men? Social relations, gender, and cardiovascular health. *Journal of Social and Personal Relationships, 26*, 63–71.

Osgood, C. H., May, W. H., & Miron, M. S. (1975). *Cross-cultural universals of affective meaning.* Urbana: University of Illinois Press.

Oster, H. (2005). The repertoire of infant facial expressions: An ontogenetic perspective. In J. Nadel & D. Muir (Eds.), *Emotional development* (pp. 261–292). New York: Oxford University Press.

Ovesey, L. (1962). Fear of vocational success: A phobic extension of the paranoid reaction. *Archives of General Psychiatry, 7*, 82–92.

Owen, J. E., Giese-Davis, J., Cordova, M., Kronenwetter, C., et al. (2006). Self-report and linguistic indicators of emotional expression in narrative as predictors of adjustment to cancer. *Journal of Behavioral Medicine, 29*, 335–345.

Owen, M. T., & Cox, M. J. (1997). Marital conflict and the development of infant-parent attachment relationships. *Journal of Family Psychology, 11*, 152–164.

Pai, A. L., Greenley, R. N., Lewandowski, A., Drotar, E. Y., et al. (2007). A meta-analytic review of the influence of pediatric cancer on parent and family functioning. *Journal of Family Psychology, 21*, 407–415.

Panksepp, J. (1998a). *Affective neuroscience: The foundations of human and animal emotions.* New York: Oxford University Press.

  (1998b). Loneliness and the social bond: The brain sources of sorrow and grief. In J. Panksepp, *Affective neuroscience: The foundations of human and animal emotions* (pp. 261–279). New York, Oxford University Press

  (2005). Why does separation distress hurt? Comment on MacDonald and Leary (2005). *Psychological Bulletin, 131*, 223–230.

  (2008). The affective brain and core consciousness: How does neural activity generate emotional feelings? In M. Lewis, J. M. Haviland-Jones, & L. F. Barrett (Eds.), *Handbook of emotions* (3rd ed., pp. 47–67). New York: Guildford.

Papadatou-Pastou, M., Martin, M., Munafò, M., & Jones, G. (2008). Sex differences in left-handedness: A meta-analysis of 144 studies. *Psychological Bulletin, 134*, 677–699.

Papolos, D., Hennen, J., & Cockerham, M. (2005). Obsessive fears about harm to self or others and overt aggressive behaviors in youth diagnosed with juvenile-onset bipolar disorder. *Journal of Affective Disorders, 89*, 99–105.

Papolos, D., Mattis, S., Golshan, S., & Molay, F. (2009). Fear of harm, a possible phenotype of pediatric bipolar disorder: A dimensional approach to diagnosis for geno-typing psychiatric syndromes. *Journal of Affective Disorders, 118*, 28–38.

Papp, L. M., Goeke-Morey, M. C., & Cummings, E. M. (2007). Linkages between spouses' psychological distress and marital conflict in the home. *Journal of Family Psychology, 21*, 533–537.

Papp, L. M., Kouros, C. D., & Cummings, E. M. (2009). Demand-withdraw patterns in marital conflict in the home. *Personal Relationships, 16*, 285–300.

Parks, M. R., & Floyd, K. (1996). Meanings of closeness and intimacy in friendship. *Journal of Social and Personal Relationships, 13*, 85–108.

Parrott, W. G., & Harre, R. (1996). Embarrassment and the threat to character. In R. Harre & W. G. Parrott (Eds.), *The emotions: Social, cultural and biological dimensions* (pp. 39–56). Thousand Oaks, CA: Sage.

Pasch, L. A., Bradbury, T. N., & Davila, J. (1997). Gender, negative affectivity, and observed social support behavior in marital interaction. *Personal Relationships*, 4, 361–378.

Pasley, K., Kerpelman, J., & Guilbert D. E. (2001). Gendered conflict, identity disruption, and marital instability: Expanding Gottman's model. *Journal of Social and Personal Relationships*, 18, 5–27.

Patrick, C. J. (2007). Affective processes in psychopathy. In J. Rottenberg & S. L. Johnson (Eds.), *Emotion and psychopathology: Bridging affective and clinical science* (pp. 215–239). Washington, DC: American Psychological Association.

Patterson, C. J., Vaden, N. A., & Kupersmidt, J. B. (1991). Family background, recent life events and peer rejection during childhood. *Journal of Social and Personal Relationships*, 8, 347–362.

Pauli-Pott, U., & Beckman, D. (2007). On the association of interparental conflict with developing behavioral inhibition and behavior problems in early childhood. *Journal of Family Psychology*, 2, 529–532.

Pelchat, M. L., Johnson, A., Chan, R., Valdez, J., et al. (2004). Images of desire: food-craving activation during fMRI. *NeuroImage*, 23, 1486–1493.

Pennebaker, J. W. (Ed.). (1995). *Emotion, disclosure, & health*. Washington, DC: American Psychological Association.

  (1997). Writing about emotional experiences as a therapeutic process. *Psychological Science*, 8, 162–166.

  (2001). Explorations into health benefits of disclosure: Inhibitory, cognitive, and social processes. In L. L'Abate (Ed.), *Distance writing and Computer-assisted interventions in psychiatry and mental health* (pp. 157–167). Westport, CT: Ablex.

Pennebaker, J. W., & Beall, S. (1986). Confronting a traumatic event: Toward an understanding of inhibition and disease. *Journal of Abnormal Psychology*, 95, 274–281.

Pennebaker, J. W., & Chung, C. K. (2007). Expressive writing, emotional upheavals, and health. In H. Friedman & B. Silver (Eds.), *Handbook of health psychology* (pp. 263–284). New York: Oxford University Press.

Pereda, N., Guilera, G., Forns, M., & Gomez-Benito, J. (2009). The prevalence of child sexual abuse in community and student samples: A meta-analysis. *Clinical Psychology Review*, 29, 328–338.

Perrine R. M. (1993). On being supportive: The emotional consequences of listening to another's distress. *Journal of Social and Personal Relationships*, 10, 371–384.

Persons, J. B. (2006). Case formulation-driven psychotherapy. *Clinical Psychology: Science and Practice*, 13, 167–170.

Pesonen, A-K, Raikkonen, K., Heinonen, K., Jarvenpaa, A-L., et al. (2006). Depressive vulnerability in parents and their 5-year-old child's temperament: A family system perspective. *Journal of Family Psychology*, 20, 648–655.

Pettit, G. S., & Lollis, S. (1997). Introduction to special issue: Reciprocity and bidirectionality in parent-child relationships: New approaches to the study of enduring issues. *Journal of Social and Personal Relationships*, 14, 435–440.

Pierce, R. A., Nichols, M. P., & DuBrin, J. R. (1983). *Emotional expression in psychotherapy*. New York: Gardner Press.

Phan, K. L., Wager, T., Taylor, S. F., & Liberzon, I. (2002). Functional neuroanatomy of emotion: A meta-analysis of emotion activation studies in PET and fMRI. *NeuroImage*, 16, 331–348.

Phelps, E. A., Labar, K.S., Anderson, A. K., O'Conner, K. J., et al. (1998). Specifying the contributions of the human amygdala to emotional memory: A case study. *Neurocase*, 4, 527–540.

Phillips, M. L., Young, A. W., Senior, C., Brammer, M., et al. (1997). A specific neural substrate for perceiving facial expressions of disgust. *Nature*, 389, 495–498.

Piferi, R. L., Jobe, R. L., & Jones, W. H. (2006). Giving to others during national tragedy: The effects of altruistic and egoistic motivations on long-term giving. *Journal of Social and Personal Relationships*, 23, 171–184.

Ping, R. M., Dhillon, S., & Beilock, S. I. (2009). Reach for what you like: The body's role in shaping preferences. *Emotion Review*, 1, 140–150.

Pinquart, M. (2003). Loneliness in married, widowed, divorced, and never-married older adults. *Journal of Social and Personal Relationships*, 20, 31–54.

Plutchik, R., & Kellerman, H. (Eds.). (1983). *Emotion: Theory, research, and experience. Vol. 2. Emotions in early development.* New York: Academic Press.

Plutchik, R., & Kellerman, H. (Eds.). (1990). *Emotion: Theory, research, and experience. Vol. 5. Emotion, psychopathology, and psychotherapy.* San Diego, CA: Academic Press.

Pogue-Geile, M. F., & Rose, R. J. (1987). Psychopathology: A behavior genetic perspective. In T. Jacob (Ed.), *Family interaction and psychopathology: Theories, methods, and findings* (pp. 629–650). New York: Plenum.

Poehlman, J., Schwichtenberg, A. J. M., Bolt, D., & Dilworth-Bart, J. (2009). Predictors of depressive symptom trajectories in mothers of preterm or low-birth weight infants. *Journal of Family Psychology*, 23, 690–704.

Pons, F., Harris, P. L., & de Rosnay, M. (2004). Emotion comprehension between 3 and 11 years: Developmental periods of hierarchical organization. *European Journal of Developmental Psychology*, 1, 127–152.

Post, S. G. (Ed.). (2007). *Altruism & health: Perspectives from empirical research.* New York: Oxford University Press.

Power, M., & Dalgleish, T. (1997). *Cognition and emotion: From order to disorder.* Hove: Psychology Press.

Prager, K. J. (1995). *The psychology of intimacy.* New York: Guilford.

Prager, K. J., & Buhrmester, D. (1998). Intimacy and need fulfillment in couple relationships. *Journal of Social and Personal Relationships*, 15, 435–469.

Pressman, D. L., & Bonanno, G. A. (2007). With whom do we grieve? Social and cultural determinants of grief processing in the United States and China. *Personal Relationships*, 24, 729–746.

Previti, D., & Amato, P. R. (2004). Is infidelity a cause or a consequence of poor marital quality? *Journal of Social and Personal Relationships*, 21, 217–230.

Prinz, J. (2010). For valence. *Emotion Review*, 2, 5–13.

Proulx, C. M., Buehler, C., & Helms, H. (2009). Moderators of the link between marital hostility and change in spouses' depressive symptoms. *Journal of Family Psychology*, 23, 540–550.

Proulx, C. M., Helms, H. M., Milardo, R. M., & Payne, C. C. (2009). Relational support from friends and wives' family relationships: The role of husbands' interference. *Journal of Social and Personal Relationships*, 26, 195–210.

Ptacek, J., Pierce, G., Dodge, K., & Ptacek, J. (1997). Social support in spouses of cancer patients: What do they get and to what end? *Personal Relationships*, 4, 431–449.

Pugliese, J., & Tinsley, B. (2007). Parental socialization of child and adolescent physical activity. *Journal of Family Psychology*, 21, 331–340.

Quirk, G. J. (2007). Pre-fronta-amygdala interactions in the regulation of fear. In J. J. Gross (Ed.), *Handbook of emotion regulation* (pp. 27–46). New York: Guilford.

Raichle, M. E., MacLeod, A. M., Snyder, A. Z., Powers, W. J., Gusnard, D. A., & Shulman, G. L. (2001). A default mode of brain function. *Proceedings of the National Academy of Sciences USA*, 98, 676–682.

Ragarajan, S., & Kelly, L. (2006). Family communication patterns, family environment, and the influence of parental alcoholism on offspring self-esteem. *Journal of Social and Personal Relationships*, 23, 655–671.

Ramirez, A., & Broneck, K. (2009). "IM me": Instant messaging as relational maintenance and everyday communication. *Journal of Social and Personal Relationships*, 26(2–3), 291–314.

Rapee, R. M. (Ed.). (1996). *Current controversies in the anxiety disorders*. New York: Guilford.

Rauch, S. L., Whalen, P. J., Shin, L. M., McInerney, S. C., et al. (2000). Exaggerated amygdala response to masked facial stimuli in posttraumatic stress disorder: A functional MRI study. *Biological Psychiatry*, 47, 769–776.

Ray, G. E., Cohen. R., Secrist, M. E., & Duncan, M. K. (1997). Relating aggressive and victimization behaviors to children's sociometric status and friendships. *Journal of Social and Personal Relationships*, 14, 95–108.

Ray, R. D., Ochsner, K. N., Cooper, J. C., Robertson, E. R., Gabrieli, J. D., & Gross, J. J. (2005). Individual differences in trait rumination and the neural systems supporting cognitive reappraisal. *Cognitive, Affective, and Behavioral Neuroscience*, 5, 156–168.

Reddy, W. M. (2009). Historical research on the self and emotions. *Emotion Review*, 1, 302–315.

Reeb, B. T., & Conger, K. J. (2009). The unique effect of parental depressive symptoms on adolescent functioning: Associations with gender and father-adolescent relationship closeness. *Journal of Family Psychology*, 23, 758–761.

Register, L. M., & Henley, T. B. (1992). The phenomenology of intimacy. *Journal of Social and Personal Relationships*, 9, 467–481.

Rehman, U., & Holtzworth-Munroe, A. (2006). A cross cultural analysis of the demand withdraw marital interaction: Observing couples from a developing country. *Journal of Consulting and Clinical Psychology*, 74, 755–766.

Reinhardt, J. P., Boerner, K., & Horowitz, A. (2006). Good to have but not to use: Differential impact of perceived and received support on well-being. *Journal of Social and Personal Relationships*, 23, 117–130.

Reis, H. T. (2002). Action matters, but relationship science is basic. *Journal of Social and Personal Relationships*, 19, 601–612.

(2007). Steps toward the ripening of relationship science. *Personal Relationships*, 14, 1–24.

Reis, H. T., & Franks, P. (1994). The role of intimacy and social support in health outcomes: Two processes or one? *Personal Relationships*, 1, 185–197.

Reis, H. T. & Shaver, P. (1988). Intimacy as an interpersonal process. In S. W. Duck (Ed.), *Handbook of relationships* (pp. 367–389). Chichester: Wiley.

Reisenszein, R., & Doring, S. A. (2009). Ten perspectives on emotional experience: Introduction to a special issue. *Emotion Review*, 1, 195–205.

Rempel, J. K., & Burris, C. T. (2005). Let me count the ways: An integrative theory of love and hate. *Personal Relationships*, 12, 297–314.

Repinski, D. J., & Zook, J. M. (2005). Three measures of closeness in adolescents' relationships with parents and friends: Variations and developmental significance. *Personal Relationships*, 12, 79–102.

Rhoades, G. K., Stanley, S. M., & Markman, H. J. (2006). Pre-engagement cohabitation and gender asymmetry in marital commitment. *Journal of Family Psychology*, 20, 553–560.

Richmond, M. K., & Stocker, C. M. (2006). Associations between family cohesion and adolescent siblings externalizing behavior. *Journal of Family Psychology*, 20, 663–669.

Rief, W., & Broadbent, E. (2007). Explaining medically unexplained symptoms-models and mechanisms. *Clinical Psychology Review*, 27, 821–841.

Rime, B. (2009a). Emotion elicits the social sharing of emotion: Theory and empirical review. *Emotion Review*, 1, 60–85.

(2009b). More on the social sharing of emotion: In defense of the individual, of culture, of private disclosure, and in rebuttal of an old couple of ghosts known as "cognition and emotion." *Emotion Review*, 1, 94–96.

Rini, C., Schetter, C. D., Hobel, C. J. Glynn, L. M., & Sandman, C. A. (2006). Effective social support: Antecedents and consequences of partner support during pregnancy. *Personal Relationships*, 13, 207–230.

Robinson, K. E., Gerhardt, C. A., Vannatta, K., & Noll, R. B. (2009). Survivors of childhood cancer and comparison peers: The influence of early family factors on distress in emerging adulthood. *Journal of Family Psychology*, 23, 23–31.

Roelofs, K., & Spinhoven, P. (2007). Trauma and medically unexplained symptoms: Towards an integration of cognitive and neurological accounts. *Clinical Psychology Review*, 27, 79821.

Roemer, L., Salters, K., Raffa, S. D. & Orsillo, S. M. (2005). Fear and avoidance of internal experience in GAD: Preliminary tests of a conceptual model. *Cognitive Therapy & Research*, 29, 71–88.

Rogge, R. D., Bradbury, T. N., Hahlweg, K., Engl, J., & Turmaier, F. (2006). Predicting marital distress and dissolution: Refining the two-factor hypothesis. *Journal of Family Psychology*, 20, 156–159.

Rogstad, J. E., & Rogers, R. (2008). Gender differences in contributions of emotion to psychopath and antisocial personality disorder. *Clinical Psychology Review*, 28, 1472–1484.

Rohrbaugh, M. J., Cranford, J. A., Shoham, V., Nicklas, J. M., Sonnega, J. S., & Coyne, J. C. (2002). Couples coping with congestive heart failure: Role and gender differences in psychological distress. *Journal of Family Psychology*, 16, 1–13.

Roloff, M. E., Putman, L. L., & Anastasiou, L. (2003). Negotiation skills. In J. O. Greene & B. R. Burleson (Eds.), *Handbook of communication and social interaction skills* (pp. 801–833). Mahwah, NJ: Erlbaum.

Roloff, M. E., Soule, K. P., & Carey, C. M. (2001). Reasons for remaining in a relationship and responses to relational transgression. *Journal of Social and Personal Relationships*, 18, 362–385.

Romero, C. (2008). Writing wrongs: Promoting forgiveness through expressive writing. *Personal Relationships*, 25, 625–642.

Ronel, N., & Lebel, U. (2006). When parents lay their children to rest: Between anger and forgiveness. *Journal of Social and Personal Relationships*, 23, 50–522.

Rood, L., Roelofs, J., Bogels, S., Nolen- Hoeksema, S., & Schouten, E. (2009). The influence of emotion-focused rumination and distraction on depressive symptoms in non-clinical youth: A meta-analytic review. *Clinical Psychology Review*, 29, 607–616.

Rook, K. S. (2009). Gaps in social support resources in later life: An adaptational challenge in need of further research. *Journal of Social and Personal Relationships*, 26, 103–112.

Rook, K. S., & Ituarte, P. H. G. (1999). Social control, social support, and companionship in older adults' family relationships and friendships. *Personal Relationships*, 6, 199–211.

Root, L. M., & McCullough, M. E. (2007). Low-cost interventions for promoting forgiveness. In L. L'Abate (Ed.), *Low-cost approaches to promote physical and mental health* (pp. 415–434). New York: Springer.

Rotenberg, K. J. (1998). Stigmatization of transitions in loneliness. *Journal of Social and Personal Relationships*, 15, 565–576.

Rotenberg, K. J., & Kmill, J. (1992). Perception of lonely and non-lonely persons as a function of individual differences in loneliness. *Journal of Social and Personal Relationships*, 9, 325–330.

Rotenberg, K. J., Mars, K., & Crick, N. (1987). Development of children's sadness. *Psychology & Human Development*, 2, 13–25.

Rottenberg, J. (2007). Major depressive disorder: Emerging evidence for emotion context insensitivity. In J. Rottenberg & S. L. Johnson (Eds.), *Emotion and psychopathology: Bridging affective and clinical science* (pp. 151–165). Washington, DC: American Psychological Association.

Rottenberg, J., & Gross, J. J. (2003). When emotion goes wrong: Realizing the promise of affective science. *Clinical Psychology: Science and Practice*, 10, 227–232.

(2007). Emotion and emotion regulation: A map for psychotherapy researchers. *Clinical Psychology: Science and Practice*, 14, 323–328.

Rottenberg, J., Shewchuk, V. A., & Kimberley, T. (2001). Loneliness, sex, and romantic jealousy, and powerlessness. *Journal of Social and Personal Relationships*, 18, 55–80.

Rottenberg, J., & Vaughan, C. (2008). Emotion expression in depression: Emerging evidence for emotion context-insensitivity. In A. Vingerhoets, I. Nyklicek, & J. Denollet (Eds.), *Emotion regulation: Conceptual and clinical issues* (pp. 125–139). New York: Springer.

Rozin, P., Haidt, J., & McCauley, C. R. (2008). Disgust. In M. Lewis, J. M. Haviland-Jones, & L. Feldman Barrett (Eds.), *Handbook of emotions* (3rd ed., pp. 757–776). New York: Guilford.

Rudy, D., & Grusec, J. E. (2006). Authoritarian parenting in individualistic and collectivist groups: Associations with maternal emotion and cognition and children's self-esteem. *Journal of Family Psychology*, 20, 68–78.

Rumbaugh, D. M., & Gill, T. V. (1976). The mastery of language-type skills in the chimpanzee (Pan). *Annals of the New York Academy of Sciences*, 280, 562–578.

Rumbaugh, D. M., & Washburn, D. A. (2003). *Intelligence of ape and other rational human beings.* New Haven, CT: Yale University Press.

Rusburt, C. A., Arriaga, X. B., & Agnew, C. R. (2003). Interdependence in close relationships. In G. J. O. Fletcher & M. S. Clark (Eds.), *Blackwell handbook of social psychology: Interpersonal processes* (pp. 359–387). Malden, MA: Blackwell.

Rusbult, C. E., & Buunk, B. P. (1993). Commitment processes in close relationships: An interdependence analysis. *Journal of Social and Personal Relationships*, 10, 175–204.

Rusbult, C. E., Kumashiro, M., Coolsen, M. K., & Kirchner, J. L. (2004). Interdependence, closeness, and relationships. In D. J. Mashek & A. Aron (Eds.), *Handbook of closeness and intimacy* (pp. 137–161). Mahwah, NJ: Erlbaum.

Rusbult, C. E., & Van Lange, P. A. M. (2003). Interdependence, interaction, and relationships. *Annual Review of Psychology*, 60, 53–78.

Ruscio, A. M., & Holohan, D. R. (2006). Applying empirically supported treatment to complex cases: Ethical, empirical, and practical considerations. *Clinical Psychology: Science and Practice*, 13, 146–162.

Russell, D., Peplau, L. A., & Cutrona, C. E. (1980). The Revised UCLA Loneliness Scale. *Journal of Personality and Social Psychology*, 39, 461–480.

Russell, J. A. (1980). A circumplex model of affect. *Journal of Personality and Social Psychology*, 39, 1161–1178.

Russell, J. A., & Barrett, L. F. (1999). Core affect, prototypical emotional episodes, and other things called *emotion*: Dissecting the elephant. *Journal of Personality and Social Psychology*, 76, 805–819.

Russell, J. A., & Carroll, J. M. (1999a). On the bipolarity of positive and negative emotions. *Psychological Bulletin*, 125, 3–30.

(1999b). The Phoenix of bipolarity: Reply to Watson and Tellegen (1999). *Psychological Bulletin*, 125, 611–627.

Russell, T. A., Reynaud, E. E., Kucharska-Pietura, K. K., Ecker, C. C., Benson, P. J., Zelaya, F. F., & Phillips, M. L. (2007). Neural responses to dynamic expressions of fear in schizophrenia. *Neuropsychologia*, 45, 107–123.

Rutter, M. (1994). Family discord and conduct disorder: Cause, consequences, or correlates? *Journal of Family Psychology*, 8, 170–186.

Ryan, R. M., La Guardia, J. G., Solky-Butzel. J. G., Chirkov, Y., & Kim, Y. (2005). On the interpersonal regulation of emotions: Emotional resilience cross gender, relationships and cultures. *Personal Relationships*, 12, 145–163.

Saarela, M. V., Hlushchuk, Y., Williams, A. C., Schurmann, M., Kalso, E., & Hari, R. (2007). The compassionate brain: Humans detect intensity of pain from another's face. *Cerebral Cortex*, 17, 230–237.

Saarni, C. (1999). *The development of emotional competence*. New York: Guilford.

(2008). The interface of emotional development with social context. In M. Lewis, J. M. Haviland-Jones, & L. F. Barrett (Eds.), *Handbook of emotions*. (3rd ed., pp. 332–347). New York: Guilford.

Safford, S. M. (2008). Gender and depression in men: Extending beyond depression and extending beyond gender. *Clinical Psychology: Science and Practice*, 15, 169–173.

Saffrey, C., & Ehrenberg, M. (2007). When thinking hurts: Attachment, rumination, and postrelationship adjustment. *Personal Relationships*, 14, 351–368.

Safran, J. D. & Greenberg, L. S. (1991). *Emotion, psychotherapy and change*. New York: Guilford Press.

Sagarin, B. J., & Guadagno, R. E. (2004). Sex differences in the context of extreme jealousy. *Personal Relationships*, 11, 319–328.

Sahakian, A., & Frishman, W. (2007). Humor and the cardiovascular system. *Alternative Therapies in Health and Medicine*, 13, 56–58.

Saitzyk, A. R., Floyd, F. J., & Kroll, A. B. (1997). Sequential analysis of autonomy-interdependence and affiliation-disaffiliation in couples' social support interactions. *Personal Relationships*, 4, 341–360.

Sakinofsky, I. (2007). The aftermath of suicide: Managing survivors' bereavement. *Canadian Journal of Psychiatry*, 52, 1295–1365.

Salmivalli, C. (2001). Group view on victimization: Empirical findings and their implications. In J. Juvonen & S. Graham (Eds.), *Peer harassment in school: The plight of the vulnerable and victimized* (pp. 398–419). New York: Guilford.

Salovey, P., Woolery, A., & Mayer, J. B. (2003). Emotional intelligence: Conceptualization and measurement. In G. J. O. Fletcher & M. S. Clark (Eds.), *Blackwell handbook of social psychology: Interpersonal processes* (pp. 279–307). Malden, MA: Blackwell.

Samter, W., Whaley, B. R., Mortenson, S. T., & Burleson, B. R. (1997). Ethnicity and emotional support in same-sex friendship: A comparison of Asian-Americans, African-Americans, and Euro-Americans. *Personal Relationships*, 4, 413–430.

Sanderson. C. A., Rahm, K. B., & Beigbeder, S. A. (2005). The link between the pursuit of intimacy goals and satisfaction in close same-sex friendships: An examination of the underlying processes. *Journal of Social and Personal Relationships*, 22, 75–98.

Sandler, J., & Joffe, W. C. (1965). Notes on childhood depression. *International Journal of Psychoanalysis*, 46, 88–96.

Sanfilippo, M. P. (1993). Depression, gender, gender role traits, and the wish to be help. *Sex Roles*, 28, 583–605.

Sanford, K. (2003). Expectancies and communication behavior in marriage: Distinguishing proximal level effects from distal-level effects. *Journal of Social and Personal Relationships*, 20, 391–402.

(2005). Attributions and anger in early marriage: Wives are event-dependent and husbands are schematic. *Journal of Family Psychology*, 19, 180–188.

(2006). Communication during marital conflict: When couples change their appraisals, they change their behavior. *Journal of Family Psychology*, 20, 256–265.

(2007). Hard and soft emotions during conflict: Investigating married couples and other relationships. *Personal Relationships*, 14, 65–90.

Sanford, K., & Rowatt, W. C. (2004). When Is negative emotion positive for relationships? An investigation of married couples and roommates. *Personal Relationships*, 11, 329–354.

Sapolsky, R. M. (2007). Stress, stress-related disease, and emotional regulation. In J. J. Gross (Ed.), *Handbook of emotion regulation* (pp. 606–614). New York: Guilford.

Sarason, I. G., & Sarason, B. R. (2009). Social support: Mapping the construct. *Journal of Social and Personal Relationships*, 26, 113–120.

Sarason, I. G., Sarason, B. R., & Pierce, G. R. (1994). Social support: Global and relationship-based levels of analysis. *Journal of Social and Personal Relationships*, 11, 295–312.

Sarwer-Foner, G. (1979). On social paranoia: The psychotic fear of the stranger and that which is alien. *Psychiatric Journal of the University of Ottawa*, 4, 21–34.

Saxe, B., & Johnson, S. M. (1999). An empirical investigation of group treatment for a clinical population of adult female incest survivors. *Journal of Child Sexual Abuse: Research, Treatment, & Program Innovations for Victims, Survivors, & Offenders*, 8, 67–88.

Saxena, S. (2008). Recent advances in compulsive hording. *Current Psychiatric Reports*, 10, 297–303.

Sbarra, D. A., & Emery, R. E. (2005). The emotional sequelae of nonmarital relational dissolution: Analysis of change and intraindividual variability over time. *Personal Relationships*, 12, 213–232.

Scarnier, M., Schmader, T., & Lickel, B. (2009). Parental shame and guilt: Distinguishing emotional responses to a child's wrongdoing. *Personal Relationships*, 16, 205–220.

Schaefer, M. T., & Olson, D. H. (1981). Assessing intimacy: The PAIR inventory. *Journal of Marriage and Family Therapy*, 7, 47–60.

Scheier, M. F., & Carver, C. S. (1992). Effects of optimism on psychological and physical well-being: Theoretical overview and empirical update. *Cognitive Therapy and Research*, 16, 201–228.

Schmitt, D. P., and 130 Members of the International Sexuality Description Project (2003). Are men universally more dismissing than women? Gender differences in romantic attachment across 62 cultural regions. *Personal Relationships*, 10, 307–332.

Schmookler, T., & Bursik, K. (2007). The value of monogamy in emerging adulthood: A gendered perspective. *Journal of Social and Personal Relationships*, 24, 819–835.

Schulte, M. T., Ramo, D., & Brown, S. A. (2009). Gender differences in factors influencing alcohol use and drinking progression among adolescents. *Clinical Psychology Review*, 29, 535–547.

Schwarzer, R., & Leppin, A. (1991). Social support and health: A theoretical and empirical overview. *Journal of Social and Personal Relationships*, 8, 99–128.

Schwarzer, R., & Weiner, B. (1991). Stigma controllability and coping as predictors of emotions and social support. *Journal of Social and Personal Relationships*, 8, 133–140.

Scinta, A., & Gable, S. L. (2005). Performance comparisons and attachment: An investigation of competitive responses in close relationships. *Personal Relationships*, 12, 357–372.

Segal, D. L., Tucker, H. C., & Coolidge, F. L. (2009). A comparison of positive versus negative emotional expression in a written disclosure study among distressed students. *Journal of Aggression, Maltreatment, & Trauma*, 18, 367–381.

Segrin, C., Badger, T.A., Meek, P., Lopez, A.M., Bonham, E., & Sieger, A. (2005). Dyadic interdependence on affect and quality-of-life trajectories among women with breast cancer and their partners. *Journal of Social and Personal Relationships*, 22, 673–689.

Segrin, C., Powell, H. L., Givertz, M., & Braokin, A. (2003). Symptoms of depression, relational quality, and loneliness in dating relationships. *Personal Relationships,* 10, 25–36.

Seime, R. J., & Vickers, K. S. (2006). The challenges of treating depression with exercise: From evidence to practice. *Clinical Psychology: Science and Practice*, 13, 194–197.

Selva, P., & Coughlin, D. (2006). Emotional processing in the treatment of psychosomatic disorders. *Journal of Clinical Psychology*, 62, 539–550.

Selvini, M. (1997). Family secrets: The case of the patient kept in the dark. *Contemporary Family Therapy: An International Journal*, 19, 315–336.

Seltzer, M. M., & Heller, T. (1997). Families and caregiving across the life course: Research advances on the influence of context. *Family Relations: Interdisciplinary Journal of Applied Family Studies*, 46, 321–324.

Senn, T. E., Carey, M. P., Vanable, P. A., Coury-Doniger, P., et al. (2006). Childhood sexual abuse and sexual risk behavior among men and women attending a sexually transmitted disease clinic. *Journal of Consulting and Clinical Psychology*, 74, 720–731.

Shabad, P. (2001). *Despair and the return of hope: Echoes of mourning in psychotherapy*. Northvale, NJ: Aronson.

Shackelford, T.K., Goetz, A. T., Buss, D. M., Euler, H. A., & Hoier, S. (2005). When we hurt the ones we love: Predicting violence against women from men's mate retention. *Personal Relationships*, 12, 447–464.

Shapiro, E.K., & Weber, E. (Eds.). (1982). *Cognitive and affective growth: Developmental interaction*. Hillsdale, NJ: Erlbaum.

Shaver, P. (Ed.). (1984). *Review of personality and social psychology* (Vol. 5). Newbury Park, CA: Sage.

Shaver, P. R., Mikulincer, M., Lavy, S., & Cassidy, J. (2009). Understanding and altering hurt feelings: An attachment theoretical perspective on the generation and regulation of emotions. In A. L. Vangelisti (Ed.), *Handbook of hurt feelings in close relationships* (pp. 92–122). New York: Cambridge University Press.

Shaver, P. R., Schwartz, J., Kirson, D., & O'Connor, C. (1987). Emotion knowledge: Further exploration of a prototypes approach. *Journal of Personality and Social Psychology*, 52, 1061–1086.

Sher, T. G., & Baucom, D. H. (1993). Marital communication: Differences among martially distressed, depressed, and nondistressed-nondepressed couples. *Journal of Family Psychology*, 7, 148–153.

Sherman, M. D., & Thelen, M. H. (1996). Fear of Intimacy Scale: Validation and extension with adolescents. *Journal of Social and Personal Relationships*, 13, 507–522.

Shortt, J. W., Capaldi, D. M., Kim, H. K., & Owen, L. D. (2006). Relationship separation for young, at-risk couples: Prediction from dyadic aggression. *Journal of Family Psychology*, 20, 624–631.

Shrout, P. E., Herman, C. M., & Bolger, N. (2006). The costs and benefits of practical and emotional support on adjustment: A daily diary study of couples experiencing acute stress. *Personal Relationships*, 13, 115–134.

Shweder, R. A., Haidt, J. Horton, R., & Joseph, C. (2008). The cultural psychology of the emotions: Ancient and renewed. In M. Lewis, H. M. Haviland-Jones, & L. F. Barrett (Eds.), *Handbook of emotions* (3rd ed., pp. 409–426). New York: Guilford.

Silverstein, B. (2002). Gender differences in the prevalence of somatic versus pure depression: A replication. *American Journal of Psychiatry*, 159, 1051–1052.

Simonton, D. K. (2008). Creativity and genius. In O. P. John, R. W. Robins, & L. A. Pervin (Ed.), *Handbook of personality: Theory and research* (pp. 679–699). New York: Guilford.

Singer, T., Seymour, B., O'Doherty, J., Kaube, H., Dolan, R. J., & Frith, C. D. (2004). Empathy for pain involves the affective but not sensory components of pain. *Science*, 303, 1157–1162.

Skopp, N. A., McDonald, R., Jouriles, E. N., & Rosenfield, D. (2007). Partner aggression and children's externalizing problems: Maternal and paternal warmth as protective factors. *Journal of Family Psychology*, 21, 459–467.

Slep, A. M. S., & O' Leary, S. G. (2009). Distinguishing risk profiles among parent-only, and dually perpetrating physical aggression. *Journal of Family Psychology*, 23, 705–716.

Slesnick, N., & Waldron, H. B. (1997). Interpersonal problem-solving interactions of depressed adolescents and their parents. *Journal of Family Psychology*, 11, 234–245.

Sloan, D. M., & Kring, A. M. (2007). Measuring changes in emotion during psychotherapy: Conceptual and methodological issues. *Clinical Psychology: Science and Practice*, 14, 307–322.

Sloan, E. P., & Shapiro, C. M. (1995). Gender differences on sleep disorders. In M. V. Seeman (Ed.), *Gender and psychopathology* (pp. 269–285). Washington, DC: American Psychiatric Press, Inc.

Smith, E. R., & Mackie, D. M. (2008). Intergroup emotions. In M. Lewis. J., Haviland-Jones, and L. F. Barrett (Eds.), *Handbook of emotions* (3rd ed., pp. 429–438). New York: Guilford.

Smith, G. T., Fischer, S., Cyders, M. A., Annus, A. M. et al. (2007). On the validity and utility of discriminating among impulsivity-like traits. *Assessment*, 14, 155–170.

Smith, S. B., Davidson, J., & Ball, P. (2001). Age-related variations and sex differences in gender cleavage during middle childhood. *Personal Relationships*, 8, 153–166.

Smith, T. W. (2006). Blood, sweat, and tears: Exercise in the management of mental and physical health problems. *Clinical Psychology: Science and Practice*,13, 198–202.

Smyth, J. M., & L'Abate, L. (2001). A meta-analytic evaluation of workbook effectiveness in physical and mental health, In L. L'Abate (Ed.), *Distance writing and computer-assisted interventions in psychiatry and mental health* (pp. 77–90). Westport, CT: Ablex.

Snapp, C. M., & Leary, M. R. (2001). Hurt feelings among new acquaintances: Moderating effects of interpersonal familiarity. *Journal of Social and Personal Relationships*, 18, 315–326.

Snyder, C. R., & Ingram, R. E. (Eds.) (2000). *Handbook of psychological change: Psychotherapy processes & practices for the 21st century.* New York: Wiley.

Snyder, J. K., Kirkpatrick, L. A., & Barrett, H. C. (2008). The dominance dilemma: Do women really prefer dominant men? *Personal Relationships*, 15, 425–444.

Solomon, S. H., & Knobloch, L. K. (2004). A model of relational turbulence: The role of intimacy, relational uncertainty, and interference from partners in appraisals of irritations. *Journal of Social and Personal Relationships*, 21, 795–816.

Somerville, L. H., Heatherton, T. F., & Kelley, W. M. (2006). Anterior cingulate cortex responds differentially to expectancy violation and social rejection. *Nature Neuroscience*, 9, 1007–1008.

Spence, J. T. (1985). Gender identity and its implications for the concepts of masculinity and femininity. In T. B. Sonderegger (Ed.), *Nebraska symposium on motivation 1984* (pp. 59–95). Lincoln, NE: University of Nebraska Press.

Spence, S. H., Holmes, J. M., March, S., & Lipp, O. V. (2006). The feasibility and outcome of clinic plus Internet delivery of cognitive-behavior therapy for childhood anxiety. *Journal of Consulting and Clinical Psychology*, 74, 614–621.

Spiegel, J. (1971). *Transactions: The interplay between individual, family, and society.* New York: Science House.

Spielberger, C. D., Reheiser, E. C., & Sydeman, S. J. (1995). Measuring the experience, expression, and control of anger. In H. Kassinove (Ed.,), *Anger disorders: Definitions, diagnosis, and treatment* (pp. 49–76).Washington, DC: Taylor & Francis.

Spitzberg, B. H. (2009). Aggression, violence, and hurt in close relationships. In A. L. Vangelisti (Ed.), *Handbook of hurt feelings in close relationships* (pp. 209–233). New York: Cambridge University Press.

Spotts, E. L., Prescott, C., & Kendler, K. (2006). Examining the origins of gender differences in marital quality: A behavioral genetic analysis. *Journal of Family Psychology*, 21

Sprecher, S., & Fehr, B. (2005). Compassionate love for close others and humanity. *Journal of Social and Personal Relationships*, 22, 629–652.

Sprecher, S., Felmlee, D., Metts, S., Fehr, B., & Vanni, D. (1998). Factors associated with distress following the breakup of a close relationship. *Journal of Social and Personal Relationships*, 15, 791–809.

Stanley, S. M., & Markman, H. J. (1992). Assessing commitment in personal relationships. *Journal of Marriage and the Family*, 54, 595–608.

Stathopoulou, G., Powers, M. B., & Berry, A. C., Smits, J. A. J., et al. (2006). Exercise intervention in mental health: A quantitative and qualitative review. *Clinical Psychology: Science and Practice*, 13, 179–193.

Stearns, C. Z. (1993). Sadness. In M. Lewis, & J. M. Haviland-Jones (Eds.), *Handbook of emotions.* (1st ed., pp. 547–561). New York: Guildford.

Stearns, F. R. (1972). *Laughing: Physiology, pathophysiology, psychology, pathopsychology and development.* Sprinfield, IL: C. C. Thomas.

Stearns, P. N. (2008). History of emotions: Issues of change and impact. In M. Lewis, & J. M. Haviland-Jones, & L. F. Barrett (Eds.), *Handbook of emotions.* (3rd ed., pp. 17–31). New York: Guildford.

Stefanacci, L., & Amaral, D. G., (2000). Topographic organization of cortical inputs to the lateral nucleus of the macaque monkey amygdala: a retrograde tracing study. *The Journal of Comparative Neurology, 421,* 52–79.

Stegge, H., & Terwogt, M. M. (2007). Awareness and regulation of emotion in typical and atypical development. In J. J. Gross (Ed.), *Handbook of emotion regulation* (pp. 269–286). New York: Guilford.

Steiner-Pappalardo, N. L., & Gurung, R. A. R. (2002).The femininity effect: Relationship quality, sex, gender, attachment, and significant-other concepts. *Personal Relationships, 9,* 313–325.

Stets, J. E., & Turner, J. H. (2008). The sociology of emotions. In M. Lewis. J. M. Haviland-Jones, & L. F. Barrett (Eds.), *Handbook of emotions* (3rd ed., pp. 32–46). New York: Guilford.

Stevens, F. E., & L'Abate, L. (1989). Validity and reliability of a theory-derived measure of intimacy. *American Journal of Family Therapy, 17,* 359–368.

Stockdale, B. (2009). *You can beat the odds: Surprising factors behind chronic illness and cancer.* Boulder, CO: Sentient Publications.

Stocker, C. M., & Richmond, M. S. (2007). Longitudinal associations between hostility in adolescents' family relationships and friendships and hostility in their romantic relationships. *Journal of Family Psychology, 21,* 490–497.

Stoff, D.M., Breiling, J., & Maser, J.D. (Eds.). (1997). *Handbook of antisocial behavior.* Hoboken, NJ: Wiley.

Storch, E. A., Ledley, D. R., Lewin, A. B., Murphy, T. K., et al. (2006). Peer victimization in children with obsessive-compulsive disorder: Relations with symptoms of psychopathology. *Journal of Clinical Child and Adolescent Psychology, 35,* 446–455.

Story, L. B., & Repetti, R. (2006). Daily occupational stressors and marital behavior. *Journal of Family Psychology, 20,* 690–700.

Strauss, M. A., & Douglas, E. M. (2008). Research on spanking by parents: Implications for public policy. *The Family Psychologist, 24,* 18–20.

Strazdins, L. M., Galligan, R. F., & Scannell, E. D. (1997). Gender and depressive symptoms: Parents's sharing of instrumental and expressive tasks when their children are young. *Journal of Family Psychology, 11,* 222–232.

Street, A. E., Gradus, J. L., Stafford, J., & Kelly, K. (2007). Gender differences in experiences of sexual harassment: Data from a male-dominated environment. *Journal of Consulting and Clinical Psychology, 75,* 464–474.

Sturge-Apple, M. L., Davies, P. T., & Cummings, E. M. (2006). Hostility and withdrawal in marital conflict: Effects of parental emotional unavailability and inconsistent discipline. *Journal of Family Psychology, 20,* 227–238.

Surra, C. A., Curran, M. A. & Williams, K. (2009). Effects of participation in a longitudinal study of dating. *Personal Relationships, 16,* 1–22.

Surra, C. A., & Perlman, D. (2003). Introduction: The many faces of context. *Personal Relationships, 10,* 283–284.

Suveg, C., Southam-Gerow, M. A., Goodman, K. L., & Kendall, P. C. (2007). The role of emotion theory and research in child therapy development. *Clinical Psychology: Science and Practice*, 14, 358–31.

Szapocznik, J., & Prado, G. (2007). Negative effects of family functioning from prosocial treatment: A recommendation for expanded safety monitoring. *Journal of Family Psychology*, 21, 468–478.

Tafa, M., & Baiocco, R. (2009). Addictive behavior and family functioning during adolescence. *American Journal of Family Therapy*, 37, 388–395.

Taft, C. T., O'Farrell, T. J., Torres, S. E., Panuzio, J., Monson, C. M., Murphy, M., & Murphy, C. M. (2006). Examining the correlates of psychological aggression among a community sample of couples. *Journal of Family Psychology*, 20, 581–588.

Taft, C. T., Vogt, D. S., Mechanic, M. B., & Resick, P. A. (2007). Posttraumatic stress disorder and physical health symptoms among women seeking help for relationship aggression. *Journal of Family Psychology*, 21, 354–359.

Tangney, J. P., & Fischer, K. W. (Eds.). (1995). *Self-conscious emotions: The psychology of shame, guilt, embarrassment, and pride*. New York: Guilford.

Taraban, C. B., & Hendrick, C. (1995). Personality perceptions associated with six styles of love. *Journal of Social and Personal Relationships*, 12, 453–462.

Taylor, J. (1996). Guilt and remorse. In R. Harre' & W. G. Parrott (Eds.), *The emotions: Social, cultural, and biological dimensions* (pp. 57–73). Thousand Oaks, CA: Sage.

Teachman, B., & Allen, J. (2007). Development of social anxiety: Social interaction predictors of implicit and explicit fear of negative evaluation. *Journal of Abnormal Child Psychology*, 35, 63–78.

Teicher, M. H., Samson, J. A., Polcari, A., & McGreenery, C. E. (2006). Sticks, stones, and hurtful words: Relative effects of various forms of childhood maltreatment. *American Journal of Psychiatry*, 163, 993–1000.

Tenser, S. A., Murray, D. W., Vaughan, C. A., & Sacco, W. P. (2006). Maternal depressive symptoms, relationship satisfaction, and verbal behavior: A social-cognitive analysis. *Journal of Social and Personal Relationships*, 23, 131–150.

Terhell, E. L., Broese van Groenou, M. I., & van Tilburg, T. (2004). Networking dynamics in the long-term period after divorce. *Journal of Social and Personal Relationships*, 21, 719–738.

Thamm, R. A. (2006). The classification of emotions. In J. E. Stets & J. H. Turner (Eds), *Handbook of the sociology of emotions* (pp. 11–37). New York: Springer.

Thayer, R. E. (1989). *The biopsychology of mood and arousal*. New York: Oxford University Press.

(1996). *The origin of everydaymoods: Managing energy, tension, and stress*. New York: Oxford University Press.

Thompson, R. (1998). Emotional competence and the development of self. *Psychological Inquiry*, 9, 308–309.

Thompson, R. A., & Meyer, S. (2007). Socialization of emotional regulation in the family. In J. J. Gross (Ed.), *Handbook of emotion regulation* (pp. 249–267). New York: Guilford.

Thompson, R. J., & Berenbaum, H. (2009). The association between rejection and depression in the context of women's relationships with their parents. *Journal of Social and Personal Relationships*, 26, 327–339.

Tolstedt, B. E., & Stokes, J. P. (1984). Self-disclosure, intimacy, and the depenetration process. *Journal of Personality and Social Psychology*, 46, 84–90.

Tomkins, S. S. (1962). *Affect, imagery, and consciousness: Vol. 1. The positive effects.* New York: Springer-Verlag.

(1963). *Affect, imagery, and consciousness: Vol. 2. The negative effects.* New York: Springer-Verlag.

Toner, B. B. (1995). Gender differences in somatoform disorders. In M. V. Seeman (Ed.), *Gender and psychopathology* (pp. 287–309). Washington, DC: American Psychiatric Press, Inc.

Tooby, J., & Cosmides, L. (1990). The past explains the present – Emotional adaptations and the structure of ancestral environments. *Ethology and Sociobiology*, 11, 375–424.

(2008). The evolutionary psychology of the emotions and their relationship to internal regulatory variables. In M. Lewis, J. M. Haviland-Jones, & L. F. Barrett (Eds.), *Handbook of emotions* (3rd ed., pp. 114–137). New York: Guilford.

Tornstam, L. (1992). Loneliness in marriage. *Journal of Social and Personal Relationships*, 9, 197–218.

Tranel, D., & Damasio, H. (1994). Neuroanatomical correlates of electrodermal skin conductance responses. *Psychophysiology*, 31, 427–438.

Trickett, P. K. (1993). Maladaptive development of school-aged, physically abused children: Relationships with child-rearing context. *Journal of Family Psychology*, 7, 134–147.

Trobst, K. K., Collins, R. L., & Embree, J. M. (1994). The role of emotion in social-support provision: Gender, empathy, and expression of distress. *Journal of Social and Personal Relationships*, 11, 45–62.

Troy, A. B., Lewis-Smith, J., & Laurenceau, J-P. (2006). Interracial and intraracial romantic relationships: The search for difference in satisfaction, conflict, and attachment style. *Journal of Social and Personal Relationships*, 23, 65–80.

Tull, M. T., Jakupcak, M., McFadden, M. E., & Roemer, L. (2007). The role of negative affect intensity and the fear of emotions in posttraumatic stress symptom severity among victims of childhood interpersonal violence. *Journal of Nervous and Mental Disease*, 195, 580–587.

Uchino, B. N. (2006). Social support and health: A review of physiological processes potentially underlying links to disease outcomes. *Journal of Behavioral Medicine*, 29, 377–387.

(2009). What a lifespan approach might tell us about why distinct measures of social support have differential links to physical health. *Journal of Social and Personal Relationships*, 26, 53–62.

Uebelacker, L. A., & Whisman, M. A. (2006). Moderators of the association between relationship discord and major depression in a National Population-based sample. *Journal of Family Psychology*, 20, 40–51.

Uehara, E. S. (1995). Reciprocity reconsidered: Gouldner's moral norm of reciprocity and social support. *Journal of Social and Personal Relationships*, 12, 483–502.

Umana-Taylor, A. J., & Yazedjian, A. (2006). Generational differences and similarities among Puerto-Rican and Mexican mothers' experiences with familial ethnic socialization. *Journal of Social and Personal Relationships*, 23, 445–464.

Unger, D. G., Jacobs, S. B., & Cannon, C. (1996). Social support and marital satisfaction among couples coping with chronic constructive airway disease. *Journal of Social and Personal Relationships*, 13, 113–142.

Urberg, K. A., Degirmencioglu, S., & Tolson, J. M. (1998). Adolescent friendship selection and termination: The role of similarity. *Journal of Social and Personal Relationships*, 15, 703–710.

van Aken, M. A. G., & Asendorpf, J. B. (1997). Support by parents, classmates, friends and siblings in preadolescence: Covariation and compensation across relationships. *Journal of Social and Personal Relationships*, 14, 79–94.

Vangelisti, A. L. (1989). *Messages that hurt: Perceptions and reactions to hurtful messages in relationships*. Paper presented at the meeting of the Speech Communication Association, San Francisco, CA.

(1994a). Family secrets: Forms, functions, and correlates. *Journal of Social and Personal Relationships*, 11, 113–136.

(1994b). Messages that hurt. In W. R. Cupach & B. H. Spitzberg (Eds.), *The dark side of interpersonal communication* (pp. 53–82). Hillside, NJ: Erlbaum.

(1997). Gender differences, similarities, and interdependencies: Some problems with the different cultures perspective. *Personal Relationships*, 4, 243–254.

(2001). Making sense of hurtful interactions in close relationships. In V. Manuson & J. H. Harvey (Eds.), *Attribution, communication, behavior, and close relationships* (pp. 38–58). New York: Cambridge University Press.

(2007). Communicating hurt. In B. H. Spitzberg & W. R. Cupach (Eds.), *The dark side of interpersonal communication* (second edition; pp. 121–142). Mahwah, NJ: Erlbaum.

(2009a). Challenges in conceptualizing social support. *Journal of Social and Personal Relationships*, 26, 39–52.

(Ed.). (2009b). Hurt feelings: Distinquishing features, functions, and overview. In A. L. Vangelisti (Ed.), *Handbook of hurt feelings in close relationships* (pp. 3–14). New York: Cambridge University Press.

Vangelisti, A. L., & Beck, G. (2007). Intimacy and fear of intimacy. In L. L'Abate (Ed.). (2007). *Low-cost approaches to promote physical and mental health: Theory, research, and practice* (pp. 395–414). New York: Springer.

Vangelisti, A. L., & Caughlin, J. P. (1997). Revealing family secrets: The influence of topic, function, and relationships. *Journal of Social and Personal Relationships*, 14, 679–706.

Vangelisti, A. L., & Crumley, L. P. (1998). Reactions to messages that hurt: The influence of relational contexts. *Communication Monographs*, 65, 173–196.

Vangelisti, A. L., & Daly, J. A. (1997). Gender differences in standards for romantic relationships. *Personal Relationships*, 4, 203–220.

Vangelisti, A. L., & Hampel, A. D. (2010). Hurtful communication: Current research and future directions. In S. W. Smith & S. R. Wilson (Eds.), *New directions in interpersonal communication research* (pp. 224–241). Thousand Oaks, CA: Sage.

Vangelisti, A. L., Mcguire, K. C., Alexander, A. L., & Clark, G. (2007). Hurtful family environments: Links with individual relationship and perceptual variables. *Communication Monographs*, 74, 375–385.

Vangelisti, A. L., & Sprague, R. J. (1998). Guilt and hurt: Similarities, distinctions, and conventional strategies. In P. A. Andersen & L. K. Guerrero (Eds.), *Handbook of communication and emotion research* (pp. 123–154). New York: Academic Press.

Vangelisti, A. L., & Young, S. L. (2000). When words hurt: The effects of perceived intentionality on interpersonal relationships. *Journal of Social and Personal Relationships*, 17, 393–424.

Vangelisti, A. L., Young, S. L., Carpenter-Theune, K. E., & Alexander, A.L. (2005). Why does it hurt? The perceived causes of hurt feelings. *Communication Research*, 20, 443–477.

Van Tilburg, T., Gierveld, J. D. J., Lecchini, L., & Marsiglia, D. (1998). Social integration and loneliness: A comparative study among older adults in the Netherlands and Tuscany, Italy. *Journal of Social and Personal Relationships*, 15, 740–754.

Verdejo-Garcia, A., & Bechara, A. (2009). A somatic marker theory of addiction. *Neuropharmacology*, 56 *Suppl* 1, 48–62.

Vescio, T. K., Schlenker, K. A., & Lenes, J. G. (2010). Power and sexism. In A. Guinote & T. K. Vescio (Eds.), *The social psychology of power* (pp. 363–380). New York: Guilford.

Vogel, D. L., & Karney, B. R. (2002). Demands and withdrawal in newlyweds: Elaborating on the social structure hypothesis. *Journal of Social and Personal Relationships*, 19, 685–702.

Volling, B. L., McElwain, N. L., Notaro, P. C., & Herrera, C. (2002). Parents' emotional availability and infant emotional competence: Predictors of parent-infant attachment and emerging self-regulation. *Journal of Family Psychology*, 16, 447–465.

Von Salisch, M., & Vogelgesang, K. (2005). Anger regulation among friends: Assessment and development from childhood to adolescence. *Journal of Social and Personal Relationships*, 22, 837–856.

Wager, T. D., Barrett, L. F., Bliss-Moreau, E., Lindquist, K. A., Duncan, S., et al. (2008). The neuroimaging of emotion. In M. Lewis, J. M. Haviland-Jones, & L. F. Barrett (Eds.), *Handbook of emotions* (3rd ed., pp. 159–179). New York: Guilford.

Wahler, R. G., & Dumas, J. E. (1987). Family factors in childhood psychology: Toward a coercion-neglect model. In T. Jacob (Ed.), *Family interaction and psycho-pathology: Theories, methods, and findings* (pp. 581–628). New York: Plenum.

Waldron, V. R., & Kelley, D. L. (2005). Forgiving communication as a response to relational transgressions. *Journal of Social and Personal Relationships*, 22, 723–742.

Walsemann, K., Geronimus, A., & Gee, G. (2008). Accumulating disadvantage over the life course: Evidence from a longitudinal study investigating the relationship between educational advantage in youth and health in middle age. *Research on Aging*, 30, 169–199.

Waring, E. M. (1980). Marital intimacy, psychosomatic symptoms, and cognitive therapy. *Psychosomatics*, 21, 595–601.

———(1981). Facilitating marital intimacy through self-disclosure. *The American Journal of Family Therapy*, 9, 33–42.

———(1984a), Marital intimacy and family functioning. *Psychiatric Journal of the University of Ottawa*, 9, 24–29.

———(1984b). The measurement of marital intimacy. *Journal of Marital and Family Therapy*, 10, 185–192.

Waring, E. M., & Chelune, G. J. (1983). Marital intimacy and self-disclosure. *Journal of Clinical Psychology*, 39, 183–190.

Waring, E. M., McElrath, D., Lefcoe, D., & Weisz, G. (1981). Dimensions of intimacy in marriage. *The American Journal of Psychiatry*, 44, 169–175.

Waring, E. M., McElrath, D., Mitchell, P., & Derry, M. E. (1981). Intimacy in the general population. *Canadian Psychiatric Association Journal*, 26, 167–172.

Waring, E. M., & Reddon, J. R. (1983). The measurement of intimacy in marriage: The Waring Intimacy Questionnaire. *Journal of Clinical Psychology*, 39, 53–57.

Waring, E. M., & Russell, L. (1980). Family structure, marital adjustment, and intimacy in patients referred to a consultation-liaison service. *General Hospital Psychiatry*, 3, 198–203.

Waring, E. M., Tillman, M. P., Frelick, L., Russell, L., & Weisz, G. (1980). Concepts of intimacy in the general population. *Journal of Nervous and Mental Disease*, 168, 471–474.

Warner, V. V., Wickramaratne, P. P., & Weissman, M. M. (2008). The role of fear and anxiety in the familial risk for major depression: A three-generation study. *Psychological Medicine: A Journal of Research in Psychiatry and the Allied Sciences*, 38, 1543–1556.

Watson, D. (2000). *Mood and temperament*. New York: Guilford.

———(2003). Subtypes, specifiers, epicycles, and eccentrics: Toward a more parsimonious taxonomy of psychopathology. *Clinical Psychology: Science and Practice*, 10, 233–238.

Weger, H., Jr. (2005). Disconfirming communication and self-verification in marriage: Association among demand/withdrawal interaction pattern, feeling understood, and marital satisfaction. *Journal of Social and Personal Relationships*, 22, 19–32.

Weigel, D. J., & Ballard-Reisch, D. (2002). Investigating the behavioral indicators of relational commitment. *Journal of Social and Personal Relationships*, 19, 403–424.

Weinberger, D. A. (1990). The construct validity of the repressive coping style. In J. L. Singer (Ed.), *Repression and dissociation: Implications for personality theory, psychopathology, and health* (pp. 337–386). Chicago, IL: University of Chicago Press.

Weinberger, M. I., Hofstein, Y., & Whitbourne, S. K. (2008). Intimacy in young adulthood as a predictor of divorce in midlife. *Personal Relationships*, 15, 551–558.

Weisberg, R. B. (2009). Overview of generalized anxiety disorder: Epidemiology, presentation, and course. *Journal of Clinical Psychiatry*, 70, 4–9.

Weiss, M. F. (2000). The aftermath of loss as a clinical issue. Clinical Update: American Association for Marriage and Family Therapy, 2, 1–6.

Weissman, M. M., Wickramaratne, P., Nomura, Y., Warner, V., et al. (2006). Offspring of depressed mothers: 20 years later. *American Journal of Psychiatry*, 163, 1001–1008.

Werner, C. M., Altman, I., & Brown, B. B. (1992). A transactional approach to interpersonal relations: Physical environment, social context and temporal qualities. *Journal of Social and Personal Relationships*, 9, 297–324

Whisman, M. A., & Uebelacker, L. A. (2010). Marital distress and the metabolic syndrome: Linking social functioning with physical health. *Journal of Family Psychology*, 24, 367–370.

Whitaker, R. C., Orzol, S. M., & Kahn, R. S. (2006). Maternal mental health, substance use, and domestic violence in the year after delivery and subsequent behavior problems in children at age 3 years. *Archives of General Psychiatry*, 63, 551–560.

Whitton, S. W., Stanley, S. M., Markman, H. J., & Baucom, B. R. (2008). Women's weekly relationship functioning and depressive symptoms. *Personal Relationships*, 15, 533–555.

Whitty, M. (2009). Technology and hurt in close relationships. In A. L. Vangelisti (Ed.), *Feeling hurt in close relationships* (pp. 400–416). New York: Cambridge University press.

Wichstrom, L., Holte, A., Husby, R., & Wynne, L. C. (1994). Disqualifying family communication as a predictor of changes in offspring competence: A 3-year longitudinal study of sons of psychiatric patients. *Journal of Family Psychology*, 8, 104–108.

Wicker, B., Keysers, C., Plailly, J., Royet, J. P., Gallese, V., & Rizzolatti, G. (2003). Both of us disgusted in my insula: The common neural basis of seeing and feeling disgust. *Neuron*, 40, 655–664.

Widen, S. C., & Russell, J. A. (2008). Young children's understanding of others' emotions. In M. Lewis, J. M. Haviland-Jones, & L. F. Barrett (Eds.), *Handbook of emotions.* (3rd ed., pp. 348–363). New York: Guildford.

Wiens, S., & Ohman, A. (2007). Probing unconscious emotional processes: On becoming a successful musketeer. In J. A. Coan & J. J. B. Allen (Eds.), *Handbook of emotion elicitation and assessment* (pp. 65–90). New York: Oxford University Press.

Wierson, M., Armistead, L., Forehand, R., Thomas, A. M., & Fauber (1990). Parent-adolescent conflict and stress as a parent: Are there differences between being a mother or a father? *Journal of Family Violence*, 5, 187–197.

Wierzbicka, A. (2009a). Language and metalanguage: Key issues in emotion research. *Emotion Review*, 1, 3–14.

(2009b). Overcoming anglocentrism in emotion research. *Emotion Review*,1, 21–23.

Williams, K. D., & Govan, C. L. (2005). Reacting to ostracism: Retaliation or reconciliation? In D. Abrams. M. A. Hogg, & J. M. Marques (Eds.), *The social psychology of inclusion and exclusion* (pp. 47–62). New York: Psychology Press.

Williams, S. I., & Mickelson, K. D. (2008). A paradox of support seeking and rejection among the stigmatized. *Personal Relationships*, 15, 493–510.

Winter, M. A., Davies, P. T., Hightower, A. D., & Meyer, S. C. (2006). Relations among family discord, caregiver communication, and children's family representations. *Journal of Family Psychology*, 20, 217–226.

Wiser, S., & Goldfried, M. R. (1993). Comparative study of emotional experiencing in psychodynamic-interpersonal and cognitive-behavioral therapies. *Journal of Consulting and Clinical Psychology*, 61, 892–895.

Witty, M. (2009). Technology and hurt in close relationships. In A. L. Vangelisti (Ed.), *Handbook of hurt feelings in close relationships* (pp. 400–416). New York: Cambridge University Press.

Wolfe, B. E. (2006). Employing empirically supported treatments: A research-informed clinical practitioner perspective. *Clinical Psychology: Science and Practice*, 13, 171–178.

Wolfe, V. V., Finch, A. J., Jr., Saylor, C. F., Blount, R. L., Pallmeyer, T. P., & Carek, D. J. (1987). Negative affectivity in children: A multitrait-multimethod investigation. *Journal of Consulting and Clinical Psychology*, 55, 245–250.

Wong, M. S., NcElwain, N. L., & Halberstadt, A. G. (2009). Parent, family, and child characteristics: Association with mother- and father-reported emotion socialization practices. *Journal of Family Psychology*, 23, 452–467.

Wood, J. T. (2001). The normalization of violence in heterosexual romantic relationships: Women's narratives of love and violence. *Journal of Social and Personal Relationships*, 18, 239–262.

(2004). Monsters and victims: Male felons' accounts of intimate partner. *Journal of Social and Personal Relationships*, 21, 555–576.

Wright, J. H., Wright, A. S., Salmon, P., Beck, A. T., et al. (2002). Development and initial testing of a multimedia program for computer-assisted cognitive therapy. *American Journal of Psychotherapy*, 56, 76–86.

Yamasue, H., Iwanami, A., Hirayasu, Y., Yamada, H., et al. (2004). Localized volume reduction in prefrontal, temporolimbic, and paralimbic regions in schizophrenia: An MRI parcellation study. *Psychiatry Research*, 131, 195–207.

Yang, S., & Rettig, K. D. (2003). The value orientation in Korean-American mother-child relationships while facilitating academic success. *Personal Relationships*, 10, 349–369.

Ybema, J. F., Kuher, R. G., Hagedoorn, M., & Buunk, B. P. (2002). Caregiver burnout among intimate partners of patients with a severe illness: An equity perspective. *Personal Relationships*, 9, 73–88.

Yonkers, K. A., & Gurguis, G. (1995). Gender differences in the prevalence and expression of anxiety disorders. In M. V. Seeman (Ed.), *Gender and psychopathology* (pp. 113–130). Washington, DC: American Psychiatric Press, Inc.

Young, J. E., & Gluhosky, V. L. (1996). Schema-focused diagnosis for personality disorders. In F. W. Kaslow (Ed.), *Handbook of relational diagnosis and dysfunctional family patterns* (pp. 300–321). New York: Wiley.

Young, S. L. (2004). Factors that influence recipients' appraisal of hurtful communication. *Journal of Social and Personal Relationships*, 21, 291–304.

Younger, J. W., Piferi, R. L., Jobe, R. L., & Lawler, K. A. (2004). Dimensions of forgiveness: The views of laypersons. *Journal of Social and Personal Relationships*, 21, 837–856.

Yum, Y. (2004). Culture and self-construal as predictors of responses to accommodating dilemmas in dating relationships. *Journal of Social and Personal Relationships*, 21, 817–835.

Zeman, J., Klimes-Dougart, B., Cassano, M., & Adrian, M. (2007). Measurement issues in emotion research with children and adolescents. *Clinical Psychology: Science and Practice*, 14, 377–401.

Zill, N., Morrison, D. R., & Coiro, M. J. (1993). Long-term effects of parental divorce on parent-child relationships, adjustment, and achievement in young adulthood. *Journal of Family Psychology*, 7, 91–103.

Zola-Morgan, S., Squire, L. R., Alvarez-Royo, P., & Clower, R. P. (1991). Independence of memory functions and emotional behavior: separate contributions of the hippocampal formation and the amygdala. *Hippocampus*, 1, 207–220.

Zvonkovic, A. M., Pennington, D. C., & Schmiege, C. J. (1994). Work and courtship: How college workload and perceptions of work environment relate to romantic relationships among men and women. *Journal of Social and Personal Relationships*, 11, 63–76.

Author Index

130 Members of the International Sexuality Description Project, 172

Subject Index